"Many years ago, Charles Malik a
saving of the soul and the saving
matter of personal discipleship but is also a matter for public discourse. The university is the seedbed for such a discourse directed at shaping the culture. In this well-timed work, Corey Miller does a masterful job of calling Christians to be salt and light on the university campus with the intention of redeeming the souls and minds of those sitting in darkness. This is a clarion call for all Christians to make the universities our next great mission field."

Matt Endris, DMin, pastor, Fairview Baptist Church, Coushatta, LA; trustee, Gateway Seminary of the Southern Baptist Convention

"What is happening in America? How did we get here, and how can we turn the tides? These are the questions Dr. Corey Miller addresses in his new provocative book, *The Progressive Miseducation of America*. He wisely diagnoses the heart of the cultural revolution in America as education, or more accurately, *mis*education. His book is part of what has motivated me to think about engaging the college campus more. Miller does not merely approach this as an academic, but as someone who has been on the front lines engaging students, professors, and the wider culture for decades. This book will open your eyes and hopefully stir you to action."

Sean McDowell, PhD, author or editor of more than 20 books; associate professor of Apologetics, Biola University

"*The Progressive Miseducation of America* is a timely and essential work that exposes the troubling devolution of American values under the influence of Marxist ideology, particularly in our academic institutions. Corey Miller not only diagnoses the problem with precision and clarity, but also offers a bold and hopeful solution: equipping Christian professors with a missional mindset to reclaim the ideological battleground of our campuses. With profound insight and unwavering conviction, Miller casts a vision for a new generation of educators who can effectively challenge false beliefs, inspire critical thinking, and cultivate a renewed commitment to truth in the hearts and minds of their students. This book is a call to action for anyone who cares about the future of our culture, reminding us that the road to lasting change begins with courage, conviction, and faith."

Lucas Miles, pastor and senior director of TPUSA Faith; author of *Woke Jesus: The False Messiah Destroying Christianity*

"Corey Miller's book is a must-read for parents, grandparents, and anyone else who cares about what the future will look like for the next generation. Recognizing the pervasive and strategic influence within the university system, as well as the downstream impact of upstream ideologies, he sounds a clarion call for needed thoughtful Christian leadership in academia. If you want to change the culture, change the universities. Providing a thorough historical analysis, he not only answers the common lament, 'How did we get here?,' but also offers a hopeful way forward. All is not lost. *The Progressive Miseducation of America* provides a roadmap to help future generations of leaders confidently find their way through the cultural wilderness."

John B. Crane, former Indiana state senator, Indiana Senate Education Committee; board member, Colson Center

"Corey Miller offers unique and powerful insights into how Christians can positively influence campus culture for the better—the vital first step in securing the hearts, minds, and souls of young Americans. He keenly understands the insidious war in academia and explains how if the problem isn't fixed in schools and universities, pastors and parents will continue to face a very treacherous battle."

Jennifer Kabbany, editor-in-chief, *The College Fix*

"It's been said that there are three kinds of people in the world: (1) those who make things happen, (2) those who watch things happen, and (3) those who wonder what happened. *The Progressive Miseducation of America* is a call for us to move from the shadows of those watching and wondering into the ranks of those who make things happen—for the good of others and the glory of God. Corey Miller's remarkable book comes from the mind and heart of one who has spent a career on the front lines in the academy. His call for revitalizing campus and culture could not be greater, his timing could not be better, and his prescription could not be clearer. Read this book and let the revolution begin."

Dondi E. Costin, PhD, president, Liberty University; Major General, US Air Force (Retired)

"In *The Progressive Miseducation of America,* Corey Miller makes a compelling case that universities are a primary source of what's wrong in our society. Most will agree. He also argues that a Christian renewal of the universities is possible. Though more will be skeptical of that aspect of the book, Miller offers a compelling case for it, based on his experience engaging the university, both faculty and students, with the gospel. And, of course, there's the Christian history behind the idea of the university and the active working of the Holy Spirit among intellectuals and college students. Perhaps Dr. Miller is on to something after all."

John Stonestreet, president, Colson Center;
coauthor of *A Practical Guide to Culture*

"University students, parents and grandparents of university students, donors, and pastors, you need to read this book. Corey Miller explains the philosophical system that has captured the American university. Many parents know that something is not right at the university, but, as Miller shows us, it is worse than they think. Giving essential details from the leading thinkers in this movement, Miller lays bare the incoherence of this philosophical system that is destroying lives, the university, and our country. He examines the epistemological, metaphysical, and ethical presuppositions supporting this philosophy and then equips his readers with sound arguments against these false beliefs. Miller reminds us of the importance of the university in shaping culture and that we cannot stand on the sidelines while it rots. Perhaps most importantly, Miller reminds us of the role of natural theology in demonstrating the falsehood of this social philosophy and in pointing us to the redemptive truths of Christianity that alone can restore us to communion with God. This is a must-read."

Owen Anderson, PhD, professor of Philosophy and Religious Studies,
Arizona State University; author and editor of
The Cambridge Companion to the First Amendment and Religious Liberty

"Discernment is not merely the ability to distinguish between true and false, but between true and almost true. Dr. Corey Miller reveals how we've been miseducated by the 'almost true' ideas preached from American universities and that we are left with a toxic culture that denies undeniable truths about reality. He not only brilliantly shows us how this problem arose—a real college education in itself—but more importantly how to fix it. An insightful read with practical solutions!"

Frank Turek, DMin, author and speaker

"As the president of a large college campus ministry, Corey Miller is uniquely positioned to provide insight on how the cultural revolution has driven the miseducation of America through control of the university. This book offers an excellent, poignant analysis of the cultural forces leading to this point, why the university is a pivotal tool in the hands of revolutionaries, and what Christians should do going forward. I highly recommend this much-needed resource for helping more believers understand the university's central role in driving culture's strident secularism."

Natasha Crain, podcaster; speaker; author of five books, including *When Culture Hates You*

the progressive miseducation of america

corey miller

HARVEST HOUSE PUBLISHERS
EUGENE, OREGON

Unless otherwise indicated, all Scripture verses are taken from the Holy Bible, New International Version®, NIV®. Copyright © 1973, 1978, 1984, 2011 by Biblica, Inc.® Used with permission of Zondervan. All rights reserved worldwide. www.zondervan.com. The "NIV" and "New International Version" are trademarks registered in the United States Patent and Trademark Office by Biblica, Inc.®

Verses marked kjv are taken from the King James Version of the Bible.

Verses marked esv are taken from the ESV® Bible (The Holy Bible, English Standard Version®), copyright © 2001 by Crossway, a publishing ministry of Good News Publishers. Used with permission. All rights reserved. The ESV text may not be quoted in any publication made available to the public by a Creative Commons license. The ESV may not be translated in whole or in part into any other language.

Cover design by Studio Gearbox

Cover images © Farhad Bek, Anastasiia Hevko / Shutterstock

Interior design by KUHN Design Group

For bulk, special sales, or ministry purchases, please call 1-800-547-8979.
Email: CustomerService@hhpbooks.com

This logo is a federally registered trademark of the Hawkins Children's LLC. Harvest House Publishers, Inc., is the exclusive licensee of this trademark.

The Progressive Miseducation of America
Copyright © 2025 by Corey Miller
Published by Harvest House Publishers
Eugene, Oregon 97408
www.harvesthousepublishers.com

ISBN 978-0-7369-9237-4 (pbk)
ISBN 978-0-7369-9238-1 (eBook)

Library of Congress Control Number: 2025930243

No part of this book may be used or reproduced in any manner for the purpose of training artificial intelligence technologies or systems.

All rights reserved. No part of this publication may be reproduced, stored in a retrieval system, or transmitted in any form or by any means—electronic, mechanical, digital, photocopy, recording, or any other—except for brief quotations in printed reviews, without the prior permission of the publisher.

Printed in the United States of America

25 26 27 28 29 30 31 32 33 / BP / 10 9 8 7 6 5 4 3 2 1

To my family.

May you forever pursue the knowledge of God (John 17:3).

ACKNOWLEDGMENTS

I'm grateful to Harvest House Publishers for being the best publishing team to work with and for bringing this project to completion and beyond.

I thank Dr. Rick James, the Ratio Christi National Director of Publishing, for providing the initial editing work on the document.

I'm indebted to members of my team—including Donald McLaughlin, Dr. Kurt Jaros, and Dr. Larry Baxter—for early encouragement to write this book.

Finally, I'm grateful to the Lord for giving me the vision for and preparing me in unique ways to write this.

CONTENTS

Foreword by Everett Piper 13

Introduction: The Dream Turned Nightmare 15

PART 1: WHAT JUST HAPPENED?
NO LONGER GRANDMA'S AMERICA

1. Woke 101 29
2. A Case of Sexualized and Genderized Insanity 49
3. The Exploitation of Race for Revolution 77
4. Math and Medicine Swoon Under the Spell 97
5. Christian Ministries and Mission Drift 111

PART 2: HOW DID WE GET HERE?
ONE WORD EXPLAINS IT ALL

6. The University as the Mind of Culture 123
7. A Brief History of the University and Extreme Mission Drift 145
8. Reasons for Failure and the Rise of the Neo-Marxism(s) of the European Axis Powers 169
9. Cultural Marxism and the Postmodern Turn 189

PART 3: HOW SHOULD WE RESPOND?
A THIRD REVOLUTION

10. Is Christianity Good for the World? 203
11. Is Christian Belief Reasonable? 227
12. Is Christian Belief True? 241
13. All Hands on Deck: Everyone Pay Attention to the University! . . . 257

Conclusion: MAGA and the Morning After 289

Notes 305

*For the world is changing: I feel it in the water,
I feel it in the earth, and I smell it in the air.*

J.R.R. Tolkien,
The Return of the King, The Lord of the Rings Series

FOREWORD

Everett Piper

Have you ever wondered about how our country got into this mess? Ever wonder about how we became the "Divided States" rather than the United States? Has it ever crossed your mind how a nation that so proudly boasted of "coexistence" seemingly only five minutes ago became so fractured, so angry, and so morally lost?

If you want to understand who and what is responsible for this cultural chaos, you need to look no further than our nation's educational institutions and how far they've fallen from their original missions.

As the parable of the prodigal son teaches us, when you squander your birthright, you're going to end up wallowing in the slop with the pigs. And what is America's educational "birthright"? Put succinctly, it is a biblical worldview.

The history of American education is clear. The guiding philosophy for nearly all of our schools up until that last handful of years, historically speaking, was to promote moral development and civic responsibility and to raise upright, honest, and trustworthy leaders. Simply stated, the primary purpose of education in America for the first couple hundred years of our country's existence was to maintain the nation's moral order. Schools were founded to galvanize future leaders in a common faith—faith in Christ. And leaders relied on their faith when stewarding America.

Harvard's founding motto, for example, was "Truth for Christ and the Church." Princeton's was "Under God's power she flourishes." Yale's is "Light and truth." These three, among America's most seminal institutions, were unquestionably charted as Christian schools.

But it doesn't end there. Seven of the eight Ivy League institutions were founded in like manner to train up future generations in a biblical ethic. Dartmouth's motto is "The voice of one crying in the wilderness." The University of Pennsylvania's is "Laws without morals are useless." After Rhode Island College became Brown University, their motto became "In God we hope." Columbia University's motto comes directly from Psalm 36:9: "In Thy light shall we see light."

The list goes on and on and literally covers coast to coast. Amherst College: "Let them enlighten the lands." Wellesley College: "Not to be ministered unto [served], but to minister [serve]." Northwestern University: "Whatsoever things are true." Kenyon College: "Valiantly bear the cross!" Ohio University: "Religion, Learning, Civility; Virtue before all things." Indiana University: "Light and Truth." Emory University: "The wise heart seeks knowledge." Valparaiso University: "In Thy light we see light." And the University of California: *Fiat Lux*, "Let there be light."

These institutions are only a few of the hundreds that explicitly cited a Christian ethic as their guiding ethos and the very reason for their existence. America's educational "inheritance" is, indeed, rich with the assumption that the highest goal of the academy should be to teach and model personal integrity within the context of those self-evident truths that are endowed to us by our Creator—truths such as respect for the law, a desire for virtue, a heart for sacrifice, and the value of sobriety, religion, morality, and biblical wisdom.

If you want to know why we are where we are today, look no further than your local schools and how far they have strayed. Corey Miller's arduous research and brilliant writing makes the case that maybe it's time for American education to follow the prodigal son's example and return home.

Everett Piper
President Emeritus,
Oklahoma Wesleyan University

INTRODUCTION

THE DREAM TURNED NIGHTMARE

Recently, maybe you awoke one morning startled by your observations of American culture only to keenly grasp a now commonly held sentiment: This is not Grandma's America! With strident trepidation, you resonate with Dorothy in *The Wizard of Oz*, who quipped, "Toto, I have a feeling we're not in Kansas anymore."

An archway into Yale University continues to read "For God, for Country, and for Yale." Yet twenty-first-century America has changed, and much that was once commonplace is now in the past; few are living now who remember it. Astonishingly, 38 percent of Americans say that patriotism is "very important," down from 70 percent in 1998. Only 39 percent say religion is "very important," down from 62 percent over the same period. Those who say raising children is "very important" fell to 30 percent from 59 percent. And what was deemed the last living virtue in America often associated with liberals, a belief in tolerance, is at 58 percent, down from 80 percent in 2019.[1]

If that is 25 years in the making, what will America look like in the next 25 years? We have a choice to make, and it must be soon.

WHAT IS HAPPENING TO AMERICA?

It's complicated. But the short answer can be simplified in one word: *revolution*. We are undergoing a cultural revolution in America and in the West. No, it isn't with tanks and guns. But not all revolutions materialize in that way—not immediately, anyway. Edmund Burke was an Irish philosopher, father of modern conservatism, statesman, and signer of the document that effectively abolished the slave trade in Great Britain. He wrote *Reflections on the Revolution in France.* It was an enormously enchanting revolution for Marx and Lenin to dream about. Famously quoting Burke about good and evil, John F. Kennedy said in a speech, "The only thing necessary for the triumph of evil is for good men to do nothing."[2]

We are in a revolution.

I've studied the primary literature on all the major revolutions, from the Russian and Chinese Revolutions in the East to the American, English, and French Revolutions in the West, to help understand our current crisis. In addition to being a philosopher and theologian, I take great interest in culture. As a student of culture, a student of the inception of the universities and their role in shaping culture, and someone published in Marxist thought who gave much reflection about this during graduate school, I'm confident that we are in a revolution in America—a soft revolution, to be sure, but a revolution nonetheless, one deeply wedded to a westernized form of Marxism. One doesn't need to know the term much less the origins to see its ideology and fruit.

Culture is broadly defined by norms, values, practices, customs, beliefs, language, laws, and shared meanings. Our culture is undergoing radical change. For many, personal anxiety is very high. We see evidence of this cultural revolution all around us; the symptoms downstream come from an ideological poison upstream. It can largely be explained in a word: *universities*. Before you cry "Conspiracy!," read on and you will understand. You cannot beware unless you are first aware of that which you ought to beware. Many liberals know that the ground underneath them has begun to tremble and do not like the way it feels. Some grasp the fact that their own foundations are being upended. Some prominent New Atheists have even converted to Christ. Yet many conservatives still fail to grasp the gravity of this threat, thinking a political election might solve the problem, or alternatively dismissing it as simply cliché talk of "political correctness," "wokeness," or "liberalism," most of whose college students will, they say, outgrow it when they get jobs.

But college students and graduates did get jobs. Then something happened. They brought the campus to the culture, to the corporations, to medicine, to elementary schools, and yes, even to churches. As the journalist Andrew Sullivan wrote, "We all live on campus now."[3] Some have rightly observed a genuine pushback against some of the apparent new norms of our culture in terms of corporate cutbacks of transgender marketing failures by companies like Bud Light or even state governments like Florida eradicating harmful university administrator positions at its public universities functioning as thought police.

But my contention is that many of these instances are only short lived. That is, billionaires pulling money from Ivy League universities due to emotive disdain for apparent radical antisemitism fostered by the universities seems brief and reactionary without any sense of permanency or resolve at the ideological level. But that is the level from where all the contention sprang. The structural core, if unchanged, will force us right back in the same direction shortly after symptoms are treated. The revolutionaries have got hold of not merely the economic means of production per se but the cultural means of production—and for good strategic reasons. The American sociologist James Davison Hunter reminds us that although a revolutionary idea might emerge from the masses, "it does not gain traction until it is embraced and propagated by elites" working through their "well-developed networks and powerful institutions."[4] This is why focusing on the locus of ideas in a culture is vital. The key locus is the college campus.

WHAT HAPPENS IN VEGAS STAYS IN VEGAS

I invoke the famous ad campaign "What happens in Vegas, stays in Vegas" here because taglines and jingles are notoriously difficult to get out of your head and I want to impress on you a central thesis of the book: What happens in the universities does not stay in the universities.

It was never intended that the goods captured in the ivory tower remain there. Like many things, the universities have been repurposed and yet still carry the highest level of influence. What has changed is the speed with which ideas make their way from the ivory tower to the village. Media and technology have seen to that, both for good and for evil. Thought precedes action. Ideas form a culture and, even, a civilization.

Typically, when you think of war, you think of blood and soil. But since the start of the twentieth century, wars have been about ideas—bolshevism, communism, fascism, democracy, socialism, and so on. Hitler was alleged to say, "Give me the textbooks and I will control Germany"; China's Cultural Revolution was a purge of ideas; Che Guevara called revolution the struggle of "masses and ideas"; and the subversive roots of cancel culture and woke ideology can be found in the ideological statement (rightly or wrongly) attributed to Joseph Stalin, "Ideas are more powerful than weapons. We don't allow our enemies to have weapons. Why should we let them have ideas?"

Ideas are powerful. They can change the world for good or evil, and the university is the cultural gatekeeper of ideas. This brings us to the second major thesis of this book: As goes the university, so goes the culture. Whatever the reasons—technology, social media, campus activism, communal housing, music, globalism, radicalizing professors, or more—the university is the epicenter of culture, and as goes the university in the US, so goes the world.

There is, in America and in the West more generally, an ever-increasing volume of voices favoring an authoritarian (or even totalitarian) spirit over a libertarian one. This extends to our cognitive liberty such that if one is deemed to have a politically incorrect thought and is found out, it can lead to ruined careers, divided families, and destroyed lives. We are in the midst of an ideological revolution that came from the college campus. What we're seeing today is the pollution downstream of what yesterday was upstream. It is clearly the case that politics is downstream from culture, culture is downstream from education, and the apex of education is the university.

Oddly, most Americans are unaware that there's a war. Sure, there's a growing divide between conservatives and progressives, Republicans and Democrats, rich and poor, Red Sox and Yankees…but not a revolution. Yes, a revolution!

It is difficult to see what you don't understand. Unlike Europe, Asia, and South America, America has no experience or understanding (or fear) of Marxism. If Marxism were a virus—and it is—America has never been inoculated, never had a near run-in with a junta or thrown a Molotov cocktail or whatever else people do in a revolution. That all happens somewhere else in the world. But it's happening here this time. And to quote the title of the song by Gil Scott-Heron, "The Revolution Will Not Be Televised."

THE CAMPUS—GROUND ZERO

American evangelicalism is unique (believers from every major denomination bound together by a higher cause), and it's a faith that formed not overnight but over centuries. According to church historian Douglas Sweeney, we—American evangelicals—are the product of four spiritual movements, all flowing from the campus.[5]

First, there's the Reformation, which began with Luther, Zwingli, and Calvin, at the universities of Wittenberg, Geneva, and Zürich. The lightning rod of the Reformation was not Father Luther or Brother Luther but Doctor Luther, professor of moral theology at the University of Wittenberg. It is from this position and post, and only from it, that the call of reform carried, answered by doctors at other universities.

Second is the Puritan movement, whose ideas about a not-so-separate church and state did not live on in perpetuity but whose universities did. As biographer Sarah Vowell puts it, "Winthrop and his shipmates" read books, wrote books, "and pretty much kept their noses in them up until the day God created the Red Sox."[6] Harvard, Yale, and Dartmouth were Puritan creations, viewing higher education as the foundation for ministry.

Third are the Pietist and Moravian movements, who gave to Christianity 24/7 prayer and were birthed in the German universities of Leipzig, Württemberg, and Halle through Christian professors like Philipp Spener and August Francke who turned their classrooms into *collegia pietatis* (colleges of piety) and their students into committed disciples.

And fourth are the eighteenth- and nineteenth-century movements of revival and awakenings in the US, many of which began at the university. In fact, of the three broadly recognized revivals of the past 75 years, one began with the students and faculty of Asbury (1970), another with the students and faculty of Wheaton (1995), and a third right back with the students and faculty of Asbury in 2023.

The conspicuous thread, common to all, is the university; nothing has been more influential or impactful to the spread of the gospel, not to mention to future leaders of culture, and let me back that with a singular example—the Mount Hermon Revival.

In 1886, a first-ever Christian conference for college students was held in Mount Hermon, Massachusetts. On the last day of the conference, 250 students were given a challenge by Princeton senior Robert Wilder to consider taking the gospel to the world as foreign missionaries. One hundred students stepped forward from schools such as Yale, Harvard, Dartmouth, and Cornell.[7]

Wilder spent the next year traveling to more than 150 campuses, giving the same challenge, with an additional 2,100 students committing their lives to foreign missions. By the time the student volunteer movement petered out in the 1940s, it had sent 20,500 students to mission fields: It was the largest missionary endeavor in the history of the church up until 1948. In 1948, student leaders left the student volunteer movement as "its activities moved steadily away from an emphasis on overseas missions and became more involved in political and social matters," and they went on to start intervarsity chapters on US campuses, which were joined by Campus Crusade for Christ, the Navigators, and others, starting a whole new student movement that would, in time, dwarf the impact of the student volunteers.[8]

Indisputably, the university has been profoundly influential for God's kingdom purposes. On the other hand, in the wrong hands, nothing has been more destructive. Knowing how we can all respond requires having knowledge about why America is in the downward spiral that it is in. Smart action requires nothing less.

THE FIRST REVOLUTION

If you want to change the world, change the university. Conversely, if you want to screw up the world, screw up the university, and to date this has occurred twice. There have been two massive ideological revolutions fought in and over the university, and the victories won by radical progressives have left the moral landscape of the country as cratered as the moon.

The first revolution took place between the Civil War and World War II (1880–1930). In *The Sacred and the Secular University*, historians Jon Roberts and James Turner lay out the revolution in meticulous detail, describing its major movements as follows:

1. *Methodological Naturalism:* As science complexified, scientists specialized, focusing exclusively on the mechanisms of cause and effect divorced from a conceptual framework. What mattered was how *A* caused *B* and not the *why* of *A* or the broader implications of *B*. This divorced science from philosophy.

2. *Philological Historicism:* The focus on material "causation" passed to the language and literature departments in the German universities, shifting attention from the language and the text to what gave rise to the language and text. Most significantly, the Bible was scrutinized, turning theology into archaeology, sifting through layers of Hebrew civilization, to find meaning in the text.

3. *Liberal Protestantism:* The highly secularized German universities had a liberalizing influence on Protestantism, and once liberalized, mainstream Protestantism became a powerful advocate for the secularization of universities in the US.

4. *Sociology:* When science is reduced to base causality, then aimed at human beings, what you get is modern sociology: the study of man, society, and culture as the passive determinant of evolutionary causality.

5. *Liberal Arts:* Following the pattern of the German language and literature schools, the humanities arose with the understanding "that the relationship between context and content was essential to establishing historical interpretation."[9]

The revolution was a reduction of all study, all learning, and all disciplines to the material explanation of cause and effect. Table scraps from the hard sciences' feasts were left over for social sciences and especially humanities. Politics and psychology became departments of "political science" and "psychological science." In other words, material cause and effect came to be regarded as a complete explanation for all that is. The total secularization of the university in scientific terms would set the stage for the second revolution.

THE SECOND REVOLUTION

The second revolution was an ideological amalgam of cultural Marxism and postmodernism whose beginnings were largely seeded in the 1930s and 1960s in Germany, France, and Italy. But it quickly moved to US universities, which have become the largest exporter of the ideology inside and outside of America.

Cultural Marxism's major influencers came from the Frankfurt School of critical theory who were forced to flee when the Nazis rose to power, still embracing fundamental aspects of Marx's conflict theory but extending its economic focus to race, class, gender, and sex (significantly appealing to Freud). Its major Italian thinker, who helped the shift from classical to cultural Marxism, was Antonio Gramsci. He was imprisoned during his final years, but his prison notes were mediated to universities in the US through the late Dr. Joseph Buttigieg, a former professor at Notre Dame and the father of Pete Buttigieg. Indeed, cultural Marxism's major thinkers became virtual faculty advisers during the sexual revolution and student protests on college campuses in the 1960s. It retained notions of dividing people into social binaries (oppressors and oppressed), seeking to enlighten them through liberational conscientiousness (what we now call "woke"), and executing on liberation through revolution. (I will address this further when we explore the subject of diversity, equity, and inclusion [DEI], and we will go down to great depths in part 2 of the book.)

Postmodernism, for its part, began in the 1960s with French philosophers philosophizing. Thinkers such as Michel Foucault, Jean-François Lyotard, Jacques Derrida, and Roland Barthes—all French communists or Marxist sympathizers—and extending to their second-generation thinkers. Their philosophy coalesced around the nature of knowledge, power, and language. Truth, they argued, is nothing other than the beliefs and values of the culture in charge (the hegemony). Cultural critics James Lindsay and Helen Pluckrose identify four themes of postmodernism.

1. *The Blurring of Boundaries:* "Radical skepticism toward objective truth…results in a suspicion of the boundaries and categories we

have generally accepted as true."[10] These include the boundaries between objective and subjective, high and low culture, male and female, man and animals, and the like.

2. *The Power of Language:* In postmodern thought, language is what defines reality. To control the language is to control mass perception of reality. Think, for example, of the way in which personal pronouns (e.g., *they, them*) have been weaponized.[11]

3. *Cultural Relativism:* Because there is no objective truth, truth is relative to the culture, and therefore, it is impermissible to critique the truth of another culture.[12]

4. *Loss of the Individual:* In postmodernism, society is stratified by socio-sexual-ethnic groups, arranged from most oppressed to least. The more oppressed, the greater the social status, with straight, white males being the bottom stratum of society.[13]

The amalgamated postmodern cultural Marxism that came to dominate the humanities has struggled with exhausting itself: If everything is relative, what is there to teach? What is there to learn? It's a one-way ticket to nihilism. But it didn't turn to nihilism. The Marxist telos inspires hope in a utopia. It turned instead to activism. Lindsay and Pluckrose wrote,

> Think of postmodernism as a kind of fast-evolving virus. Its original and purest form couldn't spread from the academy to the general population because it was so difficult to grasp and so far removed from social realities. In its mutated form, it was able to spread, leaping the "species" gap from academics to activists to everyday people as it became increasingly graspable and actionable and therefore more contagious.[14]

This applied postmodern cultural Marxism is where the third revolution begins. In this book, we will look at the rise of critical social justice (the mutated virus) on full display in part 1; then, a deeper analysis on the ideology and how we lost the universities in part 2; and finally, a broad call to action for a third revolution ("All hands on deck") in part 3, from philanthropies to churches and families and from elementary schools and universities to political alliances.

THE THIRD REVOLUTION

With all Europe under Nazi control and Germany massing to invade Great Britain, Winston Churchill took to the airwaves in his greatest speech to appeal to the British citizenry to fight for their lives:

> What General Weygand called the Battle of France is over. I expect that the Battle of Britain is about to begin. Upon this battle depends the survival of Christian civilization. Upon it depends our own British life, and the long continuity of our institutions and our Empire. The whole fury and might of the enemy must very soon be turned on us. Hitler knows that he will have to break us in this Island or lose the war. If we can stand up to him, all Europe may be free and the life of the world may move forward into broad, sunlit uplands. But if we fail, then the whole world, including the United States, including all that we have known and cared for, will sink into the abyss of a new Dark Age.[15]

The epic picture Churchill paints must have sounded exaggerated, but every word of it was true. The situation *was* that dire, the result of failure, that bleak.

Being an island, many in the UK believed it was best to hunker down, sit and wait, and not stand and fight. And there are similar voices in American Christendom, like Rod Dreher, saying, "The culture war is largely over—and we lost…Now, our mission is to build the underground resistance." But I do not believe a strategic withdrawal for the purpose of developing "creative, communal solutions to help us hold on to our faith and our values in a world growing ever more hostile to them" is the only or even the best option.[16] Where will we go? To where will we retreat? In the voice of theologian Al Mohler, "We must not exile ourselves, and we certainly must not retreat into silence while we still have a platform, a voice, and an opportunity."[17]

Harvard Magazine recently reminded us that Churchill went on to give the commencement speech at Harvard University, where he said, "The empires of the future are the empires of the mind."[18] Ironically, the article was published in 2018. In 2015, Harvard reported more atheists and agnostics entered the school as freshmen than Protestants and Catholics.[19]

We need to prepare. We need to act. And we need to do so now—together in what might be dubbed an ideological third revolution to return to our Christian roots that once made America good before America became great—that is, before it lost its greatness, having first lost a significant amount of its goodness.

A word about the title is in order. This book is not primarily political even if it has political aspects. The word *progressive* in the title may seem misleading. It is not. It points primarily to an ideological and gradual, or sometimes rapid-yet-constant, movement away from the intellectual and moral roots that formed America, roots we should also wish to conserve. That is, the Christian roots of America are what made it great. That is not to say I believe America was ever an explicitly Christian nation as such that we wish to recapture. No, America's charter, the US Constitution, as well as its preceding founding document, the Declaration of Independence, both fail to mention the name "Jesus" anywhere. Nonetheless, it was a Christian-*inspired* nation to be sure as most of its founders were Christians rather than Muslims, Hindus, atheists, Jews, Confucianists, Buddhists, or even deists. It would be preposterous to think that their Christian convictions weren't at least informing or inspiring the founding of America. Manifestly, their social contract included grounding any notion of natural rights in God. Language such as humans being "created equal" with "inalienable rights" that are "endowed by our Creator" make it clear that the founding wasn't pantheistic (note the separation of created beings from Creator), nor atheistic (note the source of our rights being given by the Creator), and nor was it reasonably theistic in any other form than Christian (note Muslims, Jews, and deists were at best a scarce minority in the colonies and among the founding fathers). As depicted in the First Amendment of the Bill of Rights, the founders opposed the conflation of church and state, or state churches, as experienced in Europe. It prompted the notion of separation. In this regard they did not want a sectarian preference (e.g., Baptist,

Presbyterian, Methodist, etc.). But they considered religion and morality to be indispensable and to a degree inseparable. John Adams, second president of the United States, captures the idea behind the founders when, on October 11, 1798, he wrote to the Massachusetts Militia that

> Because We have no Government armed with Power capable of contending with human Passions unbridled by...morality and Religion. Avarice, Ambition [and] Revenge or Galantry, would break the strongest Cords of our Constitution as a Whale goes through a Net. Our Constitution was made only for a moral and religious People. It is wholly inadequate to the government of any other.[20]

PART 1
WHAT JUST HAPPENED?
No Longer Grandma's America

*For, after all, how do we know that two and two make four?
Or that the force of gravity works? Or that the past is unchangeable?
If both the past and the external world exist only in the
mind, and if the mind itself is controllable—what then?*

GEORGE ORWELL, *1984*

1

WOKE 101

In this first chapter, my goal is to explain major ideas that are present in the conflict on campus and in the culture and the ideology that animates them. Woke 101. To make it as intuitive as possible, I'll focus on the "woke" you'll likely be most familiar with. But to start, some historical context will be helpful.

THE STORY OF WOKE

The Copernican revolution changed the fundamental way people understood the world, shifting from an earth-centric universe to a universe centered around the sun. Not a new idea but a new reality. Something like it occurred in the 1960s, and it had nothing to do with "Turn on, tune in, drop out." The newest innovation to how people viewed the world was postmodernism, formulated by French thinkers like Michel Foucault, Jacques Derrida, and Jean-François Lyotard.

Innately, as famously observed by Aristotle, man desires to know. We live to know truth, to understand the *how* and *why* of everything, and innately, we believe that truth is there to be discovered. But within modernism, many no longer believed the truth that God exists or the truth of the gospel. Everything was about science. And now, it's become even more dicey. The "gospel" according to postmodernism is "truth does not exist," and to call it a paradigm shift is to put it far too mildly. According to Pluckrose and Lindsay,

> Once postmodernism burst onto the intellectual scene in the late 1960s, it became wildly fashionable among leftist and left-leaning academics. As the intellectual fad grew, its recruits set to work producing radically skeptical Theory, in which Western knowledge and ways of obtaining knowledge—including our assumption that objective knowledge is even possible—were criticized and dismantled...This approach had its limits. Endless dismantling and de-construction were doomed to consume them in nihilistic despair, a sense that all is useless and pointless.[1]

The final sentence is extremely important: If truth is completely relative, then what's the point of the university? Of learning? What's the point of anything? But if nothing matters, one thing certainly does—power. If there is no truth, only differing perspectives and opinions (one no better than the next), then truth is, and only is, the enshrined beliefs, practices, and preferences of those in power. History, for example, is merely the telling of events from the perspective of those in power; science is the preferred data of those in power; normal sexual behavior just reflects the preferences and practices of those in power. And on and on it goes.

In a world where nothing is true and everything is relative, the only thing that matters is to be the party in power, so that *your* history, *your* facts, *your* sexual preferences, *your* concept of marriage, *your* idea of normalcy, are what is taught in the classroom.

It is the full and final realization of this fact that turned postmodernism toward activism, protesting, policing language, inciting civil chaos, dismantling power structures, controlling the narrative of the media, and moving to exile the straight, white males who held the power. But how did they do this? What do academics know about reordering society and waging a cultural revolution? It turns out, quite a lot. Pluckrose and Lindsay write,

> A new wave of Theorists in the late 1980s and early 1990s created a diverse set of highly politicized and actionable post-modern Theories that included some elements of Critical Theory. We call this more recent development *applied postmodernism*...These applied

postmodernists came from different fields, but their ideas were similar and provided a more user-friendly approach than the old postmodernism. During this turn, Theory mutated into a handful of Theories—postcolonial, queer, and critical race—that were put to work in the world to deconstruct social injustice.[2]

Critical theories (queer theory, feminist theory, race theory) are the tactics of "applied postmodernism." Postmodernism "aggressively put into action to change the existing social order, ushering out Western civilization and ushering in, well, anything but that."[3] (Postmodernism "aggressively put into action" is called critical social justice, and critical social justice is what is commonly called "woke." Moving forward, I'll be using *critical social justice*, *woke*, or *wokeism* interchangeably when referring to this.)

This is how society arrived to where it is today. To see it in more detail, we'll explore topics you've likely encountered before—cancel culture, which is everywhere; DEI (diversity, equity, and inclusion), which is probably at your workplace; and politics, which you can't avoid.

CROSS WORDS PUZZLE

Who would've ever imagined that we'd be at a place where we even need to ask the question, What is a woman? Or worse yet, that we would have a nominee for the US Supreme Court who either intellectually couldn't or politically wouldn't answer the question but who would nonetheless go on to be confirmed by the US Senate for a lifetime appointment? Lest we are preoccupied by one person or some small body of politicians, we must reckon with the fact that those officials represent the ideas of nearly half of the American populace.

In 2022, the editors of the *Cambridge Dictionary* supplemented the definition of *woman* as "an adult female human being" with "an adult who lives and identifies as female though they may have been said to have a different sex at birth."[4] That revision went beyond updating conventional usage, providing descriptive analysis of the change in language. As theologian Carl Trueman points out, it is a prescription, an assertion of power over our very words to get us to adopt a new philosophical view about reality.[5] It is here changing the very meaning of the word.

Revolutions are fought by rhetorical strategies as much as battle plans. Words are a means not just of describing reality but of changing it. Hence the focus on transforming words and inventing new ones like *heterosexualism*, *heteronormativity*, *theistic normativity*, and even *love*, *social justice*, or *woman* as adaptations with new meanings. This is a factor in how the new ideology works to transform worldviews and culture. As one radical proponent states succinctly, "Language is not a neutral transmitter of a universal, objective, or fixed reality. Rather, language is the way we construct reality, the framework we use to give meaning to our experiences."[6]

Language is given a very important role in postmodern theory and in the critical social justice scholarship that stems from it. Language is seen as the constructor of reality. Words can be a form of violence. There are trigger words that are deemed hurtful and offensive, and the intent of changing the meanings of words is also often to change our view of the world. Now, universities have long lexicons of words that ought not to be said. Stanford University, for example, had a list of hundreds of words that were off limits, which is insane. *Insane* is one of the words, which should be replaced with *surprising* or *wild*. Embarrassed, Stanford pulled it off the website.[7] But many universities adopt these ever-growing lexicons.

Besides changing the words or changing the meaning of words we commonly use, there are also new words that have come into use. Below is a glossary of important terms that recur throughout this book.

> *Critical Theories:* Critical theories are conceptual frameworks. Critical feminism, for example, is the theory about feminism. The theory includes the conceptual framework as well as strategies for cultural reeducation and activism. Critical theories are Marxist in that they seek a revolution within the social order, a reordering of the haves and have-nots. The big difference is the change in paradigm—from rich versus poor to oppressor versus oppressed—making the revolution race based instead of economic. There are many critical theories, the major ones being critical social justice (oppressor

versus oppressed), queer theory (queer versus straight), and critical feminism (female versus male).

Antiracism: Critically, *antiracism* does not mean "against racism" but is rather an essential belief of critical race theory, that everyone in the majority culture (white people) is racist, either overtly or covertly. To be an "antiracist" is to believe that every member of white society is racist and every facet of society is racist, such that sweeping cultural and political reforms are the only remedy.

Equity: In critical theory, *equality* contrasts with *equity*. It is not a synonym. Equity is a flattening of society—everyone getting the same, taking from the rich and giving it to others (which, if that sounds like communism, it is). In contrast, capitalism in America aims for equal opportunity.

Virtue Signaling: Virtue signaling is a disingenuous public display of moral sympathy and solidarity with the intent of showcasing one's own moral virtue according to the values of woke ideology.

Social Justice: Once again, we have a word that in critical theory means the opposite of what you'd think. Past injustices to ethnic minorities are "evened out" according to their social category of oppression (e.g., by inverse racism—that is, marginalizing, shaming, and blaming white people).

White Guilt: The meaning of *white guilt* is straightforward enough: white people assuming guilt, not for being racist, but for racist acts of the past done by others. The idea is, though you may have had nothing to do with those acts, you indirectly benefit from them (as a white person).

Systemic Racism: Differences in outcomes among racial groups can be explained, and only explained, by the "system" being inherently racist. Accusing the entire society of structural racism instead of accusing racist individuals is part of a strategy that seeks to justify radical, destructive political changes. If everything is racist, then everything must be torn down.

Implicit Bias: This is a theory that every person is secretly racist, even if that person doesn't feel racist, act racist, or believe in treating people differently based on race.

Hegemony: The group that maintains cultural and political dominance in a society.

Patriarchy: Racism, patriarchy, and capitalism are central facets of white, Western society, which is oppressive.

Cisgender: Someone whose internal sense of gender corresponds with the sex the person was identified as having at birth.

BIPOC: An acronym that stands for "black, Indigenous, and people of color" and is used to identify those with oppressed status.

Critical Race Theory (CRT): An academic framework examining the intersections of race, power, and systemic racism in society.

Decolonization: The process of challenging and dismantling Western education, values, political control, colonial ideologies, structures, and legacies. Decolonization involves reevaluating historical narratives and empowering Indigenous communities to reclaim their culture.

Intersectionality: The recognition of how various forms of oppression intersect and compound one another and that individuals can face discrimination based on multiple aspects of their identity. The more oppressed groups to which one belongs (for example, gay, female, and black) the more cultural and moral authority one has in society.

White Privilege: Any status, wealth, or opportunity one has by virtue of being white.

Inclusive: To be inclusive is to take pains not to exclude marginalized groups, but it has a more specific meaning in critical social justice. Inclusion typically refers to embracing the gender or sexual orientation that a person has chosen to "identify as."

You would think it impossible to introduce or implement any of these concepts into society at large, and indeed it would be—but for the university. The university is solely responsible for creating, cultivating, and spreading this highly destructive ideology. Actually, that's not quite right; it is the highly educated Marxist professors who are responsible. For example, would there be Palestinian protests on campus apart from the professors? Obviously not.

As the glossary of terms illustrates, to be woke is to see or understand everything through the lens of race, gender, and sexual orientation and to see everyone through the grid of victim/oppressor. Note that many of the words and concepts mean the opposite of their surface meaning. The confusion is intentional, and it's critical, especially for Christians, to understand that the social justice of critical theory is not the social justice of Scripture.

As Christians, we believe primary human identity lies in being made in God's image (Genesis 1:26-27) and this bestows intrinsic dignity that is worthy of Christian compassion and justice. Sin is the ultimate problem, and Christ's redemption is the ultimate solution. Redeemed people should promote genuine social justice within a biblical framework (Colossians 2:8). The social justice of critical theory is corrupted by a focus on power and privilege, and as a result, it misconstrues justice, grace, and compassion. Christians should reject any interpretation of social justice predicated on the social construct of victim/oppressor, which is a Marxist way of looking at the world.

VICTIM/OPPRESSOR NARRATIVES

Along with words and definitions, narratives play a critical role in reengineering society. To say that narratives have social significance is merely to say that human beings view the world through stories and interpret it according to narratives. Kurt Vonnegut, in a now famous video, lays out the storylines already primed in our thinking, and they are shockingly few. Taking from the video, this is what Vonnegut means by these storylines:

> Now, the simplest story…if you watch television, it'll be told again and again and again. Nobody ever gets tired of this story: I call it

> "man in a hole," but it needn't be about a man in a hole: somebody gets into trouble, and then gets out of it again.
>
> Now, another story that's very popular…I call it boy meets girl, but it needn't be about a boy or a girl. It's somebody on a day like any other day comes across something perfectly wonderful…[loses that thing], and gets it back again…[8]

We see the world, watch the news, think about the future, and see history according to a handful of *s*-shaped (up-down-up) storylines. With that in mind, consider the following example.

During the presidential election of 2012 (Obama versus Romney), some accused the media of allowing the polls to drive the national narrative. What they feared was that the rise and fall of polling numbers would enact in the mind of the American populace the "David and Goliath" storyline, one where the unlikely candidate (Romney), against all odds, takes on the establishment, comes from behind, and beats Goliath. That one. They knew that when humans anticipate a particular storyline, we can't see the story ending any other way, so it doesn't. It's self-fulfilling.

Our narrative understanding of the world makes us vulnerable to this kind of manipulation, which is why there is always a battle to control the national narrative. Typically, when you watch the local news, what you'll get is news. If you watch one of the major media outlets (CNN, Fox News, MSNBC, etc.), what you'll get is "news stories"—that is, news told as a story. For example, if you watch Fox News, a conservative narrative threads through the stories. If you watch MSNBC, the "victim/oppressor" storyline of critical race theory threads through the stories. The major media outlets take the granular facts of the local news and supply narrative details that highlight a particular storyline.

It is difficult to understate how easy it is to control the populace when you control the narrative—when you decide what people are hearing in the news, movies, classroom, etc. All critical theories exploit this fact and seize upon the media and the classroom as the commanding heights of social revolution.

But while dominating the narrative confers an ideological advantage, there's no substitute for silencing your critics. In the golden age of communism and fascism, this was done at an industrial scale—mass liquidation. Surprisingly, "canceling" people is just as effective.

CANCELLATION

In a democracy, ideally, the best ideas for a country's future will beat out—in a head-to-head competition—the worst ideas. In this case, the vision, plans, and ideas would stand on their own merit. But in the framework of a neo-Marxist revolution, a fair exchange of ideas is not what you want. You need a hostile takeover. And, as mentioned above, an initial step in that takeover is to control the messaging of educational, political, and media outlets and, in so doing, control the national narrative—tell the public a story that makes your vision seem reasonable, desirable, and inevitable. Going a step further, you probably want to silence opposing viewpoints altogether, and today, that's accomplished not by jail or murder but by cancellation. Cancel culture produces a similar result to imprisoning and executing political opponents—your opposition is indefinitely silenced.

Perhaps the most famous cancellation of any individual is that of J.K. Rowling, author of the Harry Potter series. It received global attention. Rowling summarizes the history of the controversy on her website (the blanks within the statements below represent where profanity and vulgar language are referenced):

> This isn't an easy piece to write, for reasons that will shortly become clear, but I know it's time to explain myself on an issue surrounded by toxicity. I write this without any desire to add to that toxicity.
>
> For people who don't know: last December I tweeted my support for Maya Forstater, a tax specialist who'd lost her job for what were deemed "transphobic" tweets. She took her case to an employment tribunal, asking the judge to rule on whether a philosophical belief that sex is determined by biology is protected in law. Judge Tayler ruled that it wasn't.
>
> My interest in trans issues pre-dated Maya's case by almost two years, during which I followed the debate around the concept of

gender identity closely. I've met trans people, and read sundry books, blogs and articles by trans people, gender specialists, intersex people, psychologists, safeguarding experts, social workers and doctors, and followed the discourse online and in traditional media. On one level, my interest in this issue has been professional, because I'm writing a crime series, set in the present day, and my fictional female detective is of an age to be interested in, and affected by, these issues herself, but on another, it's intensely personal, as I'm about to explain.

All the time I've been researching and learning, accusations and threats from trans activists have been bubbling in my Twitter timeline. This was initially triggered by a "like." When I started taking an interest in gender identity and transgender matters, I began screenshotting comments that interested me, as a way of reminding myself what I might want to research later. On one occasion, I absent-mindedly "liked" instead of screenshotting. That single "like" was deemed evidence of wrongthink, and a persistent low level of harassment began.

Months later, I compounded my accidental "like" crime by following Magdalen Berns on Twitter. Magdalen was an immensely brave young feminist and lesbian who was dying of an aggressive brain tumor. I followed her because I wanted to contact her directly, which I succeeded in doing. However, as Magdalen was a great believer in the importance of biological sex, and didn't believe lesbians should be called bigots for not dating trans women with penises, dots were joined in the heads of twitter trans activists, and the level of social media abuse increased.

I mention all this only to explain that I knew perfectly well what was going to happen when I supported Maya. I must have been on my fourth or fifth cancellation by then. I expected the threats of violence, to be told I was *literally killing trans people with my hate*, to be called ____ and ____ and, of course, for my books to be burned, although one particularly abusive man told me he'd composted them [emphasis Rowling's].[9]

We will return to this example in chapter 2.

I've experienced firsthand the impact of cancel culture in the ministry that I lead, which is on campuses all over the US. There are speech codes, club funding, and speech zones to contend with, along with mandates like allowing Muslim or Buddhist students equal opportunity to run the ministry. Seriously, would anyone think it rational that a vegetarian club on campus be required to allow a meat-eater to run for club president, or allow a neo-Nazi to lead the Jewish club? We've had more than 150 legal inquiries on campuses due to cancel culture, four federal victories, five appellate court victories, two assists in Supreme Court victories, as well as a victory involving atheist groups and the Department of Education that was overseen by President Biden over dismantling a regulation intended to protect religious groups on campus. There exists a campus cancel culture database. By far, most of these cancellations are happening to conservatives and Christians.[10]

The College Fix, who hosts the database, defines cancel culture as "any effort by people or groups to identify someone or something as offensive or unacceptable and seek in some way to censor or punish the transgressor or item."[11] The detailed repository of information lists nearly 2,000 successful or potential cancellations via protest this past decade or so, including everything from statues hauled off campuses to renamed buildings and mascots. It includes professors who have been suspended or lost their jobs for saying or researching something politically questionable; student groups attacked or barred for their conservative, pro-life, or libertarian views; and guest speakers shouted down or disinvited. Yours truly has been the victim of campus cancel culture as a speaker at least three times.

There is much more to be said about cancel culture that we will cover later, but for the moment, it's important to see how it fits within the tactical approach of critical social justice. Through social media, it is possible to break into the home of your ideological rival, threaten them, denigrate them, ruin them, and then make them disappear.

FROM WOKE WORD TO WOKE WORK (DEI)

When it comes to understanding critical social justice in our culture, proponents display significant aspects for us under the acronym DEI (diversity, equity, and inclusion).

As we've seen, these terms are misleading, sometimes meaning their exact opposite—for what decent human being would disparage someone's cultural background, or exclude them, or treat them unfairly? No one. And in all three cases, that's not what the word signifies in the context of critical theory. Through the lens of critical theory, *diversity* points to a concerted effort to marginalize majority culture, typically white people (when race is the topic). *Equity* means equal outcomes, not equal opportunity, and so handicapping advantage. And *inclusion* means embracing anyone's declared identity, whether someone identifies as, for example, gay or straight or trans, or pan, or even if they identify as an animal.

There are three major branches in my field of philosophy, and they can be ordered in terms of what is most to least foundational: Metaphysics concerns what exists or what is real, epistemology concerns rationality and theories of knowledge, and ethics concerns matters of good and evil. Philosophy, in a nutshell, explores what is real; then, how to know what is real; and finally, how then we should live based on what we know about reality.

Philosophy examines all worldviews through this trifold grid, and it will be instructive to view DEI through it. But to better understand it and for more than mere rhetorical purposes, occasionally we'll treat the ordering of the acronym DEI as DIE, which becomes more profound when we see actual consequences from the wages of our cultural sin that leads to death.

Diversity: Order 1—Metaphysics of Human Relations as Social Binaries

Social justice ideology teaches that all people everywhere exist in social binaries juxtaposed in conflicting relationships along the axes of class, race, sex, gender, ethnicity, ability, religion, and so forth. For every social group, there is an opposite group.

The focus of critical theory is to identify and segregate the various oppressor/oppressed, dominant/subordinate social binary groups (men versus women, white versus black, Christian versus non-Christian, rich versus poor, heteronormative versus LGBTQ+, haves versus have-nots, etc.). Oppressor groups have power and therefore privilege over other groups. Our primary identity is a group identity, not an individual identity. Groups come with identity power, ergo the focus on identity politics. Moreover, everyone has multiple group identities that often intersect in layers of power imbalance. Black female lesbians, for example, are thrice oppressed according to this matrix. This intersectionality depicts a complex interlocking power dynamic of group inequalities and therefore group injustices. To have justice for all requires having outcome equality for all.

Inclusion: Order 2—Epistemology of Standpoint

Standpoint theory or standpoint epistemology is a notion coined by early '70s feminist philosopher Sandra Harding, who concedes that she got it from Marxism. The way we know about such reality of human social relations is that our social position/location in society informs us. We have "lived experience," which, even if not supported by argument, reason, or evidential data, trumps all else. As an example, a black man knows his oppression by white men. He knows what it's like to live in a white-man world, but not vice versa. He has special knowledge simply by virtue of being black. And a black woman has special knowledge that a black man lacks.

Here, we are to assess blame by including oppressed groups and excluding oppressor groups from sharing their voices or opportunities because oppressors are often blind to their oppression and need to listen. We choose the victims in this narrative because they come with knowledge and moral authority, which resides esoterically only among the oppressed. They are the enlightened (i.e., "woke"). Such "knowledge" is grounded in social location, in one's standpoint relative to the identity of the group(s). Knowledge is also viewed as socially constructed and infused with ideology and power. The rest of the people must simply listen, learn, and lament about the oppression, with little hope for absolution from their blindness owing to their culpable group oppression of the oppressed.

Equity: Order 3—Ethics of Critical Social Justice

Whereas the original notion of "social justice" was coined by a Catholic priest,[12] contemporary social justice means something else. While traditionally equity was a finance term and inequality a mathematical term, times have changed. Again, changing the meaning of words influences the narrative. It is time to exact consequences for inequalities between groups. Inequality under this new paradigm entails injustice. Social group inequality, in every instance, entails social injustice. Because the human problem is social inequality / oppression, then the solution is social justice / liberation.

Given this context and the meaning of the term *social justice* within critical theory, meting out justice[13] implies things like reparations and payback to right the wrong of the power imbalance. Often, there is no purgatory and no forgiveness. Social justice advocates now contrast equity with equality because they think systemic oppression requires unequal treatment of groups in the power imbalance to arrive at real social justice. That is, we ought to treat white and black applicants unequally given the past. Hence, equity is equal outcome, not equal opportunity.

WOKE IN THE WORKPLACE

Now, you can see how such an esoteric worldview might thrive on the college campus; tenured professors live in an imaginary world, unconstrained by a competitive marketplace or having to make payroll. To put it bluntly, their ideas don't need to work. So how did critical social justice jump from the public sector to the private sector? How did it get out of the lab?

What happens at the university doesn't stay at the university. But for theories to affect reality, there must be a vehicle of transport, some bridge extending from the university out to the real world. DEI is that bridge.

The question must be asked: In the case of DEI, how could so much philosophical complexity be overlaid onto a corporate structure? First, you would need to hire dedicated staff whose only job is to think about group disparities in terms of race, gender, and sexual orientation. This is why many businesses do not have simply a DEI person; they have a whole DEI department.

Second, while organizing a workforce according to social identity groups based on their degree of oppression (intersectionality) may sound daunting, practically speaking, it's not—oppressors to one side of the room, everyone else (oppressed) to the other.

Third, DEI initiatives move in only two directions. There are, first, programs and events and, second, processes and protocols that buoy the "everyone-else" side. Examples of programs are diversity days, ethnic-heritage months, and BIPOC socials. An example of processes and protocols are practices like hiring and promotion quotas, making sure minority identity groups are equally represented.

Managing the main oppressor group (heterosexual, white males) requires more nuance, but in short, a concerted effort is made to treat white people in the workplace like blacks, Hispanics, and Asians were treated in the US in the 1940s. They may be passed over for promotion, unfairly subordinated to less qualified individuals, spoken of pejoratively, scapegoated for workplace failures; they may go unrecognized for accomplishments, have their opinions marginalized, and be caricatured as obtuse, lazy, and so on.

WOKE WEARS OUT ITS WELCOME

While DEI has successfully spread throughout the business world, it is losing traction, and the reason is obvious. Besides splintering the workplace, the aims of DEI are fundamentally at odds with the aims of a for-profit company, eating into the bottom line. A case in point is the now infamous Bud Light transgender activist commercials. They have cost Budweiser more than $1 billion in lost revenue.[14] Or take Target's transgender bikini apparel in the children's aisles, which led to a huge number of customers refusing to shop at the retail chain.[15] Woke ideology can cost money and stir up legal problems. For companies, whether the focus is working toward profit, the cost of legal fees, or simply hiring people who are good at their job, the bottom line will always be the bottom line.

Or consider the attempted assassination of Donald J. Trump while speaking at a campaign rally in Butler, Pennsylvania. According to an article in *The Western Journal*, 39 members of the Secret Service signed a petition demanding an investigation into whether the agency's training was adequate or whether diversity initiatives had caused lower standards.[16] This petition was submitted in May, months before Trump gave his earlobe to the cause of liberty.

At issue were DEI hiring policies. Kimberly Cheatle, head of the Secret

Service, made it "job #1" the day that she took office to make female agents comprise 30 percent of the workforce, which put the emphasis of hiring on gender, not competence.[17] As opponents of DEI like to point out, DEI could just as easily be DIE, and in this case, it was—some argued that DEI policies had led to lower standards of security and resulted in someone's death, other injured persons, and the near death of a former president.

For a Christian company, DEI not only adversely affects the bottom line, but it also adversely affects Christian values, which is why Chick-fil-A, a Christian-owned company founded by the late S. Truett Cathy, initially resisted the waves of DEI hiring that have become commonplace in the United States. But the pressure of the LGBTQ+ community was overwhelming, and if not for the support of Christians going out of their way to buy from Chick-fil-A (and a mainstream popular Kanye West song), the company would likely have had no choice but to capitulate.

Over time, however, Chick-fil-A not only showed evidence of compromise relative to pulling its own charitable donations from conservative ministries (e.g., Salvation Army and Fellowship of Christian Athletes), but it began giving donations to LGBTQ+-friendly enterprises without the awareness of most of its supporters, along with what appears to be conciliation with DEI practices and policies.[18] The web page still gives Chick-fil-A's corporate purpose, which is "To glorify God by being a faithful steward of all that is entrusted to us. To have a positive influence on all who come into contact with Chick-fil-A." But until recently, the website included content about valuing identity groups and endorsing diversity, equity, and inclusion—content that it has since removed.[19] While these moves in the corporate office don't necessarily reflect the viewpoint of all of Chick-fil-A's franchises, it is nonetheless unfortunate that a Christian company felt compelled to hire a vice president of DEI even though its most ardent supporters provided it with the ability to resist succumbing to cultural pressure.

While some companies willingly or willfully embrace DEI, others get pressured from consumers or financers. On the Blackrock Financial website, Larry Fink, a social justice advocate and CEO of Blackrock (which is one of the world's largest investment companies), said that corporate social responsibility is now part of the cost of doing business. Companies are now being given ESG (environmental, social, and governance) scores. ESG analyses evaluate risks and opportunities beyond the scope of traditional financial analyses. Fink said in his 2018 letter to investors, "To prosper over time, every company must not only deliver financial performance, but also show how it makes a positive contribution to society."[20] And by "positive contribution," he means in accordance with diversity, equity, and inclusion—DEI. Certain social credit scores are now assigned to companies and are taken into account when a business seeks to be financed. The gun of financing is being held to their corporate heads. Some corporations push back, some capitulate, most passively accept DEI and ESG as the "new normals."

DEI, cancel culture, the policing of words, and controlling the narrative—all things we've touched on—are in the category of what Joseph Nye famously called "soft power," which is defined as "the ability to influence the behavior of others to get the outcomes you want."[21] Hard power is not that. Once ideology is codified into law, dissent becomes illegal, and the state is then authorized to use "hard power" to physically enforce its laws, and that's when things get interesting.

PASSED INTO LAW

From the Justice Department and the Office of the Attorney General to the National Institutes of Health, Sandia National Laboratories, and the Federal Bureau of Investigation, these organizations have all spent years pursuing antiracism initiatives and training people to check their power and privilege. How this is supposed to assist in productivity, security, and genuine equality at America's nuclear labs is not clear. According to cultural critic Chris Rufo, what is clear is that appointing people to what ought to be meritocratic positions is endangering us all.[22] President Biden signed his most sweeping executive order of his presidency in early 2023.[23] It is an all-government expansion of equity, creating cadres of DEI officers.

In Marxist regimes, an administrative tier of political commissars monitor and police state policy and ideological adherence—foot soldiers of "the Party." To many, the intent of Biden's executive order was to create such a tier within the US government, populated by DEI officers whose mandate is

"Embedding Equity into Government-wide Processes."[24] Its intent is to redistribute resources and outcomes via coercive means even without congressional approval and oversight. In a manner best described as gestapo-esque, the department of DEI commands the heads of federal departments and agencies to establish agency equity teams within 30 days. This edict runs all the way from the most prestigious and powerful departments, such as the Treasury and Defense, to the National Aeronautics and Space Administration (NASA) and the National Science Foundation (NSF). Note carefully that Biden, in his push to further antiracism and combat systemic racism, systemic sexism, patriarchalism, heteronormativity, white privilege, and the like, did not in any way give up his seat of power to the "underrepresented" classes. It never happens.

We've been seeing this poison in public policy for some time. Until a decade ago, cultural support for same-sex marriage was in the minority. Sentiments toward LGBTQ+ have quickly become normal, and in the mind of many, it is quickly becoming normative (i.e., denoting the way it ought to be).

In his first term as president, it was difficult to tell where Barack Obama stood on the various ideologies amalgamated in LGBTQ+; in fact, he was on record for saying that marriage was "the union between a man and a woman."[25] But in May 2012, he changed his views and publicly endorsed gay marriage. A Pew Research Center poll reveals that support for the change among Democratic voters moved from 50 percent in 2008 to 65 percent in 2012.[26] It was time, both practically and ideologically, to make the move.

Consider an important aspect of voting. As people age, some "age out" of voting due to death or otherwise, and at the same time, a new generation is always "aging in," which might seem to balance out, but it doesn't. Older generations are—by and large—more conservative, while emerging generations are, by and large, more progressive, making the electorate ever so slowly lean to the left. Only now, the change hasn't been so slow, not since TikTok, social media, and progressive teachers' unions made it their mission to reeducate our youth.

That same year, 2012, the LGBTQ+ movement became a part of the party platform at the Democratic National Convention (DNC). Not unimportant is the fact that at the DNC that year, electors were in a tug-of-war over whether "God" should remain in the party platform or not. With visible perplexity and reluctance, having taken several repeat votes hearing from the "yeas" and "nays" so closely in competition, the resolutions chairman concluded in the affirmative that God could stay in the platform. But if you listen to that 2012 vote on video, it's pretty clear that the "nays" won, and God did not.[27]

The first openly LGBT nonincumbent elected to the US Senate was Tammy Baldwin (D) in 2012. (Baldwin served in the US House of Representatives from 1999–2013.) The first openly bisexual member of Congress was Kyrsten Sinema (D) in 2013. In 2014, President Obama signed an executive order protecting transgender people in matters of employment hiring, and he was the first president to use the term *transgender* in a State of the Union speech, which he delivered on January 20, 2015. Months later, *Obergefell v. Hodges*, a case in which the US Supreme Court ruled (5–4) on June 26, 2015, meant that states had to license and recognize same-sex marriages under the due process and equal protection clauses of the Fourteenth Amendment to the US Constitution. In 2020, the High Court's ruling in *Bostock v. Clayton County* confirmed the protections under the law that sexual orientation and gender identity have regarding employment discrimination.

It is important to recognize this is not a partisan observation. The internationally famous athlete who won the 1976 Olympic decathlon (who appeared on the Wheaties cereal box), Bruce Jenner, made the public announcement in April 2015 that he was now a woman—a transgender woman dressed scantily on the cover of *Vanity Fair* with a note: "Call me Caitlyn."[28] He was finally living as his true self in accordance with his truth. Just six years later, in April 2021, the new Caitlyn Jenner ran for governor of the state of California—not as a Democrat but as a Republican. What's more is that Jenner possessed various national-level Republican support. In 2023, ironically, in response to the increased involvement of men who were trans entering women's sports, Jenner launched a political action committee to oppose it.[29] While the Republicans may be trailing the Democrats in culturally changing values, clearly the face of politics is changing—and changing rapidly—with many on the left now labeled "moderate," not because of politics, but because of proximity to the far left.

For now, however, our media and many elitists in our academic and political culture have celebrated many "firsts" in our nation's progress. Here's just a partial list from the Biden early presidency:

- first black female vice president
- first gay transportation secretary
- first transgender assistant secretary for health for the US Department of Health and Human Services
- first gay and Jewish State Department spokesman
- first black female Supreme Court justice
- first black lesbian White House press secretary
- first nonbinary gender-fluid deputy assistant secretary of spent fuel and waste disposition in the Office of Nuclear Energy
- first government military recruiting video explicitly marketing to gay, feminist, and trans people to join the US Army, followed by a navy recruiting video featuring a drag queen

The list of that administration's accomplishments goes on and on, but they are only viewed as "accomplishments" through a certain philosophical window. From the perspective of merit, many are underqualified and many have underperformed.

A TOUR OF CAMPUS

To give you a basic primer on critical social justice, we've discussed the topic in contexts you likely are familiar with. In the next four chapters, you'll join me in my context, the university, where this ideology has reached a level of madness you have to see to believe.

2

A CASE OF SEXUALIZED AND GENDERIZED INSANITY

Several decades ago, a movement was launched, for which the motto was "Ideas Worth Spreading." It was called TED Talks, and the tagline "Ideas Worth Spreading" trades on similarities between ideas and viruses—and there are many. Famed atheist Richard Dawkins coined the term *mind viruses* for destructive beliefs and ideologies that spread with viral rapidity. Dawkins views human mimicry (*mimesis*) as the mechanism for spreading "mind viruses" or "social contagion," defined as "the spread of affect, attitude, or behavior 'where the recipient does not perceive an intentional influence attempt on the part of the initiator.'"[1] The incubator of social contagions, above all others, is the American university. Revolution is born and bred at the university because beliefs precede behavior, and beliefs are born of ideas, and ideas are the currency of educational institutions.

But not every idea is a good one, and the university is host to all manner of degenerative ideas and ideologies. For example, the 2023 course catalog at Princeton began offering undergraduates the educational opportunity of "Black + Queer in Leather: Black Leather/BDSM Material Culture," where BDSM means bondage, discipline (or domination), sadism, and masochism (as a type of sexual practice).[2] The course was cross-listed with the Program in

Visual Arts, the African American Studies Department, and the Gender and Sexuality Studies Department. Tiona McClodden, a 2021–2023 Arts Fellow with Princeton's Lewis Center for the Arts, was listed as its instructor. This forms part of the reading list found on the university website:

> Amber Jamilla Musser, *Sensational Flesh: Race, Power, and Masochism*
>
> Ariane Cruz, *The Color of Kink: Black Women, BDSM, and Pornography*
>
> Jennifer C. Nash, *The Black Body in Ecstasy: Reading Race, Reading Pornography*
>
> Emily Apter and William Pietz (eds.), *Fetishism as Cultural Discourse*
>
> Joseph Beam, *In the Life: A Black Gay Anthology*
>
> Mireille Miller-Young, *A Taste for Brown Sugar: Black Women in Pornography*

But educational opportunities aren't limited to course offerings at Princeton. There are also visiting professors and lecturers who expose students to the latest ideas in scholarship. Recently, Princeton invited a professor from the University of Washington to visit: a "queer-trans-feminist river scientist" to discuss research grounded in a "queer and trans focus on love and grief for rivers and fish." It was the topic of Cleo Wölfle Hazard's recent book, titled *Underflows: Queer Trans Ecologies and River Justice* (Feminist Technosciences Series), published in 2022 by the University of Washington Press.[3]

I've been to Princeton. I've seen the school's motto on the building architecture as well as the website, a motto as old as its founding in 1746: "Under God She Flourishes." On the seal, there is a Bible with the words *Old New Testament* in Latin. Things have changed. Examples of such courses or venues can be enumerated endlessly at our nation's most prestigious (and expensive) public and private universities.

But remember, what happens in the university doesn't stay in the university, so the madness on campus has become the madness of corporate America. At one time, big business remained neutral and avoided the culture war's controversial issues in order to reach the broadest customer or client base. That changed in 2015. My state of Indiana's legislature passed a religious freedom bill that would've provided protection for businesses refusing to go along with the LGBTQ+ agenda. But a coalition of elite businesses—including Apple, Salesforce, Eli Lilly, eBay, and others—threatened economic boycotts against Indiana if it didn't reverse course.

Then-Governor Mike Pence capitulated. Big-business leftism learned that you could bully states into submission and began a practice of it elsewhere. The standard thinking of the past was that when kids leave universities, they'll grow up, get jobs, and leave the nonsense behind. They did get jobs, and they brought the university ideology with them. Now, the (critical) social justice ethos is viewed as "corporate social responsibility." Human resources departments have begun to function as social justice commissariats. It has become commonplace for Fortune 500 companies to hire diversity, equity, and inclusion (DEI) officers whose sole job is to flush social justice ideology throughout the corporate world. But with the push of the second-term Trump administration to eradicate DEI throughout the federal government, many in the corporate world began to roll it back as well.

ALPHABET SOUP

LGBTQ+ is a political force unlike anything we've seen; this isn't the neat bifurcation of right and left, conservative and liberal, but an array of sexual and ethnic identities, all claiming victim status, all demanding to be recognized, and all bundled together (via intersectionality) for maximum political clout so that they can subvert, dismantle, reimagine, and ultimately, transform America and the West.

One atheist philosopher whom I've forged communication with is none other than the (in)famous Peter Singer of Princeton University. Singer's progressivism has "progressed" further than most because he affirms that one might consider sex with animals so long as it is mutually consensual and no harm is inflicted on the animal.[4] This is perfectly consistent with his ethical theory of consequentialism. While his discernment of "consent" is itself intriguing to some academics (and disgusting to the rest of us), the mutual consent idea in our sex-saturated society has primed the way for both sex with minors and with animals. Ironically, politics has yet to catch up, because every state (except West Virginia) retains laws against human intercourse with animals.

A gay cleric acquaintance of mine was once visibly shocked by the question I posed during a lunch conversation with him. In trying to grasp the ever-changing and perhaps growing alphabet LGBTQQIAAP+ (the plus sign represents an openness for additional non-cis-heteronormative minorities), I asked about MAP being added to the ever-growing list. Laughing almost embarrassingly, he said, "We're always trying to add more." This was followed by him inquiring into the meaning of MAP. When I told him that it was an acronym at an academic conference standing for minor-attracted persons (because the term *pedophile* is now being slowly dismissed as hurtful and harmful speech), in a visceral response, he placed one hand on his forehead and the other on his gut, gasping, "I know, I know. I see where the logic is going. But there is just something about that which is just wrong." I said nothing. Silence. He said he understood the logic, but he was clearly uncomprehending, in some sense, of the arbitrary nature of moral relativism. Why is it "just wrong"?

Indeed, according to Singer, who some consider to be the most famous moral philosopher alive and who adopts what is perhaps the most popular normative ethics position among academics, utilitarianism, a view in which "nothing is just wrong." Another atheist friend of mine once told me that he has gay kids at home, and he thinks that they ought to be able to have sex with whoever they want because he doesn't believe in sin. Fair enough, I suppose. No God. No way to violate a divine moral law. If God is dead, everything is permissible. But he followed that by claiming, "This trans stuff is just nuts." But by whose or what standard is it "just nuts"? Whose rationality or morality?

I've traveled to several universities to speak and conducted hours and hours of student interviews from places like Indiana and Purdue Universities to Florida State and Florida A&M Universities. Shockingly, not a single student (including those claiming to adhere to Christianity) failed on some level to be a moral relativist. The buzz words are "my truth" and "your truth." People today quite literally believe what we were told as children—namely, that we can be whatever we want. Literally anything. A different gender. A different race. A different species. And more, so long as one self-consents or self-identifies as such, each can follow his or her or its own truth. "I think I am a woman. Therefore, I am a woman."

In 1995, we were told that kids who were homeschooled were "weird." But today, in our public schools, kids self-identify as *furries*, *fursona*, or *otherkin*, members of a made-up species. One is reminded of a conversation between Alice and the queen addressing beliefs in Lewis Carroll's children's story *Through the Looking Glass*:

> The Queen remarked… "Now I'll give YOU something to believe. I'm just one hundred and one, five months and a day." "I can't believe THAT!" said Alice. "Can't you?" the Queen said in a pitying tone. "Try again: draw a long breath, and shut your eyes." Alice laughed. "There's no use trying," she said: "one CAN'T believe impossible things." "I daresay you haven't had much practice," said the Queen. "When I was your age, I always did it for half-an-hour a day. Why, sometimes I've believed as many as six impossible things before breakfast."[5]

Six impossible things before breakfast. Matters have become much worse. Only we aren't in Wonderland; we are one-quarter into the twenty-first century in the most affluent, most formally educated, most influential, and formerly one of the most devoutly Christian countries on earth.

Through mass miseducation and social contagion, we have an entire society experiencing mass psychosis or else conforming to group pressure to appear virtuous in what church historian Carl Trueman calls "virtuous victimology."[6] The sexual revolution of the past, and that which is manifesting on campuses today, is but a symptom, not the cause, in the search for human identity. Trueman's work is motivated by the curiosity of how statements like "I am a woman trapped in a man's body" can register as coherent and meaningful. His book *The Rise and Triumph of the Modern Self* masterfully traces the path of the self being psychologized, psychology being sexualized, and sex being politicized. The current revolution is now celebrated so widely as to include promoting celebrity 11-year-old drag queen children on mainstream media.

The classical children's story *The Emperor's New Clothes* illustrates, in an alarming way, what many see happening in our culture. The central theme of Hans Christian Andersen's story is that illusion depends at least in part on self-deception on the part of those being deceived. The emperor and his courtiers pretend he is wearing clothes because they do not wish to appear foolish but, in the end, only look more so.

THE HUMAN GE-NONE

Here's an interesting fact: There is no "gay gene." This often comes as a shock to people when I say it because news of the research was so obfuscated by the media at its release. I will assume, however, that leading lesbian academics like Dr. Lisa Diamond, professor of psychology and gender studies at the University of Utah, have read the research because, along with the American Psychological Association, Diamond now concedes that the argument of "born that way" should be abandoned.

Professor Diamond studies the expression of sexual attractions and sexual identity over a person's lifetime and the influences of early life experiences on later sexual development. She is known for her research on sexual fluidity, which describes the capacity for individuals to experience shifts in their pattern of same-sex and other-sex attractions over time. She is coeditor of the *APA Handbook of Sexuality and Psychology* and is a fellow of two divisions of the APA. She has published more than 100 articles and book chapters and has been invited to present her research all over the world. Diamond states,

> As a community, the queers have to stop saying, "Please help us. We were born this way, and we can't change," as an argument for legal standing. I don't think we need that argument, and that argument is gonna bite us in the ass because now we know that there's enough data out there that the other side is aware of it as much as we are aware of it.[7]

For years, "born that way" has been used to gain equality. "Born This Way" is the title of a Lady Gaga song that became an unofficial anthem for the gay community. The plea for victimhood based on inborn genes is false and no longer necessary. It's not scientifically accurate, no longer legally necessary, and it is unjust, according to Diamond. Sexual orientation isn't fixed, according to her research. She doesn't advocate people trying to change others but concedes that our preferences and desires and orientations change themselves all the time. According to Diamond, we aren't born that way and no longer need the phrase to legally prove the legitimacy of the lifestyle—that's already been accomplished.

According to Diamond, "we all deserve equality," but she never tells us what that equality is based on. Apparently it's based on justice, but according to whose or what standard of justice? For Diamond, sexual autonomy is now the central issue: "Our genes are not the issue. It is our lives that are at stake. Either we are a society that protects and defends all individual sexual autonomy, or we are not."[8] Of course, we now want to ask if she really means that. Or does she simply fail to grasp the significance of her words? All individual sexual autonomy—really? Pedophiles? Animals?

Things have become quite queered (meaning blurred or blended) these days. Linn Tonstad, a systematic theologian at Yale Divinity School (and open lesbian), wrote a book that forms the basis of a course she teaches. It's called *Queer Theology: Beyond Apologetics* (Cascade, 2018). She says, "I warn students that much of what we'll be reading will not be theology, but texts from an academic discipline known as queer theory."[9] This flags our attention that her approach to theology is guided by a philosophy—a philosophy of what might be called "critical queer theory," cousin to critical race theory. According to Tonstad, we no longer need to justify or argue for homosexuality. It and much more are here to stay. We now need to assume its normativity and get on with making it mainstream. In a paradoxical way, the very notion of what is queer is anything but normative, or a way that things ought to be. She says, "One of the most famous definitions of 'queer' calls it 'an identity without an essence,' that is 'defined wholly relationally, by its distance to and difference from the normative.'"[10] She explores ways in which God and Christianity can be queered. She has adopted and teaches queer theory, and queer theology at Yale Divinity School, no less.

One can begin to surmise from this philosophical pit—not science—how theories of trans identity begin to find their way. Biology is not bigotry. It's simply science. A man is a man, and a woman is a woman—binaries that are as fundamental as anything we know. John Adams once remarked that "facts are stubborn things."[11] Returning to homosexuality, one of the most comprehensive studies to date, mentioned in *Science* magazine, has confirmed that there is no gay gene.[12]

When research on exhaustive genetic study was released, however, the news headlines didn't read "There is no gay gene" but rather "Homosexuality has a biological basis." What does it mean to say that "homosexuality has a biological basis"? Nothing. Absolutely nothing—at least nothing at the level of importance those invested in the topic sometimes hope for. My preference for cotton candy has a biological component to it; every heritable trait or predisposition or polygenetic influence has a biological component, but that isn't determinative. I may be drawn to cotton candy, but I can choose to never try cotton candy, and if I never try it, I will never come to love or need it. Here are some concluding takeaways from the largest study ever as documented in *Science* magazine:

> Thus, although they did find particular genetic loci associated with same-sex behavior, when they combine the effects of these loci together into one comprehensive score, the effects are so small (under 1%) that this genetic score cannot in any way be used to predict same-sex sexual behavior of an individual...Sexuality is dynamic, with the ability to express and realize sexual preferences, and is thus also shaped and regulated by cultural, political, social, legal, and religious structures.[13]

The bottom line is that homosexuality lacks a "gay gene" like adultery lacks an "adultery gene" and having multiple sex partners lacks an "I-want-multiple-sex-partners gene." Some people may have heritable traits that incline them to desire chocolate or prefer the color blue, but there is no specific genetic determination for this. Never was. Never will be. We've mapped the human genome since 2004. We know the answer to the question, Are we born that way? And the social impact of the answer is precisely nil; it matters not a whit because the gay-parade rhetoric of "hate or celebrate" won the sentimental war—the battle for hearts and minds. As Abraham Lincoln famously said, "Public sentiment is everything. With public sentiment, nothing can fail; without it, nothing can succeed. Consequently, he who molds public sentiment goes deeper than he who enacts statues or pronounces decisions."[14]

OF COURSE THERE ARE HARD CASES

I'm not saying that no hard cases exist. They do. For example, there is a condition called *intersex*. Just as there exists the abnormality or defect of being born blind, so also one can be born with abnormality leading to confusing sexual "parts." It's a fallen world. People are to be loved regardless. Embryos will develop with every cell carrying two Xs or an X and a Y. Typically, XX means female, together with parts like a vulva, ovaries, and a uterus. XY means male, together with parts like a penis, testes, and a prostate. The former, not the latter, will eventually have periods and, unless some future defect occurs, is able to reproduce.

But a lot can happen in embryonic development. In rare cases, there is confusion because the fusing of the egg and sperm goes wrong. Babies can develop XXX, XXY, or XYY without hard physiological signs appearing. Sometimes people can lean male genetically but female anatomically or vice versa, and sometimes in between. Sometimes a baby is born with disagreeable genitalia, resulting in some cases in which doctors do surgical sex reassignment, and that sex doesn't always align with how that person sees themselves as an adult. Most of this is a growing social inclination as it becomes popular, but it isn't likely all blamed on that. One surgeon I spoke with told me he usually sides with genetics in which operation to conduct or advise, and then into adulthood, most things go the normative route. But intersex is real, and we need to make thoughtful and careful accommodation for that.

Nonetheless, a biological defect, abnormality, or anomaly in no way establishes anything beyond the normative gender binary of male and female. Encouraging laws that destroy girls' sports and privacy and encouraging sex-reassignment surgeries and hormone therapy at early ages is child abuse, and the medical community should know better. But these days, it is not hard to find a doctor willing to make a buck. Playing on suicide statistics and implying that children's freedom to express themselves and "their truth" through gender-reassignment surgery is necessary to curb suicidality is without evidential support.[15] Black people in American history from slavery to Jim Crow were often treated far worse, and we don't see evidence for suicidality being caused by their social ostracization. Suicidality associated with transgender dysphoria seems more resident to the person for other reasons than causal pressure from society. And the Hippocratic oath medical doctors have taken since the ancient world is supposed to be about helping, not harming. Love wills the good of the other. But many doctors today are more concerned about virtue signaling and/or prospering than "doing no harm" in accordance with their oath. Copycat trans activity among middle school and elementary school kids has increased in this social contagion because of many irresponsible and unloving adults (including parents) who encourage this plague on civilization.

FRICTION BETWEEN LETTERS

It is assumed that the various factions that make up LGBTQ+ are a harmonious and happy family, but that's far from the case. It's a marriage of convenience, by which I mean the amalgamation of these eclectic communities is for purposes of political clout, not collegiality. The relational reality is that significant infighting occurs among the members of the LGBTQ+ community.

There has been, for example, a heated exchange on the side of LGB against T, displaying an X (formerly Twitter) hashtag issued largely by members of the gay community, #LGBdroptheT. The return fire from T was to call those oppressing them, including lesbians and feminists, TERFs (trans-exclusive radical feminists). The bickering among these factions is far more than sibling rivalry or jealousy over transgender people hogging all the public sympathy. It is rather a substantive disagreement over the question, What is a woman?

How can one be a lesbian if there is no such thing as a woman? Yet this thinking is becoming so accepted in our culture that even the most recently confirmed member of the US Supreme Court failed to answer the question, claiming that she didn't know what a woman was because she wasn't a biologist. What is a gay man? How can one know unless one first knows what a man is? Lesbians often claim that they have a choice but *choose* not to sleep with the enemy (men). Gay men, by contrast, claim to be "born that way"—that is, males attracted to males. Matters are apparently just as confusing for members of the LGBTQ+ community as they are for everyone else.

These internal rifts are real and the tension palpable, as seen in everything from high school girls' sports and women's Olympic teams having been dominated by males claiming to be transgender women to transgender women entering women's prisons and bathrooms only later to have actually raped women. (A transgender woman is a biological male at birth but claims to have a psychological identity as female.)

Although the creative alphabet has proved a productive political alliance, there are signs of the alliance unraveling. Lesbian women who are typically feminists and gay men who claim to be born men with a natural orientation toward men don't always appreciate the T.

In 2019, a bias-reporting complaint was filed at the University of Michigan by a student identifying as a transgender woman. The complaint was that the group this student sought involvement with, Lez Get Crafty, was a lesbian group made exclusively for women and they denied her membership on the grounds that "she" was "he" and their group was for radical feminist women, indeed, lesbian women who are women as such. The group Lez (for lesbian) Get Crafty began posting flyers around the University of Michigan campus seeking members. The group limited its membership to lesbians who wanted to "express their creative side." But the group's problem was that it was "exclusively for 'lesbian Womyn-born-Womyn,' excluding transgender women born male." This was reported to the University of Michigan's bias response team by a student offended by the membership requirements. Apparently, dozens of such complaints were filed.[16] (Bias response teams have become a common forum for people to submit their grievances against things by which they have been offended.) You see the problem? Such cases are submitted on many campuses but not always picked up by the media, which often wants to avoid providing coverage that reveals an unwanted divide in an otherwise unified block of people.

But in the middle of 2020, when the infamous COVID-19 pandemic was in full swing and the George Floyd riots were sweeping America (and cultures around the world), none other than J.K. Rowling got involved. As we've previously discussed, Rowling, author of Harry Potter, the bestselling book series in the history of literature, is an avid feminist and defender of women and yet targeted by the trans community.

Rowling went public in her defense of women as women and against the charge of TERF lobbied at her and others simply because they "didn't believe that lesbians should be called bigots for not dating trans women with penises." She said, "Dots were joined in the heads of twitter trans activists… I expected the threats of violence, to be told I was *literally killing trans people with my hate*" (emphasis Rowling's). She went on to explain that her passion wasn't only over free speech in support of a classically liberal order but over so many detransitioners now reporting regret for being misled while young, as the number of little girls now making decisions toward transitioning has skyrocketed at alarming rates.[17]

In quick response, *The Guardian* ran an article titled "UK's Only Trans Philosophy Professor to JK Rowling: Harry Potter Helped Me Become a Woman,"[18] which pushed back against Rowling. The author, Timothy Chappell (now called Sophie Grace Chappell), was a transgender woman (a man claiming to be a woman) heavily involved in the trans community and, more consequentially, turned out to be the external examiner when I defended my PhD in Scotland in 2013.

In the British system, there is an internal and external examiner in the dissertation defense. The one to fear is the external examiner, who has no connection to the university from which you'll potentially graduate and thus has no "dog in the fight," so to speak, for your success. So, I researched him before arriving and found his work interesting: He was a moral philosopher who had written on virtue theory as well as Saint Augustine, among other topics. He was a father of four and enjoyed hiking and skiing, among other things. He was involved with the leadership of the LGBT community of the Church of Scotland, which had approved of gay marriage shortly before my arrival.

During my defense, or "viva," as they call it in the United Kingdom, Dr. Chappell and I disagreed over the role of God in Aristotle's *Nicomachean Ethics*. Aristotle's main point in his most famous treatise cannot so much as get off the tarmac without appeal to God, and ultimately, Chappell conceded, though he did have me rewrite my final chapter, and by the time I rewrote it, he was she.

In his response to Rowling in *The Guardian*, Chappell revealed his intense struggles during his childhood, exclaiming, "I was desperate to escape, to be someone else, to be in another world where I could be me." The claim was that she was a woman trapped in a man's body, had married, fathered four children, and finally had her moment of realization. Chappell was evidently triggered by *Harry Potter and the Philosopher's Stone*: "The mirror of Erised… struck me as a really heartbreaking image for my own condition," he wrote in his letter to Rowling. "If I looked in the magic mirror and saw myself exactly as I most long to be, what would I see?" The answer, Chappell goes on, was "a woman, of course." This is why Chappell was shocked at Rowling's essay saying trans activism was dangerous to cis women (women born women).

Chappell continued, "But we have to fight for our rights—and the thing people fail to realize is: who stands to gain from setting gay women and trans women against one another? The answer, of course, is the right: they want a society that's misinformed, ignorant, terrified of otherness and divided, because that makes it easier for them to run it."[19] Clearly, the LGBTQ+ coalition is a political but not a natural coalition.

Chappell's point was to draw together the disparate and often unnatural elements of the LGBTQ+ fighting one another so that they could again, as an intersectional group, possess power to resist those who seek to run others in the world via misinformation, ignorance, and fear.

Today, the T has eclipsed other members in the LGBTQ+ community to the point where they receive the greatest of all victims' status, some earning $1,200 per month in San Francisco, California, for being transgender individuals who are of low income. In 2017, California enacted a law that threatened jail time for healthcare workers who refuse to use patients' requested gender pronouns. New York had earlier adopted a similar law applicable to employers, landlords, and business owners.[20]

Previously in my career, I was teaching an ethics class at Indiana University, using notable texts and articles by atheist ethicists whose views I did not agree with. I taught nine different courses in the department in both religion and philosophy, had good reports from the students, and was in good standing with the administration. Once, I had a student who, when I covered the sexuality area of the text and offered an educated alternative, yelled at me, berated me as a homophobe, and later turned me in to the department for creating a hostile and suicidal environment. The student insinuated that because LGBTQ+ individuals were already prone to suicidality due to cultural pressures, I was adding to the problem. The student wanted an apology; they wanted me to "correct" the information and a guarantee that I'd never hurt anyone ever again. They wanted to make an example of me. *What misinformation?*

I told the class that with or without God, homosexuality is unnatural and unhealthy because of our anatomy and physiology. It's a biological fact that whereas the vagina can expel a baby (akin to a ten-pound bowling ball) given its natural elasticity, an anal sphincter has no such elasticity. Rectal intercourse creates immune system problems, explaining why the immune systems of homosexual men break down leading to early deaths.[21] Also, the vagina has a protective double-membrane lining, whereas the anal cavity has only a single lining and is susceptible to tears and fissures that open the bloodstream to bad viruses and diseases wholly apart from HIV/AIDS.

Further, this isn't a homophobic argument because rectal intercourse is likewise discouraged among male-female monogamous couples for the same reasons. It's neither healthy nor loving to harm the one you claim to love. "Love is love" is as meaningless as "water is water," whether from a tap or a toilet. Love means something. It means to will the good of the other. When I tried to have a private discussion with the student and asked about tolerance rather than trying to get me fired, they responded, "I don't believe in being tolerant to the intolerant." Did they recognize what they had said? Yes, under the rubric of critical theory sweeping academia and our country, "tolerance" is only a selective tool.

At the time, I was confused by the student's outrage and irrationality, and only later, through the lens of the new Marxist left, did it make sense to me. I was also confused when a representative of the university accused me of bias, which I thought was odd because everyone is biased, yet we can still be rationally objective while aware of our bias. At least, that is what I taught my philosophy students. I had yet to learn the new lexicon with imported definitions from critical race theory. Bias, as the university official meant it, was not bias as I or anyone else outside the university understood it.

Although some at the university wanted me fired, thanks to Alliance Defending Freedom and two atheist students of mine in the class who defended me, I was exonerated. The student went on for a PhD in psychology and may well have become an activist. I never recanted my position even though I faced the tribunal, and I kept teaching for another several years, giving that same lecture, not out of defiance, but out of wanting to stand up to the bullies. I was hired to educate, not indoctrinate—or so I thought. But a true education is increasingly uncommon in classrooms and disciplines overrun by ideology.

CELEBRATE WHAT WE OUGHT TO HATE

Recently, I was on a tour of the main campus of Indiana University, which my daughter was considering attending. I stomached the tour for a while, but it didn't last. Midway through the tour, the guide pronounced with exuberance that "bias reporting" on campus was now more accessible, with campus phones all along the pathways to report someone. For relevant uses, like someone's safety, that's certainly helpful, but coming to understand the breadth of bias reporting, it conjured ideas that seemed almost Soviet. I could imagine someone picking up the phone and saying, "I'd like to report a cisgendered white male heterosexual able-bodied Christian capitalist who dared vote for Trump." Perhaps outlandish, but then again...

And there were other new installations on the campus of Indiana University: a newly erected statue of Alfred Kinsey, the self-described "sexologist" who, after his death, was revealed to have falsified research and legitimized child abuse and exploitation of infants and whose information was used to help provide the "science" for the sexual revolution.

Kinsey had been a researcher at Indiana University during the 1940s, setting up an Institute for Sex Research in 1947 to conduct his expansive research into human sexuality. His books *Sexual Behavior in the Human Male* (1948) and *Sexual Behavior in the Human Female* (1953) were bestsellers and are now known collectively as the *Kinsey Reports*. Kinsey campaigned for the repeal of any legislation that restricted sexual freedom, believing people would only be "free and fulfilled" when the restraints of Judeo-Christian morality were removed.

At the statue's dedication, Indiana University's president, Pamela Whitten, proudly declared, "Around the nation and around the world, the Kinsey Institute is the trusted source for information on critical issues in human sexuality, relationships, gender, and reproduction. And its reputation for excellent, relevant scholarship bolsters Indiana University's reputation."[22] Excellent scholarship indeed, if the goal is to use data to be studied on small children as sexual objects.

Groupthink, a theory developed by social psychologist Irving Jans, initially focused on political dynamics, with the free-thinking university seen as the ideal. Today, the university is a case study in groupthink, but there are dissenters, and sadly, some of the most vocal are not the Christians. Abigail Shrier, for example, is a graduate of Columbia, Oxford, and Yale and, like Rowling, is now attacked as transphobic, but for different reasons. Shrier, a religious agnostic and someone who embraces transgenderism for adults, is nonetheless fearlessly concerned for the spike among teenage girls whose social contagion came without notice. Speaking of gender dysphoria, which refers to a person's discomfort over their biologically sexed body and ordinarily disappears over time, Shrier said,

> Before 2012, in fact, there was no scientific literature on girls ages eleven to twenty-one ever having developed gender dysphoria at all. In the last decade that has changed and dramatically...for the first time in medical history, natal girls are not only present among those so identifying—they constitute the majority.[23]

Transgenderism is increasingly popular among middle school girls. It is like a contagious virus but is mental, not physical. Social contagion involves behavior, emotions, or conditions spreading spontaneously through a group or network. This notion is an apt expression of the massive sweep of middle school girls suddenly claiming to be trapped in boys' bodies as if something were in the water changing people's psychology for the first time in history.

Approximately 40 percent of Brown University students now self-identify as LGBTQ+.[24] So we shouldn't be surprised if it were likewise popular among middle school and elementary school students identifying with LGBTQ+, whose movement enjoys popularity in mainstream and social media and has made its way to our youngest population via drag queen story hours. Keep in mind that public K–12 teachers are educated in universities. Shrier explains,

> America has become fertile ground for this mass enthusiasm for reasons that have everything to do with our culture frailty: parents are undermined; experts are over-relied upon; dissenters in science and medicine are intimidated; free speech truckles under renewed attack; government health care laws harbor hidden consequences; and an intersectional era has arisen in which the desire to escape a dominant identity encourages individuals to take cover in victim groups.[25]

CONVENIENTLY FORGOTTEN MEMORIES

Dr. John Money, a prominent psychologist and sexologist in the 1960s, was one of the earliest pioneers of the gender theories now taught in grade schools and universities. He was among the first to take the word *gender* out of the realm of grammar and apply it to people, coining the expressions *gender role*, *gender identity*, and *sexual orientation*.

In 1965, twins were born by the names of Bruce and Brian Reimer. The boys were born healthy except for a condition called phimosis, which affects the foreskin. It was decided that the best treatment was circumcision. Bruce's procedure went horribly wrong, and his penis was essentially burned off. His parents eventually decided to take him to see the renowned Dr. John Money. Eager to prove the legitimacy of his theory that gender is a product of environment and culture, Money recommended sex-reassignment surgery. Before age two, Bruce's testicles were removed, some crude approximation of female genitalia was formed, and Money instructed the parents to raise him as a girl from that day forward and never tell him about his real identity.

While seeking to follow the advice, the parents nonetheless found that Bruce was still Bruce, even while calling him Brenda and coddling his false female identity. He wanted to pee standing up, play with boy toys, and not wear a dress. Yet they were told gender is a social construct (like everything else in the new ideology). Why should his boy-like tendencies materialize even while socializing him as a girl? The boys also attended regular therapy sessions with Money. Despite mixed results, Money was convinced that his project had been a success, which he reported in publications.

But the female identity never took hold for Bruce. He was confused, miserable, and on the verge of suicide until, as a teen, his parents told him the truth. Almost immediately, Bruce chose to detransition, taking the name of David. He underwent another reassignment surgery. He felt better for a brief period of time but never overcame being a sexual project for John Money. David (Bruce) would go on to speak out publicly against Money. Eventually, he even got married at age 22 and adopted three children. But all was not well. In 2004, at the age of 38, David drove to a grocery store parking lot and took his own life.[26]

In recent years, there has been an explosive rise in gender confusion among children. Kids are given drugs and sometimes physically mutilated. But many extensive studies have shown little evidence that sexual reassignment surgery alleviates the suicidality of a patient, and in some cases, it seems to make it worse unless controlling for psychiatric needs.[27]

As David Reimer's parents discovered, you cannot "reassign" someone's genetically and biologically hardwired sex. You can dress them in different clothes and conduct irreversible surgeries, but none of that can change their DNA. You can alter a person's looks, but you cannot alter their biological nature. It's just science. Believe the science. Even after this sad story, a major psychology textbook in its seventh edition tells college undergraduates, "Let us remind ourselves, though, that (here as always!) biology is not destiny."[28] Listen to ideology, not science, is what we are told.

I DEMAND YOU FEEL SORRY FOR ME

To heap insult upon insult and harm upon harm, while debate over race reparations is a matter of course, few are aware of conversations among other victimhood groups regarding their "right" to reparations. There is, for example, a recent book by a Princeton PhD student called *The Case for Gay Reparations*. Apparently the activism for victimhood wants to reach deep into people's pockets for years of oppression by allegedly dominant groups subjugating minoritized groups who find their strength in the broad alliance of the LGBTQ+ alphabet. The common thread among all these groups is a "virtuous victimology" that manipulates public sentiment through an emotional appeal to oppressed, marginalized, and victim status. Oppose them in any way, or fail to celebrate them, and you open yourself up to being called an oppressor, a bigot, a phobic, or a hater even to the point of contributing to erasing their existence or pushing them to suicide. The mantra is "hate or celebrate" without a third option, which amounts to "comply or else." It's simply bullying.

This sticky sentimentalism for the oppressed, turned maniacal bullying of the oppressor, has even crept into Christian academic societies, seminaries, and colleges, where there ought to otherwise be a Christian academic mind. In 2016, Richard Swinburne, the distinguished Oxford philosopher, delivered a lecture at a Midwest Society of Christian Philosophers (SCP) conference. The topic? Christian sexual ethics. That seems innocent enough and perfectly fitting for a Christian academic society. Yet Dr. Michael Rea, a Notre Dame philosopher and then-president of the SCP, wrote this shocking entry on his social media following the event:

> I want to express my regret regarding the hurt caused by the recent Midwest meeting of the Society for Christian Philosophers. The views expressed in Professor Swinburne's keynote are not those of the SCP itself. Though our membership is broadly united by way of religious faith, the views of our members are otherwise diverse. As President of the SCP, I am committed to promoting the intellectual life of our philosophical community. Consequently (among other reasons), I am committed to the values of diversity and inclusion. As an organization, we have fallen short of those ideals before, and surely, we will again. Nonetheless, I will strive for them going forward.[29]

Swinburne, one of the world's top Christian philosophers, was shamed for being faithfully Christian in his treatment of sexual ethics. The executive director of the SCP, female philosopher of gender at Calvin College (a college noted for mission drift), asserted on Facebook that views like Swinburne's "have caused incalculable harm to vast numbers of already disadvantaged people" and that "having someone in a position of power [like Swinburne] advocate that position furthers that harm."[30]

From one notable Catholic philosopher's blog we find even more disturbing commentary.[31] Ed Feser's blog connected with another, following many others' comments outside of the Facebook group. What follows is a sample. (The blanks within the statements below represent where profanity and vulgar language was used.)

"My friends, I give you North America's finest philosophical minds."

Then the response to Swinburne and his defenders put forward by Jason Stanley, the Jacob Urowsky Professor of Philosophy at Yale University, went like this:

> "____ those _____. Seriously."

After this comment was publicized, Stanley posted this charming follow-up remark on Facebook:

> I really wish now I hadn't said that!! I PROFOUNDLY regret not using much harsher language and saying what I really think of anyone who uses their religion to promote homophobia, you know that sickness that has led people for thousands of years to kill my fellow human beings for their sexual preferences. Like you know, pink triangles and the Holocaust. I am really, truly, embarrassed by the fact that my mild comment '____ those _____' is being spread. This wildly understates my actual sentiments towards homophobic religious proponents of evil like Richard Swinburne, who use their status as professional philosophers to oppress others with less power. I am SO SORRY for using such mild language.[32]

Other philosophers soon joined in this well-ordered "Socratic discussion" in agreement with Stanley, sharing similar sentiments. It went on and on. "Christian" philosophers, all.

I am one of only 100 philosophers who signed a petition urging Rea and the SCP to rectify the manner and even offer an apology to Dr. Swinburne, but to no avail. Swinburne's sin was that he referred to homosexuals as "disabled," which was to be understood by philosophers in the room in value-neutral terms that specify what one is unable to do in reaching toward the telos (i.e., gays cannot reproduce). Indeed, after the petition, other more progressive philosophers piled on, and Rea did nothing except offer laughs at the profanity used by Swinburne's agitators.

In their public apology, the SCP leadership spoke of "inclusive" standards. But how is it non-inclusive to invite the ethical perspective of a Christian philosopher, especially by a Christian society? If the woke can effectively cancel Richard Swinburne in and among a Christian society, there is no place and no one out of reach.

GOING WHERE NO ONE HAS GONE BEFORE

Once upon a time, transgenderism was on the fringe of society. Now it's mainstream. What now occupies the margins are those who self-identify as transracial, transspecies, transabled, transaged, and so on, among other such dysphoria.

Transgenderism is about persons whose sense of personal identity and gender does not correspond with their birth sex. Those whose gender does match are referred to as cisgender. Transagism is about those persons who feel they are a child trapped in an adult's body or vice versa. Transracialism is about persons who claim to have a racial identity that differs from their birth race and who have tanning injections administered to darken their hair and skin, hair jobs, or surgeries. Transableism is about persons who desire and sometimes become disabled by choice because they feel like impostors in their fully working bodies. Transspeciesism is about people who pretend to be animals, claim that they are animals, and sometimes have surgical enhancements to further match their bodies to their species orientation. All of these cases of identity dysphoria divorce biology from psychology, and cases can be found in the real world representing all of them.

For example, Joe Biden wasn't the only major politician who appeared to have some level of cognitive impairment. Indeed, John Fetterman was running against a celebrated heart surgeon, Dr. Mehmet Oz, for the US Senate seat in Pennsylvania. Tragically, Fetterman was the genuine victim of a stroke. The campaign and the political party used his (genuine) status as a victim to rally support for his election even though it was widely known that his condition would make him less able to do his job, which was helping to run the most powerful country in the world.

Months later, an NBC reporter asked Fetterman about whether he'd be able to do the job, and the liberal media set the reporter's hair on fire (not literally). Indeed, his wife went on record demanding that the reporter apologize for her "ableist" comments or face consequences. Ableism, as a "woke" social construct, takes the victim/oppressor model from critical theory and applies it to bodily status. In this paradigm, able-bodied people form the oppressor group making the disabled the oppressed.

Gisele Fetterman also said that Burns (the reporter) and NBC should apologize for the interview, expressing concern that it caused harm to the disability community, making those with disabilities more reluctant to ask for accommodations. She said, "I would love to see an apology towards the disability community from her and from her network for the damage they have caused."[33] John Fetterman went on to win the election and, predictably, struggled to do the job. Shortly after the election, he entered a mental hospital for depression and cognitive problems without anyone taking his seat, so at the time, the potential "damage" to the disabled community was averted by "damaging" the entire country—well played!

But the scope of group identities regarded as oppressed is unimaginably large, and therefore, those who identify as "disabled" must be sorted from the "transabled." Transableism is the desire to acquire a disability through choice rather than happenstance. This belongs to a larger cluster of part of body identity dysphoria (BID), a mental disorder characterized by a desire to have a sensory or physical disability.

In the simplest terms, a person who is transable can, say, see or hear perfectly well but chooses to identify as blind or deaf. And as with transgenderism, doctors are encouraged to match the body to the identity—e.g., take away their ability to see and hear. So rather than treating these people with compassion by recognizing some psychosis, our society has lost its mind and normalizes and then makes normative these conditions, seeing those who identify as such as being oppressed by others who think they are normal. In reality, those who are transable are abnormal.

On April 10, 2021, the famous geneticist and anti-theist Richard Dawkins tweeted the following query: "In 2015, Rachel Dolezal, a white chapter president of NAACP, was vilified for identifying as Black. Some men choose to identify as women, and some women choose to identify as men. You will be vilified if you deny that they literally are what they identify as. Discuss."[34]

The tweet made headlines for its comparison between the identity claims of transgender people and those of Rachel Dolezal. He took much flak and quickly went on an apology tour. On April 12, two days later, Dawkins tweeted, "I do not intend to disparage trans people. I see that my academic 'Discuss' question has been misconstrued as such and I deplore this. It was also not my intent to ally in any way with Republican bigots in US now exploiting this issue."[35] Evidently, Dawkins was shamed into submission. He tried to scapegoat Republicans but couldn't, and ultimately, the American Humanist Association Board stripped him of his 1996 Humanist of the Year award, claiming that he

> accumulated a history of making statements that use the guise of scientific discourse to demean marginalized groups, an approach antithetical to humanist values. His latest statement implies that the identities of transgender individuals are fraudulent, while also simultaneously attacking Black identity as one that can be assumed when convenient. His subsequent attempts at clarification are inadequate and convey neither sensitivity nor sincerity.[36]

Like Swinburne, if the woke can do this to celebrity atheists like Dawkins, they can do it to anyone. Apologizing often only serves in such cases to self-incriminate.

The case of Rachel Dolezal is an interesting one. Dolezal is a white American woman who attended Howard University, an HBCU (historically black college and university) and sued the school in 2002, claiming it had discriminated against her for being white. Somehow, she was persuasive. Increasingly, she presented herself as black, eventually becoming president of a local

NAACP chapter. When she was outed by a journalist in 2015 as being white, she said, "I identify as black."[37]

The media coverage died down, but less than two years later (2017), the controversy returned when a feminist professor, Rebecca Tuvel, published an article in the philosophy journal *Hypatia*, titled "In Defense of Transracialism." Tuvel compared the situation of Caitlyn Jenner, who self-identifies as a woman, to that of Rachel Dolezal, a white woman who self-identifies as black, claiming that if we accept one, then we should accept the other on equal grounds. Tuvel wrote that society should accept people's gender transitions regardless of whether any biological basis for transgender identity can be found. Gender identity, for some people, does not need to be biologically grounded; it can be political or personal, and that is sufficient. She then pointed out that "race is not biologically based" either, and that "one's 'actual' race is a matter of social definition."[38] Thus, can't we just accept people's assertions about their own identities, including the decision to change race? The "*Hypatia* Gate," as it was called, was picked up by *The New York Times*, and amid mounting pressure, *Hypatia* apologized for its publication, listing various harms caused and leading to editorial resignations.

STRANGE BEDFELLOWS—BUT NOT IN A QUEER WAY

In 2017 and 2018, Peter Boghossian, along with two liberal atheist colleagues previously referenced, James Lindsay and Helen Pluckrose, attempted to pull off the veil of leftist academia by showing that they could publish nonsense papers in various high-level social science and humanities journals by simply using the right language and ideology as a cover. The trio dubbed various academic fields—postcolonial theory, queer theory, gender studies, fat studies, critical race theory, and intersectional feminism—as "grievance studies" because the fields begin with the presumption of a grievance and then bend evidence to support the theory.

"The grievance studies affair," as it was called, entailed submitting bogus papers to academic journals in queer, cultural, fat, race, gender, and sexuality studies to determine whether they would pass through peer review and be accepted for publication. Of 20 papers, two-thirds had been published, accepted for publication, or were under consideration before someone from *The Wall Street Journal* realized the hoax and blew the whistle.[39]

These papers contained "arguments" such as dogs engage in rape culture based on observations at dog parks in Portland, Oregon, and they also featured elements such as rewriting parts of Adolf Hitler's *Mein Kampf*, overlayed, however, with feminist language. They were all hoaxes and yet proved remarkably successful in showing how ideological and shoddy scholarship had become so prevalent in so many university fields now dominated by New Leftist ideology. Critics came after Boghossian with a vengeance. He eventually succumbed and resigned from Portland State University. In his highly publicized resignation letter, he said, "[Woke ideology] has transformed a bastion of free inquiry into a social justice factory whose only inputs were race, gender, and victimhood and whose only outputs were grievance and division."[40]

The next year, in 2019, I was made very aware that alliances make strange bedfellows, or rather, speaking partners. I was connected to Peter Boghossian through a mutual friend. Boghossian was teaching a 300-level course on atheism at Portland State University, and he invited me to give a lecture on the rationality of religious belief. We had lunch afterward and realized we shared significant similarities. Both were actively engaged on opposite sides in the philosophy of religion debate and both were keenly aware of the encroaching revolutionary ideology in academia about to overwhelm the culture. It was then that he proposed an alliance.[41]

Boghossian reached a point where he saw that something worse than the Christian religion had emerged in America and the West for what he determined to be a more pressing matter than the atheism-versus-theism debates. Within four months, and just before COVID transformed travel, we lectured together on numerous university campuses. He now concedes a point I had made back then: that it was in part his tribe, New Atheism, that created the conditions for this new virus that morphed into a Frankenstein for which his side lost control, a thing we call "woke" or "social justice" (greater elaboration will come below).[42]

We lectured on "viewpoint diversity" in the universities as a liberal atheist and a conservative Christian, respectively. Is there any other sort of diversity that ought to be prized in the university? The full title of our presentation was "Viewpoint Diversity: The Death of Intellectual Diversity in the University." That might sound harmless enough. One note of description on the flier read, "How Social Justice and Identity Politics Are Negatively Impacting the University and Culture." Some groups sought to cancel us. One group known as the Anti-Racist Solidarity Group, at Utah State University, wrote a letter to the university president denoting our efforts as that which "promotes logical fascism and anti-identity politics," among other choice terms, claiming our views were making them "not feel safe."[43] Since when did viewpoint diversity become a code word for racist, using "logic" to dominate subdued minorities? If any kind of diversity is on exhibit at a university, shouldn't it be viewpoint diversity?

Boghossian was correct. The atheist groups on campus would not come out to support him or his side, even though he was a former champion of their previous cause (atheism without woke ideology). These are the same people who later withdrew Dawkins's Humanist of the Year Award. Surprisingly, the same mind virus had begun to infiltrate Christian campus ministries, and the local chapter of Cru (formerly Campus Crusade for Christ) wouldn't come out in support either but chose instead to have their staff watch a video on white privilege. Notably, I used to be on staff with Cru and tried to communicate with the leadership. When I inquired about what was happening and challenged that this new "social justice" being promoted may have some good components but that it may also have some Marxism built into a Trojan horse, it was suggested to me that maybe we can learn from Marx.

In some respects, Cru has likewise succumbed to the mind virus and has lost numerous staff over the past decade. There are signs that perhaps they've "stopped the bleeding" at least partly given the challenge posed by many of its donors and staff.[44] After the Trump reelection, however, Cru sent out a comfort email to all possible afflicted BIPOC (black, Indigenous, and people of color) staff.[45] More will be said later. I was soon thereafter disinvited from a Christian seminary because I failed to have the proper skin pigment required for having the right "lived experience" to speak on the topic. Boghossian and I realized that in this new cultural revolution, we have more in common with one another than we each do with some within our respective camps—atheist and Christian. But things were about to spike to new levels in the next few months following the death of George Floyd.

COURAGEOUSLY RECLAIMING THE INTELLECTUAL VOICE OF CHRIST

If you go to the website of Riley Gaines, former All-American swimmer at the University of Kentucky, there on the home page, in extra-bold, 16-point Helvetica type, you read the following:

> I can attest to the tears that I witnessed from finishers who missed being named an All-American by one place. I can attest to the extreme discomfort in the locker room from 18-year-old girls exposed to male body parts and having to undress with a male watching in the same room.[46]

In even larger type, the website says, "Riley Gaines: Athlete, Advocate, Woman." Three qualities strike me about Riley. First is courage: She has been willing to stand up to the most formidable special interest group since the Teamsters. The trans community doesn't play nice, and it doesn't play fair, but Riley couldn't care less, and that's the second quality I admire about her: She's unapologetic. How many times do you think "I'm sorry" was uttered in the US last year? A trillion? Being white shouldn't require an apology; being straight shouldn't require an apology; having an opinion shouldn't require an apology; being a Christian shouldn't require an apology; and the sins of the Founding Fathers shouldn't require an apology—not from us anyway. It's refreshing to see someone who is gracious, kind, yet unapologetic.

But here's what really inspires me. Riley borrows from the language of critical social justice, calling herself an advocate and a voice, but *she* twists the meaning, being an activist for truth and traditional morality. Wise rhetoric. I don't know if Riley Gaines is a Christian, and it doesn't matter. She can fight on my side any day, or rather, I can fight on hers.

Riley is just one person, but because she is fearless and relentless, she has had an enormous influence on the culture, and when I see her, I'm confident we can do this too.

3

THE EXPLOITATION OF RACE FOR REVOLUTION

Nearly 40 years ago, the Reverend Jesse Jackson led a crowd of protestors at Stanford University over a college course, Western Culture. They loudly chanted, "Hey hey, ho ho, Western Civ has got to go."[1] Stanford capitulated in 1987, and it was a sign of things to come. In the decades that followed, nearly all academia in the Western world would follow suit. The history of Western thought, philosophy, culture, and even art was increasingly absent—at least in terms of being taught favorably or neutrally. It became somewhat of an embarrassment, the product of a bunch of "dead white males," as the new term entered our lexicons along with a host of other dazzling descriptions. Today, you can't pay universities enough to teach such a course.

In 1995, *The New York Times* ran the headline, "Yale Returns $20 Million to an Unhappy Patron." Four years after giving Yale University $20 million to expand its Western civilization curriculum, billionaire Lee Bass, a Yale alumnus, requested that the money be returned because Yale never instituted the courses. The university communicated that it had agreed to return the donation after concluding it could not accept his conditions. Mr. Bass wanted to approve the faculty members for the courses. After all, he didn't want to give $20 million to undermine his grandma's America, his own, or the future of civilization.

Liberal faculty members, of which there was no shortage, had criticized the restrictions placed on the donation, arguing that the money could be better spent on courses with a multicultural perspective. But a few other faculty members lauded the proposed program as a powerful antidote to the rush to embrace multiculturalism on the country's elite campuses. In the end, the dispute spoke volumes about the trajectory of our culture. The donation, one the biggest ever received by Yale, is also believed to be the biggest that a university has ever agreed to return. His gift, along with the gifts of other members of his family, invested nearly $85 million between 1990 and 1992.[2]

Having been to Yale and seen the words over the archway entry, "For God, for Country, and for Yale," I had to wonder whether teaching Western Civ was really that bad? For those influenced by postcolonial theory, America is horrible. Postcolonialism is the critical academic study of the legacy of colonialism and imperialism, focusing on the impact of power over and exploitation of colonized people.

In the West, there is an obvious European genetic heritage, which ostensibly comes along with a lighter skin pigment. To delegitimize the West, as bestselling author Douglas Murray says, "It appears to be necessary first to demonize the people who still make up the racial majority in the West. It is necessary to demonize white people."[3] America is the most prominent Western country, and so why not demonize America? In late 2021, the US census revealed that the number of white people had decreased.[4] As late-night comedy hosts seek to do, Jimmy Fallon thought he'd say something funny. He pointed out that for the first time in America's history, the number of white people declined. The audience cheered, he smiled, and then he piled on that Fox News had probably declared an emergency, which generated even more laughter and support.[5]

THE SMASHED DREAM OF MLK AND THE RISE OF OBAMA

Not long ago, it had become unfashionable, to say the least, to lump people together and dismiss them simply because of their skin color. It seemed Martin Luther King's dream was coming true. At the turn of the century, most people in America had come to realize that treating people with respect as individuals and not by the color of their skin was best. This wasn't to say that they were entirely or literally color blind—they were color aware but not color obsessed—but only that they had adopted King's message where the focus should and shouldn't be. Thomas Sowell, who has lived through the Jim Crow laws, the civil rights era, and this present century, is one of the finest black scholars alive. A graduate from Harvard, Columbia, and the University of Chicago, now in his nineties, he's as bright as ever. Having written numerous books on race and himself a former Marxist, he chastises "social justice" as fallacious.[6] Just a decade ago, Sowell echoed what seemed to be common sentiment—namely, that "racism is not dead. But it is on life-support, kept alive mainly by the people who use it for an excuse or to keep minority communities fearful or resentful enough to turn out as a voting bloc on Election Day."[7]

In the early years of this century, stemming from universities where suspect ideas increasingly emerge, people began looking for hidden mechanisms of race—everywhere. Publicly, race discussions began in fervor up to and during Barack Obama's presidency (2008–2016). Indeed, the playing of the race card can be argued to have worked in his favor, as he was, by merit of experience, one of the least-qualified candidates to have ever run and won the presidency. His résumé reveals only being a US Senator for no more than 18 months before running for the highest office in America. Regardless, Obama's inauguration corresponded with polls indicating that most Americans thought race relations were doing well and heading in the right direction—especially having just elected the first black president.[8] But early on in his presidency, people's image of such race relations began to change with noticeable actions and policies.

In 2009, Obama's Attorney General, Eric Holder, flagrantly disregarded obvious voter intimidation of whites by New Black Panther Party members at election polling places dressed in military garb while swinging billy clubs.[9] The same year, a white police officer was referred to by Obama of acting "stupidly," something the white officer (and his black partner) never conceded to even after Obama had the white officer to the White House for a beer at what was dubbed the "Beer Summit."[10] The two officers had arrested a black Harvard professor for disorderly conduct. It was professor Henry Louis Gates Jr., who claimed the officers' actions against him were racially motivated. The arrest caused backlash for the black officer, being characterized by some as an "Uncle Tom." It was as if the officer wasn't truly black or at least didn't fit the new black ideology. It was activity like this that began to make people wonder about racial optics and relations during the Obama presidency, if things were different than expected. Regardless, despite having the first black president, academics (well beyond Gates) were sure to push race front and center, as it had been brewing in a certain ideology for decades.

Obama, in a rather revealing remark in his bestseller *Dreams from My Father*, said, "I chose my friends carefully. The more politically active black students. The foreign students. The Chicanos. The Marxist professors and structural feminists and punk-rock performance poets. We smoked cigarettes and wore leather jackets. At night, in the dorms, we discussed neocolonialism, Franz Fanon, Eurocentrism, and patriarchy."[11]

THE YEAR WAS 1989

From 1988–1991, Obama attended Harvard Law School and studied under Derrick Bell, the godfather and founder of critical legal studies (CLS) and fountainhead contributor to critical race theory (CRT), not surprising because CLS itself is a spinoff of critical theory. Critical legal studies looks at law fundamentally from the lens of race. Pictures and videos can be seen online with Obama and Bell hugging and speaking alongside each other. CRT was being used as a title in the 1970s alongside and as an offshoot of CLS, even though it hadn't yet formally launched as a movement. One of Bell's other former students, Kimberlé Crenshaw, a black law professor at Columbia and UCLA, coined the expression *intersectionality* in 1989 and is widely believed to have also coined *critical race theory*.[12] She, along with some other activists, officially founded CRT in 1989 in the Midwest. Their initial conference was held in the same year Westerners thought Marxism was on life support, given the fall of the Berlin Wall and bad public relations coming out of China from the infamous Tiananmen Square incident. Marxism had not fallen. It had simply spread out and adapted.

In a puzzling twist, the group began in a Wisconsin church that had stained glass windows—the Marxist thinkers joked about the irony of their new movement.[13] Richard Delgado, one of the original members, said, "We gathered at that convent for two and a half days, around a table in an austere room with stained glass windows and crucifixes here and there—an odd place for a bunch of Marxists—and worked out a set of principles."[14]

That is interesting for an additional reason. Liberation theology is race Marxism pretending to be Christian. The father of Black liberation theology, James Cone, had two notable students. One was Jeremiah Wright, Obama's pastor for 20 years in Chicago, and the other was Raphael Warnock, a US Senator from Georgia and the person who performed the eulogy at Cone's funeral. All this proximity shows Obama was influenced by Marxist thought in both academics and religion, providing a lens through which to understand certain governing decisions.

But surely, the progress away from past racism in America can be seen. Not according to critical race theory. As can be imagined, "progress" in race relations according to CRT advocates is a ruse. Bell himself said in 1987, "Progress in American race relations is largely a mirage obscuring the fact that whites continue, consciously or unconsciously, to do all in their power to ensure their dominion and maintain their control."[15] For CRT advocates, it's often about theory in search of evidence. Evidence offers nothing when compared to lived experience. This idea that CRT is a theory in search of evidence is partially derived by some of its founders. Take Richard Delgado, for example. In the book he coauthored, *Critical Race Theory: An Introduction*, he describes CRT as a "movement." That's not scholarship. That's activism. He admits it is a

> collection of activists and scholars interested in studying and transforming the relationship among race, racism, and power. The movement considers many of the same issues that conventional civil rights and ethnic studies discourses take up...but unlike the former which embraces incrementalism and step-by-step progress, critical race theory questions the foundations of the liberal order, including equality theory, legal reasoning, Enlightenment rationalism, and neutral principles of constitutional law...unlike some academic disciplines, critical race theory contains an activist dimension. It not only tries to understand our social situation, but to change it.[16]

And this, of course, was Marx's impetus when he said, "Philosophers have historically sought to understand the world. The goal is to change it."[17] As Douglas Murray points out, "This is the language of revolutionary politics, not a language traditionally used in academia."[18]

In 2012, large media outlets began raising national attention to the killings of black men by nonblacks (over the years, Trayvon Martin, Michael Brown, Philando Castile, and Ahmaud Arbery are just a few). On February 26, 2012, Trayvon Martin was killed by George Zimmerman (who is partly Hispanic). Shortly after and in response to Zimmerman's eventual acquittal, the hashtag #BlackLivesMatter (BLM) went viral, and the website with the same name was founded in 2013, by three young black female activists, two of whom identify as queer. The claim was that the BLM website was supposed to raise awareness, foster demonstrations, and protest police brutality and systematic racism that they believed overwhelmingly affects the black community. The cofounders are on record numerous places as being "trained Marxists" with ties into critical theory.[19] Around the same time, notions like intersectionality, whiteness, and systemic or institutional racism from academia began pouring into culture, from sports personalities and journalists to politicians and celebrities. They were now present in pop culture. These ideas were surging by factors of two, three, and four in major newspapers and "systemic" racism and its cognates by a factor of eight between 2012 and 2020, marking the year of the death of George Floyd, showing that the media's embrace of "wokeness" did not begin in response to the death of George Floyd.[20] But as we'll see later, those new terms that have entered our common vocabulary, and more that are connected to critical theory, preceded their entry into pop culture by decades in academia.

THE YEAR IT ALL BROKE LOOSE

Then 2020 happened, and the fires began to roar. Black Lives Matter used the video of George Floyd's May 2020 death to create the impression that those frightening nine minutes defined America and its justice, alleged to be undergirded by systemic racism. This, in turn, sparked nearly a year of riots costing lives and billions of dollars in damage. Despite a Gallup poll that showed following Floyd's death, 61 percent of blacks wanted the same amount of police presence and 20 percent wanted an increase—not less police presence—woke politicians, media, and academia spawned massive calls to defund the police.[21] It stunned the country and the world. Traffic to the BLM website surged massively as the protests got underway, spiking just eight days after Floyd's death, when nearly two million people flooded the website.[22] Not two days later, critical race theory trainer Robin DiAngelo was rushed into a conference call with no fewer than 184 members of Congress, all from the Democratic caucus.[23]

Recorded in its 2020 Impact Report, in the second half of 2020, the BLM website was visited by more than 24,000,000 people and it raised more than $90,000,000.[24] Many gave out of white guilt or to virtue signal, or they were simply naive. Sadly, much of the money was squandered by its leader, Patrisse Cullors, on multiple-million-dollar luxurious homes in places from Los Angeles to the Bahamas, much of which people have ignored until recent times (including paying her brother nearly $1,000,000 to provide security without him having any serious background in security training).[25] All this while, since 2020, BLM has been calling for the defunding of police and redirecting public funds to low-income African American communities, who never received anything. In November 2020, a complaint letter drafted by several BLM chapters, upset at the actions of the Black Lives Matter Global Network (BLMGN), stated, "To the best of our knowledge, most chapters have received little to no financial support from BLMGN since the launch in 2013…This is not the equity and financial accountability we deserve."[26] This seems to clash with her being an avowed Marxist and opponent of private property. After these revelations, she resigned from the organization but remains closely affiliated with it. Marxists often turn out to be the best capitalists.

In 2018, the formerly obscure academic Robin DiAngelo, who is white, wrote a book called *White Fragility*. Her view was that not only were all white people racist, but those who deny it show proof of it in their denial. In other words, you are wrong no matter what you do. It's a no-win situation. She claims that "positive white identity is an impossible goal. White identity is inherently racist; white people do not exist outside the system of white supremacy."

So, what can white people do? Her suggestion is that they should "strive to be 'less white'" since "to be less white is to be less racially oppressive."[27] Her voice led to many companies following suit, including Coca-Cola training its employees to "be less white."[28] Apparently, whites aren't sufficiently fragile to talk about racism as the title and subtitle of her book suggest. Up until spring 2020, her book had sold more than three-quarters of a million copies, and one month after Floyd's death, she sold another half million copies.[29] DiAngelo, like Cullors, embraces critical theory, an iteration of Marxist thought. Again, ironic evidence that Marxists make the best capitalists.

THE TOXICITY OF THE NEW RACISM

DiAngelo's views are poisonous for race relations. After the death of Floyd, black speakers were sought everywhere. Indeed, I was attending an all-black church prior to the Floyd incident. The church shut down due to COVID, but one of the pastors was called upon to address the topic of race at another church following the Floyd event. In the talk, he recommended DiAngelo's book. When I asked the pastor about it later, he said he didn't even know what critical theory was, much less CRT, and yet he recommended the book simply because it was a bestseller.

Together we were involved in a racial reconciliation campus ministry. Such an endeavor now counts for little, if DiAngelo and CRT are correct. Further, I'm always going to be walking on eggshells attending a multiethnic church wondering what others are thinking of me and my agenda for attending the church. DiAngelo says, "Racism invariably manifests itself within cross-racial friendships...Racism cannot be absent from your friendship."[30] She writes elsewhere that "from an antiracist perspective, the question is not, 'Did racism take place' but 'How was racism taking place' because the assumption is that racism is always at play, always operating."[31]

Being consistent with critical theory, another author applies the same reasoning to identity factors beyond race. She writes, "If you are white in a white supremacist society, you are racist. If you are male in a patriarchy, you are sexist. If you are able-bodied, you are ableist. If you are anything above poverty in a capitalist society, you are classist." To white people, she says,

> Do not try to absolve yourself of responsibility with your good intentions…Remember that you do not have all of the pieces. You are not living as a person of color. You will never fully understand the impact that sustained, systemic racism has on people of color. You will never be able to fully empathize with the pain your actions may have caused. Nothing will get you there…Nobody owes you a relationship…In a hostile world, people of color have the right to cut off contact with people who have harmed them.[32]

Choice words to be sure. You might ask, What might it be like to be interracially married in that context? Every disagreement can simply be boiled down to racism by the lighter-skinned spouse? Or what about the parent-child relationship? Consider a child whose parents are different races. When the lighter-skinned parent scolds or disciplines the child, it's racism? It's power and privilege, nothing more? And there is no point in apologizing? They are simply guilty. This is social poison.

The senseless killing of George Floyd brought with it an explosive and exploitive judgment day in America. Not only were protests taking place around the world—with America taking a scolding from the likes of China, a nation that is not quite a bastion of human rights—but an unnerving declaration was made, and one could feel it in the air.[33] There was even a BLM protest in Japan, where 98 percent of the population is Japanese.[34] Statues were being toppled in the US, including ones of Abraham Lincoln (who ended slavery in the US) and Ulysses S. Grant (who brought about the surrender of the Confederacy). Even statues such as that of David Hume in Scotland were demoralized, and one of the tallest buildings at the University of Edinburgh had his name ripped off and renamed with the poetic moniker "40 George Square."[35] The argument was that Hume had made racist statements. One wonders why Marx's statues don't come down for more plentiful and obvious statements that he made?[36]

The killing of George Floyd wasn't simply something that just happened in America. It was apparently emblematic of America, revealing something in the heart of all white Americans—not just its cops. It is something America had been primed for, the skids had been greased, as it were, by voices who were applying critical race theory. This was especially true of college-aged Americans. Thomas Sowell's statement about racism being largely dead wasn't merely reflecting his own sentiment. A *CBS / New York Times* poll revealed that 66 percent of Americans thought race relations were generally good at Obama's inauguration in 2009.[37] But polling evidence showed how badly they were souring over time,[38] suggesting that either America had become more racist over this brief time, or the university-trained journalists were simply operating under the philosophy that they had consumed in the universities.

What academia theorized, the media then popularized, and the state finally politicized. Were there really that many CRT professors who introduced such language in academia that then became the language of America? If 25 percent of sociologists claim to be outright Marxists and possibly another 25 percent are at least sympathetic, what can we infer from this?[39] Race Marxists even claim that whiteness is contagious, which they assert is the only way to explain how not all black people understand or see racism everywhere. They've not achieved liberational consciousness. Prior to Floyd's death, and after the 2020 US presidential election, the media put forth the concept of "multiracial whiteness" to explain why nonwhites would vote for a Republican president.[40] But the trigger of the murder of George Floyd set off a time bomb whose clock had been ticking. According to race Marxists, it wasn't just an individual racist killing; it was a racist killing indicative of the nature of racist policing in America, sparking a movement to defund, not reform, the police. It was systemic racism because America was allegedly intrinsically a racist nation dominated not merely by white people but by whiteness and white supremacy.

ACAB (ALL COPS ARE BASTARDS)

So broad was the media presentation that one black author living for a few years in Zambia felt compelled to write his book on CRT because so many Zambians were inquiring about police brutality in America and why police officers were actively "hunting down black men."[41] But the understanding of the links from university to media to culture was wildly out of touch with reality by orders of magnitude. When a poll was taken by Americans about how many unarmed black men had been shot by police in 2019, around 22 percent who identified as "very liberal" said they thought the police shot at least 10,000 unarmed black men annually. Among self-identified "liberals," nearly 40 percent thought it was between 1,000 and 10,000. The actual figure? Just slightly more than ten. Even among conservatives, the numbers are alarming. Nearly 34 percent thought it was 1,000 or more. Media and a genuinely uneducated (even though college-educated) citizenry are to blame. The truth is that more police officers were killed that year by black Americans than unarmed black Americans were killed by the police.[42] But when evidence doesn't support theory, so much the worse for evidence over hype it seems. This is not an uncommon coincidence when it comes to critical theory in its various iterations, including race.

This disconnection (of one's beliefs) to reality also explains why individuals on sports teams began to take the knee before each game as a sign of protest against massive and unjust racial killing by a nation and its law enforcers systemically mistreating blacks rather than standing (as is tradition) for the national anthem. Also, it is why on June 8, 2020, Democratic politicians took a knee for nearly nine minutes (to honor the time in which Floyd was kneeled on by former police officer Derek Chauvin), wore kente cloth scarves (many not realizing that the cloth had also been worn by black African slave traders), and drafted legislation against police brutality.[43] It is why CEOs and the business world began in earnest to virtue signal their opposition to police brutality as though it were a nightly routine by racist police. It was a time when silence was considered violence, when one must speak out against racial violence, all the while excusing massive racial riots resulting in real harm to others (including blacks) and their businesses and excused as a part of speech.

Former mayor of Seattle Jenny Durkan dubbed that summer the "summer of love," even as a part of her city was literally dubbed as occupied territory by rioters who christened the area the Capitol Hill Autonomous Zone (CHAZ). Ideas have consequences; bad ideas have victims. Not only were police property and buildings destroyed, but multiple shootings leading to deaths and injuries occurred during the occupation. The riots were so frequent and so long across the nation that one Marxist transgender woman (Willie/Vicky) even wrote a book defending the destruction and violence titled *In Defense of Looting*, with one chapter titled "All Cops Are Bastards."[44]

Many defended the most destructive rioting in US history by quoting Martin Luther King out of context: "Riots are the voice of the unheard." I recall, one of my PhD student colleagues who had become a tenured professor posted his comments on Facebook: "I want the entire world to burn until the last cop is strangled"[45] Was all of this necessary? Minneapolis Mayor Jacob Frey, in response to Floyd's death, said, "Being black in America should not be a death sentence."[46] Granted, George Floyd's killing was heinously wrong, and the police officer who did it faced swift justice. But to this day, there was no evidence of it being a racist killing and therefore an instance of racial injustice.[47] No matter.

Was Floyd's death unique, and did it reveal evidence of a particular callousness toward black men on the part of the police? Have you ever heard of Tony Timpa? Likely not. His story didn't fit the theory media sought to popularize on the backs of that which academics theorized. While Derek Chauvin kneeled on the back of George Floyd for nine minutes, prompting Nancy Pelosi and others to kneel for nine minutes, where were the politicians kneeling for 14 minutes as "Timpa wailed and pleaded for help more than 30 times as officers pinned his shoulder, knees and neck to the ground"?[48] Tony Timpa died in 2016. In the 2020 Floyd case, Floyd died on May 25, officers were fired on May 26, protests spread across to other cities on May 27, the government activated the Minnesota National Guard on May 28, and 20-year police veteran Derek Chauvin was arrested on May 29, eventually sentenced to 22.5 years in prison, and later stabbed 22 times in prison.[49]

In the Timpa case, knees were also placed on the back of the neck, which lasted for 14 minutes with 30 cries for help from Timpa, while officers laughed. One officer in the Timpa case was black, another Hispanic. Where was Pelosi? Where was the media? No one knew his name, and few had ever heard of the case. The footage was withheld for three years during legal battles. In July 2020, just two months after the Floyd riots had begun, a federal judge threw out a suit brought against five Dallas police officers. Was the judge influenced by the racialization narrative? Seven years later, in 2023, no officer was criminally charged or arrested, one retired, and one was promoted.[50]

Why the difference? Floyd was black, but Timpa was white. Only the former advanced the narrative's theory.

Racism, understood anew, is unidirectional from the vantage point of power. Whoever is in power is the only one that can be racist. This explains why the initial confusion was quickly clarified when, in January 2023, five cops were reported for killing a young black male, Tyre Nichols. Media instantly went into preprogrammed action decrying racist police brutality. But then it was discovered that not one, not two, but all five cops involved were black. What was the media to do? Well, when applying a theory in search of evidence, go with theory. The act was still deemed as racist because it is the racist system or policies that crush the oppressed, and oftentimes it is blacks who are forced by the system to do the dirty work of the system. The assertion being: Even black cops act under white supremacy. Judgment was swift, and all were charged.[51]

It seems that very few want to be a cop these days, and departments are hard pressed to find good police officers. Politicians and media demean and condemn them, which places spotlights on them and somewhat handcuffs their abilities. Police officers who do remain after a "defund the police" rampage are reluctant to do their jobs, lest they risk their own lives and livelihood. Consequently, the streets are more dangerous now than ever before. In 2021, police deaths skyrocketed by around 25 percent, to their highest level in US history.[52] The breakdown of law and order because of this new ideology strikes at the heart of our civilization. A society that looks away when law enforcement is attacked is one that is headed for anarchy. According to *The Washington Post*'s police shootings database, between 2015 and 2020, approximately 122 unarmed black men were fatally shot by a cop. The year after Floyd's death, murders of police officers shot up 59 percent, the same year in which 11 unarmed black men were slain by cops.[53] Nonetheless, the perception remains that cops are part of systemic racism, and because of that, the pressure on cops is immense. This puts lives at risk—all lives. It destroys law and orderly society. Much of the devastation in lost lives and property that occurred in the summer of 2020 was at the loss of blacks and the poor. But according to revolutionary "critical race theorist, Kimberlé Williams Crenshaw, 'consternation over the loss of goods' in rioting is nothing more than fear of 'marauding Black masses undermining white people's well-being,' just another example of 'violence-enabling pearl-clutching about looming social disorder.'"[54]

By 2020, America was prepared and primed for its self-interpretation to be judged, sentenced, and executed. That interpretation was first theorized in academia, then popularized in media, and finally politicized in government. Today, America is perceived by many as a racist nation through and through.

RACIST GHOSTS

In 2016, there was an instance of panic on the campus of Indiana University, an institution where I taught philosophy and comparative religions for a dozen years. One evening, it was believed that a Ku Klux Klan (KKK) member was spotted with a weapon on the campus in Bloomington, Indiana. Social media went to work. Resident assistants started messaging residents, pleading with their students not to go outside. Eventually, it was discovered that the person in question was a Dominican Catholic monk walking around campus in his robes not with a whip but with his rosary.[55] This of course is not an isolated incident.

In 2013, there was a similar report of a KKK member at Oberlin College in Ohio. All classes were canceled during the day. When the police arrived, it was determined that it was most likely a homeless man walking around in a blanket or a girl wearing a blanket keeping warm across campus.[56] In November 2015, a queer black activist caused an uproar at the University of Missouri when he claimed that the KKK was spotted. The former student-body president warned people to take precaution, exclaiming on social media to "stay away from the windows in residence halls. The KKK has been confirmed to be sighted on campus. I'm working with the MUPD, the state trooper and the national guard." The student eventually apologized for his misinformation.[57] Numerous other campus stories are told, too many to list, of similar farce episodes of students seeing KKK ghosts, followed by university officials making bold statements against racism. Everyone seems to be primed on campus to look for the ghost of racism.

Then there was the infamous case of Hollywood actor Jussie Smollett, who claimed that in January 2019, he was accosted by two white men shouting racist and homophobic slurs who then attacked him and put a noose around his neck. This was followed by prompt responses of support that went as high as the California senator and later US vice president Kamala Harris, who denounced the incident as "an attempted modern-day lynching."[58] Smollett continued the story, adding creative components and gaining wide support against white supremacy, until camera footage by police and other evidence revealed that the two "white supremacists" were Abimbola Osundairo and Obabinjo Osundairo, two weight-lifting brothers from Nigeria who knew Smollett.[59] What is interesting is how quickly support built in the spread of Smollett's lies, not just from Harris, but from the likes of Nancy Pelosi and media elites like Stephen Colbert, who quickly took Smollett's story at face value because it sounded true. It's the narrative. It is theory in search of evidence.

None of this is to say that racism is completely dead in America or to ignore that there was a war fought over it. Rather, it is simply highlighting the dangerous assumption that behind everything is a racist story haunted by a racist ghost. It is a story we've been fed and come to believe about America, and it's important to get it correct. Life and death are at stake.

RACIST BABIES TO RACIST GRANDMAS, A NEW EDUCATION FOR ALL

The rise of the Third Reich wasn't simply an overnight power coup; the conditions precipitating it existed for some time, making a radical cultural revolution possible. "Teachers in Germany joined the Nazi party at twice the rate of the population as a whole before World War II."[60] So, too, we're raising the next generation of little revolutionaries. In the 2010s, during the Obama presidency, publishers were busy marketing radicalization. Innosanto Nagara's book *A is for Activist* (2013) is a case in point. It's an alphabet book for ages one through four that doesn't begin with *A is for apple* but rather *A is for activist*, and so on. It was dubbed one of NPR's top 100 books for young readers.[61] And it is listed on Amazon as a "teachers' pick."[62] Of course, it is never too early to start a "good" education.

Ibram X. Kendi has become the high priest of antiracism and has produced five *New York Times* bestsellers. *Time* listed him as one of the 100 most influential people in the world.[63] Kendi too has a children's book. It is titled *Antiracist Baby* (2020), a book similar to his famous adult book *How to Be an Antiracist* (2019) but for kids and babies.[64] He has another book for parents on how to raise antiracist kids, *How to Raise an Antiracist* (2022). And yet another for young adults, said to be for ages 12 and up, *How to Be a (Young) Antiracist* (2023). This one is supposed to help young people think critically to make the world more equitable. In other words, the focus isn't on critical thinking but critical theory. Kendi is not opposed to racism, only certain kinds of racism—that is, white-to-black racism. Everyone is considered either racist or antiracist depending on whether you agree with his view. He says, "There is no neutrality in the racism struggle. The opposite of 'racist' isn't 'not racist.' It is 'antiracist.'"[65]

Because antiracists see racism primarily as a system of racial dominance rather than as personal racial prejudice, they believe that personal rejection of racial prejudice is insufficient to combat racism. If we adopt the antiracist definition of *antiracism*, it's possible for someone to abhor and even publicly denounce personal racial prejudice and to still fail to qualify as an antiracist if they do not commit to dismantling racist systems and structures. He defines racism in terms of policies where "racist policy" is simply any measure that produces or sustains racial inequity. These redefinitions lead to numerous problems. For example, the institution of marriage perpetuates racial inequities for many reasons (differential marriage rates, inheritance laws, tax breaks, etc.). Thus, according to Kendi's definitions, a federal law that abolished marriage would qualify as "antiracist," while opposition to such a law would be "racist." Given that most people realize that the abolition of marriage would be horrifically destructive and unjust, we're then put in the awkward position of arguing that some "antiracist" policies (like the abolition of marriage) are evil, while "racist" opposition to such policies is good and just.

While he's not entirely consistent, Kendi rejects the idea that "Blacks can't be racist."[66] He contradicts his fellow antiracists in that he believes blacks can be racists but only when they're acting on whiteness or white-supremacist policies. So long as they reject systems of racism—that is, any policy or practice that creates or perpetuates racial disparities—then they're fine. They're antiracist. But there is more. Like others who embrace critical race theory, he embraces intersectionality. He says, "Antiracist policies cannot eliminate class racism without anticapitalism policies. Anticapitalism cannot eliminate class racism without antiracism."[67] Also, "To truly be antiracist is to be feminist. To truly be feminist is to be antiracist."[68] And, "We cannot be antiracist if we are homophobic or transphobic...To be queer antiracist is to understand the privileges of my cisgender, of my masculinity, of my heterosexuality, of their intersections."[69]

Kendi thinks of antiracism as a sort of gospel akin to religious strivings. He tells us at length,

> At Urbana '70, Ma and Dad found themselves leaving the civilizing and conserving and racist church they realized they'd been part of. They were saved into Black liberation theology and joined the churchless church of the Black Power movement...[Dad] began reading the work of James Cone..."What is your definition of a Christian?" Dad asked in his deeply earnest way. Cone looked at Dad with equal seriousness and responded: "A Christian is one who is striving for liberation"...Receiving this definition was a revolutionary moment in Dad's life. Ma had her own similar revelation in her Black student union—that Christianity was about struggle and liberation. My parents now had, separately, arrived at a creed with which to shape their lives, to be the type of Christians that Jesus the revolutionary inspired them to be... This new definition of the Christian life became the creed that grounded my parents' lives and the lives of their children. I cannot disconnect my parents' religious strivings to be Christian from my secular striving to be an antiracist.[70]

In addition, Kendi writes, "When you truly recognize that racial groups are equals, then you also recognize that racial disparities must be the result of racist policy."[71] Hence, he's not just a national socialist but a globalist socialist. America, by its nature, is iniquitous. Kendi thinks "systemic racism" is redundant because racism is by its nature systemic, institutional, and structural. He prefers the synonym "racist policy":

> A racist policy is any measure that produces or sustains racial inequity between racial groups. An antiracist policy is any measure that produces or sustains racial equity between racial groups. By policy, I mean written and unwritten laws, rules, procedures, processes, regulations, and guidelines that govern people. There is no such thing as a nonracist or race-neutral policy. Every policy in every institution in every community in every nation is producing or sustaining either racial inequity or equity between racial groups.[72]

Another way of saying this is that any policy or practice that creates or sustains racial disparity or inequality is what is popularly called "systemic racism." What does taking that perspective look like when applied to something like marriage? Marriage is a practice that creates or sustains racial disparity, when in the black community, the single-parent rate is extraordinarily high.

Kendi quickly became the front-runner of antiracism, which is nothing more than justified racism of another form. In 2020, Purdue University was also responsive to the cry of racism in America, launching a lecture series on "Pursuing Racial Justice Together." Kendi was the series' first speaker.[73] Note that Purdue is among the more conservative of top universities. Yet right off the bat, series speakers they announced included not only Kendi but Patrisse Cullors, Robin DiAngelo, and Kimberlé Crenshaw. After I communicated with then-President Mitch Daniels about the worldview being advanced by all the many speakers sympathetic to critical theory, I like to think he might have been willing to embrace bringing in at least one of my recommended speakers, Dr. Shelby Steele, who finished the series.[74] Later that month, Kendi tweeted that Amy Coney Barrett is a colonizer for having adopted two Haitian children. The *New York Post* reported on his tweet:

> "Some White colonizers 'adopted' Black children," he wrote. "They 'civilized' these 'savage' children in the 'superior' ways of White people, while using them as props in their lifelong pictures of denial, while cutting the biological parents of these children out of the picture of humanity."[75]

Empires rise and empires fall, and like BLM, so too we see the possible collapse of Ibram X. Kendi.[76] But sadly, the ideas persist even if the actors change.

REFOCUS AND CONTROL THE NARRATIVE

As Christians, our response to this new brand of racism is to begin with our position of strength, which we'll focus on in part 3 of the book. Suffice it to say for now that we need to begin by showing Christianity to be good, true, and rational. We must be anchored in our proper identity and the one that best establishes equality for all—our being made in God's image (Genesis 1:26-27). The Christian worldview is incomparable in its ability to provide the philosophical framework for that which everyone intuitively knows is right but has little rationale to ground it. Even secularists are beginning to see this and lamenting the apparent demise of Christianity in the West.

4

MATH AND MEDICINE SWOON UNDER THE SPELL

When it comes to knowledge, there are various ways of knowing. Rationalism or rational knowledge concerns the *a priori*, things known prior to investigation, as a way one can know things simply by rational reflection. Items include math (e.g., 2 + 2 = 4), logic (e.g., the law of noncontradiction), and introspective philosophy (e.g., notions like "I think, therefore I am"). This is often the area where we think we might have certainty. After all, you cannot deny the laws of logic without assuming them in your denial. They are literally preconditions of rational thought. Empiricism or empirical knowledge concerns the *a posteriori*, wherein items of knowledge are ascertained after investigation has taken place, often by a process of inductive reasoning such as found in science and medicine. This results in high levels of confidence in the probability or likelihood of our beliefs being true. We see its fruit in examples such as improving our eyesight or flying to the moon. Special revelation is given by God through Scripture, and Christians are to test personal reflections against Scripture. Often, fields relative to rationalism and empiricism can be used to confirm revelation, and in fact, the very ground of revelation can ground those fields. The father of modern calculus, Gottfried Leibniz, once reasoned that the atheist can be a geometer, but without God, there would be no geometry. He believed that reason itself is governed by the laws of logic and the principle of sufficient reason. From reasoning comes reason, which itself needs an ultimate explanation. Using, as an example, a geometry book whose content is copied from a chain of copies, there must be a reason for the content. Indeed, for a geometric mind (even if he were an atheist) and geometry itself, there must be a Mind. For the Christian, Jesus is referred to as the logos in John 1:1-3. God is the ground for rationality itself.[1] The very notions of rationality and our minds seem to be best explained by an ultimate Mind.

But now, all these traditional ways of knowing have been targeted during the current revolution with disastrous consequences for common sense, life-and-death medical technology, and spiritual health, ranging from ministry mission drift by institutions to the exchange of the gospel for a false gospel.

The cultural revolutionary movement is serious in its efforts to impact all areas of human existence; it's not simply interested in the back alleys of humanities departments at universities. As Douglas Murray asserted, "[Theory] might work in lesbian dance theory classes, it would halt at the borders of the hard sciences and mathematics. It would stop at the doors of engineering, because at some point the bridges have to stay up."[2]

Long before Robin DiAngelo influenced the Smithsonian Institution to dismiss whiteness on their web page by downplaying things of white culture like rationality, hard work, being on time, delayed gratification, and so on (for which they faced massive backlash),[3] there were race Marxists of CRT claiming in the workbook *Dismantling Racism* that "sense of urgency," "individualism" and "objectivity," as well as logic and more were all white-supremacist notions.[4]

MATHEMATICAL INCARCERATION AND JUSTICE FOR ALL

Mathematics, an area thought to be untouchable and objective that serves as the grounding for sciences such as engineering, physics, and chemistry, is now viewed through a skeptical lens. Revolutionary ideology stemming from Marxism even problematizes fields like mathematics. Enter "equitable math."

Math is elitist, white privileged, and inherently racist, and Western too. But hasn't math been around since, well, forever? The book *A Pathway to Equitable Math Instruction* claims to be a guide to teachers of students of grades six through eight for examining their own biases with the goal of dismantling racism in mathematics. It cites *Dismantling Racism*, quotes Ibram X. Kendi as well, and asks readers to imagine what it means to be an antiracist math educator. It seems to give homage to other ways of knowing.[5] But just what are those other ways?

In the summer of 2020, several academics in the education fields tried to deconstruct or dismantle our common understanding of math, beginning creatively with two plus two makes four. In fact, it was deemed that $2 + 2 = 4$ is obviously part of a hegemonic narrative people use, and they shouldn't get to decide what is true. Two plus two can equal whatever we want it to be. A brief skirmish happened on Twitter that included doctoral students and professors, some calling on people to attack the haters who think two plus two must equal four.[6] One commenter, a critical math educator and PhD student at Rutgers who believes in "math identities," posted, "Nope the idea of 2 + 2 equaling 4 is cultural and because of western imperialism/colonization we think of it as the only way of knowing." Other professors piled on in agreement, one saying, "Critical mathematics education research plays an important role in dismantling injustices," and then, as if we should be surprised, she kindly shared her pronouns. This was followed by ways others could help support the position that two plus two can equal anything. Of course, this didn't last long. An open letter was signed by 750 math teachers and professors shutting down the absurdity.[7] This incongruity is due to the presumption of mass racism. The American Mathematical Society has pledged to "address systemic inequities that exist in mathematics community."[8]

Critical math proponents think in terms of proportionality. The assertion is absent some unfairness or injustice, it is presumed that racial demographics of every institution would match that of the population at large, and this is true of math as well. On the face of it, it is absurd. Disparate outcomes do not necessarily entail disparate treatments. Case-by-case examinations are required. If that were the case, then just as it is claimed the rates of incarceration of black males show systemic racism, the rates of incarceration of males over the rates of females show sexism. In math, as in some other fields, gifted-and-talented programs are being dismantled because minorities are not proportionally represented there. Doing things like this dumbs us all down rather than builds us all up. As of 2021, University of California campuses began refusing to consider SAT and ACT scores in undergraduate admissions because of the proportionality, claiming the SAT test was a racist test—that is, until 2024, when many universities began sensing pushback against DEI and began reversing course.[9] But racial disparities in outcomes are overwhelmingly the result of measurable differences in achievement and behavior. Is this replacing meritocracy with mediocracy?

MEDIOCRE MEDICINE IS GOOD FOR EVERYONE

It gets worse. Many times, false ideologies become a matter of physical health or even life and death. In 2020, the biggest pandemic in American history was underway. COVID-19 was a clear medical science issue with life-and-death implications on a mass scale. The leading journal of the medical world, *The Lancet*, ran a piece titled "Racism Is the Public Health Crisis"[10] and along with it published an antiracism pledge. The pledge professed to "educate ourselves about racism," "pledge our solidarity with the Black Lives Matter movement," and "turn that pledge into concrete actions in our own work."[11] Other major science journals did the same. We were seeing discussions by medical experts advising the CDC to consider racial preferencing of blacks over the elderly because "older populations are whiter…society is structured in a way that enables them to live longer."[12] In a culture where structural racism is now a given, the older white people have apparently lived too long already.

One year after Floyd's death, *Nature*, the leading science journal, stated that "systemic racism is science" and that the staff at *Nature* had to recognize their part in it and the role of science as a whole in perpetuating racism. According to *Nature*, "Too often, conventional metrics—citations, publications, profits—reward those in positions of power, rather than helping to shift the balance of power."[13] In response to this, while we recognize that some people might be made to feel guilty or to want to virtue signal that they're not racist by going along to get along, one might also wonder whether the aim of scientific journals isn't simply to publish the best and most important research, whoever comes up with the ideas and for whomever it benefits. Surely, understanding the physical world is of some value that is important to everyone. Surely, understanding the human body and disease and encouraging ways of knowing in a conducive manner that produces good health is a good we should all be concerned about. Apparently not.

In 2021, an eye-opening incident happened at the *Journal of the American Medical Association* (*JAMA*). The deputy editor said in a podcast discussion that he thought "structural racism" (synonymous with systemic or institutional) was an unfortunate term and that "many people like myself are offended by the implication that we are somehow racist." For this he was not only fired (after apologizing for the harm he caused, of course), but his editor was forced out of a job and a DEI specialist was to take their place (a black epidemiologist specializing in racial disparities).[14]

In June 2022, people called on Congress to require that the National Institutes of Health (NIH) fund science researchers for proportionality, those who "look like the country."[15] For example, if blacks represent 13 percent of the country, then 13 percent should be funded. But what if that 13 percent doesn't merit the public funding? Justice, classically understood, is getting what you deserve. Social justice is getting what you do not necessarily deserve. All objective measures document an average skills gap that makes the expectation of proportional representation across all meritocratic institutions unrealistic. America today does not conclusively show that our system or individuals behind the system seek to keep blacks and other underrepresented minorities down. The hunt for racist ghosts is destroying America's core institutions and putting at risk meritocratic scientific advances in favor of racial "progress," which may actually result in racial regress. If anything, everyone is in competition to privilege and hire more minorities—quotas. Yet no one can seem to fill their quotas because there aren't enough meritocratically qualified candidates to go around.

What is never asked is the proportion of competitively qualified BIPOC candidates in the hiring or promotion pool. It is simply assumed that such candidates are available. Yet the underrepresentation in many professions is the result of the unequal distribution of skills, not bias. Also in 2022, Boeing announced plans to raise hiring quotas. Boeing decided to make its management bonus structure based in part on hiring for underrepresented groups, not for airplane safety. DEI poured into hiring, and by 2024, a door flew off a Boeing jet operated by Alaska Airlines in the middle of a flight. This prompted billionaire Elon Musk to thunder, "People will die due to DEI."[16]

Has there been a demonstrable death? The risk is nearly mathematically inevitable. Let's consider the pressure on businesses to hire someone who is black. Around 13 percent of the US population is black.[17] To match, businesses should have around 13 percent representation in their staff. In 2023, there were more than 33,000,000 small businesses in the US (this does not include big businesses)[18] and 48,300,000 black people in the US (including children, who are not of eligible age for employment).[19] These numbers would indicate that a threshold of 13 percent representation in every company in the United States is not achievable. It's not just Boeing; it is medical schools, nuclear power plants, and many others. Companies are searching for a token, even if unqualified, and there are not enough people to fill the openings.

This is what one *New York Times* bestselling author terms "The Bias Fallacy."[20] In Heather Mac Donald's well-researched book *When Race Trumps Merit*, physicists, mathematicians, and the most cutting-edge medical researchers and engineers are ordinarily drawn from an applicant pool with the uppermost range of math scores. It is a meritocratic system. The most high-level jobs in law and finance will have similar requirements, seeking to find the best. Yet research shows that when looking at our nation's report card, black student math scores are significantly lower than white student scores, which are lower than Asian student scores.[21] The ACT and SAT measure a more selective group of students for those intending to go to college, and the gaps remain. Whites are five times as likely to be ready for college-level work in all four ACT subject areas.[22] Moving to the job market and seeking those with the highest academic degrees, there simply aren't enough black candidates in STEM subjects who have PhDs to place individuals in every company. Yet people protest to shut down STEM.

Do we want mediocre medicine, mediocre technology, mediocre everything? In 2021, blacks made up 1 percent of all who were awarded doctorates in physics to US citizens and permanent residents, according to the annual

Survey of Earned Doctorates from the National Center for Science and Engineering Statistics. They earned 3 percent of math and statistics doctorates. There were none in many fields.[23] The LSAT for law school is similarly skewed. It isn't because of racism but because of skills gaps. Yet according to UCLA law professor Richard Sander, because firms are trying to hire black candidates, they get a disproportionate number of internship offers compared to white candidates.[24] It is the same with the GRE test, and consequently, most top graduate programs have been dropping GRE test requirements entirely, just like the ACT and SAT.

It is absurd to drop objective standards. Knowledge and skills exist and can be measured. They're being dropped not because of justice but because of social justice. Yet ironically, the SAT was developed in the middle of last century to overcome potential biases that favored some groups over others. It was developed to make things fair and just—equal, not equitable. Now the woke movement deems merit-based measurables like this to be racist. Mac Donald makes the astute observation,

> America's elites have apparently decided that if, after five decades of massive financial outlays on inner-city education, income transfers [socialist redistribution], and social services, the academic skills gap has still not closed, it is time to break up the objective yardsticks that measure it. The same will happen regarding crime data.[25]

EXAMS ARE RACIST

Ibram X. Kendi opposes standardized testing in schools. In 2019, he said, "I'll say it again and again: Standardized tests have become the most effective racist weapon ever devised to objectively degrade Black minds and legally exclude their bodies."[26] He and other race Marxists loathe discussion about the "achievement gap" that Mac Donald's data reveals. He says,

> The acceptance of an academic-achievement gap is just the latest method of reinforcing the oldest racist idea: Black intellectual inferiority. The idea of an achievement gap means there is a disparity

> in academic performance between groups of students; implicit in this idea is that academic "achievement" can only be measured by statistical instruments like test scores and dropout rates. There is an even more sinister implication in achievement-gap talk…Intellect is the linchpin of behavior, and the racist idea of the achievement gap is the linchpin of behavioral racist ideas. Remember, to believe in a racial hierarchy is to believe in a racist idea. The idea of an achievement gap between the races—with Whites and Asians at the top and Blacks and Latinx people and Natives at the bottom—creates a racial hierarchy, with its implication that the racial gap in test scores means something is wrong with the Black and Latinx and Native test takers and not the tests. From the beginning, the tests, not groups of people, have been the racial problem.[27]

Kendi doesn't clearly think things through here. One can't ignore the inequalities of other groups and only focus on whites and blacks. One needs to be open to the fact that life is complex and there may be other causes of disparities. He's not open to that. He says, "Racial discrimination is the sole cause of racial disparities in this country and in the world at large."[28] Ignoring, for example, Hispanic and Asian inequalities is a convenient way to simply invoke the legacy of slavery hardships. The fact is that disparities and inequalities don't always entail injustice.

Black Stanford economics professor Thomas Sowell points this out in a multitude of ways in *Discrimination and Disparities*. The central target in his book is the false dilemma that either "those who have been less fortunate in their outcomes are genetically less capable" or they "are victims of other people who are more fortunate."[29] He aims to show that this is false. Indeed, statistical disparities can be produced by any number of causes, which certainly includes but is by no means limited to discrimination. He says that geographical differences will produce dramatic disparities quite apart from any human intervention. For example,

> Coastal peoples around the world have long tended to be more prosperous and more advanced than people of the same race

living farther inland, while people living in river valleys have likewise tended to be more prosperous and more advanced than people living up in isolated hills and mountains around the world. Transportation costs to and from mountain communities have long been prohibitively expensive...Climate and soil are likewise geographic obstacles to equal prospects or equal outcomes. Most of the most fertile land in the world is in the temperate zones and little or none in the tropics...Areas that are located both near the sea and in the temperate zones have been found to have 8 percent of the world's inhabited land area, 23 percent of the world's population, and 53 percent of the world's Gross Domestic Product.[30]

This is true in Africa, not just America, an important factor to note since the left often wants to tie disparities to slavery. Numerous other examples exist, demonstrating that disparities between societies and people groups even in the same families as twins do not necessarily indicate nefarious activity. Sowell asks, "If there is not equality of outcomes among people born to the same parents and raised under the same roof, why should equality of outcomes be expected—or assumed—when conditions are not nearly so comparable?"[31] Disparate outcomes do not necessarily entail disparate treatment. Inequality does not necessarily entail injustice. Yet that is the whole house of cards that social justice narratives are built on. In terms of the legacy of slavery often brought up, Sowell offers a profound statement:

> If we wanted to be serious about evidence, we might compare where blacks stood a hundred years after the end of slavery with where they stood after 30 years of the liberal welfare state. In other words, we could compare hard evidence on "the legacy of slavery" with hard evidence on the legacy of liberals. Despite the grand myth that black economic progress began or accelerated with the passage of the civil rights laws and "war on poverty" programs of the 1960s, the cold fact is that the poverty rate among blacks fell from 87 percent in 1940 to 47 percent by 1960. This was before any of those programs began. Over the next 20 years, the poverty rate

among blacks fell another 18 percentage points, compared to the 40-point drop in the previous 20 years. This was the continuation of a previous economic trend, at a slower rate of progress, not the economic grand deliverance proclaimed by liberals and self-serving black "leaders." Nearly a hundred years of the supposed "legacy of slavery" found most black children being raised in two-parent families in 1960. But thirty years after the liberal welfare state found the great majority of black children being raised by a single parent…If we are to go by evidence of social retrogression, liberals have wreaked more havoc on blacks than the supposed "legacy of slavery" they talk about. Liberals should heed the title of Jason Riley's insightful new book, "Please Stop Helping Us."[32]

Sowell is arguably one of the best and most relevant economic and social philosophers alive. He's been the senior fellow at Stanford University's Hoover Institution for the last 40 years. He grew up during Jim Crow and the Great Depression. His father died prior to Thomas's birth, and his mom was too poor to keep him and gave him up for adoption. He grew up without running water and electricity at his house. He dropped out of high school, joined the Marines during the Korean War, and then became a Marxist. He returned and completed a bachelor's degree (Harvard) and a master's degree (Columbia) in economics and then earned his PhD from the University of Chicago, studying under the Nobel Prize winner Milton Friedman. He now despises Marxism and sees the dangers happening in our culture.

Now we'll address the major cause of wealth disparity in the black community. As of 2021, 63 percent of black children are growing up in fatherless homes.[33] Fatherlessness is the single most accurate predictor of poverty for *all* social groups. As supported by the data, children from fatherless homes are more likely to be poor, become involved in drug and alcohol abuse, drop out of school, and suffer from health and emotional problems. Boys are more likely to become involved in crime, and girls are more likely to become pregnant as teens.[34] What people fail to realize is that the poverty rate among black married couples has been less than 10 percent every year since 1994.[35] Let that sink in. If someone marries and stays married, they have a nine in ten chance of escaping poverty. No government-sponsored "war on poverty" can compete with that success rate. Follow God's ways, get married and stay married, and the poverty problem largely disappears. What is needed is not more government but more God. The gospel of Jesus Christ, not the "gospel" of Karl Marx.

If society chooses social justice and quotas over justice and merit it will erode excellence in all facets of life for all people—including blacks. It is a choice between meritocracy or mediocrity. Yet we're moving into a zone where any test or evaluation on which blacks and Hispanics score worse than whites and Asians is considered biased and should be eliminated. Consider the United States Medical Licensing Exam (USMLE). In their second year of medical school, students take step 1 of their exams, which measures knowledge of the field and predicts success in residency. Highly sought-after residency programs such as surgery use step 1 scores to select the best meritocratic candidates. Blacks are not admitted at the same rate as whites because scores reveal a massive knowledge gap.[36] In the world of antiracism, this can only mean one thing. The test must be to blame rather than a legitimate comparison of medical knowledge. What is the solution?

Abolish step 1 grading and make the test pass/fail, which is what has recently occurred at Yale's medical school, starting in January 2022.[37] Membership in the medical school honor society Alpha Omega Alpha influences residency selection and faculty hiring. White students are six times as likely to be inducted, according to *JAMA*.[38] Hence, in 2020, the president of the honor society suggested adding a potential inductee's relationship skills and any unequal barriers he or she may have faced to the consideration criteria.[39] Voilà! The University of Pennsylvania's medical school, among others, converted to a new system in 2021, including community activities (like diversity, equity, and inclusion). And minority students' selectees more than doubled according to one researcher.[40] Every other step in the process is similar.

To make room for diversity, while attempting to overcome real obstacles, the bar is being lowered, with the result that at every step of the way, we're encouraging mediocrity and eroding excellence in all fields. How will you feel knowing that your surgeon barely passed medical school with competence in medical expertise but overcame significant trauma in life as a teenager?

While MCAT tests are rigorous to get into medical school, they've already been watered down such that, as of 2021, a notable number of the questions now focus on social issues and psychology.[41] How that is helpful during a heart surgery is unclear.

Yet the gap persists, so the bar continues lowering. Acceptance variables now include GPA, MCAT, state of residence, and unsurprisingly, ethnicity. Blacks and Hispanics are now accepted at far higher rates yet with lower scores.[42] They are not being excluded; they are being catapulted. Doing this in other doctoral programs will inhibit scientific progress, but doing it in medicine could cost lives.

Recently, the US Supreme Court delivered rulings on several issues. One ruling was *Students for Fair Admissions v. President and Fellows of Harvard College* and *Students for Fair Admissions v. University of North Carolina*. The ruling found that race-based affirmative action in admissions policies violated students' rights; for example, Harvard cannot discriminate against Asian students in favor of black students. The decision is a win for students who can receive justice (rather than social justice) in being judged on the basis of merit rather than skin pigment. Racism is wrong, everywhere, even when it is reverse racism dictated by critical race theory.

When the US Supreme Court seat that Justice Ketanji Brown Jackson (the same justice who, when asked, couldn't or wouldn't answer the question, What is a woman?) came to fill first became open, Joe Biden was very clear that he was selecting his nomination based on race and sex,[43] not necessarily merit. In the affirmative action case above, she offered a minority dissenting opinion against the 6–3 majority. She said that black doctors give black babies twice the chance of survival and therefore we should advance racial preferences (i.e., be racist) in medical school admissions because it saves lives.[44]

Numerous writers on both sides—supporters and opponents of her confirmation—have pointed out her erroneous thinking.[45] Citing a study in an amicus brief, she said, "For high-risk Black newborns, having a Black physician more than doubles the likelihood that the baby will live, and not die."[46] That claim was taken from an amicus brief filed by the Association of American Medical Colleges, which in turn was referencing a study that appeared in the Proceedings of the National Academy of Sciences. As one author argues,

First, the study does not claim to find a doubling in survival rates for black newborns who have a black attending doctor. Instead, in its most fully specified model, it reports that 99.6839 percent of black babies born with a black attending physician survived, compared to 99.5549 percent of black babies born with white attending physicians; a difference of 0.129 percent. The survival rate of 99.6839 percent is clearly not a doubling of 99.5549 percent.[47]

Thus, it is misleadingly false to claim that the black newborn survival rate doubles when they have black attending physicians. Further, assuming the results of the data were correct, the fallacious interpretation needing correction is that black newborns on average have greater complications. For example, one study shows that one in 13 births of all babies born in California in 2023 was of low birthweight, and yet in 2021–2023, black infants were nearly three times more likely to be born with lower birthweight than white infants and two times more likely than Hispanic infants.[48] This usually requires a specialist rather than a family practitioner or regular pediatrician, who is likely to be white given the meritorious reasons cited earlier. Finally, apart from that, the justified racial preferences (i.e., racism) that the schools were applying in their admissions practices are not morally tenable, much less legally tenable, as the 6–3 majority showed.

If the logic of mathematics and care of medicine can be so infected, is there anything beyond the reach of this ideological poison in the universities? We must remember that as Christians, we serve a God who is the ground of rationality and compassion. We have something to offer. Christ is the logos of God and demonstrated care when he became incarnate and showed his love through sacrifice. We have the opportunity—and we should view it as an opportunity—to be salt and light to a culture. But this can only be done intentionally when we know what and where the problems reside. The fact that we can identify the problems, and we have many people serving in the relevant areas, provides us with a potential map with which we can strategically plan to reclaim the heart, hands, and head of Christ to again make an impact in these fields and in culture. As Paul said in Galatians 6:9, "Let us not grow weary of doing good, for in due season we will reap, if we do not give up" (ESV).

5

CHRISTIAN MINISTRIES AND MISSION DRIFT

During the Winter Olympics in Russia in 2014, President Vladimir Putin shocked leftist sensitivities when he warned homosexual activists about their attempts to influence children, telling them to "leave children alone."[1] While I'm no fan of Putin, he is apparently dealing with similar concerns we share in America.

In Chattanooga, Tennessee, in 2022, someone took video footage of a Pride month celebration that one might think would have come from San Francisco. The now-viral video captures a child seemingly stroking the groin of a drag queen.[2] During Pride month 2023, we witnessed parades of LGBTQ+ activists in New York City chanting, "We're here, we're queer, and we're coming for your children."[3] Upon viewing them, images of the mob in Sodom and Gomorrah immediately come to mind. Except we're not in Sodom. We're in America. Should we believe them when they tell us what they're doing? Perhaps there is some relief in knowing that it's happening "out there" and not in our churches, where our children are safe.

That same month, the Washington National Cathedral in Washington, DC, put on a light show inside the chapel featuring a dazzling rainbow. The Reverend Canon Leonard L. Hamlin, the Canon Missioner and Minister of Equity and Inclusion, celebrated Pride month by saying, "Love always wins."[4] Other churches hosted events from coast to coast. At Calvary Presbyterian

Church in San Francisco, we witnessed not merely a drag queen story hour on the streets or in a public library but a drag queen Bible story hour in a church with an audience of three- and four-year-olds taught by a transgender activist named Flamy Grant.[5] And there now exists a Bible version known as the Queen James Bible (2012), in which "valid" corrections were made for all the texts dealing with homosexuality. Any student of history cannot help but think of the infamous Greek tyrant Antiochus Epiphanes of Syria, who entered the Jewish Temple on December 25, 167 BC, and desecrated it by sacrificing a pig (an unclean animal) on the altar, dedicating it to Zeus. Christianity is now being co-opted by cultural morality.

During February 2020, the archbishop of Canterbury, Justin Welby, gave a speech to the Church of England, apologizing for the "institutional racism" of the church, claiming that it was still institutionally racist (even though the next important bishop in the church beside himself, John Sentamu, was from Uganda). Nonetheless, while the Church of England shut down over COVID, its leadership worked tirelessly at policy changes. Following the George Floyd killing, the church came out with a 71-page report, *From Lament to Action*, which described Floyd as "a 46-year-old practicing Christian, who worked to mentor young people and oppose gun violence," which is certainly a different interpretation of Floyd's varied career. Not only were there to be sweeping personnel changes (note that the grand bishop himself wasn't calling for his own removal or opting for someone of color to displace him—perish the thought), but there was also a call to "decolonize theology, ecclesiology, and possibly examine official teachings of the Church that follows prejudicial theological value system." The curriculum for ordinands must include participation in "an introductory Black Theology module." They must "diversify the curriculum," "produce a workable plan for increasing racial diversity," and "formally adopt Racial Justice Sunday in February of each year."[6]

In February 2021, the Episcopalian Church in America sprang into action and conducted a racial audit at the cost of $1,200,000. Verdict: guilty as presumed. For their part,

> the goal of this research has not been to determine whether or not systemic racism exists in the Episcopal Church, but rather to

examine its effects and the dynamics by which it is maintained in the church structure...To this end, we have employed the guiding tools of grounded theory and the theoretical framework of critical race theory.[7]

Enough said. Theory in search of evidence. All the while, the church was led by a black bishop but was still convinced of its inherent institutional racism. Most bishops polled in the audit defined racism in terms of critical race theory, not in terms of the classical definition. Note that Episcopal bishops throughout the denomination are enamored with the work of Ibram X. Kendi. One suspects which "gospel" the church has embraced.

But of course, that's just liberal Protestantism. Surely the Catholics, with all their tradition, won't be so moved. They boast of being the least likely church to shift with the times. In June 2020, the chaplain of MIT, Daniel Patrick Moloney, sent an email of caution to the university's Catholic community, saying that the protests over Floyd's death may have had nothing to do with racism. He also questioned Floyd's character given his previous convictions, never coming remotely close to saying that his death was right. Moloney's email leaked out and his sentence was swift: guillotine. A vice president and dean for student life was incensed and scolded Moloney for failing to acknowledge systemic racism. The regional leadership of the Catholic Church gave in to the pressures of the new gospel. The archdiocese of Boston distanced itself from the comments, and Moloney followed by doing what so many wrongly do in response to the woke mob—namely, he issued an apology for the hurt he had allegedly caused. Moloney resigned immediately at the behest of the archdiocese.

THEOLOGY DECOLONIZED AND LIBERATED

The emergence of liberation theology (a combination of Marxist and Christian thought, in which Christ is the shell and Marx is the core) began within Roman Catholicism in Latin America during the 1950s. Whereas Pope Benedict XVI condemned liberation theology for an overemphasis on Marxist social analysis, Pope Francis emerged from Latin America and was seemingly sympathetic. For years, Pope Francis actively sought to bring together Marxism and Christianity. Not long ago, the dialogue was formalized, but there has long been a name for it: liberation theology.[8]

Mentioned already, James Cone, the father of Black liberation theology, revamped the Latin version of oppression theology for consumption among the US's black Christian population in 1970, 20 years before CRT was a formal movement. The twentieth-anniversary edition of Cone's *A Black Theology of Liberation* had a foreword written by Paulo Freire, one of the most cited authors in all the humanities, especially in education, for his work in critical pedagogy. He is a known Marxist and identified his views with Cone's. Most people going through schools of education (including teaching K–12) can hardly avoid his influence in the field. The fiftieth-anniversary edition's foreword is by Peter J. Paris, a visiting professor at Boston University who teaches alongside Ibram X. Kendi.

I first became aware of liberation theology during seminary in the 1990s. At the time, I thought its potential for impact was nebulous and somewhat irrelevant for us in America. Little did I realize what a pregnant ideology it was, only later to study Marxism at Purdue under a famous Marxist professor and with numerous Marxist classmates.

Cone's now-decolonized theology was to "analyze the satanic nature of Whiteness" and "prepare all non-whites for revolutionary action."[9] Cone, like other woke "Christians," seems more in tune with sociology and the culture of lived experience rather than with theology and Scripture. For Cone, "In order to be Christian theology, White theology must cease being White theology and become Black theology by denying Whiteness as an acceptable form of human existence and affirming Blackness as God's intention for humanity."[10] The focus of liberation theology generally is that salvation is liberation—it stresses worldly liberation just as Marx himself did. Cone says, "Jesus is not a human being for all persons; he is a human being for oppressed persons, whose identity is made known in and through their liberation."[11]

Further, "To participate in God's salvation is to cooperate with the black Christ as he liberates his people from bondage. Salvation, then, primarily has to do with earthly reality and the injustice inflicted on those who are helpless and poor."[12] It doesn't end there. It smacks of, well, revolution: "What we need is the divine love as expressed in black power, which is the power of blacks to destroy their oppressors, here and now, by any means at their disposal."[13] Remember that among Cone's many disciples were Jeremiah Wright, Obama's pastor for 20 years, and Reverend Dr. Raphael Warnock, US Senator from Georgia, who gave the eulogy at Cone's funeral.

Cone's Jesus isn't the biblical Jesus. As one author points out,

> The ironic fact lost on Cone, as well as on most Woke social justice warriors, is that a great number of the early patristic church fathers who had shaped what he referred to as "White religion," such as Augustine, Origen, Tertullian, Cyprian, and Athanasius, were all People of Color from various parts of Northern Africa.[14]

Sadly, it is not only mainline or ethnocentric denominations that are being affected. When I was invited to speak at a Christian apologetics conference in Chicago in 2021 on the topic of critical race theory, I asked those in the audience to raise their hands if they wanted to be a racist. Expectedly, no one did. I then asked them to raise their hands if they wanted to be antiracist. Astonishingly, more than half the people raised their hands well before knowing what that word meant.

In our culture, sometimes one suspects that it is almost more acceptable now to be accused of being a rapist than a racist, as if racism is the big sin in culture. The very charge of being a racist seems to be a death sentence. The poisonous ideology of critical race theory has infiltrated all layers of American Christianity, including campus ministries. Cru, for example, lost major staff and donors over the issue of critical race theory within.[15] I'm friends with some Cru leaders and was on Cru's staff for many years myself teaching in their continuing education program and leading in faculty ministry at Purdue University. My current ministry has numerous former Cru staff members. We've lamented over and prayed for our colleagues there, and I've personally been engaged with their leadership, with whom I maintain genuine friendships even at the highest levels. They've recognized that mistakes have been made and are making some effort to remedy them, and yet still there are concerns about the extent to which remedy is necessary.

So subtle is this philosophical ideology that even renowned churches and pastor-theologians like Tim Keller of Redeemer Presbyterian Church in New York City are not immune from being infected. I've delightfully used and recommended his works on apologetics and marriage. But in certain respects, he's been influenced by the philosophy of the age while also stating his resistance to it. Kirsten Powers is a well-known television news anchor who says she became a Christian under his ministry. But she wrote a memorial to him on her Substack titled "My Complicated Feelings About Tim Keller." She claims that she heard one thing from the pulpit but not other things that she later came to resent, feeling like she was a victim of "bait and switch." She said,

> I signed up for what I heard from the pulpit, which never included teaching about homosexuality or abortion being sin…But as I became more involved in the church, I learned that these were in fact core teachings. Keller may well have been orthodox on those things but apparently was not very public about it. It is easy to hold views and be influenced by the culture around you to the point where you conceal certain teachings for sensitivity of making the main thing, the main thing: i.e., the Gospel.[16]

Powers no longer refers to herself as a Christian.

But it is another thing to ingest and then digest some of the poisonous philosophy from our culture back into our culture as Keller has done with tenets of critical race theory, for which some theologians have gone to lengths to criticize him for.[17] In the year before his death, Keller claimed that what convinced him of the proof of "systemic racism" was evidence that missionaries of color couldn't raise support as easily as white missionaries. As much as I appreciate Keller's writings as well as the positive impact he's had on the kingdom, he arrived at a hasty conclusion without fully understanding the complexity of the issue, which is both intellectually and practically problematic.[18] Pastors have always needed to be on guard to make sure they are guided primarily by theology and Scripture rather than sociology and culture. We see the problem of syncretism (blending biblical thought with cultural ideology) in the New Testament with tension between the Hebraic Jews and the Hellenistic Jews (influenced by Greek thought) of the first century.

We see this syncretism phenomenon visible in a range of Christian institutions, from Christian colleges and universities to Christian academic societies[19] to parachurch ministries like Christian adoption agencies.[20] An organization that connects Christian colleges is itself compromised. The Council for Christian Colleges and Universities' (CCCU) mission is "to advance the cause of Christ-centered higher education and to help our institutions transform lives by faithfully relating scholarship and service to biblical truth."[21] Yet how faithful are they to biblical truth? Its website advances Kendi-style antiracism and endorses readings from some of the worst CRT popular offenders.[22]

One of the main problems is that institutional administrators often accept donations from donors with subversive motives and strings attached. As the saying goes, "Mission drift is but a donor away."[23]

Following the money trail can help show who an organization is being funded and influenced by and, therefore, that organization's future trajectory. Megan Basham, in her book *Shepherds for Sale*, has compiled data on Christian ministries who are candidates for this. For example, *Christianity Today*, the magazine founded by Billy Graham in 1956, has increasingly been viewed by many evangelicals as moving in a more progressive direction over the last decade. Basham helps trace in her *New York Times* bestseller where significant funds have come from and where the top-brass leaders are heading based on the contributions they receive—including from proabortion and pro-LGBTQ+ Democrats.[24]

Another problem I've learned from my own experience and research is that many of these Christian institutions have boards made up mostly of "money people." I'm not saying Christian board members who are wealthy are to be viewed with suspicion. Their influence becomes a problem when they unwittingly or knowingly take the mission in an unbiblical and sometimes nefarious direction. Affluence is fine, but not at the expense of doing what is biblically right, especially when the institution is connected to higher learning. I've seen numerous cases of entire boards at Christian institutions (campus ministries, colleges, etc.) being seated by members who lack the theological or biblical training that makes one capable of sniffing out the subtleties of critical theory and the like. This is especially egregious when such institutions are somehow related to ministry connected to higher education. Having board members with impressive degrees or credentials is no guarantee that ideological mission drift will be averted. But it is almost a guarantee that if there is no one intellectually and spiritually prepared to guard the mission, then it will go adrift. Mission drift is like entropy. It's the natural course if it's not guarded against.

How did this radical cultural revolution come about at what seems to be lightning speed? No doubt, it is radical. In one respect, it has occurred rapidly. In another respect, it's been incubating for longer than we know. In the Steven Spielberg movie *The War of the Worlds*, starring Tom Cruise, alien life forms with mechanical parts were embedded in the subterranean soil across the earth many, many years before the radical event took place. A trigger mechanism worked, in concert, to bring them all out from under the soil and unleashed terror on the world.

In our world, culture and politics are the soil, but beneath the soil lie ideas generated most articulately and influentially in the universities. As one noted Holocaust survivor quipped,

> The gas chambers of Auschwitz were the ultimate consequence of the theory that man is nothing but the product of heredity and environment—or, as the Nazis liked to say, of "Blood and Soil." I am absolutely convinced that the gas chambers of Auschwitz, Treblinka, and Majdanek were ultimately prepared not in some Ministry or other in Berlin, but rather at the desks and in the lecture halls of nihilistic scientists and philosophers.[25]

It is not a war of the worlds but a war of ideas that is changing our world. And it all begins in the universities.

In the movie, the aliens were eventually defeated. The war of ideas begins in the universities, but it doesn't end there. Nor will our response to this ideology. As we're often reminded, every "square inch"[26] belongs to Christ, and we should seek to bring the heart, hands, and mind of Christ to bear on all areas of life. The apostle Paul admonishes us in 2 Corinthians 10:3-5,

> For though we walk in the flesh, we are not waging war according to the flesh. For the weapons of our warfare are not of the flesh but have divine power to destroy strongholds. We destroy arguments and every lofty opinion raised against the knowledge of God, and take every thought captive to obey Christ (ESV).

Jesus, from small beginnings, worked in and through His disciples, who were trained by Him and committed to sowing seeds that have gone on to have a great impact on civilization, including bringing about and sustaining for centuries the very universities in question in this book. May it be so again!

PART 2

HOW DID WE GET HERE?

One Word Explains It All

The university is a clear-cut fulcrum with which to move the world…More potently than by any other means, change the university and you change the world.

CHARLES MALIK

6

THE UNIVERSITY AS THE MIND OF CULTURE

niversity. At one time, that word was not part of my vocabulary. I held a 0.666 GPA in school (yes, you read that correctly). I was *that* smart kid. Smarter than the system, or so I thought in my own head. I wasn't much interested in knowledge. But then, I had an encounter that would be a game changer forever. I met Christ later in my high school years, and when I did, I was given an insatiable desire to know—to know God and His world. As a new believer, I was very serious about the good news in Christ and had a strong desire to share it with others. My engagement in conversations with people at the University of Utah and in downtown Salt Lake City became routine. However, something about the university stood out. It was special. There was an aura of influence about the institution that drew me in very early on, and I would only come to understand the significance of that later.

While an undergrad at Salt Lake Community College in 1991, I was in a Humanities 101 class where the professor spent six weeks focused on myths, and he lumped Jesus in with many other great "myths." When the term project approached, we were assigned to do a presentation that could be on virtually anything humanities related. Classmates presented pet spiders, exhibits from Greece, an excursus on snow skiing with skis in hand, and more. I thought, *What could be more central to humanities than the founder of the largest worldview or religious movement that shaped Western civilization?* I decided I would challenge my professor about Jesus as a myth and show instead how Jesus was not. My presentation was called "Myth Became Fact: The Fulfillment of Bible Prophecy." It was only fair. I gave a presentation arguing that Jesus Christ is the Messiah, citing evidence from Bible prophecy concerning His identity, historical support for the Bible, and important facts about Jesus' resurrection.

The professor, a '70s hippie, literally cut me off midway through my presentation to the large class and told me it was over. I couldn't proceed. Later, he informed me that I was no longer welcome in the course because I was proselytizing. Funny, I was doing what he was doing in his lectures. I thought the university was a fine place to present ideas, debate, and pursue truth in the free exchange of competing ideas. What's more, he gave me an F for proselytizing. I called a lawyer, met with a college administrator to notify them that a legal letter was on its way, then waited to see who would flinch first. They persuaded the professor to let me back in the classroom so long as I stayed quiet. I received an A.

I wish I could say things got better after that. But they got much worse.

Universities claim to prize diversity and inclusivity. But these days, this means little more than a fixation with skin pigment and private parts. It doesn't include viewpoint diversity—at least, not if the viewpoint is a conservative Christian perspective.

Fast-forward several years. I went to Bible college and seminary and was completing a time of working in pastoral ministry with high school and college students. But I became nauseated over seeing my students fall away from their faith whenever they'd attend the secular baptismal font: universities. That is when an idea struck. I pondered the valiant story of the Greeks and the city of Troy. For a decade, the Greeks failed to broach the walls of the city. But then they devised a creative and stealth plan to enter the walls via the infamous Trojan horse. By analogy, I realized that Christians had largely failed to engage the secular universities. The walls were too large. I thought that we needed a stealth plan to reclaim—at least a portion—of the intellectual voice of Christ from within institutions that Christians founded, sustained (for centuries), and then became exiled from. Christian influence went from the predominant voice within to barely allowed. By *reclaim*, I do not mean to convey a hostile takeover. But can we at least have a seat at the table to be influencers at the institutions we founded? Yes, indeed. We're called to be salt and light, but we cannot be that if we're absent. So I reasoned, Why not start with me? To be honest, many had preceded me, and I knew many would come after me. But I wanted to be part of such a movement. Unfortunately, finding others with a kindred spirit on campus was rarer than one would hope.

After completing yet another master's degree in preparation for a reputable doctoral program, I entered the PhD program in philosophy at Purdue University in 2004. Six weeks into my studies, I was shocked that I was receiving prank calls at three o'clock in the morning from fellow graduate students. They were mocking me for my faith. The next semester, I took a class on Marxism, a topic I remembered studying in seminary under the title "Liberation Theology." I recall receiving a permanent note in my file from the distinguished professor, himself a Marxist. In the note, he claimed that I was schizophrenic. While he was not a clinical psychologist who was capable of diagnosing me as schizophrenic, like any good Marxist, he believed religion was the opiate of the masses and that my beliefs were delusional.

I reached a point where I tried to be as stealth as possible and keep my head down just to graduate. Nonetheless, I could not avoid the hostility. While in my fifth year, I was sabotaged near the finish line. I was ABD (all but dissertation) with a 3.5 GPA. I completed all my course work, languages, and exams, and my funding was provided independent of the department. But my dissertation committee chair informed me, and everyone else, that he dropped me. He told me that it was because I had too much of a faith perspective. Never mind the fact that part of my dissertation topic was on the virtue of faith.

I had no adviser and no legal recourse. Professors need only "publish or perish." If they do not want to advise a graduate student, then they don't have to do so. The water was soiled. I couldn't find an adviser willing to touch me. Without an adviser, I couldn't even register for research hours. Without research, you're gone a semester later. So much for academic freedom and viewpoint diversity, even in a philosophy department. I had no choice but to terminate with a five-year master's in philosophy. I was effectively forced out of the PhD program.

Seeing university operations at the highest levels and realizing what was at stake, I enrolled in another PhD program abroad. Meanwhile, I joined a campus ministry in order to reach out to professors, hoping to influence them. I directed the ministry to professors at Purdue while pursuing doctoral work once again. Simultaneously, I taught as an adjunct professor of philosophy and comparative religions at Indiana University. As a professor, even though I typically stacked the deck of course materials with textbooks that were unfavorable to my position, one semester brought a new challenge. I was charged with bias and creating a suicidal environment in the classroom. How so? We discussed this incident earlier.

Following these experiences as an undergrad, graduate student, and professor, I came to realize how hostile universities can be at all layers of strata if you don't believe the "right" doctrines or are unwilling to simply accept them without challenge. Higher education has become so thoroughly secularized that an alternate viewpoint is foreign, unwelcome, attacked, and often pushed out. There are numerous exceptions, but anyone who has gone the distance I have can, at least, relate. At the end of a long road, I arrived in Scotland to defend my PhD dissertation. As providence would have it, I was forced to defend it before someone who self-identified as the first transgender philosopher in the United Kingdom. Ultimately, I finished my PhD in philosophical theology from the University of Aberdeen in 2014. With some pride and trepidation, I pulled myself up to the highest peak only to see that the peak I had climbed to was blocking my view of numerous other peaks and valleys laid before me. A new horizon had dawned.

This chapter will be *an* education *about* education and modern universities. We are going to embark looking first at what makes the secular university secular. We will follow with an excursion through the history of the university and what went wrong. To grasp the gravity and grandiosity of an attempt at a solution for the problem requires us to seriously grapple with the scale and depth of the problem.

THE MIND OF THE SOUL AND THE MIND OF CULTURE

Charles Malik was the former president of the United Nations General Assembly, leading architect of the 1948 Universal Declaration of Human Rights, and author of *A Christian Critique of the University*. He understood the nature and value of ideas that are sufficiently powerful to shape the world. Malik studied philosophy under the famous German atheist Martin Heidegger before fleeing Germany when the Nazis took power. Consequently, Malik completed his PhD in philosophy in the US, under the process philosopher Alfred North Whitehead at Harvard. Later, he went on to teach at Harvard, Dartmouth, and Notre Dame. Notably, his acclaim has garnered him the reputation as the man who may hold the world record for the number of honorary doctorates (more than 50). During his lifetime, he learned a thing or two about the connection between ideas upstream and their real-life impact downstream. In a quotation often attributed to Malik and certainly consistent with his focus on the battlefield of ideas written about in his *A Christian Critique of the University*, we have this reflection: "You may win every battle, but if you lose the war of ideas, you will have lost the war. You may lose every battle, but if you win the war of ideas, you will have won the war." And he realized that the most prominent battle of ideas exists at the universities. Revolution is upon us. But it is fundamentally one whose source is explained in reference to the most influential institution in civilization—universities.

In 1980, Malik joined Billy Graham and many others to dedicate the Billy Graham Center at Wheaton College. Malik lectured on what he called the "Two Tasks": that of saving the soul and saving the mind. He said, "The problem is not only to win souls but to save minds. If you win the whole world and lose the mind of the world, you will soon discover you have not won the world. Indeed, it may turn out that you have actually lost the world."[1]

He continued,

> All the preaching in the world, and all the loving care of even the best parents between whom there are no problems whatever, will amount to little, if not to nothing, so long as what the children are exposed to day in and day out for fifteen to twenty years in the school and university virtually cancels out, morally and spiritually, what they hear and see and learn at home and in the church. Therefore, the problem of the school and university is the most critical problem afflicting Western Civilization.[2]

One may wonder whether people who become "saved" or "redeemed" can do so without also redeeming the mind. That answer is yes. In 1 Corinthians 3:1-3,

Paul addressed true believers who remained infants drinking milk rather than eating meat for far too long. There are plenty of examples both in Scripture and culture where we see the menace of mindless Christianity, which is defenseless against false philosophies and false teachers. Genuine believers can be fooled by worldly philosophies, which is why the apostle Paul admonished us to beware of false philosophy (see 1 Corinthians 3:19; Colossians 2:8).

Concurring with the sentiments of Charles Malik, my friend and fellow philosopher Paul Gould observes, "The university in general and professors in particular are the gatekeepers of ideas, influencing directly or indirectly all aspects of thought and life in our world."[3] According to the National Center for Education Statistics, in 2020, there were approximately 1.5 million faculty teaching at nearly 4,000 degree-granting institutions (55 percent full time, 45 percent part time), out of which 25 percent were tenure track.[4] These influencers are changing the world through the institution that possesses the most leverage over ideas that shape culture. That the university and professors have a powerful influence on the world is not a radically new idea; what is new is that we have radically different professors. Professors used to be scholars, researchers, and intellectuals. Today, many of them are first and foremost activists. They don't necessarily want Christians to teach. They want to change the world, all the while influencing students (in part, Christian students) to do it. The implications of this are so vast that it is necessary to not only have a robust presence in these institutions but also discover the most prominent thought currents flowing out of them into culture. There are three major ideologies subversive to Christian faith in the universities. They are scientism, cultural Marxism, and postmodernism. All sprang from the root of naturalism but are not necessarily tied to it in practice. The former dominated the last century and privileges the natural sciences. The latter two are significantly intermixed and both emerge from the social sciences and humanities. We'll look at these in turn beginning with scientism.

TRANSFORMING CULTURE BY EMBRACING SCIENCE AND COUNTERING SCIENTISM

Today, Christian faith is often viewed as countercultural to the university, specifically by running counter to science. But is Christianity countercultural to science or to a certain naturalistic philosophy of science? Our culture underestimates the role of faith and overestimates the role of science. People who lived during the mid-nineteenth century seem to have had more in common with Moses or Abraham than with us. This can largely be attributed to the explosion of information and technology produced through science. To be sure, science is a very good means of acquiring knowledge about the physical world. Flowing from the university, however, contemporary culture often treats faith in a pejorative sense as if juxtaposed to science.

The common viewpoint in the university is articulated by Steven Weinberg, a Nobel Prize winner in physics, who said, "The World needs to wake up from the long nightmare of religion. Anything we scientists can do to weaken the hold of religion should be done and may in fact be our greatest contribution to civilization."[5]

Opposite to this thinking, in 2013, Weinberg declined to participate in a debate I moderated at Purdue University, out of which came my book *Is Faith in God Reasonable? Debates in Philosophy, Science, and Rhetoric*. But another atheist, a philosopher of science, did participate. In his book *The Atheist's Guide to Reality*, Alex Rosenberg sings a similar note, asking a plethora of questions:

Is there a God?

No.

What is the nature of reality?

What physics says it is.[6]

He informs us that the best reason to embrace atheism is that science adopted "scientism," the conviction that the methods of science are the only reliable ways to secure knowledge of anything. After the scientific revolution, departments of academic disciplines began changing their names, ostensibly showing the new philosophical assumptions within the disciplines. For example, politics became political science. Psychology became psychological sciences. Scientism has come to dominate the intellectual landscape of academia for more than a century with a remarkable impact on culture. However, is science really the be-all and end-all of knowledge?

Certainly, Jesus thought that the concept of knowledge was broader than science. Indeed, in John's Gospel, Jesus is called the *logos,* from which we derive the English word *logic*. Logic is a precondition to science. The laws of logic are invisible (perhaps abstract) entities that are true for all people of all time and in all places. They are known with certainty and yet elude sense perception. Jesus viewed the central purpose of human life to consist in the knowledge of God. Knowing God isn't something we gain by taste, touch, smell, and the like, yet it is nonetheless knowledge. Psalm 34:8 says, "Taste and see that the Lord is good." But that is simply metaphorical. Christianity is a knowledge tradition, not a mere faith tradition. What we have is knowledge. The major concern of philosophers and theologians during the Middle Ages was largely a project expressed in Latin, *fides quaerens intellectum,* which means "faith seeking understanding."

The great halls of reason, the modern universities, were for centuries largely established in the context of and motivated by the Christian faith. Most of the founders of the subdisciplines of science were Christians. Faith informed and inspired their scientific efforts and reflections. Consider Mendel in genetics, Pasteur in bacteriology, Kepler in astronomy, Linnaeus in taxonomy, Newton in physics, Boyle in chemistry, and Maxwell in electrodynamics. The list goes on and on. These were innovators who saw themselves as reading the two books of God, God's world and God's Word, nature and Scripture, as said by the father of modern science, Francis Bacon. Ironically, Weinberg is found to be in the minority. From 1901–2000, more than 65 percent of Nobel laureates were Christians.[7] Not only is faith shown to be compatible with science, but it motivated its emergence and flourishing.

Worldview and the Limits of Science

The practice of science is done within the context of a worldview. Many assume when a scientist puts on a white lab coat and pulls measurements, they merely gather evidence, faithfully delivering facts, things they've proven to be true. But this is an oversimplification.

Science does not prove things to be true. Science cannot prove things to be true. Why? Because science relies on inductive reasoning. Inductive reasoning in science commonly works by examining repeated instances of an event, and then drawing a conclusion about what must be true for that event to happen again. This is a method of inference. While this form of reasoning is powerful to science, it is also a limitation. It forces us to be content with probabilistic conclusions—not proof or absolute certainty—concepts related more to the fields of mathematics and logic.

This reveals something very significant. Not only can science never attain certainty, but there are certain things science can never know. For example, first-person knowledge. No matter how much neurologists learn about my brain, they can never know, for instance, what it's like to be me—not even in principle. There are numerous beliefs for which science cannot account for, good as it is. Some examples suffice: (1) logical and mathematical truths (like the law of noncontradiction), (2) metaphysical truths (e.g., beliefs about such things like other minds, the external world beyond my mind, and the past), (3) ethical/value beliefs, and (4) aesthetic beliefs. Even broader, science itself cannot be accounted for by the scientific method.[8]

Worldview and the Philosophical Assumptions of Science

In addition to internal limitations intrinsic to science, science is also limited by several external underlying philosophical presuppositions, which cannot be settled or justified by science.

First, the scientific enterprise assumes that nature exists independent of our minds. While this may seem like common sense, it is taken for granted. How do you know that you're not being deceived by an evil demon or in a dream state thinking that what you are seeing is reality? Or perhaps your brain is in a vat being controlled by a superscientist who is plugging you full of electrodes to provide you with virtual images. What is to say that's not reality? Throughout history, many do not and have not believed in the full reality of the external world. This is typical for Eastern thinkers. It cannot simply be assumed. But it makes sense within a Christian worldview.

Second, science assumes that nature has an intelligible order that can be known. But appearances and reality are not necessarily the same. Again, this seems to be plain common sense, but it too is embedded in a philosophical framework. The physical structure of the world is describable using the language of mathematics. We learned from Einstein that underlying matter is energy, and since then, we've learned that underlying energy is information.[9] This all points to a world that is, at bottom, fundamentally mind, not matter, which resonates within a Christian worldview that began with a divine Mind who created matter.

Third, science assumes the existence and applicability of the laws of logic, which are central to rational thought. But note that this is a category of philosophy, not of science. Scientists borrow from philosophy and use the laws of logic, such as the law of noncontradiction, the law of identity, and the law of excluded middle. They use these in discussing their experimental observations, inferences, and conclusions. Because knowledge of the world itself is something requiring argument, then the status of scientific statements about the world also requires such. These laws are the preconditions of thought, including scientific thought. They are inescapable truths known with certainty, unlike in matters of science, and are not even known by science but instead rationally discerned. But this assumption makes best sense given a certain worldview.

Fourth, science typically assumes the reliability of our senses such as taste, touch, sight, hearing, and smell. They generally assume that our senses accurately deliver bits of truth to us about the world. But how do we know that our faculties provide accurate information about the external world? And even if they do, how do we know whether they are truth conducive, which is to say, whether they are designed at giving us true beliefs? This is not unimportant. If scientific naturalism is true, then perhaps they are aimed at survival instead; in which case, is it possible that giving false perceptions of the world could provide a survival advantage? Having a false sense of depth perception where you think a predator is much closer than it really is serves as an example that would send you into flight for survival. This might seem to undermine our confidence in sense-perceptual beliefs being aimed at truth rather than merely survival.

But it is worse for naturalists who embrace evolution. As observed by atheist philosopher of science Alex Rosenberg, "Natural selection sometimes selects for false beliefs and sometimes even selects against the acquisition of true beliefs."[10] One implication of this is that the composed beliefs of naturalism plus evolution, or naturalistic evolution, seem to carry their own defeater.

If both naturalism and evolution are true, we cannot trust that our minds are delivering for us true beliefs about reality, including the beliefs about naturalism and about evolution.[11]

Unfortunately, our modern notion of science has largely come to mean whatever can be explained in terms of chemistry and physics. But science was not always this way and has taken a decidedly philosophical turn toward scientific naturalism. The term *science* comes from its Latin origin, *scientia*, which denotes all fields of knowledge—not just the hard sciences or those who want to be so associated. The Greek equivalent of *scientia* is *episteme*, or epistemology, the second major branch of philosophy pertaining to theories of knowledge.

The medieval thinkers who founded the modern universities used to say that "theology is the queen of the *scientia* and philosophy is its hand maiden." Imagine the hub of a wheel representing theology and the spokes representing the diversity of academic disciplines like economics, psychology, language, and mathematics. Philosophy is the glue that anchors the diversity of disciplines into the unity of knowledge that constitutes the university. This explains why everyone who possesses a PhD, whether formally trained in philosophy or not, possesses a doctor of philosophy in their respective field. Unity in diversity forms the university, the modern university being largely a product of faith seeking understanding.

Some of what counts as science today is not really science but philosophy hidden in scientific clothing. Our culture has confused science with "scientism," the view that the only things that can be known to be true are those which can be tested by science. But that statement itself can't be tested by science. It is self-defeating. It is a philosophical statement about science and not a scientific one. No amount of discovery will ever make it true. Considering intrinsic limitations and external presuppositions of science, science requires certain philosophical foundations. These foundations are best provided by the Christian worldview, which is why science emerged from within that worldview. We can disabuse ourselves, then, of the false philosophy that is scientism and rejoice in the good that is science. The Christian faith is countercultural not to science but to scientism. People must be educated on this point because the myth exists that science and the Christian faith are incompatible.[12]

As the former atheist scholar who became Christian C.S. Lewis reminds us, "Men became scientific because they expected Law in Nature, and they expected Law in Nature because they believed in a Legislator."[13] Our culture became scientific because of the knowledge of God.

Having worked for years with faculty in ministry, I've seen not just this scientism at work among atheists like Alex Rosenberg above but a sort of soft scientism at work among even evangelical scholars. A personal friend of mine, and mentor in many respects, was the late Paul Simms. He was a professor of physics for many years at Purdue University. I once introduced him to literature on intelligent design. For a long time, he rejected it. I finally asked him to explain this. He said that it isn't science, otherwise it would be in the best journals like *Nature*. I replied by pointing out that journals such as *Nature* have gatekeepers, and unless you embrace their same thought, it makes it difficult to get papers published however stellar the quality may be. Doubling down, he stubbornly asserted that intelligent design just wasn't science. So I asked him to define science. He said, among other things, that it was a practice that sought to explain phenomena by invoking all, and only, natural laws. I quickly helped him see that isn't science per se but scientism. I could repeat this sort of story a dozen times over. My experience is that far too many evangelical Christians, not just atheists, are guilty of embracing scientism rather than simply science.

In one respect, it is no surprise because the *Ph* behind the *D* in PhD stands for *philosophy*, and unless trained in philosophy, many of our best and brightest hold a disintegrated rather than integrated view of the world and don't even realize it. They're enveloped by non-Christian (and in this case, nonscience) philosophical assumptions. You might say they are metaphysical theists on Sunday, but Monday through Friday, they are methodological naturalists (methods that are more closely related to atheism than to theism). They may or may not take Saturdays off. Christians need to beware of false philosophy infiltrating their own worldviews and counter it with truth.

But scientism and its kin, like methodological naturalism, aren't the only major ideas or thought currents running antithetical to Christian thought in the universities. Making its ascent known is an iteration of Marxist thought.

TRANSFORMING CULTURE BY EMBRACING JESUS AND COUNTERING CULTURAL MARXISM

As we previously observed, Marxism didn't die when the Berlin Wall fell or when the Tiananmen Square incident gave Marxism a public relations black eye. It was operating in our universities a bit more clandestinely and has now launched into our culture and even our churches. Christians are called to always begin our discernment through the lens of Scripture and theology, not through culture and sociology. Our primary lens is a Christocentric lens. Tragically, many within Christianity are doing the opposite. Christianity is under assault in our culture by yet another insidious ideology, further corrupting our universities from their original goal—the pursuit of truth—opting instead for the pursuit of social justice. But as we've seen, it has quickly moved downstream to our culture, including Christian subculture via campus ministries, seminaries, churches, and Christian academic societies.

Christianity has long been considered a tour de force that positively shapes Western civilization. But in recent times, it has been challenged for being a negative force denoted for its hegemonic power of colonialist oppression throughout the world and undermining the perception that Christianity's contribution has been ultimately good. Where does this come from? Popular terms swirl around us in culture like *social justice, critical theory, cultural Marxism*, or *identity politics*. Next to one another, you can see the common ideology even without a full comprehension of the terms.

Sometimes, when people say "social justice," they are referring to activities like helping the poor, oppressed, and downtrodden or fighting sex trafficking—all good things. But when other people, perhaps the majority within the culture, use the term, they are referring to topics like reproductive justice (abortion), economic justice (socialism), environmental justice (climate change laws), sexuality and gender justice (homosexuality, transgender, polyamory, etc.), racial justice (equity, reparations, payback, etc.), and even research justice (not using majoritarian or dominant group texts). Much of this is, in fact, injustice.

Most universities are no longer interested in viewpoint diversity. Rather, they are interested in a diversity of skin color, body parts, and group identities.

Indeed, cancel culture itself is rooted in this insidious philosophy. We used to agree with a statement commonly attributed to Voltaire: "I may disagree with what you say, but will defend to the death your right to say it." No longer. Now, culture seems to operate based on a statement that Joseph Stalin allegedly said: "Ideas are more powerful than guns, we don't let our enemies have guns, so why let them have ideas?" That which once had Marxist and atheist roots has somehow infiltrated not just educational institutions but even religion, including Christianity. Of course, the goal of cultural Marxism all along, we were told, entails "the long march through the institutions."[14] That is well under way.

This ideology looks at human relations from the standpoint of social binaries: haves and have-nots, bourgeoisie and proletariat, oppressors and oppressed, victimizers and victims. Society is separated into dominant oppressor groups and subordinate oppressed groups along the axes of race, class, sex, gender, ability, age, nationality, and even religion. Your primary identity is a group identity, either as an oppressor or the oppressed. In identity politics, life is about privilege and power dynamics. A white male is an oppressor to a black male simply due to their respective skin color.

A few years ago, I was invited to speak at a university on the topic of race and critical theory. I was the odd person out on the speaker panel. I am white. I am male. I began my talk like one might begin in a common meeting of Alcoholics Anonymous: "Hi, my name is Corey. I'm white." The expected response, "Hi Corey!" never came. I was using that moment to point out the obvious—namely, I was the odd white man invited on a stage with black guest panelists. My intent was to address the proverbial elephant in the room and get to the business of why it might be assumed without argument that I might have nothing to contribute to the conversation other than confession and admission of guilt. But I quickly discovered that there was yet another layer to this. The speaker after me was a black man who was subsequently subverted in his oppressor level or layer by the speaker following him, who was not only black but a black female. He now may as well have made a similar confession.

According to the concept of intersectionality, each person exists at the intersection of multiple group identities, like being a black male juxtaposed to a black female, having oppressor status as male but oppressed status as black.

The more you share identification within oppressed groups, the more enlightened to the problem you allegedly become, and you carry authoritative knowledge relative to that group oppression. That is, you become "woke." This is because knowledge is socially constructed based on your social location. If you can't see the problem, then intersectionality says it is because you're blinded by your privileged standpoint (i.e., you suffer from internalized oppression or lack liberational consciousness). It's all about power and privilege.

As we discussed earlier, one cannot simply view issues of race, class, sex, and gender in isolation because they are interlocking systems of oppression. It's all intersected. In sum, if the problem in society is oppression, then the goal is liberation. According to the theory, any group inequality entails group injustice. Hence, the goal is social justice.

Notice nothing is said here about true justice, getting what you deserve. Nothing about forgiveness. Nothing about other virtues. While Christianity concurs that oppression is bad, the biggest conflict between Christianity and critical theory is that both function as a metanarrative framing all of reality. "Coexist," says the bumper sticker. But that doesn't work. Secular social justice advocates see the Bible as the ultimate hegemonic power metanarrative responsible for oppressions. Sadly, some Christians aid and abet that notion.

But instead, the Bible views man as made in God's image, worthy of dignity and respect, condemning real oppression on the grounds of the sacredness of all human lives. It sees the ultimate problem as human sin and its corresponding solution as salvation by faith alone through the work of Christ. Salvation is not accomplished through mankind's works of dismantling all inequalities as injustices and by moving ourselves from the slavery of oppression to the promised land of equity—a veritable utopia.

From a truly Christian point of view, the one who fails to see this is either blinded by sin or else, if seeking to baptize social justice, is looking at life primarily through the lens of culture and sociology rather than through the lens of Scripture and theology, creating inadvertent mission drift. In the gospel, there is forgiveness available to everyone in all social locations. We don't need the tools of critical theory to know the good for society. Scripture gives us an objective standard of right and wrong, all that we need for godliness, with goodness grounded in God.

This is not a mere theoretical or philosophical issue. Marxism has real-life consequences. People have died by the tens of millions and much of the world has been wrecked by it. It must be countered. It is not alone, however, as there is yet another major thought current running counter to Christian thought in the universities.

TRANSFORMING CULTURE BY EMBRACING TRUTH AND COUNTERING POSTMODERNISM

A third dominant current of thought running through the universities that is hostile to Christianity and Western civilization is postmodernism. It is the dominant perspective in the humanities and social sciences and has wreaked havoc on the culture at large. In one respect, postmodernism is derived from Marxism, which was a spinoff of naturalism. The apostle Paul says to beware of false philosophy, but one can't beware unless one is first aware, right? So what is postmodernism, and how did we get here?

It's notoriously difficult to define. But some have tried. The *Encyclopedia Britannica* defines postmodernism as "a late 20th-century movement characterized by broad skepticism, subjectivism, or relativism; a general suspicion of reason; and an acute sensitivity to the role of ideology in asserting and maintaining political and economic power."[15]

Perhaps we can best understand it if we think of it in relationship to its historical predecessors. Postmodernism is a reaction to modernism, or as some have suggested, it is hypermodernism, or modernism on steroids. Modernism was the intellectual movement characteristic of the Enlightenment.

Prior to AD 1650 is considered the premodern era. In this era, the dominant focus was on reality as was shared by the major Greek thinkers and Christian, Muslim, and Jewish thinkers. The sorts of questions philosophers asked about reality, or metaphysics, were, What is real? Does God exist? Are souls real? Do humans have free will? The modern era, or modernism, began in 1650 with Rene Descartes, who professed belief in God and was the father of modern geometry. Intellectual thought changed the focus from reality to epistemology—how we know what we know about reality. One might say that Descartes got "de-cart before de-horse." Premodernists were concerned with knowledge too. As we covered, the medieval motto was "faith seeking understanding," and the sixteenth-century cry of Martin Luther during the Protestant Reformation was "Unless I am convinced by the testimony of the Scriptures and by clear reason."[16] But for premodernists, it wasn't by mere human reason alone. Knowledge certainly included divine reason via revelation.

In modernism, instead of authority or revelation, the focus going forward was on human reason alone, and the project was the pursuit of certainty—geometric certainty to be sure, often called "Cartesian certainty" in the spirit of Descartes. Descartes famously began with skepticism in method to ferret out what we can know with certainty, like geometric proofs. He even put his own existence on the chopping block as a question to doubt. He placed himself in a Dutch oven and queried about what things he knows or can know that are foundational to knowledge, not derived, and that cannot be doubted. He inferred that doubting is a form of thinking and only thinkers think. He concluded, "I think, therefore I am." He at least knew that he was real. He was a rationalist.

Over time, others like John Locke who were empiricists (as opposed to rationalists) likewise focused on knowledge but began with the sciences. Great gains were made in developing scientific methods, liberal democracies, capitalism, and so forth. There was optimism and progress in this age of reason and humanism. Yet the cracks and the fissures in the foundation of mere human reason were present, and it was just a matter of time. Divine reason was supplanted by human reason and the focus on reality supplanted by the focus on knowledge. Whereas modern philosophy began with Descartes and a method of skepticism where we start with doubt, the truth is that it ended with Immanuel Kant by whose philosophy it is remembered, "I *Kant* know ultimate reality." Agnosticism. Modern philosophy began with a bang in the quest for certainty grounded in the (over)confidence of human reason in the Enlightenment, but it ended with a whimper in agnosticism, setting the stage for postmodernism. The Enlightenment project was, in one sense, a failure. Following in the wake of Kant, religious belief was coined "leap of faith," or blind faith by Soren Kierkegaard, and in the other direction was coined "God is dead" by Friedrich Nietzsche. The options seemed to be to either believe blindly or disbelieve. With the death of God, there was no absolute Mind that underwrote absolute truth and meaning.

The Death of God and the Death of Man

Today, we live in a world where transcendent meaning and purpose are elusive at best. When reflected upon and realized that this is the state of the universe, many in fact do move toward suicide or even homicide. If there is no truth, then we've lost the anchor to any notion of the good or the beautiful in life. Indeed, respect for life itself is called into question. We see this in the rise of secularism correlating with several examples. Consider the rise in the number of school shootings pervading America since Columbine High School in 1999. Or consider the broadening of abortion stances from "safe and rare" in the 1990s to abortion on demand and even the consideration of infanticide in cases of botched abortions in the 2020s. If there is no sanctifier, there is no sanctity of life. We're reminded of the statement "If God is dead, then everything is permissible."[17] This is an outcome of postmodern thinking to take seriously.

While there is disagreement over the precise time, the formal postmodern era didn't really take shape until around 1950. But its roots go to a time much earlier, tied with Nietzsche and Kant. A primary concern in postmodernism is deconstructionism, tied both to truth itself but also to hermeneutics—the method of interpretation, which in this case was a hermeneutic of suspicion. This deep suspicion was about grand metanarratives, truth, and knowledge—including the biblical text. It was all to face the hatchet of deconstruction (or destruction).

To help illustrate these three positions of premodern, modern, and postmodern, consider an umpire calling the pitches in a baseball game.

The premodern referee says, "I call them like they are." Truth is that which corresponds to reality. Aristotle held to this and Jesus held to this, as did virtually everyone in the premodern era. This view was predominant for 2,500 years.

The modernist says, "I call them like I see them." First, you must see it to believe it. But then notice the switch from "truth corresponds to what is real" to "truth is now somehow mediated by sense datum." Our understanding of truth is one step removed from reality.

The postmodernist declares, "They are nothing until I call them." Truth isn't found or discovered "out there"; it is made within but created by social construction through language.

Postmodernism took the baton from modernism in its skepticism of religion but ended with skepticism also of science. More than this, it ended with radical skepticism and even cynicism. There was no truth, no religious truth, no scientific truth, no moral truth. Truth and knowledge related to power and language as social constructions of reality. Even the individual is a social construction. One's gender is a social construction. All knowledge is a social construction in accordance only with the language games of our communities.

Modern times in Western culture were characterized by metanarratives promising progress through human reason and science. But faith in these metanarratives was dashed by revolution, like the French Revolution in the age of reason. Revolution gave us the guillotine, bloody wars, totalitarianism (from fascism to the Marxism of the twentieth century), and genocide, along with many intellectual dead ends by mere human reason. Indeed, we saw the first atheistic state religion, called "the cult of reason," in France. With the crumbling of an Enlightenment man of humanism, a man of mere reason, a man of progress, all would come crashing down on humanism, ending instead with nihilism: no meaning, no truth, no knowledge. There was only power. In fact, truth was linked to systems of power. There is truth and then there is political truth. But clearly, they are not the same. That is, unless you adopt postmodernism.

When Skepticism Becomes Cynicism

Postmodernism was so radically skeptical that it became cynical. It posited not only a lack of knowledge but a distrust in knowledge claims whatsoever. This is why some say that it isn't simply a reaction to modernity but rather takes modernity one step further down the rabbit hole of skepticism. It now looks with suspicion on many of the great developments within modernism, including the rise of representative democracy, individual liberty, capitalism, and the age of science. It radically rejects the foundations upon which today's advanced civilizations are built and seeks to undermine and subvert them.

While it includes skepticism about objective reality, it claims that all knowledge is a social construction of reality, where *knowledge*, so to speak, is always tied to power. Language is the tool with which to communicate or construct the so-called reality. Postmodernism is particularly skeptical of science, revelation, or any other culturally dominant way of legitimizing claims as truths and of the grand, sweeping explanations or metanarratives that support them.

What we're left with is that everything exists in a subjective, situational perspective. We're left with only a social power struggle to have one's own subjective value system prevail. Jean-François Lyotard, who coined the term *postmodernism*, summarized in 1979 what he called "the postmodern condition," characterized as a profound skepticism and the move away from the metanarrative toward local narratives and lived experiences.

In postmodern theory, truth and knowledge are believed to have been constructed by the dominant discourses and language games within a society, and because we cannot step outside our society, no one set of cultural norms can be said to be better than any other. The postmodern belief that individuals are vehicles of discourses of power, dependent somewhat on where they stand in relation to power, makes cultural critique hopeless except at the hands of those said to be marginalized or oppressed. Consequently, according to postmodernists, the notion of the autonomous individual is largely a myth. The individual too is a social construction, as is the universal—whether a biological or theological universal about human nature or an ethical universal like equal rights and freedoms, regardless of race, class, gender, and so on.

The four dominant figureheads of postmodernism are Michel Foucault (1926–1984), Jacques Derrida (1930–2004), Jean-François Lyotard (1924–1998), and Richard Rorty (1931–2007). In the words of Richard Rorty, truth is "what our peers will, *ceteris paribus*, let us get away with saying."[18] Truth is relative. Even that "truth"? Yes.

FAITHFUL STEWARDSHIP OVER THE SOUL

Clearly, one cannot beware of false philosophies unless we are aware that they exist. As Christians, we must be able to understand them to effectively communicate the truth of the gospel. Most of the major ideas that are present in culture now seem to come from the university. We have two ears and one mouth for a reason. We need to listen more. We need to know and understand to properly diagnose the acuteness and source of the problems before advancing a prescription or solution. Hence, later, we'll trace the history and ideological revolutions as they occurred, bringing greater depth and insight into the nature of what we're up against. Then we'll move to a plan of action. Suffice it to say that Scripture does not merely speak against Christians living in perpetual intellectual infancy (1 Corinthians 3:1). Paul commands the immature believers in Corinth, "Do not be children in your thinking" (1 Corinthians 14:20 ESV). Stop it. Be adults. Move beyond baby's milk to eating meat. It's a choice to love God with our minds. This means that it is possible for true believers to have slack minds. This is neither helpful, nor is it a badge of honor. It's troublesome for the soul and has societal impact, stretching from families to communities to civilization. We honor God and can best represent Christ when we love God not with only our hands and hearts but with our heads. May we be faithful stewards.

7

A BRIEF HISTORY OF THE UNIVERSITY AND EXTREME MISSION DRIFT

have visited all 50 states, spoken at numerous universities, and canvassed all the earliest colonial colleges in America, most of which are now Ivy League. Despite their best efforts, these universities all continue to reveal the genesis of the institution and its purpose. Most people are scarcely aware of the history of universities and thus have no vision for the future. Universities are not what they once were. Christians largely started the universities. But at great cost, we later lost them. Now, we must look on and lament that our children are swallowed up by the very institutions we founded and, later, forfeited.

Losing the American universities to post-Christian secularism is one of the greatest debacles and tragedies of world history. Why does it matter? It matters because the university is the most influential institution of Western civilization, having become the gatekeeper of thought for culture and civilization. From the universities come our journalists, artists, doctors, lawyers, businessmen, political leaders, K–12 educators, and future professors. As goes the university, so goes the culture. Indeed, as goes the university in the US, so goes the world. Remember, ideas have consequences, and bad ones have real victims. Abraham Lincoln is alleged to have said, "The philosophy of the school room in one generation will be the philosophy of the government in the next." Whether he said this or not is irrelevant. There is profound truth in that statement. It is hard to underestimate the ubiquitous influence of the modern university. The university is one of the most important institutions in the world today because of its disproportionate opportunity to train the leaders of the world. One cannot truly understand an institution, however, without knowing something of its origins.

The Greeks and the Romans are foundational in the story of why the West became so prominent in its impact on the world. Plato's Academy (academia) and Aristotle's Lyceum were the first to consider the makings of such an academic institution. The Romans, with their Stoic philosophers, built on that of the Greeks and built a republic—consequently, the name of one of Plato's books. Acts 17 shows us when Paul, on Mars Hill, addressed both Stoic and Greek philosophers. But those early institutions, important as they were, are nothing like the modern university. It was not the Greeks or the Romans who invented universities. They established no scholarly communities and no permanent institutions.[1]

Universities emerged most prominently in Christian European areas, and their development was more than coincidental.

WHAT HATH JESUS TO DO WITH KNOWLEDGE?

Jesus said that our purpose in life is to know God (John 17:3), establishing that knowledge is central, not peripheral, to the Christian faith and experience. The New Testament's Gospel of John starts with the words "In the beginning," sounding exactly like Genesis 1:1, intentionally grabbing the Hebrew reader's attention. It continues, "Was the *Word*, and the *Word* was with God, and the *Word* was God...All things were made by him...And the *Word* was made flesh, and dwelt among us (and we beheld his glory, the glory as of the only begotten of the Father)" (John 1:1, 3, 14 KJV, emphasis added). The term *word*, repeated many times, was chosen by John to include Greeks to his audience. Other Greek terms could have been used, but John chose a special one: *logos*. Jesus is denoted in John 1 as the Word, or *logos*, from which we derive the English word *logic*. In Greek philosophy, the logos was impregnated with the reason or mind of the world. The Latin equivalent is *ratio*, from which we derive *reason* and *rationality*.

Knowledge being central to Christian experience and the logos being at the heart of existence itself seems to lend credibility to the idea that it was more than a mere coincidence that great universities emerged most prominently in the Christian world. One might argue that high-level education would be a predictable product of the worldview. Right as the imperial structures of the Roman Empire were in decline, Christians were in preparation mode, articulating a vision for education by the likes of Saint Augustine—not many years after three to four centuries of terrible Christian persecution.

Through the Dark Ages, there began to emerge a phenomenon spanning from the monasteries to the throne rooms of the Frankish King Charlemagne—one of the most remarkable educational reforms in the world that, as historians have noted, began in the eighth century. Educational and religious reforms went hand in hand in the Carolingian Renaissance. Just as the early Christians eventually popularized books (Bible means collection of books), with the codex supporting the connection of the pages over and against the standard scroll for purposes of missionary endeavor, so text production was ignited and revived. Historian Mark Graham notes that "we have seven times more surviving texts than the total number of texts that survive from all of human history up to the year 800. Every bishop was commanded to set up a local school for teaching these classic texts and Scripture."[2]

The lower-education programs upon which higher education would be built began with the trivium and quadrivium, terms first used in a Christian context. It was in these Carolingian cathedral schools that Western higher education as we understand it began. Philosophers as famous as Anselm would become masters in such schools. Even those who point to the golden years of Islamic education must recognize the influence of Arabic Christian authors such as the sixth-century theologian and literary scholar John Philoponus, whose works influenced Arabic philosophy and the textual translation movement. Eventually, we would see the rise of the likes of Peter Abelard and Thomas Aquinas. The latter wrote more than 100 books without the aid of the printing press, one work being 60 volumes long, *Summa Theologica*.

These men were associated with the earliest universities of Paris, Oxford, Cambridge, and Bologna, all of these of Christian origin.

Thoughts about God—that is, theology—became the central field of study, and as such, theology was sometimes thought of as "the queen of the *scientia*." *Scientia* denoted all disciplines of knowledge. Abelard coined the term *theology*. The medieval project was born and, as we covered earlier, was known as *fides quaerens intellectum* ("faith seeking understanding"). This thinking and practice would eventually spread to America and worldwide. Institutions were founded that were Christ centered and the first of their kind in places like India and South Korea as recently as 150 years ago. Vishal Mangalwadi, the Indian thinker and writer, reminds us that it is neither colonialism nor commerce that spread modern education around the world. Soldiers and merchants do not educate people. Education was a Christian missionary enterprise.[3]

The American model emerged from Europe's Christocentric universities. Most of the modern universities, in their origins over the centuries, were largely established in the context of and motivated by the Christian faith. The first college in America was established by the Puritans within a decade of their arrival, Harvard (1636). Chapel attendance and freshmen taking courses in Hebrew were mandatory. Harvard's original mission statement concerned knowing God in Christ. More than half of the graduates in the seventeenth century became clergy.[4]

As one noted historian of American universities writes, "Contemporary university culture is hollow at its core. Not only does it lack a spiritual center, but it is also without any real alternative."[5] The contemporary university has lost its heart, its soul. Disputation through the rigorous pursuit of truth as the *telos*, the purpose, of universities was a mainstay from its inception. One wonders how long the university can function apart from its historical and philosophical (and indeed, theological) roots? We have theory without theology, often under the guise of critical theory.

Mark Graham reflects, "In my field of history, and not too long ago, to not pursue research on race, class, and/or gender, would likewise consign one to a mop and broom closet of the hall of academia."[6] Today's indoctrination of critical theory is far removed from the educational element of critical thinking that was part and parcel of the telos of the medieval European and early

American universities. But this ideology is somewhat recent, all things considered, as we'll see later. The goal was to teach not what to think but how to think. Today's practice in universities seems far more economic—get answers to exams to get passing grades to get a degree as a means to get a job.

The sixteenth-century reformers of Europe quipped along with Martin Luther something like "Here I stand, I can do no other. Unless I am convinced by Scripture and by reason, I will not recant."[7] They stood for and revealed the value of the Bible and rational thought. They subsequently sought to create a Bible in every major language of the day so that the common man could read it. Over time, the Puritans emerged as dissenters from one movement—the Church of England—and traveled to the new land of America. As Missionary Protestantism spread out from Europe, it placed a high level on literacy so that people could read the Bible. The Bible directly inspired roughly 90 percent of the first 120 universities in America, beginning in the early seventeenth century. For brevity's sake, we will survey only a few of them that predate the United States' origins in 1776. These are colonial colleges of the early colonies, most of which went on later to become Ivy League universities.

Harvard University (1636)

The Puritans established one of the most compelling examples of the symbiosis between the Bible and education by establishing Harvard within the first decade of arriving in America, even before they set out to build any industry. It began as a ministers' training center. Their seal lasted until the late seventeenth century, when it was replaced by *Veritas Christo et Ecclesiae*, "Truth for Christ and Church." The two top books face up, the bottoms down, symbolizing the limits of reason and the necessity of God's revelation. In 1936, Harvard's 300-year anniversary, it dropped all reference to Christ, leaving only *veritas*. Although that history is hardly discoverable on its website, I've seen it with my own eyes, as it is etched on old buildings around campus. Harvard is now, in some respects, one of the most anti-Christian universities in America.

College of William and Mary (1693)

Originally for Anglicans or American Episcopalians, the institution was named after the two comonarchs, King William III and Queen Mary II, resulting from the Bloodless Revolution of 1688. It is another example of an elite American university launched in the name of Christ. It was founded to establish "a perpetual college of Divinity."[8] Today, important insight can be gained about how closely the mission has been preserved. By reading the school's website listings about the religious studies program, one is informed that it is housed in the oldest academic building in continuous use in the US. Among other items, it is noted that "through studying religions, we gain insight into important aspects of social life: gender and sexuality, race, power, art, literature, and media, to name a few."[9] An impression I am left with is that the components of the department that are related to a history of oppression and the subjects of critical theories are forefront for the school, rather than a focus on preserving its founding mission. At many schools, religious studies departments treat the Bible as a mere book of human origin, with inspiring parts, some resulting in good and some in bad.

Yale University (1701)

Yale's origins were Congregational. Remember, it has a slogan, "For God, for Country, and for Yale," etched in stone above a massive arched gate in one of the most visible locations on campus. Like Harvard, Yale began as a missionary-training seminary. It was founded because Harvard began to drift. Considering Harvard's drift, Yale's founders and some academics decided to up the ante when they coined their motto *lux et veritas*, "Light and Truth." This motto has significance grounded in Scripture, for the pursuit of the Hebrews was idealized and symbolized by light—"The LORD is my light and my salvation" (Psalm 27:1). Yale's most famous child prodigy, Jonathan Edwards, entered Yale in 1716 at age 13, and he graduated as valedictorian. He went on to become the president of Princeton Theological Seminary and one of America's most famous theologians. He penned the sermon "Sinners in the Hands of an Angry God." But now, Yale is a secular bastion featuring an event they call Sex Week that has been taking place for more than a decade. Events like it have now spread to other universities where certain feminist professors or lecturers have been reported to speak while nude.[10] And recall, one lesbian professor at Yale has a book titled *Queer Theology* that is about "queering God."[11]

Princeton University (1746)

Princeton also was created to train ministers. Its motto is *Dei sub numine viget*, "Under God's power she flourishes." The open book on the shield says *Vet nov testamentum*, "Old New Testaments." Professor Peter Singer, now perhaps the most (in)famous living moral philosopher, teaches there and contemplates the merits of both bestiality and infanticide.[12]

Columbia University (1774)

The school's motto is *In lumine tuo videbimus lumen*, meaning "In your light we see the light," citing Psalm 36:9. Today, Columbia has professors like Joseph Massad who say they were "invigorated" by the October 7, 2023, slaughter of Jewish women and children and called the attack by Hamas "awesome."[13]

At their outset, the colonial-aged colleges all mainly trained ministers and served their respective sectarian religious interests. Other universities include the University of Pennsylvania (Anglican, 1740), Rutgers (Dutch Reformed, 1766), Dartmouth (Congregationalist, 1769), and Brown (Baptist, 1774). There were many others, like the University of Delaware (Presbyterian, 1743), but these schools aren't considered colonial colleges because their official charters came in the years that followed 1776. The same religious origins are true of most of the early colleges and universities. But over time, serving the broader public and succumbing to subversive philosophies took precedence.

This is all very foreign to most people. Many believe that the universities must have been founded by secularists because religion is only about faith and not about reason. According to a recent survey by *The Harvard Crimson*, the single largest religious group of the class of 2019 is atheist/agnostic.[14] Erstwhile Harvard alumnus Bill Gates dubs *Enlightenment Now*, by Harvard professor Steven Pinker, his "new favorite book of all time."[15] Pinker, like a great number of his colleagues, is a self-proclaimed Jewish atheist and liberal. From top to bottom, Harvard isn't what it once was. Pinker points out that in 1990, 42 percent of all faculty in the country were far left or liberal, 40 percent moderate, and 18 percent conservative, for a liberal-to-conservative ratio of 2.3 to 1.[16] Today, for those ages 65 and older and preparing for retirement, it is 12:1; and for younger scholars, ages 40 and under, it is 23:1.[17] In religion departments, it is a whopping 70:1![18]

Michael Bloomberg, billionaire and former Democratic mayor of New York City, gave the three-hundred-sixty-third commencement address at Harvard. He said that Harvard, like other Ivy Leagues, is a "good school but not a great school." Why? Because it is not ideologically diverse. He goes on:

> Today, on many college campuses, it is liberals trying to repress conservative ideas, even as conservative faculty members are at risk of becoming an endangered species. And perhaps nowhere is that more true than here in the Ivy League. In the 2012 presidential race, according to Federal Election Commission data, 96 percent of all campaign contributions from Ivy League faculty and employees went to Barack Obama. Ninety-six percent. There was more disagreement among the old Soviet Politburo than there is among Ivy League donors…When 96 percent of Ivy League donors prefer one candidate to another, you have to wonder whether students are being exposed to the diversity of views that a great university should offer. Diversity of gender, ethnicity, and orientation is important. But a university cannot be great if its faculty is politically homogen[e]ous.[19]

IMPLICATIONS FROM EXTREME BIAS IN EDUCATION

Today, there is an extreme bias against hiring evangelical Christians in academics. African American sociology professor George Yancey admitted that it is easier being a black than an evangelical Christian in academics. In his seminal work on hiring-preference biases among faculty, he shows that when faculty are given 27 different group identities ranging from Democrat, NRA member, atheist, Mormon, Catholic, divorced, homosexual, communist, hunter, Republican, and others, the identity that would provide the best chance of getting hired is Democrat. The least likely to be hired would be in the category of Fundamentalist Christian, beating out Evangelical for the final spot.[20] It seems like there is an all-out assault on the Christian faith where the major battlefield is the universities. Some professors have been very explicit in targeting faith. Peter Boghossian remarks, "Employing universities in the struggle against faith is a cornerstone in the larger strategy to combat faith, promote reason and rationality, and create skeptics."[21]

The implications of this are staggering. Put 100 professors in a room and there might be only four conservatives. And the number may drop by one for the poor chap who raised his head above the foxhole and let his position be known. That leaves three scared and hiding. Many who hold to the truth are scared to speak out, and it's to the point that they may even passively work in the advancement of cancel culture. "Punch right and coddle left" seems to be the national motto. Many nonleftist groups self-censor or partake in cancel culture themselves to secure their own positions.[22] The universities are a monolithic echo chamber, whose ideological monopoly is anything but diverse. It creates a very unhealthy situation, and coupled with pressure created by blasphemy laws for those who violate political truth, is it any wonder huge percentages of Christian students lose their faith upon entering the secular baptismal font known as the university? This has a leavening effect on the culture after they graduate. It creates a situation where Christian parents and grandparents are literally paying for the apostasy of their own children.

The story of what went wrong is complex but not mysterious. It wasn't simply Darwin, Marx, Freud, and Nietzsche, although their ideas were present. In the famous paraphrase of D.L. Moody, "Don't polish the brass on a sinking ship."[23] In other words, the Titanic is going down. Forget everything else, and just save the souls. During the great revivals of the past, the focus was mostly on saving the soul, getting as many people to heaven as possible. In some corners of cultural Christianity, where Christian anti-intellectualism was setting in, Christians abdicated their roles and responsibilities in high culture. They didn't have a robust vision for the future or for discipling the mind. This didn't help students on university campuses. And as for the professors, the old guard graduated or was gradually forced out as the new guard that possessed a new ideology ascended to the top ranks of the top universities. The result was that we lost our universities and, with them, many of our children and grandchildren for generations.

Detached from their foundations, universities have undergone two ideological revolutions: (1) modernity's scientific naturalism and (2) a blood-curdling stew of postmodern cultural Marxism.

THE FIRST REVOLUTION: SCIENTIFIC NATURALISM

From philosophical ideas to secular methods and practical needs, the masses of conservative Protestant leaders in education diminished and were replaced by those who were more liberal, or even secular, and the result was universities eventually succumbed to the spirit of the European Enlightenment and modernism. First becoming liberal Protestants, they undermined the core teachings of the Bible, promoting only its moral and social fruit. Liberal Protestants liked the Bible's morality but not its historicity. Eventually, liberal Protestants evolved into the secular humanists of today, many of whom control state-funded education, having dismissed the Bible's authority altogether, including its morality.

In the mid-eighteenth century, Protestant colleges that served the public good moved from a denominational or sectarian focus, like Presbyterian or Baptist, to a pluralistic one—albeit Protestant pluralism (along with some deism). Academic freedom was celebrated for the competition of ideas in pursuing truth as the telos—the end goal—of the university. Historian George Marsden observes, however, that even a century later (1840), "four-fifths of the college presidents of denominationally related colleges were clergymen, as were two-thirds of state college presidents. Students typically learned 'evidence[s] of Christianity' or 'natural theology.'"[24] Because belief in God was essential to establishing a moral order, apologetics concerns were closely related to courses in moral philosophy. Such a course was taught by the university president, and students took it during their senior year. Every president was also a member of the clergy. Nonsectarian moral philosophy was now the capstone of the program. Most of the university builders were active Protestants, and even in the 1890s, almost all state universities continued to hold mandatory chapel and required church attendance.

In the early nineteenth century, denominational offshoots of the colleges, such as seminaries and divinity schools, emerged to perform distinctly ecclesiastical functions. While most new colleges were still church related, each moved to serve the public beyond its own sect. Theology was becoming professionalized in the seminaries, and the colleges could focus on other things, including morality. No matter the sect, each had to deal with the same American market with ever-changing demographics as the nation grew. Theological distinctions limited a college's constituency, becoming a liability. Hence, colleges emphasized socially unifying aspects of Christianity, especially morality rather than theology.

Several emerging commitments precipitated cataclysmic changes in the university that would take place over 50 years. These commitments cast the die for the direction in which the university was set adrift. First, with respect to religion, the defining feature of the university was no longer training clergy. The majority of students were preparing for other professions. Ministerial education shifted to sectarian divinity schools placed in locations no longer central to the campus.

Second, Enlightenment thought was exported from Europe. Before we had the opportunities of graduate school in America, many of our bright minds would travel to Europe for graduate work and return with a new philosophy. The reverence for scientific authority took hold as a major new commitment. The corollary was that moral philosophy replaced theology as the defining feature of Christian intellectual life. The former involves reasoning about the human good, which became divorced from the grounds for that good. Good without God was considered good enough. Pressure was applied to jettison sectarian Christian aspects or broaden Christianity into moralism.

Third, universities had commitments to serve the public in practical ways via a free market economy in the face of their struggle for institutional survival. Colleges were competing for students for their new graduate, technology, and professional schools, and their efforts took a decidedly secular approach. Here I mean not merely juxtaposed to sectarianism but rather juxtaposed to orthodox religion as well.

Through the latter half of the nineteenth century, German universities served as America's graduate schools. It was rare to find a university leader or prominent scholar who hadn't studied in Germany. Ideas have consequences. This was true for colleges and sectarian seminarians.[25] German philosophy and secular research methodology were enormously influential. The philosopher Immanuel Kant culminated the Enlightenment project, undermining natural theology and giving us agnosticism that would later support the undermining of science.

He was famous for what became known as the fact-versus-value dichotomy. He believed that we do not have access to the noumena (i.e., the thing in itself) but instead only have access to the phenomena (i.e., the thing as it appears). That is, one cannot know reality, but only their view of reality. Essentially, one is trapped in their own mind.

Subjective approaches to truth were being given more validity. Biblical criticism was on the rise. The trend to reduce religion to morality and theology to anthropology was growing. Did God create man in his image, or was it that man created God in his image? Marsden comments, "When the advanced German theological views became commonplace in American educational circles, these theological changes played an important role in allowing adjustments to the latest academic trends, such as scientific historical investigation and emphasis on development of character."[26] In short, even if most scholars weren't metaphysical naturalists (i.e., atheists), many had adopted methodological naturalism in practice. Even classical Marxism was modernist in origin and prided itself on being scientific.

German universities were strongly controlled by the state, guaranteeing a measure of academic freedom from sectarian interests. Sectarian theological interests became scandalous outside of divinity schools. Near the end of the nineteenth century, universities were still claiming to be Christian in religion, however, sectarianism was anathema. Because religion was being reduced to morality and human progress, it was on a fast track to becoming obsolete. With the increasing strength of the scientific research university developing in conjunction with methodological naturalism,[27] the introduction of Charles Darwin's theory of evolution in 1859, and biblical criticism, Christianity was being severely challenged. Christianity was becoming broadly humanistic. The claim was being made that universities were Christian, non-sectarian, dedicated to high moral values, but also working toward a value-free, theology-free scientific inquiry, which co-opted the Protestant rhetoric of the evangelical establishment. Eventually, this led to the establishment of nonbelief. The modern research universities were being born from the colleges, and the defining methodology of graduate education that followed the German model was, again, a value-free and theology-free science. Virtually all university teachers eventually would be trained in graduate schools built on the purely naturalistic assumptions of the new science and professionalism. Methodological naturalism became the reigning paradigm in practice even before metaphysical naturalism—that is, atheism—became the reigning paradigm in theory. Indeed, one would eventually lead to the other.

Yale historian Julie Reuben examines the transition from the nineteenth century's broad conception of truth to the twentieth century's division between *facts* and *values* (roughly from 1880 to 1930).[28] In the late nineteenth century, intellectuals assumed that truth had spiritual, moral, and cognitive dimensions. By 1930, however, intellectuals had abandoned this broad conception of truth. Instead, they embraced a view of knowledge that drew a sharp distinction between "facts" and "values."

Cognitive truth was now associated with empirically verified knowledge. By this standard, moral values could not be validated as true. Only science constituted true knowledge. Moral and spiritual values could be true only in an emotional or nonliteral sense. While the hard sciences became dominated by scientific naturalism, the humanities took a postmodern relativistic turn that eventually put even scientific truth as suspect. "All truth is God's truth" eventually became "Truth is what my peers will let me get away with"—at least in the humanities.

By the 1870s, the enlightened critics of historical Christianity who had traveled abroad, mostly to Germany, became so numerous and influential that they could and did take control of key institutions. They proceeded to dismantle the old college, severing the ties to religious denominations. Liberal Protestantism, which dominated American universities from the Civil War to World War II, eased the transition from secular method to ideological separation. Liberal Protestantism contributed to its own demise by equating religion with morality. Under the theory of knowledge known as scientism, neither could stand.

According to Reuben, the university's narrative during this period was the separation of knowledge and morality. The Bible was no longer viewed as trustworthy, and science became the new authority. Departmental disciplines began changing their names from politics to political science and from psychology to psychological sciences, indicating the shift in worldview of both the "queen of the *scientia*" and its philosophical handmaiden that had taken root in the ideological revolution that occurred between 1880 and 1930. The queen of the sciences (or knowledge disciplines) was no longer theology, as it were, but a-theology.

Both the scientific naturalism of the modernists and the skeptical relativism of the postmodernists deny moral and religious knowledge. Neither of them sees Christianity as a viable worldview that ought to be invited back to the table. They are squatters on what was Christian land. They moved in and kicked out the Christian influence—with the notable exceptions of (1) Christian children, and (2) Christians' money.

THE SECOND REVOLUTION: POSTMODERN CULTURAL MARXISM

The current revolution in American universities is rapidly pouring into culture. Just as the dust from the first revolution was settling in the universities of the United States, the seeds were being revealed for both the second and current revolutions. Among the European Axis powers of World War II—with their fascist governments in Germany and Italy—those who were not so friendly to national socialism of the Nazis (i.e., the international or globalist socialists known as Marxists) were very active. In Germany, Marxists had established the Frankfurt School of critical theory. Most of the founders were Jewish atheists. They were seeking to discern where Marx's predictions had gone wrong and to retool the ideology for the future. In 1933, being a globalist socialist, as well as a Jew, in Germany meant being faced with ostracism and danger. Germany was not a safe place for these Jewish Marxists when the national socialists rose to power. So they quickly evacuated and ended up in the United States.

In Italy, after Mussolini had changed from being a Marxist to becoming a fascist, he had the Italian Marxist leader Antonio Gramsci imprisoned for life without the option of escaping the country. Gramsci's inspiring writings combined with the outputs of the Frankfurt School gave us what we might consider today as *cultural Marxism, Western Marxism, neo-Marxism, critical social justice*, or other roughly synonymous expressions. While Marxism proper was modernist in its thinking given the time of Karl Marx, in America,

Western Marxism became fused with postmodern thinking, and the result was postmodern cultural Marxism as we see it in our country and in what is being exported abroad.

One of the difficulties in discussing this topic is due, in part, to the ambiguity of the language. For example, let's imagine a hypothetical scenario. You make a statement saying that you oppose *social justice*, and someone else hears that and thinks what you mean is that you hate one or more marginalized or oppressed groups. Call it *critical theory* instead, and it's enough to make an average academic's eyes glaze over. Call it *identity politics* and people simply think you are referring to political correctness or some view that you merely don't like. The other person is already repulsed by political discussion and doesn't want to hear any more about it. But they can't escape it. As is popularly stated, "You may take no interest in politics, but politics takes an interest in you." Call it *cultural Marxism* or *neo-Marxism* and people think you are waving the banner for a conspiracy theory. Yet all of those terms reside in the ballpark of what you wish to discuss; however, gaining understanding through discourse remains elusive.

Aside from the Bible, *The Communist Manifesto* is the bestselling book in history. To assume that the ideas it espouses are dead would be terribly naive. To assume that its practitioners aren't serious believers is dangerous. Christianity promises liberation and the ultimate good life in the hereafter, but Marxism promises those things in the here and now. Christianity has one view of justice, Marxism another. And at different times in history many have tried to conflate two. It is happening right now. To be sure, the term *social justice* is a Trojan horse. While first coined by a Catholic thinker, it was later co-opted by Marxist thinkers and now pervades society without precise understanding by the masses. Hence, on the website of the organization over which I preside, we have distinguished biblical social justice from the Marxist version. The entry reads thus:

Social Justice

> We believe primary human identity lies in being made in God's image and this bestows intrinsic dignity that is worthy of Christian compassion and justice. Sin is the ultimate problem and Christ's

redemption the ultimate solution. Redeemed people should promote genuine Social Justice within a biblical framework. So-called Critical Social Justice is corrupted by a focus on power and privilege rather than truth as the way to understand human relationships. "Social Justice" corrupted in this way misconstrues justice, grace, and compassion, and ultimately undermines the mission of the church and its gospel. We reject as anti-biblical any interpretation of Social Justice as a metanarrative inspired by the false components of Critical Theory (or Cultural Marxism). This views primary human identity in terms of opposing oppressor/oppressed groups along the axes of race, class, sexuality, gender, etc., granting special knowledge found only in the "lived experience" of the oppressed.[29]

What is justice? Going back to thinkers like Aristotle and Thomas Aquinas, it is understood as "giving to each his due." Aquinas was an Aristotelian and one of the most influential thinkers in all of Christendom. He spoke about the three theological virtues of faith, hope, and love. He also addressed the classical virtues known to the Greeks as courage, prudence, temperance, and justice.

Interestingly, Aquinas's treatises give us a glimpse into his thinking, which is highlighted by how much space he allocated per topic. For example, for faith he allocated 16 questions, hope 6 questions, and charity 24 questions. Yet justice is one of the largest topics in the *Summa Theologica*, covering 66 questions. He defined justice as "rendering to each one his due."[30] Justice, by its very nature, is social. Yet in Scripture, it is never called social justice; it is simply justice. In biblical justice, there is also an element of compassion. Contemporary culture seeks to conflate these. Biblically, we can see various characteristics of justice such as protecting the vulnerable (Isaiah 1:17), impartiality (Leviticus 19:15), and punishing evil and promoting good (Romans 13:1-4). And Micah 6:8 is perhaps one of the most cited verses in ecclesiastical circles concerning social justice: "He has shown you, O mortal, what is good. And what does the Lord require of you? To act justly and to love mercy and to walk humbly with your God."

Revolutionaries always view themselves to be fighting for a just cause. But views about what is just or unjust, like other ethical concerns, develop within the backdrop of a deeper worldview—about reality (metaphysics), knowledge (how or what do we know), and ethics (what is good or right, if anything). We ask questions within the three branches of philosophy culminating to these: What is real? How do I know what is real? How then should I live based upon what I know about reality? So asking questions about justice entails asking questions about what is good. This, in turn, entails questions about knowledge and reality, which are more basic.

Cultural Marxism and the Non-Conspiratorial Revolution

Richard Weaver once said that "ideas have consequences."[31] Some ideas are harmless, others are revolutionary for good or for evil, and they're shown to be so through their histories. For this reason, the philosopher George Santayana said, "Those who cannot remember the past are condemned to repeat it."[32] Mapping the movements of the past and evaluating their effects on the present can help us avoid pitfalls in the future by recognizing them before it's too late.

Nonetheless, some movements encapsulated in various terms (especially if they accrue divisive political overtones) can become words that provoke an almost visceral reaction of either disgust or delight, denunciation or celebration.

Such is the case with cultural Marxism (a.k.a. neo-Marxism, identity Marxism, or Western Marxism). It is real and revolutionary.[33] Once, I worked with a philosophy student from China who told me that he came to the West to finish his final year of doctoral studies for the purpose of studying Western Marxism as it exists in the West. It's alive. What is Western Marxism or cultural Marxism? The phrase *cultural Marxism* seems to have been coined around 50 years ago by Trent Schroyer in his 1973 book *The Critique of Domination: The Origins and Development of Critical Theory*. But the idea itself preceded the term. Cultural Marxism is a well-established concept in academic circles. It simply refers to a twentieth-century development in Marxist thought that came to view Western culture and its colonizing of other places as a key source of human oppression. It is the application of Marxist theory to culture. But over the last decade it's become explosive—so much so that Wikipedia's editorial team took the rather extraordinary step of archiving its rather tame entry on the subject and tried to let you know what they "know," namely, it's only a conspiracy theory by right-wingers.[34] Most people who adopt the viewpoint or strains of it are oblivious.

Why the commotion? Because of public intellectuals like Jordan Peterson, a famous psychologist from the University of Toronto. The expression *cultural Marxism* has come to function as "shorthand for left-wing ideology," manifesting in various "progressive" or "social justice" causes.[35] For this reason, most on the left side of the contemporary culture war not only hear cultural Marxism as an accusatory "snarl word" but claim that it has zero validity. To really understand today's cultural Marxism, we must first understand Marxism version 1.0.

Introducing Karl Marx (1818–1883) and Classical Marxism

While we're well aware of the fascism that developed in Germany and Italy, it is the Marxist thinking within those two movements that threatens to be the most successful Marxist revolution ever, if it can take hold in America and America's influence on the world scene. Marx could not have foreseen that America would have the potential to become a prized capture of his ideology.

Marx was born shortly after the French Revolution, and he was very intrigued by it. He observed the American Civil War from afar and provided comment on it. He was alive when the first ideological revolution was occurring in American universities from 1880 to 1930.

Marx's parents converted to Christianity—albeit a very liberal form of Lutheranism—so that Karl's father, Heinrich (the son of a rabbi), could continue working as a lawyer with an abundance of Christian clients. Karl Marx was baptized in 1824 and became an atheist in college, influenced by his professor and colleague Dr. Bruno Bauer at the University of Bonn. Together, they sought to launch a journal, *Archives of Atheism*. He later studied philosophy under Hegel. Marx soon came to embrace the idea that history follows a natural and inevitable dialectical process. However, in contrast to Hegel's idealism—that regarded matter as dependent upon mind and history as the progressive self-realization of an absolute Mind—Marx proposed dialectical materialism, a view that saw matter as primary and change as inherent in the nature of the material reality. Marx was a kind of social philosopher seeing a distinct human problem and solution.

Marx's Diagnosis of the Problem and His Solution to the Human Condition

When reading Marx, I can understand his frustration. I was frustrated along with him when I first read his book *Das Kapital*. He gave the notion of capital in capitalism a pejorative meaning. In the initial phases of industrial capitalism, not only were working conditions frequently dangerous and unhealthy, but work arrangements were often cruel and exploitative. Consequently, "wealth inequality soared as the industrialists...made excessive profits while denying their workers sufficient income to flourish."[36]

This led Marx to view the fundamental human problem through two lenses: oppression and alienation. Oppression is a consequence of living in a society of stratified classes, an arrangement exacerbated by the exploitation inherent in capitalism. The capitalist class (the bourgeoisie), as the owners of the means of production, use the working class (the proletariat) to make profits for themselves, a brand of slave labor. Such oppression leads to a four-fold experience of alienation for the worker: first, from the act of production; second, from the product made; third, from other workers; and fourth, from his or her humanity.

Although capitalism had intensified this problem, Marx contended that the problem itself was nothing new. He believed that all of history has been about the inequalities of the rich oppressing the poor. But Marx was convinced that the capitalist system contained within it the seeds of its own destruction. Continued exploitation of the proletariat by the bourgeoisie would lead to mounting resentment. This would eventually and inevitably boil over into a proletarian revolution in which the bourgeoisie would be violently overthrown and out of which a new, classless society would finally emerge.

Marx's "dialectical materialism" inferred that the transition from capitalism to communism would be unstoppable due to the natural evolution of the material forces of production. Nevertheless, he clearly believed that violence was a necessary part of the process. He thus spoke freely of "the violent overthrow of the bourgeoisie"[37] and even felt justified in inciting such violence. This is borne out by the closing lines of *The Communist Manifesto*:

> The Communists disdain to conceal their views and aims. They openly declare that their ends can be attained only by the forcible

overthrow of all existing social conditions. Let the ruling classes tremble at a Communistic revolution. The proletarians have nothing to lose but their chains. They have a world to win.[38]

This is not a conspiracy. For something to be a conspiracy, it must be secret. This is explicit and it is violent. As the Chinese revolutionary Mao Zedong is often invoked as saying, "A revolution is not a dinner party."[39]

The call was "Working men of all countries, unite!"[40] For what purpose? Revolution.

Now, between the time of revolutionary terror and the arrival of a communist utopia, a transitional government of the working class—what Marxists called "the dictatorship of the proletariat"—would also be necessary. Elsewhere, he makes clear that this intermediate state is what he means by "socialism."[41]

Supposedly, all the bloodshed would be worth it. After capitalism's demise, a truly humane society would appear, governed by the principle "From each according to his abilities, to each according to his needs!"[42] In modern vernacular, "Paying our fair share." We're asked to consider a world of equality where wealth is shared. Many in our own time have sought support from Christians by invoking the false claim that even Jesus was a socialist and that the early church was likewise socialistic.

The Beatles legend John Lennon charmingly pieced this idea together in the hit song "Imagine," which has impacted millions, if not billions, of people. The song begins by asking us to dream about a world with no heaven, hell, or religion. That would be a world of peace. He tells us that we might think he's dreaming, but he's not alone. He asks us to join him in his vision. Imagine not having any possessions, he continues, and you'll be happy. The song finishes like an evangelistic altar call for us to join him and many others in this utopian dream world so we can live as one.

In such a society, all land, industry, labor, and wealth would be held in common and freely shared. Nothing would be privately owned. This makes sense in classical Marxism, where the special property is the inequality of capital or wealth. This is why "the theory of the Communists may be summed up in the single sentence: Abolition of private property."[43]

Today's Marxism has changed, of course. In later iterations—that originated and evolved in America—like critical race theory, the key "property" to be abolished is the property of "whiteness." In critical queer theory, it is "cisgender heteronormativity." The list goes on with other key "properties" that must be shed as defined by some social category along the axes of race, class, sex, gender, and so on.

Such an abolition would also bring about another of communism's stated goals: the eradication of the family. The family had to go. For "the bourgeois family will vanish as a matter of course when its complement [private property] vanishes, and both will vanish with the vanishing of capital."[44] Again, in our own time, there have been recent writings explicitly calling for the abolition of family and a reimagining of it in the current Marxist iteration.

Marx and His Religion of Revolution

Marx was not a good man. He was a bum and a loser.[45]

In 1989, as many in the West expressed relief at the fall of the Berlin Wall, Marxism, in fact, wasn't dead. Bill Ayers (former professor of education at the University of Chicago) and Bernardine Dohrn (former law professor at Northwestern) were founders of the terror group Weather Underground in the early 1970s. They bombed government buildings in protest of the Vietnam War. In 2008, controversy stirred around Barack Obama's connections to Ayers that began in the 1990s in Chicago.

In 2015, we saw Black Lives Matter (BLM) emerge at the popular level. Despite Marxism's failures, it has many adherents in America. Cofounder Patrisse Cullors explains the origins of BLM: "We actually do have an ideological frame. Myself and Alicia in particular are trained organizers. We are trained Marxists."[46] *The Communist Manifesto* called for the abolition of the family and the forceful overthrow over all existing institutions. The BLM website stated, until it was scrubbed, that "we disrupt the western prescribed nuclear family…We foster a queer affirming network…heteronormative thinking."[47]

Marxism was never about economics. Marx was a philosopher set on overthrowing Christianity and replacing it with a system that gives meaning to the world apart from God. The famous anti-theist Richard Dawkins quipped, "The universe we observe has precisely the properties we should expect if there is, at bottom, no design, no purpose, no evil, and no good, nothing but blind pitiless indifference."[48] Unlike many who seek to find meaning and purpose individually, Marx thought there was a right and wrong side of history. In place of struggle, he promised a world of utopia. In place of sexual and economic limitations, he promised total freedom, including sexual freedom. It is said that Darwin gave atheists a creation myth, but Marx gave them an eschatology—a telos. Marx said, "Communism abolishes eternal truths, it abolishes all religion, and all morality, instead of constituting them in a new basis; it therefore acts in contradiction to all past or historical experience."[49]

Marx's ideal was the French Revolution.[50] He sought to overthrow not simply an earthly king but God Himself. Marquis de Sade spent years in prison as a rapist and pedophile. His perverse eroticism and sexual writings gave rise to the term *sadism*. The French revolutionaries not only released him but made him a delegate to their convention. The new government didn't want the calendar to be connected to the birth of Jesus. So they sought to declare a new calendar with the year 1789 marked as the beginning of the new world, wanting a ten-day week rather than a seven-day week. In 1791, the government repealed laws against sodomy and incest. They established the atheistic cult of reason as the official state religion. They paraded a prostitute through streets of Paris and placed her naked upon the altar of the Notre Dame Cathedral (she represented reason and freedom), insisting men would not be free until the last king was strangled with the entrails of the last priest. This reign of terror didn't bring freedom. Robespierre was himself put under the guillotine of his own making. No sooner did his head come off than Napoleon became the new dictator.

Like Friedrich Engels, Marx was a pampered son of bourgeoisie parents. His parents were despised by him, loathing their insistence that he get a real job. The small fortune they left him was less than he thought he deserved. *The Communist Manifesto* demands the abolition of private property and inheritance, but somehow this is not seen as a contradiction in Marx's mind, who received his inheritance because he was doing humanity a favor. Marx wanted us to imagine a world where government simply withered away and somehow all would be well, and people could do what suited them. His solution was destructive, not constructive. Apart from a small job here or there, Marx lived off the charity of his family and Engels. His wife was gifted a maid from her mother. The maid is alleged to have become pregnant by Marx, who never supported the child. Sadly, two of Marx's daughters committed suicide.

Everywhere his ideas have been implemented—Russia, China, Cambodia, Cuba, Burma, the Democratic Republic of the Congo, Zimbabwe, East Germany, North Korea, or Venezuela—the results have been nothing short of catastrophic: dystopian, not utopian. With a body count of around 100 million, the Marxist experiment has led to more deaths than any other ideology our world has ever known.[51]

Yet it is unlikely that any of this would have troubled Marx. For despite having much to say about exploitation and oppression, he seems to have been more or less indifferent to human misery. Humans are a means to an end rather than an end in themselves. Marx was driven less by a love for the proletariat and more by a hatred of the bourgeoisie.[52]

OUR UNIVERSITIES MAY HAVE BEEN OVERRUN, BUT THE STORY IS NOT OVER

As Christians, we need to be students of the culture around us to better understand our current circumstances and how to respond. We can see how the ideological revolutions happened in the universities and their impacts downstream. Scientific naturalism impacted the church by giving us the "social gospel" that is embraced by liberal Protestants. Marxism was grounded in naturalism, but it has evolved. While it was capable of a frontal assault in countries like Russia and China, the West seemed somewhat impenetrable. It would come to have a significant impact eventually, but only after it morphed to effectively infiltrate our cultural institutions. Cultural Marxism, as we can see and will cover in more depth, has come to infiltrate areas of Christianity in America with a form of social justice subversive to Christianity. Like the apostle Paul, who engaged the intellectual elites on Mars Hill in Athens, we must engage with not only the ideas pouring forth from the universities but the intellectual elites themselves.

This entails rebelling against world systems by being faithful to Jesus and His way. He is "the way" (John 14:6). As we've seen, the universities in America—not to mention Europe (beginning half a millennium prior) and major institutions in Southeast Asia—were largely founded by Christ followers, initially to train ministers but also to bring good to the world. This should be no surprise because knowledge has, at least historically, been seen to be in concert with the Christian faith. Indeed, it is central, not peripheral, to the Christian faith. Jesus Himself declared that eternal life involves the knowledge of God (John 17:3). And Jesus is likewise referred to as the logic of God (John 1:1-3 refers to Christ as the *logos* [Greek]). Our worldview begins "in the beginning," with mind and not matter. Christian faith is most reasonable, and we need to demonstrate its plausibility to a skeptical world. It is no accident that the universities emerged within Christendom. But we lost them, and in that, we've paid an exorbitant price. If we want to be most influential in culture as salt and light and leverage an enormous platform for the gospel, we need to think seriously about how to reinfiltrate the universities from which we've largely been exiled. Consequently, our influence has waned, and instead, the world's influence has crept into our churches and ministries.

We will address more specifics in part 3 of this book, but the silver lining of observing that not one but two ideological revolutions took place in the universities is that it obviously is not impossible for there to be another. Each time, the dominant paradigm was infiltrated, and a new paradigm took root and became the majority voice that influenced and shaped ideas, cultures, and civilization. We can and should rise to the occasion to be salt and light in the universities. Christians may be on the outside now, but we must seek to enter the conversation as we gain further understanding of our audience. I agree with Al Mohler, who said to me in a recent conversation, "I refuse to enter into a self-imposed exile," and while the battle may seem uphill and our optimism levels low at times, "the opportunity is closing but not gone."[53] We must learn and adapt.

8

REASONS FOR FAILURE AND THE RISE OF THE NEO-MARXISM(S) OF THE EUROPEAN AXIS POWERS

Motivations aside, Marx's economic philosophy is riddled with numerous flawed assumptions and mistaken claims, as subsequent history has repeatedly shown. He assumed that economics was a zero-sum game. But it is not. He also assumed that human nature is basically good or at least neutral (shaped by society). But it is not.

Marx was wrong about virtually everything he predicted. For example, he claimed that the working class would increase in number and decrease in wealth, while the capitalist class would decrease in number and increase in wealth. Neither happened. He also predicted that socialist revolutions would first take place in the most advanced capitalist nations (Britain, America, and France). Instead, they took place in some of the least-developed regions of the world, places still in a feudalist system (Russia, Latin America, and parts of Asia). The claim was that capitalism was exploitative and socialism humane and that capitalism is less productive than socialism. None of this has been ultimately persuasive over the years in theory, nor has any of the evidence proven Marx to be correct, leading one to consider that Marxism is based on resentment and envy more than anything else.

But Marx was more than a false prophet. He was an intellectual fraud. As has been painfully demonstrated ever since the 1880s, when two Cambridge scholars first started fact-checking his work, they noted that Marx was chronically dishonest in his use of sources and regularly engaged in the deliberate distortion of data. Why would he do this? Paul Johnson explains,

> The facts are not central to Marx's work; they are ancillary, buttressing conclusions already reached independently of them. *Capital*...should be seen, then, not as a scientific investigation of the nature of the economic process it purported to describe but as an exercise in moral philosophy...It is a huge and often incoherent sermon, an attack on the industrial process and the principle of ownership by a man who had conceived a powerful but essentially irrational hatred for them.[1]

None of this is to deny the inspirational nature of Marx's vision or that he got some things right. Indeed, his condemnation of the evils of child labor is easily understood. Moreover, his philosophy has spawned a range of reductionistic conflict theories that tend to exacerbate (if not create) the very problems they claim to address. And yet despite his destructive views, not only does Marx's reputation survive among millennials and Generation Z, but his ideas are making a marked comeback![2] In fact, the new Marxists (neo-Marxists) of the Axis powers, such as Germany and Italy, fighting against fascism formed the bases for the current revolution in the United States.

THE ITALIAN AND HIS DIAGNOSIS OF AND SOLUTION TO THE PROBLEM: ANTONIO GRAMSCI (1891–1937)

In the early part of the twentieth century, however, many of Marx's most ardent disciples were fast becoming aware of insoluble problems with classical Marxist theory. This brings us to the Italian neo-Marxists and the contribution of the Italian communist philosopher Antonio Gramsci. He has been referred to as "the most dangerous socialist in history."[3]

Born in Sardinia in 1891, Gramsci became the head of the Italian Communist Party in 1924. During this time, he was befriended and influenced by

Hungarian Marxist György Lukács, one of the founders of critical theory. Mussolini's fascist regime came to power in 1922. In 1926, he had Gramsci imprisoned as an enemy of the state until his death in 1937. During that time, Gramsci developed most of what came to be known as the *Prison Notebooks*. But they weren't published until after the war, in 1948. Not until 1970 were they translated into English, French, and German. Notre Dame professor Joseph Buttigieg is the father of 2020 Democratic presidential candidate Mayor Pete Buttigieg, who went on to work in the Biden administration. Professor Buttigieg was the president of the International Gramsci Society and mediated to the English-speaking world thousands of pages that he translated from the *Prison Notebooks*.

Gramsci metamorphosized Marx. While in prison, Gramsci turned his mind to the question that haunted classical Marxism: Why hadn't Marx's predictions worked out in practice? For instance, why hadn't the Russian Revolution of 1917 replicated itself in Western European nations? The answer, Gramsci believed, was because of the persistence of capitalist ideas embedded in the institutions of "civil society" (e.g., the family, the church, trade unions, the education system)—all the consensus-creating elements of society that are independent of "political society" (e.g., the police, the army, the legal system).[4] The cultural Marxists realized that a revolution requires a cultural war over an economic war. The revolutionaries could no longer rely on factory workers but instead needed to persuade intellectuals. With that in mind, the university was to become the factory floor. For Marxists to fundamentally transform America, they had to seize the "cultural means of production," the hegemonic narrative via academia, media, and ecclesia (churches).

The problem, then, was that the "culture" of Western society was blocking the proletarian uprising. This required a modified strategy that called for a kind of "cultural Marxism." As Gramsci wrote in *Notebooks*: "The state was only an outer ditch, behind which there stood a powerful system of fortresses."[5] Furthermore, these fortresses were inseparable from the West's Christian heritage and, despite the secularizing impact of the Enlightenment, remained undergirded by a latent Christian worldview. Consequently, until Christianity's cultural hegemony was broken, no communist revolution would take place and no utopia could arrive.

Hegemony derives from a Greek word meaning "lead out," denoting the control of the ideology of a society. This is the domination by the ruling class via establishing and maintaining the cultural worldview as normative (beliefs, values, etc.). By the way, Marx wasn't completely blind to this. As I'll show later, he believed that tertiary criticism was economic criticism, secondary was political, and primary criticism was and is religious. Nominal religion could stay, but serious religion could not.

Marx clearly believed that religion dulled people to their oppression by giving them hope beyond it. It thereby dampened their revolutionary instincts (hence his calling religion "the opiate of the masses"). Religion itself would naturally disappear in a socialist system. It is "the sigh of the oppressed creature," and religion itself creates self-oppression.

For Gramsci, culture was not downstream from economics, like Marx thought, but economics was downstream from culture. What this meant was that Marx was fundamentally wrong, and Hegel was essentially right. Gramsci thus turned Marx upside down (or right side up).

The significance of this inversion of classical Marxism is profound. What it means is that if you want to change the economic structure of society, you must first change the cultural institutions that socialize people into believing and behaving according to the dictates of the capitalist system. The only way to do this is by cutting the roots of Western civilization—particularly its Judeo-Christian values, for these (supposedly) are what provide the capitalist root-system. In short, unless and until Western culture is de-Christianized, Western society will never be decapitalized.

To accomplish this would require an army of Marxist intellectuals undertaking what was later called "the long march through the institutions of power"[6]—that is, by gradually colonizing and ultimately controlling all the key institutions of civil society. Gramsci is often cited as if he said, "In the new order, Socialism will triumph by first capturing the culture via infiltration of schools, universities, churches and the media by transforming the consciousness of society."[7] This is fully consistent with his thinking, but this quote isn't found in his literature.

The larger goal Gramsci promoted was control of all the major institutions of political society (e.g., the police, law courts, civil servants, local councils). Gramsci referred to this process as "becoming State."[8]

The program, then, at least in theory, is simple: Subvert society by changing its culture and change its culture by infiltrating its institutions. The goal is likewise clear: Destroy capitalism and replace it with a communist counter-hegemony. This is why many see cultural Marxism as an accurate description of Gramsci's neo-Marxist philosophy. This requires a "war of position" (consent) before a "war of movement" (coercion). Once the former is successful, the result is decisive victory. Cultural Marxism doesn't necessarily require violence, but it seeks a sustained methodical infiltration into and takeover of institutions—a soft revolution.

The goal here is not merely a flattening of the system but a flipping of the system—the creation of what Gramsci called a "periphery-centered society."[9] In other words, insiders must be turned into outsiders and underdogs into overlords. Likewise, oppressors must now be oppressed and those formerly privileged must have their privileges taken away. Remember, as Mao popularly said, "A revolution is not a dinner party."[10]

Above all, Christianity must be replaced. As Gramsci wrote in 1916, "Socialism is precisely the religion that must kill Christianity. [It is a] religion in the sense that it too is a faith…[and] because it has substituted for the consciousness of the transcendental God…trust in man and his best strengths as the sole spiritual reality."[11]

The whole discipline of cultural studies is largely the result of Gramsci's influence, and his impact on the humanities and social sciences has been nothing short of immense.[12] As Andrew Roberts summarizes, "Gramsci was perhaps the most important communist thinker in the West since Marx himself… and nowhere were his ideas followed more effectively than in academia."[13]

Cultural Marxism advocates a sustained ideological subversion rather than a violent political revolution. But the end results are the same: the destruction of Western culture and the replacement of the Christian church with the communist state. That's why we call this a soft revolution, but it is no less of a revolution. It is about the disrupting, dismantling, and destroying of Western civilization. If these revolutionaries can overtake America—and their work is in process—then they will have achieved the most successful Marxist revolution ever. The Chinese need only to buy popcorn and watch the show.

Here, then, is a strategy for the communist conquest of capitalist cultures.

Nor was Gramsci alone in thinking along these lines. While he was dying, a group of German Marxist intellectuals, quite unaware of the *Prison Notebooks*, was exploring similar ideas. This brings us to consider the work of the Frankfurt School.

THE FRANKFURT SCHOOL OF CRITICAL THEORY AND ITS MAIN CHARACTERS

The origins of the Frankfurt School (also referred to as "Freudian-Marxists"[14]) can be traced to 1923, when the radical Hungarian Marxist György Lukács was invited to chair a week-long symposium in Frankfurt, Germany. He corresponded with Antonio Gramsci, the leading Italian Marxist. Out of this came a vision for a Marxist think tank and research center, originally to be called the Institute for Marxism. But for public relations purposes, a more benign name was chosen: the Institute for Social Research.[15]

While the early work of the institute moved in a classically Marxist direction, this all changed in 1930 when Max Horkheimer (1895–1973) moved in a decidedly neo-Marxist direction.[16]

I'll explain critical theory in greater detail shortly. In brief, it is a form of biting social critique aimed at exposing and dismantling the corrupt foundations and oppressive nature of capitalist society. Like Gramsci, Horkheimer was convinced that the major obstacle to human liberation was the capitalist ideology embedded in traditional Western culture. That, fundamentally, was what needed exposing, criticizing, and changing.[17]

Horkheimer recruited Theodore Adorno and Herbert Marcuse, who would help to blend classical Marxist doctrines with both Darwinian sociology and Freudian psychology.

In 1933, when the Nazis came to power, most members of the Frankfurt School (being not only communists but also Jewish) were forced to flee the country. Initially, they went to Geneva. But eventually, they settled in the United States near Columbia University in New York City, and they renamed their journal *Studies in Philosophy and Social Science*.[18]

In 1941, Horkheimer moved to Los Angeles, followed by Adorno and Marcuse. Horkheimer and Adorno returned to Frankfurt to resume their work, and Marcuse stayed in the US as a professor—first at Brandeis University in Boston, then, in 1965, at University of California, San Diego.

Before we look further into Marcuse's work (especially his impact on the 1960s revolution—1968 specifically with M-M-M, which stands for Marx, Mao, and Marcuse), we will find it helpful to learn more about some of the other members and associates of the Frankfurt School and their main contributions to the cultural Marxist cause.

György Lukács (1885–1971)

Lukács chaired the week-long symposium that led to the Institute of Social Research's founding. As a personal acquaintance of Gramsci, Lukács may have been a conduit for Gramsci's ideas entering the Institute for Social Research. Lukács's *History and Class Consciousness* (1923) reveals that he still held to the classical Marxian tenet that it is "not the consciousness of men that determines their existence, but, on the contrary, their social existence that determines their consciousness."[19]

What is especially noteworthy is Lukács's brief stint, in 1919, as the People's Commissar for Education and Culture under the Bolshevik regime in Hungary. He launched a program called Cultural Terrorism, and its purpose was "the annihilation of the old [cultural] values and the creation of new ones by the revolutionaries." For Lukács, "the revolutionary destruction of society" was "the one and only solution to the cultural contradictions of the epoch."[20]

One of the chief goals of Lukács's short-lived campaign was the destruction of Judeo-Christian sexual ethics and the weakening of the bourgeois family. To this end, he introduced a radical sex-education program into all schools. As a result, "Hungarian children learned the subtle nuances of free love, sexual intercourse...the obsolete nature of monogamy, and the irrelevance of organized religion, which deprived man of pleasure."[21]

Lukács's commitment to Marxist ideology was quasi-religious. He described it in terms of "conversion,"[22] and he quoted with approval the words of the German idealist philosopher Johann Gottlieb Fichte: "If theory conflicts with the facts, so much the worse for the facts."[23]

According to Roger Scruton, the only way to account for such blind dogmatism is to see that "the root fallacy of Marxism, the belief in a real 'essence' of which our social life is only an 'appearance', had colonized Lukács's brain, and taken the form of an immovable religion."[24] As Scruton remarks, "With Lukács…the devil is 'capitalism,' and hatred of capitalism is total and unconditional, justifying every moral breach."[25] Consequently, "Communist ethics," declared Lukács, "makes it the highest duty to accept the necessity to act wickedly."[26]

Erich Fromm (1900–1980)

Erich Fromm was a social psychologist who became an associate of the Frankfurt School in 1930 and was the first to attempt to integrate Marxian and Freudian thought. He was also one of those who not only sought refuge in the United States but remained there until only a few years before his death.

Among Fromm's books were *The Art of Loving* (1956), *The Heart of Man* (1964), and *Escape from Freedom* (1941). In the latter, he argued that early capitalism had created a social order that had bred within some people a sadomasochistic and authoritarian character, of which Martin Luther and Adolf Hitler were prime examples.

Fromm's views on human sexuality, at least in his earlier writings, were also marked by a radical constructionist outlook. For instance, as Jeffrey Breshears says concerning Fromm,

> Fromm contended that sexual orientation is merely a social construct, that there are no innate differences between men and women, and that sexuality and gender roles are socially determined. Furthermore, he argued that sexually repressed societies discourage sexual experimentation and practices such as homosexuality due to manmade legal codes and moralistic taboos that are psychologically inhibiting and counterproductive.[27]

Theodor Adorno (1903–1969)

It was this particular concern that motivated Adorno, along with several other members of the Institute, to author *The Authoritarian Personality* (1950).[28] Based on analytical studies of German society that were begun in 1923, the book claimed to have identified what Adorno called "a new anthropological type"—the authoritarian character. This character was a product of capitalism, Christianity, conservatism, the patriarchal family, and sexual repression. And according to the Frankfurt School, it was precisely this combination that induced the prejudice, antisemitism, and fascism that had engulfed Germany in the 1930s and 1940s.

However, according to Martin Jay, *The Authoritarian Personality* was really trying to study "the character type of a totalitarian rather than an authoritarian society."[29] In this light, it can be faulted for drawing an exclusive connection between authoritarianism and fascism. Why not communism also? As Jay asks, "Why was political and economic conservatism seen as connected with authoritarianism, while the demand for state socialism was not? In short, why was the old left-right distinction upheld, when the real opposition was between liberal democracy and totalitarianism of both extremes?"[30]

The answers are not obvious. Likely, their personal experience of Nazi Germany made them hypersensitive to dangers on the right but far less attuned to equal dangers on the left.

Herbert Marcuse (1898-1979)

Given Marcuse's influence, we'll spend a bit more time learning about him. Like Eric Fromm, Herbert Marcuse was convinced that for cultural liberation to be complete, sexual liberation was vital. This was the case he sought to make in *Eros and Civilization: A Philosophical Inquiry into Freud* (1955), a further attempt to combine neo-Marxism with neo-Freudianism.

Marcuse's book caught the attention of the 1960s counterculture and soon became one of the founding documents of the sexual revolution. It also helped to bring the work of the Frankfurt School to the attention of numerous student activist groups and introduced their various writings into colleges and universities around the world. Thus, of all the members of the Frankfurt School, it was Marcuse who did the most to provide the intellectual justifications for the adolescent sexual rebellion of the 1960s, and *Eros and Civilization* became the textbook.

The main thesis of *Eros and Civilization* is that the only way for human beings to escape the one-dimensionality of advanced industrial society is to rebel against "technological rationality" (i.e., the repressive values of capitalist morality)[31] and to liberate our erotic side, our sensuous instincts. This means casting off sexual restraint in favor of "polymorphous perversity"—a term Marcuse borrowed from Freud.[32]

Not unsurprisingly, it is here that we see the now widely known Princeton academic Peter Singer appear on the radar. Singer is a Jewish atheist moral philosopher (yes, that is an oxymoron) and a polyamorous sex philosopher (entertaining possibilities of both pedophilia and bestiality). Is he also a Marxist? Yes, that too. Singer completed his BA in 1967, was in grad school during 1968, and did his Oxford thesis in 1971 on civil disobedience.

The slogans "Make love, not war" and "When I rebel, I want to make love" were popular at the 1960s student protests. Mao backed North Vietnam, and Marcuse met with a North Vietnam official in Germany.

Marcuse was as enamored by Freud as fish are by water. And Freud explains what he means by this expression: "What makes an infant characteristically different from every other stage of human life is that the child is polymorphously perverse, is ready to demonstrate any kind of sexual behavior, with any kind of pleasure, without any kind of restraint."[33] But the child is not meant to remain like this, argued Freud. Indeed, maturation and "civilization" emerge only after such polymorphous perversity is restrained and responsibly rechanneled. Moreover, in Freud's mind, such restraint and rechanneling are profoundly necessary, for heterosexual procreation is necessary for the continuation of our race, and so heterosexual coupling is essential for civilization itself.

In 2021, a major critic of the scientist of the sexual revolution died, and a year later in 2022, Indiana University erected a statue of the trained zoologist and self-proclaimed sexologist Alfred Kinsey to celebrate the seventy-fifth anniversary of the Kinsey Institute. The sculptor was a graduate of Wheaton College. The president of Indiana University gushed over the unveiling of the statue. Not only did this represent the rise of a statue; it represented the rise of an ideology coming to dominate the American landscape. Apparently it didn't matter that Kinsey was posthumously discovered to have fudged his research results and to have committed child sexual abuse on hundreds of children, including young infants. Dr. Judith Reisman documents how Kinsey had his own staff engage in intercourse with each other's wives and between men while being filmed.[34] From claims that were then used for gay propaganda that 10 percent of adult males were homosexual to proclaiming abortion a human right and advocating humans having sex with animals, Kinsey's views were instrumental in the revolution.

Kinsey was also an early partner with Planned Parenthood in the creation of sex-education curricula. As *The Washington Times* announced, together "they spread the gospel of unrestrained sex of all kinds at earlier and earlier ages."[35] Even Hugh Hefner credited Kinsey's "findings" to inspire him to launch *Playboy* magazine, saying, "If Kinsey had done the research, I was the pamphleteer, spreading the news of sexual liberation through a monthly magazine."[36]

When cultural Marxists like Herbert Marcuse were envisioning ways to subvert the West, they surely had someone like Hefner in mind. Worst of all, Kinsey, known as the father of the sexual revolution, conducted or procured monstrous experiments on children. He believed there were no sexual norms and that people would not be free and fulfilled until they overcame Christian sexual values. His publications prior to the 1960s were bestsellers, and together, were called the Kinsey Reports. Kinsey's research has been used to weaken laws against pornography, rape, and child molestation and open pathways for the *Roe v. Wade* ruling legalizing abortion.[37]

Not unsurprisingly, perhaps the most (in)famous moral philosopher alive today is none other than Peter Singer. In a 2014 book, Singer came out declaring his position to be that of hedonistic utilitarianism. Singer's pleasure ethic, where the end justifies the means, advocates controversial views embracing bestiality and chastising those who demur as being guilty of a form of discrimination he calls "speciesism."[38] Singer is also a Jewish Marxist who did his graduate work during the Marcusian sexual revolution. In 1973, he published a book titled *Democracy and Disobedience*, which was based on his 1971 PhD thesis from Oxford. Through people like Singer, Marxist revolutionary thinking is at the most prominent levels in American academia.[39] These revolutionaries have taken over the highest positions in academia today.

For Marcuse, true sexual liberation involves the disciplining of not our polymorphous desires but their indulgence. The goal is "to make the human body an instrument of pleasure rather than labor."[40] Human emancipation is said to be tied to "the primacy of pleasure and the liberation of Eros."[41] Behind this thought was the conviction that because advanced capitalist society had effectively de-eroticized the human body (except for the genitals), liberation required "the eroticization of the entire organism."[42] As Marcuse explained, "This spread of the libido would first manifest itself in a reactivation of all erotogenic zones and, consequently, in a resurgence of pregenital polymorphous sexuality and in a decline of genital supremacy."[43]

Think of this "genital supremacy" the same way you might think of the familiar term *white supremacy*. Privilege is said to always entail power. Privilege and power by the oppressor class uses their hegemonic discourse narrative to suppress and oppress the subordinate group. Marcuse is open about the fact that this "change in the value and scope of the libidinal would lead to a disintegration of the institutions in which private interpersonal relations have been organized, particularly the monogamic and patriarchal family." Nevertheless, he did not believe that the "transformation of the libido" would lead to "a society of sex maniacs."[44] Supposedly, "eroticizing previously tabooed zones, time and relations, would minimize the manifestations of mere sexuality by integrating them into a far larger order." Indeed, "the libido would not simply reactivate precivilized and infantile stages but would also transform the perverted content of these stages."[45]

And yet, as far as Marcuse is concerned, behaviors traditionally regarded as perversions—like homosexuality and coprophilia (enjoyment of the smell, feel, or taste of feces)—particularly when employed in "a free libidinal relation," can be expressed in ways that are "compatible with normality in high civilization."[46] Marcuse even speaks affirmingly of the classical Greek notion that "the road to 'higher culture' leads through the true love of boys."[47] It is little wonder that Marcuse is regarded as having had a major influence not only on the sexual revolution of the 1960s in general but on the gay liberation movement in particular.[48]

Marcuse insisted that if we want to maintain our "mental health," our instincts must be expressed, not repressed. He thus called upon Western youth to "live and fight for Eros against Death" and to engage in counterorganization. He concluded by saying, "Today the fight for life, the fight for Eros, is the political fight."[49]

Marcuse's other lasting political contribution was his radical redefinition of tolerance, presented in his 1965 essay "Repressive Tolerance."[50] The concept of repressive tolerance was his way of referring to the kind of "pure" tolerance championed in classically liberal societies, typified by the writings of John Stuart Mill and expressed in the famous saying "I disapprove of what you say, but I will defend to the death your right to say it."

In Marcuse's estimation, while such a view of tolerance may sound good in theory, in practice, it fosters inequality and serves the cause of oppression. How so? Because "the stupid opinion is treated with the same respect as the intelligent one." The only way to overcome this problem is by "censorship, even pre-censorship." This is the way of "liberating tolerance." Marcuse expanded on his thinking as follows:

> Tolerance cannot be indiscriminate and equal with respect to the contents of expression, neither in word nor in deed; it cannot protect false words and wrong deeds which demonstrate that they contradict and counteract the possibilities of liberation. Such indiscriminate tolerance is justified in harmless debates, in conversation, in academic discussion; it is indispensable in the scientific enterprise, in private religion. But society cannot be indiscriminate where the pacification of existence, where freedom and happiness themselves are at stake: here, certain things cannot be said, certain ideas cannot be expressed, certain policies cannot be proposed, certain behavior cannot be permitted without making tolerance an instrument for the continuation of servitude.[51]

Marcuse went on to explain that such "liberation" would mean not only "the withdrawal of toleration of speech and assembly from groups and movements which promote aggressive policies, armament, chauvinism, discrimination on the grounds of race and religion" but also the oppression of those who "oppose the extension of public services, social security, medical care, etc."[52] In other words, "liberating tolerance" means (and Marcuse is completely candid about this) "intolerance against movements from the Right and toleration of movements from the Left."[53]

Here, again, we see something of the extent of Marcuse's commitment to a root-and-branch disintegration of Western culture. First Amendment thinking must go: "Heigh-ho, heigh-ho, Western Civ has got to go," chanted students at Yale. Marcuse himself put it this way:

> One can rightfully speak of a cultural revolution, since the protest is directed toward the whole cultural establishment, including the morality of existing society…there is one thing we can say with complete assurance: the traditional idea of revolution and the traditional strategy of revolution has ended…What we must undertake is a type of diffuse and dispersed disintegration of the system.[54]

THE LEGACY OF FRANKFURT

As Western Civilization courses seem to be on the demise with all the criticism against colonization, on the rise are not only teachings but also whole departments such as that found at Occidental College: "Critical Theory and Social Justice (CTSJ) is the only undergraduate academic department of its kind in the U.S."[55]

Cornell University recently hired a "critical pedagogy and equity librarian" whose sole job is to encourage "research justice,"—that is, to root out or decolonize white Western authors and build library-wide interest in critical information literacy.[56]

Critical theory is a form of incisive social critique that aims to undermine the status quo in the hope of changing society for the better: hope and change. It thus stands opposed to what Horkheimer called traditional theory, which aimed only to explain society. The way here had been paved by Marx, who, in the last of his famous "Theses on Feuerbach," had criticized philosophers for only having sought to interpret the world when "the point is to change it."[57] Critical theory is also indebted to Marx in that it took its starting point from his injunction to engage in a "ruthless critique of everything existing."[58] Like Marx, Horkheimer had no idea what kind of world such criticism would produce.

Whatever its "positive" desired outcomes, critical theory is essentially negative and destructive rather than positive and constructive. It's like skepticism, which has the benefit of never holding a false belief but only at the expense that it does so because, by definition, the negative philosophy results in never holding any beliefs whatsoever, including true beliefs. Critical theory was long on trenchant, unremitting criticism of any aspect of Western culture that was deemed to be oppressive or dehumanizing, but short on alternative proposals.

No proper assessment of the Frankfurt School can be made without appreciating the historical context in which it developed and its work was carried out. Living through the horrors of World War I (1914–1918), the failed Spartacist uprising in Germany (1919), the experience of the Great Depression (1929–1939), and the rise of both Nazism and antisemitism (1932–1945), not to mention, the absolute destruction of Hiroshima and Nagasaki by a powerful United States and the rise of McCarthyism with its watchful eye on Marxist infiltrators in America, gave the members of the institute plenty to critique and genuine reasons for pessimism. The dislocation of being "émigré scholars," the destructiveness of World War II, and finally, the Jewish Holocaust (1939–1945) only added to their anxieties. For all these reasons, it appeared to these Frankfurt School neo-Marxists "as if Western civilization had generated not human development but an unparalleled barbarism. They knew that something more was required from radical thought than the usual stale critique of capitalism."[59]

Critical theory needs to be understood against this backdrop. It is a reactionary theory, generated by the emotional, intellectual, and indeed, civilizational traumas of the first half of the twentieth century. The subtitle of Adorno's *Minima Moralia* (1951) illustrates the point powerfully: *Reflections on a Damaged Life*.

While majoritarian systems always have the potential to become tyrannous, and the track record of Western civilization is far from unblemished, to demonize the key elements and attainments of Western culture—for example, Christian morality, family, hierarchy, loyalty, tradition, the rule of law, sexual restraint, universal suffrage, property rights, patriotism, capitalism, and technology—is both myopic and ungrateful (and resentful envy). Furthermore, criticizing an imperfect system when you have no idea how to build a better one is more than idealistic; it is irresponsible.

To make matters worse, the school's skepticism extended beyond a general critique of Western civilization to a specific critique of Western rationality. Indeed, the proponents charged "instrumental reason" (i.e., practical or scientific reason) with producing the oppressive industrial culture of capitalism, as well as a heartless domination of nature.

In addition to this, the charge is philosophically vague, as critical theory never really defined what it meant by reason nor its relationship to truth. Perhaps the explanation for this is that (in Horkheimer's mind, at least) there is no absolute truth; rather, each historical era has its own truth.[60] This led Horkheimer to the conclusion that "logic is not independent of content"[61] and that truth "is whatever fosters social change."[62]

Beyond this, there is also the problem of hypocrisy. The members of the Frankfurt School were highly privileged individuals, each benefiting from the commercial success of his father and the education that wealth provided. In this, they followed in the footsteps of Marx. And yet their entire intellectual enterprise was "Oedipally fixated on bringing down the political system that had made their lives possible."[63] While such rebellion was not without its reasons, did they practice their own theory? The short answer is no. This earned them the ire of many classical Marxists, prompting Lukács to refer to the school as the "Grand Hotel Abyss."[64] These days, one need not look beyond all the capital being paid to the pop-level teachers of CRT and the millions they've raked in personally while burning down the Western house as they go (e.g., Ibram X. Kendi, Robin DiAngelo, and Patrisse Cullors).

The Frankfurt School is plagued by an unresolved tension between utopianism and pessimism. Critical theory turns out to be a manifestation of the very disease of which it purports to be the cure—a utopian dream of a classless society versus the reliability of a Christ-centered society.

Such was Marcuse's hatred of capitalism that he had long set himself to the task of "erasing the residues of puritan morality as well as the constraints of the Protestant ethic."[65] Note the reference to *The Protestant Work Ethic and the Spirit of Capitalism* (1905), a book by German sociologist Max Weber. Puritan ethics and ideas influenced the development of capitalism. In Weber's view, the Puritan wanted to work in his calling. We are not forced to do so. Yet 1 Corinthians 10:31 intimates that everything we do, including what we eat or drink, can be viewed through the lens of worship. Thus, working in the secular realm is sacred and a matter of worship. Even the most mundane work is to be a form of worship, a vocation (calling) instead of an occupation (job). Workmanship was spiritualized to worship.

It is easy to see why Marcuse was to become popular during the 1960s—the Vietnam War, the civil rights movement, and the student revolt all spoke for his theory. Consequently, at the Paris riots of May 1968, as well as those in Rome, students held up placards with the names "Marx/Mao/Marcuse" emblazoned on them, "hailing a new revolutionary trinity."[66] Nor is it surprising that Marcuse gave his public support to the leader of the Communist Party USA and member of the Black Panther Party, a former student of his who was a lesbian and CRT advocate who was awarded the Lenin Peace Prize, Angela Davis. *Time* magazine was right to call Marcuse "the guru of the New Left,"[67] and later, Davis was listed by that magazine as being among the 100 most influential people of 2020.[68] Davis ran on the Communist Party USA's presidential ticket, and she still teaches at UCLA. She claimed the aftermath of Hurricane Katrina in New Orleans in 2005 was the result of structural racism.[69]

Marcuse's impact also extends far beyond the 1960s. The main reason for this is that he "tutored a generation of young radicals, who, after the 1960s, gained a toehold in tenure by writing university press books."[70] Moreover, these radicals not only became lecturers and authors, but they also became "teachers, media employees, civil servants and of course politicians."[71] They and their later progeny are endowed with a sense of mission and the illusion of being on the side of moral righteousness and justice. In thousands of important but always influential positions of authority, they have succeeded in injecting entire generations with a disgust for their own culture and history and a selective inability to think. With their allegedly liberating tolerance, they have torn down natural or culturally nurtured inhibitions and replaced them with chaos.

CHRISTIAN RESPONSE

Marxists did not accept defeat after the failures of classical Marxism. They evolved. They learned from their errors, morphed, and even moved to greener pastures: America. The European Axis powers of World War II were deemed fascist as to the actual war, but there was another set of Axis powers who weren't national socialists and depended on the national socialists being destroyed in World War II. These global socialists, neo/cultural Marxists whose views stemmed mainly from Germany and Italy, migrated—or at least had their works translated, in the case of Gramsci—in order to infiltrate America. We've seen how they've done so in academia, media, all facets of culture, and even ecclesia (churches and parachurches). Their pervasive influence is deep and wide, and as Christians, we have our work cut out for us.

Contrary to those who think Jesus was a socialist—that is, Jesus saw things the way Marx (who was of Jewish descent) saw them—Jesus was consistent with the biblical revelation. Unlike Marx, Jesus' views didn't kill 100,000 people. Marx arguably proved to be worse than Hitler. We ought to have real compassion for people, like Jesus, not that drummed up by conflict theory that only divides. Our worldview isn't grounded in naturalism or some sort of revolutionary atheism connected to Marx. It is grounded in theism, whereby God is author of both Scripture and nature and has shown us, through revelation and reason, that human dignity and attending inalienable rights reside not in the sphere of secularism, where it is hard to become grounded. Rather, it is grounded by virtue of our being image bearers of God (Genesis 1:26-27). We are commissioned to be salt and light in the culture.

Strategically speaking, this most certainly includes leveraging our light in the most influential places, including the universities. We want to create conditions that enable us to present the light of the gospel while navigating conversations and cultures that oppose it.

Let us not forget that during the French, Russian, and Chinese revolutions, many Christians lost not only their views but their lives. This happened in Germany and Italy as well. We would be foolish to think America is somehow immune to conduct more typical of the world. What happened in Germany, which at the time was one of the most educated countries in the history of the world, can happen in America, another one of the most educated countries in the history of the world. We cannot remain silent. But to speak up, we need to understand our audience to know what to say, when to say it, and why.

As we'll see, even cultural Marxism has changed. Like a chameleon, it has continued to reach deep into the American heart, even into our religions. It has successfully infiltrated the West, and America in particular. This is where pastors, shepherds, and parents and grandparents must seek to understand enemy ideologies that seek to destroy the Christian world and life view.

9

CULTURAL MARXISM AND THE POSTMODERN TURN

Political correctness,[1] the new intolerant-tolerance (i.e., repressive tolerance) and ever-increasing erotic liberty are part of the legacy of cultural Marxism. Similarly, Antonio Gramsci's ideas have generated rotten fruit in the rise of today's resentful victimhood culture (or class consciousness), as well as in the fact that in the fields of media and academia (and politics too), the "long march through the institutions" is well underway to being virtually complete.[2]

The main problem with all the conspiratorial versions of cultural Marxism is the same: For something to be a conspiracy, it needs to be a secret. But there never was anything secret about the publications of Gramsci or the members of the Frankfurt School and any of their disciples. Rather, contemporary proponents of cultural Marxism (whether or not they own the label) are usually loud and proud, making no secret of their aims and ambitions.

This highlights the most important issue of all. The philosopher Alasdair MacIntyre, a former Marxist turned Christian, once described Marxism as "a secularism formed by the gospel which is committed to the problem of power and justice and therefore to themes of redemption and renewal."[3] Its diagnosis is superficial and its cure fatal. Marxism, in all its various iterations, is a corruption of the gospel—together with its own false prophet (Marx), false Bible (*Das Kapital*), false doctrine (conflict theory), false apostles (Lenin, Stalin, Mao, Marcuse), and false hope (a communist utopia).[4] Therefore, the fact that cultural Marxism is a real ideology making a real impact on our world is not good news. It must be confronted and countered.

It has been said that Marxism precipitated postmodernism. Stephen Hicks, an atheist philosopher and expert on postmodernism, has argued that it was Marxist thinkers who led us to postmodernism.[5] The claim is not that Marxism became postmodernism. Rather, a segment of Marxist thinkers became the leading figures of the postmodernist movement. The postmodern vanguard set the trajectory and tone for the postmodern milieu and intellectual world.

The four dominant figureheads were Michel Foucault (1926–1984), Jacques Derrida (1930–2004), Jean-François Lyotard (1924–1998), and Richard Rorty (1931–2007). As we'll see, Foucault and Marcuse have not fallen far from the Freudian tree of sexual perversion. All four postmodernists were Marxist sympathizers or activists. If you're paying attention to the historical line, you can see how close they are in proximity to the Frankfurt School of critical theory and of Antonio Gramsci.

But first, let's see what they've had to say about their view of truth and knowledge in a postmodern perspective. Michel Foucault said, "It is meaningless to speak in the name of—or against—Reason, Truth, or Knowledge."[6] Richard Rorty helps us understand this by saying it's not that postmodernism is true or that it somehow provides knowledge, but that effort must be given

> to avoid hinting that this suggestion gets something right, that my sort of philosophy corresponds to the way things really are. For this talk of correspondence brings back just the idea my sort of philosopher wants to get rid of, the idea that the world or the self has an intrinsic nature.[7]

The goal is to deconstruct the notion that reason, truth, or the very idea that our thought somehow corresponds to reality—that a statement, sentence, or thought, squares with the way things are—is laughable. With inspiration,

Jacques Derrida helps us see the connection with the philosophy of Marxism—he explains that "deconstruction never had meaning or interest, at least in my eyes, than as a radicalization, that is to say, also within the tradition of a certain Marxism, in a certain spirit of Marxism."[8]

Yet again, in the words of Richard Rorty, truth is "what our peers will, *ceteris paribus*, let us get away with saying."[9] Truth is relative and it simply reduces to power. That is why we can refer to it as political truth or political correctness.[10] Putting this together, one of their disciples nicely sums it up declaring that postmodernism "seeks not to find the foundation and the conditions of truth but to exercise power for the purpose of social change."[11]

We see then that their postmodernism is anti-realist—it holds that we cannot speak meaningfully about, or know, objective reality. Instead, it substitutes a sociolinguistic account of constructing reality. Neither reason, nor any other method, can get us to reality. The best we can do is construct our own reality via sociolinguistic groups. And because truth simply reduces to power, we're talking about group power or identity politics structuring political truth. This is then done via language games of group dynamics.

Hicks, a modernist, understands postmodernism to be an attack on modernism and on reason itself. He says, "The Enlightenment confidence in reason, however, upon which all progress had been based, had always been philosophically incomplete and vulnerable."[12] In my view, modernism is incomplete because it is divorced from a stable grounding in theism. And this is the case for many reasons, not the least of which is that modernity, at best, disregarded revelation in favor of rationalism or empiricism as the ways of knowing, and at worst, dismissed it as rubbish to be cast into the flames.

Second, without an adequate grounding in theism, modernism is hard pressed to account for morality and meaning as well as certain notions in America's founding documents, such as inalienable rights endowed by our Creator. Theism can easily account for human dignity, which all mankind possesses by virtue of its being grounded in the image of God. All human life matters and matters equally, which carries with it moral obligations that we have toward one another, without which we can hardly talk about human rights. Civil rights grounded in a social contract are insufficient because legality isn't moral, per se. Legality shouldn't determine morality, but vice versa.

Our civil rights must be grounded in deeper metaphysical rights by virtue of our membership in human persons as such.

THE CLIMATE OF COLLECTIVISM AND THE STRATEGY OF THE NEW LEFT

In postmodernism, the focus is often on skepticism leading to relativism. But the problem lurking here is with postmodern politics. As Hicks points out, "If a deep skepticism about reason and the consequent subjectivism and relativism were the most important parts of the story of postmodernism, then we would expect to find that postmodernists represent a roughly random distribution of commitments across the political spectrum."[13]

But that is most definitely not what we find. Postmodernists are monolithically left-wing thinkers and activists. The four major figureheads and all their major disciples are demonstrably so. As Derrida long ago remarked, "My hope as a man of the left, is that certain elements of deconstruction will have served or—because the struggle continues, particularly in the United States—will serve to politicize or repoliticize the left with regard to positions which are not simply academic."[14] He wanted activism from the left and for the left. Hicks says, "Of the major names in the postmodernist movement, there is not a single figure who is not Left-wing in a serious way."[15]

Postmodernists have taken to heart that, in the last analysis, everything is political. It's all about power—power and privilege. Postmodernists claim that epistemology is merely a tool for power, that all claims to rationality and objectivity mask oppressive political agendas. Yet Marxists used to say scientific socialism represented their movement.[16] Socialists once argued that the validity of socialism could be proven by evidence and rational analysis. But all their claims were shown false, and hopes were dashed. Hicks observes that "postmodernism is born of the marriage of Left politics and skeptical epistemology."[17]

Many French intellectuals joined the Communist Party during the early 1950s following World War II, including Michel Foucault—or they were at least very strong sympathizers, like Jacques Derrida. Left-wing socialists were happy that right-wing socialists (i.e., fascists) were utterly defeated in World

War II. But repeatedly, there have been crises of faith in Marxist predictions theoretically and empirically. Foucault became disenchanted with Marxism's credibility as practiced. Seeing what was happening in the USSR under Stalin, for example, dispirited many. Derrida reported that many began to drift away even at that time:

> For many of us, a *certain* (and I emphasize certain) end of communist Marxism did not await the recent collapse of the USSR and everything that depends on it throughout the world. All that started—all that was even *deja vu*, indubitably—at the beginning of the '50s.[18]

By 1956, left-wing socialism was dealt a devastating blow (in contrast with what might be denoted right-wing socialism, or national socialism or fascism). Nikita Khrushchev revealed Stalin's actions toward millions of his own citizens—he had tortured, deprived, and executed many of them, as well as put many into labor camps. His cruelty made right-wing socialism look small by comparison and dashed hopes for many for a socialist utopia. The fascists had lost, leaving Marxists to look to the USSR, but with increasing concern. The questionable morality of the USSR caused many to shift their devotion from Leninism to China's Maoism, until revelations of the horrors there during the early 1960s showed China to be worse than the USSR. Cuba was next, then Vietnam, then Cambodia, and many new hopefuls were on the horizon, but none ever panned out. Left-wing socialism has killed more than 100 million of its own citizens.[19] This problem with left-wing socialism was compounded by the fact that capitalist and classically liberal countries were booming economically and going in the right direction morally.

At first, leftist believers responded to the crisis by changing their ethical standard, claiming that none of the socialistically monstrous countries were truly socialistic, including the national socialists of Germany. This is the familiar excuse that "socialism has never truly been tried." Those who opposed capitalism claimed it causes poverty, but that's not what was happening. So socialists shifted their rhetoric from the mantra from "each according to his ability, to each according to his need" to "equality." They no longer argued that people were failing to get their needs met in capitalism. They were getting their fair share. Yet they weren't getting an *equal* share. "Equality" served as opportune rhetoric because Western governments used that language. So, the left began focusing on poverty in the 1960s, claiming that capitalism causes not absolute poverty but relative poverty. This sense of envy would help the proletariat experience psychological oppression. Leftists also began shifting their focus from internationalism to narrower subdivisions of humans, like women and racial and ethnic minorities, carrying the broadly Marxist themes of conflict and oppression into discussions of equality.

Another strategy was to claim that wealth is bad. Capitalism was so good at producing wealth it was creating a dulling sensation for people who could no longer feel or sense their alienation and oppression. This was a strategy used by Marcuse, who had become the leading philosopher of what was being branded the New Left. His views were being promulgated heavily in the English-speaking world, especially America. Following Marx, Marcuse believed that the purpose of the proletariat was to be a revolutionary class. But under capitalism, the proletariat had now become comfortable with his goodies rather than miserable. Marcuse, along with members of the Frankfurt School, had begun marrying Freudian psychology and Marxist philosophy and saying that capitalism not only oppresses the masses but also represses them psychologically. During the 1960s, Marcuse's work inspired many radicals to the point of Maoist violence. Indeed, Marcuse met with Vietnamese (Mao-inspired) Marxists in Europe during this time.

The New Left was facing collapse just as the older left had. What would be the next step? In 1974, Marcuse was asked whether he thought the New Left was history. He replied, "I don't think it's dead, and it will resurrect in the universities."[20] Indeed.

Recall now the prominent figureheads of postmodernism (Foucault, Lyotard, Derrida, and Rorty). Foucault was a member of the French Communist Party from 1950 to 1953,[21] eventually declaring himself a Maoist in 1968, the year of the famed 1968 riots (the same riots with the repetitive chant "Marx, Mao, and Marcuse"). He went on to teach in US universities such as UCLA, UC Berkeley, NYU, and others. He is the single most-cited scholar in all the humanities.

Lyotard studied under Foucault and worked for a dozen years for a radical-left socialist group. He taught at numerous US universities, such as UC Irvine, Emory, Johns Hopkins, Yale, UCSD, UC Berkeley, and others. Derrida never joined the party but was certainly a French Communist Party sympathizer. He taught at UC Irvine and did graduate work at Harvard. Rorty considered the Socialist Party candidate whom his parents worked for (A. Philip Randolph) one of his great heroes. He taught at Princeton, University of Virginia, and Stanford.

All had remarkable influence in top universities, thus spreading their seed for generations. All were born within a seven-year period and at the time critical theory began. All studied philosophy (and some psychology) at top universities. All were associated with Marxism, were committed to leftist politics, and entered their academic careers during the 1950s, living through the crises socialism experienced in the 1950s and 1960s. By the 1970s, they were at the top of their academic game and had achieved a high standing among the intellectual left.[22] When the left collapsed, it turned to these men who were the most up to speed on the latest trends in the field of the theory of knowledge. They signaled the direction for the academic left.

If one is an academic foe of capitalism, one's weapons are words and rhetoric. *Rhetoric* refers to the art of persuasion. As far back as Aristotle, rhetoric has been defined in terms of logos, ethos, and pathos. That is, logos has to do with logic; ethos relates to ethics, credibility, or competence; and pathos is about emotional connectivity. And if one's epistemology tells one that words are not about truth or reality, then the battle becomes rhetorical in the language games played leading to the politics of social change. Rhetoric masks rationality, but its focus of persuasion is on ethos and pathos for social change. Remember that for postmodernists, language doesn't connect to reality "out there." Rather, it connects only to other languages, and we can never escape language. It becomes self-referentially coherent only as it is used. Rorty said, "I'm not going to offer arguments against the vocabulary I want to replace. Instead, I am going to try to make the vocabulary I favor look attractive…"[23] As we learned at the beginning of the book, "language is the way we construct reality." So for these social justice activists, its design is to circle the wagon train, create new social discourses, and attract the sentiments of its audience via virtuous victimology.

Consider the expressions surrounding abortion. The language by those on the pro-choice side uses rhetoric like "reproductive justice," "women's health," or simply "pro-choice." Or consider the way to persuade public sentiment on LGBTQ+ with language like "love is love," "born that way," "homophobia," or "transphobia." Conflict theory is the idea that social order is maintained by power and domination over the otherwise underprivileged. Given the context of conflict theory that all Marxists adopt, in a scenario involving conflict resolution, the sort of tool one needs in a language is the development of a weapon. That is, weaponizing language.

Unsurprisingly, then, the left regularly uses ad hominem attacks against people rather than arguments about truth. This is a logical fallacy in critical thinking, but even critical thinking has now been hijacked by critical theory. For example, consider the LGBTQ+ mantra "hate or celebrate." If you say you disagree with any belief or behavior expressed by LGBTQ+ adherents, you will be blasted as a hater. That's true about race matters when it comes to critical race theory. In this day, it appears that it is worse to be called a *racist* than a *rapist*. The left regularly attempts to silence the opposition rather than argue with them. That's why they claim that debate is a form of hate. Cancel culture comes almost entirely from the left. Truth or falsity is not the issue. What matters primarily is the language's effectiveness in achieving socially desired outcomes.

WHEN THEORY CLASHES WITH FACT

We've had two centuries to try socialism in every way conceivable, and defenders of it keep making excuses for why it never works. The latest failure is Venezuela, the most oil-rich country in South America. But oil is no substitute for toilet paper, which is hard to come by in that dismal socialist country. Recall, as John Adams said, "Facts are stubborn things." But what happens when socialism is repeatedly found wanting? If one is interested in truth, one throws out anything that doesn't measure up. But truth and rationality aren't virtues in postmodernism. As noted, leftist Richard Rorty, the author of *Achieving Our Country: Leftist Thought in Twentieth-Century America*, has said, "I think that a good Left is a [political] party that always thinks about the future and doesn't care much about our past sins."[24]

Postmodern thinkers see their job as a sort of what Hicks calls "reverse Thrasymacheanism."[25] In Plato's *Republic*, Thrasymachus was a Sophist. Plato hated the Sophists, who weren't viewed as real philosophers. Their arguments sounded good on the surface, but like most politicians, ultimately, they were terrible and they would manipulate an audience for selfish gain. Postmodernists are seeking to rehabilitate Sophists. The Sophist Thrasymachus said that "justice is the advantage of the stronger," or paraphrased, "justice is in the interest of the strongest party."[26] In other words, might makes right. This was essentially the position of Nietzsche, who influenced Hitler to "roll in the tanks" as it were with respect to the Aryan race having the natural right to conquer. But postmodernists are reversing Thrasymachus's concept of justice to be on the side of the victim or oppressed. That is, "justice is in the interest of the weakest party." They want to make certain identity groups feel victimized or oppressed—to conjure up sympathy or empathy as part of the pathos or suffering on behalf of made-up victims so they can divide people. They trade on the emotions of resentment and envy. They want to divide and conquer. As one leading postmodernist (and Marxist sympathizer) says, the theory of postmodernism "seeks not to find the foundation and the conditions of truth but to exercise power for the purpose of social change."[27]

Postmodernists use contradictory discourse as a political strategy. In postmodern discourse, truth is consistently rejected. Consider these pairs of ideas:

"Truth is relative" and "Postmodernism tells it like it is."

"All cultures are equally deserving" and "Western culture is uniquely destructive and bad."

"Values are subjective" and "Sexism and racism are evil."

The contradictions here reveal relativism in one breath and absolutism or dogmatism in the next. Postmodernists use such expressions and are frequently charged with being contradictory. But they are often content with living in this way because they have an agenda. It is a fair question to ask which side of the contradiction, relativism or absolutism, is the one they're most committed to, and which is the one they use for their agenda.

Consider some additional statements by postmodernists that put attitude over and against the facts of history:

"America is deeply racist." Yet postmodernists know that America is the only country ever to terminate slavery at the cost of its own blood and resources. It was called the Civil War (1861–1865).

"America is deeply sexist." But postmodernists know that America is a great place for women's rights. A comparative study of the treatment of women based on national laws motivated by worldview undercurrents makes this clear (e.g., Islam in Saudi Arabia, atheism in China, Hinduism in India, and Christianity in America).

"America cruelly exploits its poor." But postmodernists know that America's poor are rich by many nations' standards. America's poorest, the homeless, have access to shelters, three meals per day, and free entry in hospital emergency rooms. Many low-income households get food stamps, some people receive free college, and more. Even illegal immigrants who aren't US citizens realize this, or they wouldn't risk their lives on the trek to America.

So, are postmodernists committed to relativism while using absolutism rhetorically, or are they committed to absolutism while using relativism rhetorically, or do they knowingly embrace contradictions without pause or psychological shiver?

The first option doesn't seem very plausible. If postmodernists are committed to relativism, then maybe they're living on their borrowed capital of the Marxist leftist value system without recognizing it because they are uniformly—to the man—associated with leftist politics. Postmodernism is thus firmly a political movement.

The second option seems to indicate that when postmodernists are backed into a corner in an argument, they simply put on the skeptic's hat for convenience. When a leftist wants to keep Christian critics off his back, he'll quickly cite Jesus out of convenience: "Don't judge," all while still holding dogmatic judgments himself about the Christian. This option, then, simply uses relativism as a strategy but does not believe it. This also has merit given Marcuse's double standard of tolerance as articulated in his concept of repressive tolerance. At the end of the day, no one is really a relativist. Everyone has a threshold area of things they consider right or wrong beyond mere opinion.

Third, perhaps because contradiction is a form of psychological destruction, it's fine to live with it. Yet it doesn't matter for postmodernists because for them, everything is meaningless anyway. Nihilism is close to the heart of postmodernism.

Whatever the case, it is clear postmodernists have a leftist agenda, one that is indubitably poised to subvert Christianity:

> We try to arrange things so that students who enter as bigoted, homophobic, religious fundamentalists will leave college with views more like our own...The fundamentalist parents of our fundamentalist students think that the entire "American liberal establishment" is engaged in a conspiracy. The parents have a point. Their point is that we liberal teachers no more feel in a symmetrical communication situation when we talk with bigots than do kindergarten teachers talking with their students...When we American college teachers encounter religious fundamentalists, we do not consider the possibility of reformulating our own practices of justification so as to give more weight to the authority of the Christian scriptures. Instead, we do our best to convince these students of the benefits of secularization. We assign first-person accounts of growing up homosexual to our homophobic students for the same reasons that German schoolteachers in the postwar period assigned *The Diary of Anne Frank*...You have to be educated in order to be...a participant in our conversation... So we are going to go right on trying to discredit you in the eyes of your children, trying to strip your fundamentalist religious community of dignity, trying to make your views seem silly rather than discussable. We are not so inclusivist as to tolerate intolerance such as yours...I don't see anything *herrschaftsfrei* [domination free] about my handling of my fundamentalist students. Rather, I think those students are lucky to find themselves under the benevolent *herrschaft* [domination] of people like me, and to have escaped the grip of their frightening, vicious, dangerous parents...I am just as provincial and contextualist as the Nazi teachers who made their students read *Der Stürmer*; the only difference is that I serve a better cause.[28]

It bears listening to and believing postmodernists when they're clear about what that agenda entails.

These ideas have morphed over the last half century, but the core has remained. Once you begin understanding these main ideologies running through our universities, you begin to see them everywhere in culture and cannot unsee them. DEI everywhere finally makes sense, from the corporate world and government to churches and parachurch ministries. Most everything downstream comes from upstream, academia. Critical race theory applies the ideas to race, queer theory to gender and sex (which are allegedly distinctly psychological and biological), critical pedagogy to education, postcolonialism to colonialism, "research justice" to the books carried in libraries and curriculum even by Christian ministries, medicine, sports, and eventually even to icebergs. Can anyone be surprised at the secularizing of our culture as generation after generation of students attend these secular baptismal fonts called universities?

Christians have remarkable resources. Most simply have no idea what they are or where to find them. But Christian spiritual and intellectual leaders should know where to find them and be able to unlock the potential for masses of Christians, otherwise defenseless, to meet these subversive ideologies head-on, and do so persuasively and graciously. A thoughtful sort of Christianity might be foreign to many Christians today, but that needn't be so, as it isn't true of the majority of Christian history. We can and must unlock the resources for Christians to adequately address our cultural thought currents as if lives depend on it—because they do.

So, how can and should we respond to these currents rapidly flooding into our culture? To this we now turn.

PART 3

HOW SHOULD WE RESPOND?

A Third Revolution

*Cultures change from the top down,
rarely if ever from the bottom up.*

JAMES DAVISON HUNTER, *To Change the World*

*Though we walk in the flesh, we are not waging war according
to the flesh. For the weapons of our warfare are not of the
flesh but have divine power to destroy strongholds. We destroy
arguments and every lofty opinion raised against the knowledge
of God, and take every thought captive to obey Christ.*

2 CORINTHIANS 10:3-5 (ESV)

10

IS CHRISTIANITY GOOD FOR THE WORLD?

We've seen the nature, source, and significant size of the problems we're facing. What can be done to thwart the coming apocalypse? We must begin with realizing that the sky is not falling and that this problem is not the apocalypse. The durability of America is being significantly tested, and we're getting ever closer to the breaking point, such that if the trajectory is to change, it will demand decisive action and focus. There are quite a few practical steps Christians can take to turn the tide on what seems to be a very grim future. But it requires a thoughtful sort of Christianity. If there is to be a renaissance of Christian thought, it will take a concerted effort. It does not require a reconquest of the universities, but it does involve a substantial Christian presence.

First, because the ideological currents creating this mess are significant, we need to be able to respond to our culture with answers to some basic questions (especially against the assaults from scientific naturalism and postmodern cultural Marxism that dominate the intellectual landscape): Is Christianity good or bad for the world? Is belief in God rational? And does the Christian God exist?

Second, we need to think about our institutions and how we can and must play a part in the effort, from pastors and parents to educators and philanthropists. We need to forge alliances and think strategically about targeting certain influential institutions, one of the most influential being the university.

Let's begin by considering the question of whether Christianity is good for the world.

THE BENEVOLENT IMPRINT OF JESUS IS UNMATCHED IN HISTORY

Whatever one's evaluation of whether Christianity is good or bad for the world, the greatest mark left in history seems to be the imprint of Jesus. Earning a PhD and speaking eight languages by age 22, Yale historian Jaroslav Pelikan minced no words in the introduction to his book *Jesus Through the Centuries*:

> Regardless of what anyone may personally think or believe about Him, Jesus of Nazareth has been the dominant figure in the history of Western culture for almost 20 centuries. If it were possible, with some sort of super magnet, to pull up out of that history every scrap of metal bearing at least a trace of His name, how much would be left?[1]

Harvard psychology professor and Jewish atheist Steven Pinker authored a recent bestseller, *Enlightenment Now*.[2] Recall, the book is so influential that the billionaire Bill Gates provided a cover endorsement dubbing it as his "new favorite book of all time." The volume is an apologetic, a defense, for secular humanism and science for that which made the world good. Yet Pinker seems to offer somewhat of a revisionary history compared to the work by Pelikan, a historian.

Pinker's message is that reason, science, and humanism—which he claims are the key themes of the Enlightenment—have led to mass progress in most areas of life. No doubt they have contributed. He asserts that they are our best means of continuing this progress into the future. Concerned, he thinks these ideals are not consistently upheld and are often under attack. Therefore, he calls people to fortify and defend them against counter-Enlightenment enemies like socialism and religion.

The goodness or badness of Christianity isn't the full concern. While we should not believe something simply based on how good or useful it is, it is certainly relevant, especially in an era when Christianity's critics claim that Christianity is not only false but harmful and an enemy of human flourishing. Showing Christianity's net good creates plausibility for its veracity, especially if the reasons for its goodness connect to its truth-claims. Goodness and truth aren't mutually exclusive, and they're both important.

Undoubtedly, Christians have been guilty of harm and evil in the past. We cannot ignore that. But neither should we forget the good that Christians have done. And to be fair, one must also separate the malicious actions performed by professing believers away from the teachings of the founder. Such actors may not be genuine believers. If they are, then such actions often turn out to be the illogical outworkings of the teaching of Jesus—that is, hypocrisy—and thus aren't properly Christian actions even if performed by actual rather than merely professing Christians.

The existential question about God asks whether God exists, but the axiological question about God addresses the question of what value-impact, if any, God's existence does (or would) have on our world. Two antithetical answers emerge at the top. Protheism is the view that God's existence does (or would) add value to our world. Antitheism, by contrast, is the view that God's existence does (or would) detract from the value of our world.

One way of approaching our first question from a protheistic stance is to locate values or goods whose existence entails God's existence (i.e., they couldn't exist without God). A more modest approach would be to locate such goods or values that are widely considered such and to show how their existence makes God's existence more likely. That is the endeavor here. The argument is not that some of the goods couldn't emerge aside from Christian theism, but that they didn't and there are good reasons for this.

Most in the West don't realize the richness of their heritage. Secular humanists like Pinker point to the various goods that made the West great yet fail to see that Christianity offers the best explanatory power and scope that underwrites the existence of those goods. In essence, such people are living on borrowed capital from the Christian worldview, just as Pinker is doing while waxing eloquent from the fruitful perch of Christendom's first university established in the new world. If the Christian God exists, then He would make a substantive difference bringing added value to the world. We will consider some widely affirmed values or goods whose most prominent manifestations are best explained by Christianity.

What Is Good?

We often think of *good* as an exclusively ethical notion. But it is broader than ethics. Take for example, health. What constitutes good health is neither subjective nor relative; health is an objective notion providing some normativity in terms of how humans should behave to flourish as healthy individuals. Artifacts are like this too. A pair of scissors is good when it cuts well, when it functions properly as designed in the mind of the artisan.

When considering various goods, it is important to distinguish between something that is good *for us* and something that is merely good *to us*—the first is objectively good and the second only subjectively good. The former is desirable, whereas the latter is only desired (a preference). It is a happy occurrence when they're aligned—that is, when we can cultivate our desires such that they align with what is most desirable. It is there where we discover human flourishing.

For example, parents may wrestle with the same challenge my wife and I have—namely, convincing our kids that broccoli is good and cotton candy is, well, not so good. Only the former is good for kids in an objective sense, leading to their flourishing. Our job as parents is to cultivate tastes such that they harmoniously come to desire what is desirable. In this respect, *desire* is related to *desirable* much like *belief* is related to *truth*. Just as it is appropriate that we should want our beliefs to correspond with what is real, for the sake of truth, so it is appropriate that our desires correspond with what is desirable, for the sake of goodness. Indeed, we want to look at desirable goods as a clue to what is true. Being and goodness are first principles in theoretical and practical reason.

Prosperity, Jesus, and Responsibility of Persons and Societies

Systems that are helpful to human flourishing are desirable for our good, whereas ones that detract from it are not. Absent from the minds of many is the reality that Jesus impacted economics long before it was a field of study. Pinker endorses the capitalist enterprise as a means of greatest prosperity, as a civilizational good, and shows how capitalism has lifted man from abject poverty. He mentions Adam Smith, the moral philosopher and economist. But he fails to see that the father of modern capitalism was a Christian who appealed to the "invisible hand of God" to reveal the brilliance in the working of free market systems in his classic work *An Inquiry into the Nature and Causes of the Wealth of Nations* (1776).

More than a century later, sociologists were apt to explain the phenomenal growth of wealth in the world. In the late eighteenth and early nineteenth centuries, most of the world was in extreme poverty. But today, billions of people have been lifted out thanks, in part, to capitalism, and billions more have been helped by charity. While Pinker likes to credit this to secularism, his Harvard colleague and department head of economics disagrees. Benjamin Friedman defends the vital role Christianity played in the birth of capitalism, even if the contemporary scene has long since divorced itself from its origin.[3] The contemporary scene, we might say, is living on borrowed capital.

Pinker demurs concerning Marxism as a system for social good. Granted, this is disputed by Marxists, but in terms of bringing people out of poverty, it is an observable fact that credit goes to capitalism, not to socialism. Notably, no Marxist leader ever took his own poison when the revolution occurred, and the dictatorship of the proletariat came to power to "share all things in common." Leaders like Lenin, Stalin, Mao, Castro, Pol Pot, Kim Jong-il, and so on never lived in tents of squalor like their people, whom the leaders claimed to liberate. Their quest for social good led to their killing more than 100 million of their own citizens.

Far from Marxism's socialistic impetus of noncharitable, coercive, statist redistribution, "from each according to their ability to each according to their need,"[4] Jesus modeled giving by giving Himself. The early church followed, and it continued down the line through history. They gave to the poor via voluntary charity. Marx, despite his Judeo-Christian heritage, did not follow suit. We might say that Jesus was the more faithful of the two to the principles of Judaism. Judaism (including most of the Jewish authors of the New Testament) taught that if a man doesn't work, then he shouldn't eat. The biblical world embraced private property and the responsibility and fruit of one's labor. Without property, the commandment forbidding theft is pointless. Abuses notwithstanding in the Industrial Revolution, which began in the English world and was criticized by the likes of Karl Marx, proper use has revealed great fruit and even spawned certain virtues from self-interest (not selfishness). Among these are innovation, excellence, wealth accumulation, hard work, and so on.

The great sociologist Max Weber first observed a correlation between being Protestant and being involved in business, such that the notion of (spiritual) "calling" for Protestants shouldn't be relegated to being a minister or missionary. Wealth making took on a spiritual character. Reformational thinking broke down the wall between priest and parishioner with its emphasis on "calling," previously applicable only to pastors and missionaries. The motto was that every member was a minister in his own calling. He argues that the modern spirit of capitalism sees profit as an end in itself and the pursuit of profit as virtuous. Protestantism offers a concept of the worldly "calling" and gives worldly activity a religious character.[5] While important, this alone cannot explain the need to pursue profit.

One branch of Protestantism, Calvinism, does provide this explanation. Calvinists believe in predestination—that God has already determined who is saved. As Calvinism developed, a deep psychological need for clues about whether one was genuinely saved (or elect) arose, and many Calvinists (even long after some had shed their Calvinism) looked to their hard work and fruitful success in worldly activity for those clues of confirmation.

Thus, they came to value profit and material success as signs of God's favor. Other Protestant groups had similar attitudes to a lesser degree. Weber argues that this new attitude broke down the traditional economic system, paving the way for modern capitalism and thinkers like Adam Smith. So it doesn't matter whether the work is on Main Street or Wall Street, many today fail to make explicit reference to the Christian heritage of yesterday. They live on the borrowed capital of the Christian worldview.

The common caricature of capitalistic greed doesn't apply when grounded in the Christian ethic of love and treating one's workers well ("The worker is worthy of his wages"). However, once capitalism emerged, the Protestant values were no longer necessary, and its ethos took on a life of its own. Today, we are locked into the spirit of capitalism because it is so useful for modern economic activity to the benefit of human flourishing. Even if capitalism is sometimes charged with being inspired by greed and socialism by envy, these are spiritual and moral problems to which the Christian ethic has answers.

Jesus, not secular humanism, is the greatest motivator for charitable distribution of wealth in history. As a Jew, He embraced the sanctity of human life, a high view of humanity, and provisional Christian humanism, whereby property ownership was a matter of stewardship, and He taught about our responsibilities owed to others. Jesus taught and demonstrated the highest form of love. Christianity is the largest movement in history. Followers recognize this movement's substantial value-impact on civilization. Hence, there is some natural predictability downstream. The compassionate Jesus community emerged very early on. This fact is recognized by even the most ardent atheist thinkers. Princeton moral philosopher Peter Singer confesses,

> The doctrine of the sanctity of all human life, and the seriousness with which the killing of any member of our species is regarded, mark off the Christian ethical and cultural tradition from almost all others...That very many different societies have seen no moral objection to abortion and infanticide is, I think, well-known. Even if we restrict our attention to infanticide, the list is almost endless...Both Plato, in the *Republic*, and Aristotle, in his *Politics*, propose that the state command the killing of deformed infants... We find nothing resembling the doctrine that the lives of all born of human parents are sacred in the pre-Christian literature. There can be no doubt that the change in European attitudes to abortion and infanticide is a product of the coming of Christianity.[6]

Christian Humanism and Organized Charity

Far more beneficial than secular humanism is Christian humanism. When the abortion issue is brought up, it is common to hear critics claim that Christians—the most prominent defenders of the right to life—are concerned only for the preborn but not for the postborn. A favorite scathing aphorism from critics of the pro-life movement is "Life begins at conception and ends at birth." But nothing could be further from the truth.[7] There are nearly

600 Planned Parenthood centers in America[8] that offer health services in addition to beheading, ripping off limbs, and burning babies alive—the elaborate results of abortion methods in these "women's health" facilities. But there are more than 3,000 pregnancy centers[9] that offer women's health and pregnancy services that provide compassionate medical care for mothers and children that don't include abortion services. Furthermore, they offer help to mothers and their babies long after a child is born. Numerous churches offer personal help to young mothers. Given the Christian impetus toward life and loving the poor, it is unsurprising that the Christian community is responsible for more than twice that of the general population when it comes to adoption.[10]

Critics should consider that the name of a hospital in which they've received care likely bears a religious denominational title in the hospital's name. Examples include Saint Elizabeth, Presbyterian Hospital; Saint Jude, Methodist Hospital; Saint Mark, Good Samaritan; and so on. Hospitals were invented by and exponentially multiplied because of the efforts of Jesus' apprentices following the Council of Nicaea in AD 325. The idea of the hospital rose to prominence in the fourth century with the building of Basil's hospital in the city of Caesarea in the Roman Empire. Basil the Great, a monastic leader, church bishop, theologian, and one who suffered from sickness himself, envisioned and established the first hospital.[11] A mere accident of history? I think not. Followers follow.

Today, inspired by Christ, the largest disaster relief organizations in the USA with operations around the world are the Red Cross, Salvation Army, Samaritans Pursue, and Southern Baptist Convention. Not only were they founded by Christians, but they continue to be staffed predominantly by Christians and have given birth to global movements. They work in tandem. For example, every hot meal served by the Red Cross in the US is prepared by the Southern Baptists.[12] The largest child relief and adoption organizations are likewise Christian.[13] The same goes for anti-sex-trafficking organizations that assist women and girls to escape their situations and work with local governments and other agencies to get them help and back into society.[14] America has become the most prosperous nation in the history of the world, and it is also the economic mothership of organized charity across the globe. Notably, America is among the most heavily influenced by Christianity.

Private Charity and Mentality

Beyond institutions, when it comes to individual charitable giving, on average, conservative Christians are the most charitable. By conservative, I mean those who see the Bible as God's Word and the need for personal conversion and apprenticeship to Jesus. Ironically, they're even more charitable to secular causes than are secular people. And this goes beyond monetary charity to other commitments like giving blood.

One professor at Syracuse University, Arthur Brooks, admits that he began as a liberal and skeptic about the thesis that religious conservatives were the largest group of givers per capita. But after having spent decades researching philanthropy in the US and Europe, he was converted. He writes, "In years of research, I have never found a measurable way in which secularists are more charitable than religious people."[15] From his research, he observes:

> Religious people were 25 percentage points more likely to give than secularists (91 to 66 percent). Religious people were also 23 points more likely to volunteer (67 to 44 percent)…religious people—who, per family earned exactly the same amount as secular people, $49,000—gave about 3.5 times more money per year…They also volunteered more than twice as often.[16]

Additionally, the data shows that "People who pray every day…are 30 percentage points more likely to give money to charity than people who never pray"[17] Similarly, "The churchgoer will be 9 points more likely than the secularist to give to non-religious charities…25 points more likely to volunteer for secular causes."[18] Nationwide survey evidence shows that "if the workplace has a blood drive and a colleague asks them to donate, the churchgoer is two-thirds more likely to say yes than the secularist."[19]

Brooks shows that even one's view about the role of government has measurable consequences. Someone affirming strong governmental care for the poor will give far less than someone skeptical about the government's role. Data also shows that people who have children are, on average, more generous than those who don't. Christians have a theological, not merely sociological, view of the family. People who were raised in church, even if they don't currently attend, are more generous than those who never regularly attended church. Ironically, Bill Gates, who endorsed the Pinker book and whose foundation gives millions to charity, claimed in his 2014 interview with *Rolling Stone* magazine to believe in God and to have been raised in church, and he currently raises his family with three kids in church...even if he doesn't quite understand the faith or its value.[20]

Human Rights

And what about human rights? The Holocaust of World War II—the attempted genocide of the Jewish people—provided a major impetus for the human rights movement. In 1948's Universal Declaration of Human Rights (UDHR), we see that humans have a special moral status. It demands "recognition of the inherent dignity and of the equal and inalienable rights of all members of the human family."[21] The grounding of this intrinsic dignity is universally shared by humans in virtue of their being human as such. It is because such rights owed to human dignity are inherent that they are likewise inalienable. One of the key architects of UDHR is Harvard-trained philosopher and former UN Secretary General Charles Malik, a devout Christian.

It is this notion of inalienable rights that we also find in the US Declaration of Independence, penned two centuries prior. The state cannot take away what it had no authority to grant. The rights are something transcendentally endowed by our Creator. It is why all lives matter because all lives are sacred. Moral rights are deeper and more durable than civil rights because they are connected to humanity as such. Legality ought not determine morality; rather, morality ought to determine legality. The modern expression "human rights" didn't emerge in a vacuum. Like modern capitalism, it has deeper historical roots deriving historically from "natural rights," whose concept is derived from "natural law" and further derived from "eternal law."[22]

Few documents have provided as much of a platform for freedom and human flourishing as the US Constitution. Significantly, it gives pride of place in the Bill of Rights to the First Amendment. The highest glory of the American Revolution connected in one indissoluble bond the principles of civil government and the principles of Christianity. Our constitutional republican form of liberal democracy was designed to preserve rather than curtail human freedom given the Christian insights on human persons. The seed of the self-destruction of slavery was embedded in thought, even though it would take another century to be realized. It was Christians in England, then in the US, who were the first in their communities to oppose slavery—at great cost.

Scarcely is there a nation or people to consider who have been more free, prosperous, and charitable than America, due to its founders' recognition of inalienable human rights. This is not to argue that America was ever a Christian nation, much less one without blemishes. Christ isn't mentioned in the founding documents, and sinners do sin—blemishes and all. Indisputably, however, America is a social contract informed and inspired not by its Christian citizenry and history.

Darwin, operating from a naturalistic perspective, once said,

> If…men were reared under precisely the same conditions as hive-bees, there can hardly be a doubt that our unmarried females would, like the worker-bees, think it a sacred duty to kill their brothers, and mothers would strive to kill their fertile daughters; and no one would think of interfering.[23]

Examples abound. Our moral sense would be radically different had we developed like lions. Male lions notoriously kill offspring of other males to alleviate competition. Both moral facts and our moral sense depend in this case on evolution. Prominent atheistic ethicist, James Rachels, comments, "We are not entitled—not on evolutionary grounds, at any rate—to regard our own adaptive behavior as 'better' or 'higher' than that of a cockroach, who, after all, is adapted equally well to life."[24] Even if there were moral facts on this account, it isn't clear that we would know them because of the impediment of the account of our minds aimed at survival rather than truth. Pinker, a cognitive psychologist, states, "Our brains were developed for fitness, not for truth."[25] The severity of such is far greater than mere moral knowledge. It impacts the possibility of all knowledge.

It does not appear that this provides a satisfactory ground of human rights, our knowledge of them, and attending obligations—unlike Christianity. The great anti-theist Richard Dawkins now concedes that theistic belief seems to have greater moral motivation than not. He announces this much to his chagrin in his recent book in a chapter titled "Do We Need God in Order to Be Good?" He wrote, "Whether irrational or not, it does, unfortunately, seem plausible that if somebody sincerely believes God is watching his every move, he might be more likely to be good."[26]

The imprint of Jesus is clear. Jürgen Habermas, an atheist philosopher and one of Europe's leading intellectuals, observed that democracy, human rights, equality, and freedom as we know it are "the direct heir to the Judaic ethic of justice and the Christian ethic of love" and that any other attempted explanation for them is "just idle postmodern talk."[27]

THE GOLDEN RULE IN COMPARATIVE EXPLORATION AS EVIDENCE FOR CHRISTIANITY

Some claim that the major world religions teach the same moral values. In one sense, from a Christian perspective, everyone has knowledge of the fundamental moral principles. This is explained by virtue of their being created in God's image with moral knowledge, even if suppressed, corrupted, and distorted to varying degrees. Thus, from a Christian perspective, we would expect all people to have some level of moral knowledge, which they in fact have even if application of such moral principles differs widely.

The expression "Do to others what you would want others to do to you" is an example of a moral principle or facet that is widely known. It is one of the most well-known ethical principles throughout time and across continents. Since the seventeenth century, it has been called the Golden Rule (GR), ostensibly claiming supremacy among ethical principles.[28] While most understand the GR only as a principle in ethics, less known is the evidence it provides for Christianity. It reveals further evidence of a moral law implying a moral Lawmaker.

From science to religion (East and West), we have knowledge of the GR. Although it has been variously represented across cultures and worldviews for millennia, not all worldviews can equally explain or account for it. Through analysis of representational statements of the rule from various worldviews and reflection on how these worldviews account for the rule, the Christian worldview seems to best explain or account for the GR.

Evidence of the Rule's Universality

The rule is pervasively known. Consider the discovery of neuroscientist Donald Pfaff:

> For several years now, I have been reading far and wide in the literature of religions throughout the world, looking to answer just one question: "Can I find an ethical command that seems to be true of all religions, across continents and across centuries?" Well, I found one, and you'll recognize it instantly. You probably know it as the Golden Rule. Once I found abundant evidence for a universal ethical principle, I was convinced there must be a biological reason for it.[29]

Pfaff assumes without argument a biological rather than theological origin of the rule but nonetheless sees evidence for the rule's universality. His tenacity toward a biological explanation seems to stem from his *a priori* naturalist worldview rather than following the evidence where it leads.

Western Religious Perspectives

Of the rule's various expressions, a common one is what some call the Silver Rule (SR) because of its negative formulation construed as a do-no-harm principle. In Rabbinical Judaism, the famous Rabbi Hillel said, "That which is hateful to you do not do to another; that is the entire Torah, and the rest is its interpretation."[30]

In Christianity, we see Jesus offer a most-familiar version of the Golden Rule: "In everything, do to others what you would have them do to you, for this sums up the Law and the Prophets" (Matthew 7:12).

In Islam, we see a qualified positive version: "None of you believes until he loves for his brother what he loves for himself."[31] This saying of Muhammad is in the Hadith, a source second in authority to the Qur'an. The passage stipulates loving only fellow Muslims. This qualified statement is as close as the Qur'an gets to the GR.

Thus, among the great Western religions, we have the SR, the GR, and a qualified GR.

Eastern Religious Perspectives

In Confucianism, we again see the negative version, the SR: "Do not impose upon others those things that you yourself do not desire."[32]

In Buddhism, we find the SR in a canonical passage by Buddha: "On traversing all directions with the mind, one finds no one dearer than oneself. Likewise, everyone holds himself most dear. Hence, one who loves himself, should not harm another."[33]

In Hinduism, again we find the SR, "One should not behave towards others in a way which is disagreeable to oneself. This is the essence of morality. All other activities are due to selfish desire."[34]

Eastern religions seem governed by the SR.

Scientific Worldview Perspectives

Consider the GR from a naturalistic scientific (i.e., scientist) perspective consistent with the assumptions above by Pfaff. Darwinism can be taken as a worldview describing man's origin, destiny, and in the scheme of things, purpose. Indeed, one prolific Darwinian author notes the elastic nature of defining religion, placing Darwinism in that category. He argues that Darwinism is a "secular religious perspective," a mild statement given the astonishing title of his book, *Darwinism as Religion*.[35]

Darwin himself recognized and spoke about the GR: "The social instincts—the prime principle of man's moral condition—with the aid of active intellectual powers and the effects of habit, naturally lead to the golden rule, 'As ye would that men should do to you, do ye to them likewise,' and this lies at the foundation of morality."[36]

Explanation of the Evidence for the Rule

Evidence is one thing, explanation another. Some provide an evolutionary explanation from science for the GR in terms of cooperation. They observe reciprocal benefit and invoke kin selection for an apparently altruistic sort of behavior that seems self-sacrificial. It implies the decrease of individual survival for the sake of one's kin. Consider the behavior of squirrels or apes when predators are within striking distance. They make sounds to warn their kin, posing a benefit to their kin while endangering themselves.

But a problem emerges. This behavior promotes survival and reproduction but does not entail a moral principle. As one atheistic philosopher of science quips, "If Darwinism is true, then anything goes!"[37] This seems supported by a famous statement from Darwinian philosopher of science Michael Ruse:

> The position of the modern evolutionist...is that humans have an awareness of morality...because such an awareness is of biological worth. Morality is a biological adaptation no less than are hands and feet and teeth...Considered as a rationally justifiable set of claims about an objective something, ethics is illusory. I appreciate that when somebody says "Love thy neighbor as thyself," they think they are referring above and beyond themselves...Nevertheless... such reference is truly without foundation. Morality is just an aid to survival and reproduction...and any deeper meaning is illusory.[38]

On a naturalistic evolutionary account of ethics, the GR becomes descriptive, not prescriptive. It reveals that beasts do in fact cooperate to get more by hunting in a pack than by going it alone. But this descriptive behavior doesn't entail prescriptive morality. It doesn't (and can't) tell us what we *ought* to do in a moral sense. It lacks the fundamental normative ("oughtness") dimension of morality.

Explanatory Scope and Power

The Christian view has greater explanatory scope and power.[39] It is consistent with our ethical intuitions that we owe something to others. This obligatory "ought" is grounded in fundamental human dignity in virtue of being created in God's image (Genesis 1:26-27; 9:6; James 3:9). It accounts for how fundamental morality is pervasively known because that divine image entails a moral imprint (Romans 1:18-20; 2:14-15). Thus, we should expect everyone to have an awareness of certain moral obligations to fellow humans created in God's image with intrinsic dignity.

Christianity explains the GR better than Western scientific naturalism or Eastern pantheism. The Greek philosopher Plato famously asked this question: Why should I be moral? He offers a story about the Ring of Gyges where we're asked to imagine a magical ring with the power of invisibility. If we had such power, would we use it for good or for evil? He concludes that most people would be moral either for fear of the consequences of getting caught or motivated by a love for the good because it is the right thing to do. While the naturalist may appeal to cooperation as to why *we* should be moral, the question is why should *I* be moral if I know I can get away with gain by being immoral?

Unless there are objective moral facts, morality is subjective. But more than mere objectivity, we want a deeper explanation of moral facts. Christian ethics moves from superficial precept on the outside of a concentric circle (like "don't murder" or "don't lie") to deeper principles underwriting such precepts (like the sanctity of human life or the principle of credulity—i.e., truth telling). Some atheists will assert that such bare objective moral facts or principles simply exist but that explanation is weak. Even if justice exists somewhere floating around, to what or whom am I obligated? I don't owe anything to nonpersonal physical or abstract objects, such as the number two or a light bulb. Morality is always a property of persons. I owe something to you and you to me. Hence, the Christian not only has a more sensible option but one with greater explanatory power—namely, going a step beyond precept and principle to grounding morality in a personal being, God. Because God is life and God is truth, whose personal ground explains the principle on which the precepts derive, Christian morality is far deeper than precepts.

Versions and Worldview Impediments to the Rule

From the perspectives of the major religions, two considerations emerge. First, most of the competing views assume the SR, which is ethically inferior to the GR both intuitively and in scope of coverage. To see why, consider the parable of the good Samaritan (Luke 10:25-37). The first two men who come across the hurt man in the road simply pass him by. Yet the third man, the unsuspecting Samaritan, is the one who helps the injured man. Upon reading the story, most people can easily discern independent from one's worldview who are the villains and who is the hero. Our natural moral intuitions about the rule when considering the narrative are clear that the GR is ethically superior to the SR. It directs us to pursue good and not simply avoid evil or do no harm. It is about virtue, not merely avoiding vice. The GR is good for humanity. Using the SR, one would simply pass by the hurt individual—that individual isn't harming me, so I won't harm him. But nothing follows in the SR that tells me that I ought to help the individual. That concept is only captured in the GR. Further, it is captured in a robust formulation of the GR that isn't merely descriptive but prescriptive, having moral force or obligation—Christ gave a command. *A fortiori*, the Christian worldview has an objective frame grounded in God that explains why we know the GR through our created moral conscience. In fact, it is among many objective moral truths that we cannot be unaware of.

Second, there are worldview considerations relevant to understanding and applying the rule. For instance, we indicated that Islam has a qualified GR focused on the brotherhood of Islam exclusive of non-Muslims. In confirmation, Muhammad indicated elsewhere something less than GR or SR: "He who changes his religion [i.e., apostatizes], kill him."[40] In the Qur'an, Surah 9:4-5 tells us that Allah loves only those who obey, and the text talks about killing certain non-Muslims. Chronologically, this Surah is one of the last passages on Jihad. Per the Islamic principle of abrogation, the most recent comments take precedence. Contrast this with Jesus, who taught us to love our enemies (Matthew 5:44).

From the Buddhist perspective, it seems incoherent that one ought to treat others the way one wants to be treated. This is because the GR assumes one is a self. Yet core to Buddhism is the "no-self" doctrine. Part of the grand illusion said to cause suffering includes self-conception as a self. In fact, "no-self" serves as a major point of contention between Buddhism and Hinduism relative to what it is exactly that is being reincarnated. The Buddha's view about the self is not only that it is false; rather, holding the false view leads to selfishness and egoism.

Ultimately, Hinduism may not fare much better if all is maya (illusion). For Hinduism, even if we can make sense of a self, one's duties to others are hierarchically qualified in a caste system. One isn't expected to treat members of a lower class the same way (much less those outside the caste like Dalits or "untouchables"). Similarly, one's dharma (duty) is relative to one's caste such that a warrior caste's dharma seems to run into deep internal conflict with the principle of *ahisma* (nonviolence).

Confucianism is a bit different. It suffers from the problem of authority or the moral force of the obligation. If there is no Creator to ground the obligation, even with respect to SR, then we are left with mere human wisdom without moral force, much like getting moral advice from a fortune cookie. To what or whom are we obligated?

From the scientistic perspective, the GR is universal and is explained in terms of its being an aid to survival and reproduction. Atheistic philosopher of science Alex Rosenberg admits, "There are fundamental principles endorsed in all cultures at all times."[41] Yet for him, what explains this is simply that "nature just seduced us into thinking it's right. It did that because that made core morality work better; our believing in its truth increases our individual genetic fitness."[42] We are often told by those who reject design in nature or in the moral order that our strong perception of design is simply illusory as evolution has blinded us to reality.[43] But if we cannot adequately know truth about the world, including moral truth, then why communicate this as if it is supposed to be a truth in which we should believe?

Naturalistic evolution gives us reason to doubt many of our beliefs if our cognitive faculties are allegedly aimed at survival rather than at truth. In a self-defeating way, this undercuts our confidence in the ability of our faculties to produce true beliefs (rather than false beliefs conducive to survival), including the belief in naturalistic evolution itself. This "blind to reality" notion seems shared by the religion of Darwinism and some Eastern religions.

The Golden Rule is universally known, but it is uniquely shown. Some might raise the threat of relativism because "Do to others what you want others to do to you" hinges on what we *want* or *desire*, where these refer to personal preferences that might be highly dubious in terms of their virtue. Though GR is universally known, it doesn't exist in a vacuum. The immediate context of Jesus' statement includes a robust view of love situated in a broader theological context for understanding good in terms of what is objectively desirable, not merely what is subjectively desired. Christianity claims that the very source of goodness made the world such that everyone can reliably map onto it and intuit the basic moral order, making relatively accurate inferences about reality. Christianity makes the best sense of both the universality of the GR and its most robust intuited formulation. The Golden Rule is most at home in a Christocentric view of the world.

RATIONALITY AND THE RISE OF THE UNIVERSITIES AND SCIENCE

Aristotle began his greatest work with this statement: "Man by nature desires to know."[44] This concept of desire is impregnated with reason. Knowledge is a good thing. Scarcely would someone deny that education is a good thing. We will again briefly look at the history of the university; however, now we will consider its contributions to society in more detail.

The bulk of Pinker's bestselling book is devoted to an empirical analysis of human progress along multiple dimensions (health, quality of life, education, life expectancy, etc.). His data is relatively good. His explanation of the data for secular humanism is not so good—it fails, but he tries. He fails to underwrite most of it because he fails to give credit where credit is due.

After having made the case for progress, Pinker returns to the themes that provided its foundation, which he identifies as key themes of the Enlightenment, and calls for these ideas to be fortified against counter-Enlightenment movements in the culture like religion.

Reason, he points out, is fundamental, and anyone who opposes it is unreasonable. But from whence comes reason and the halls of reason, the universities? While some may claim that religion is an impediment to reason and science, history says otherwise. Indeed, it is more than a fact of history that the universities were birthed in Christian medieval Europe. This is best explained by the Christian worldview, making it more than a mere fact of history.

Recall, some argue that universities were around long before the Christian era. But entities like Plato's Academy and Aristotle's Lyceum were nothing like the modern university. It was not the Greeks or the Romans that invented universities. They established no scholarly guilds and no permanent institutions.[45] The major universities did not emerge in the East, in atheism, or in Islam but, instead, in the West in the Judeo-Christian context. Jesus, a Jew, said that our purpose in life is to know God (John 17:3). This fits with Aristotle's observation. Mankind desires to know ultimate reality. Knowledge is not peripheral to the biblical mindset about the good life.

The knowledge of God was central to some of the greatest thinkers in the West for more than 2,500 years.[46] The medieval project was faith seeking understanding. The medieval philosopher-theologian Thomas Aquinas and others used to say that theology is the queen of the *scientia* and philosophy is its handmaiden. Again, like the spokes connected to the hub of a wheel, the diversity of academic disciplines is connected in unity to the hub of theology with philosophy as the glue that holds the spokes onto the hub. We have the unity in diversity constituting the university.

The medieval monasteries kept education alive, and Christian thinkers birthed the major universities. The rise of the universities in Europe at institutions like Bologna, Paris, Cambridge, and Oxford weren't mere accidents of history but were intentionally formed with Christ at the center. This spread to America and around the world.[47]

Adherents of Missionary Protestantism desired that people would be able to read the Bible in their own language and it was their movement that was the major impetus for teaching people to read and resulted in higher levels of global literacy. Sociologist Robert Woodberry demonstrates through careful research that mass education and mass printing followed wherever Protestant missionaries went. This biblical literacy encouraged religious freedom, which became the staple First Amendment in the US, whose freedom is now coveted throughout the world. Woodberry challenges anyone to look at any map to see for himself. Countries with more Protestants are more democratic and have more stable democratic transitions. Wherever they have been, there we find evidence of more printed books and more schools per capita.[48]

The American model emerged from Europe's Christocentric universities, later spreading to Southeast Asia. For centuries, most of the modern universities were largely established in the context of and motivated by the Christian faith. Ironically, Pinker reveals tremendous ignorance as he saws off the branch on which he sits. The very university of Harvard from which he luxuriously pontificates was founded by the Puritans, devout apprentices of Jesus—its original motto, *Veritas Christo et Ecclesiae* (Truth for Christ and the Church).[49]

Yale, sensing Harvard (1636) drifting left, began anew affirming *Veritas* but adding a notion that represented salvation in the Hebrew scriptures, *lux* (light). The motto of Yale (1701) is *lux et veritas* (Light and Truth) in reference to Psalm 27:1, where light represents the salvation of the Lord. Yale's great prodigy Jonathan Edwards then went on and became the president of Princeton. The motto of Princeton (1746) is "Under God's power she flourishes." The motto of Columbia (1754) is "In thy light we shall see light," quoting Psalm 36:9. These are only the first four universities in America, all preceding the United States' independence in 1776. I've visited most of the early colonial schools, and the same can be said for them.

Since the rise of educational institutes, Christian intellectuals have seen themselves contemplating what the father of modern science Francis Bacon called the two books of God. That is, God's Word and God's world; Scripture and nature (yet without conflict). If there is conflict, it rests not at the level of the facts themselves (nature or Scripture) but at the level of the interpretation of the facts (science or theology). While Harvard's current head chaplain is an atheist, the student body are largely nonbelievers, and the school's motto has reverted to "truth" with a small *t*, the root cause is present. The centuries old motto "Truth for Christ and the Church" that is extant on numerous buildings is emblazoned on the Harvard shield whose source of inspiration stands. Remarkably, the top two books on the shield are face up while the bottom book is face down. This symbolizes the limits of reason, and the need for God's revelation. With the secularization of the school, the current shield now contains only the word "Veritas" with three open books.

This Christian influence spread as far east as South Korea and India with their initial major universities founded as Christian institutions, the same as in America and Europe.

As for the nature of many of these seminal universities, their central purpose was training missionaries and pastors. At Harvard, chapel attendance and freshmen Hebrew courses were mandatory. Harvard's original mission statement concerned knowing God in Christ. More than half of the graduates in the seventeenth century became clergy.[50] Up until 1840, all university and college presidents in the US were members of the clergy, and almost all were Protestant. As late as 1890, chapel and church attendance were required in every college in America. Clearly, the universities, the cultural center of ideas and influence, were Christ centered until just over a century ago. That seminal historical influence is not to be credited to secular humanism but to Christian humanism.

There is a long history revealing how the universities moved from Christocentric sacred to godless secular.[51] Universities and education are good for the world. Christianity deserves credit. Connected to the rise of universities is modern science. Pinker says that science is the proudest accomplishment of our species.[52]

Ironically, reason and science come not from matter but from mind, that which is fitting for a Christian theistic worldview more than an atheistic one. At one point in the Enlightenment, it was thought that everything was reducible to matter. Later, we discovered that underlying matter is information. Below that, we came to see intelligence. While pantheism in the East struggles to explain matter, atheism in the West struggles to explain the mind. Theism accounts for both with the primacy of mind over matter.

Darwin revealed his own doubt about considerations of knowledge that included moral knowledge assuming the veracity of both evolution and naturalism together. "With me," says Darwin, "the horrid doubt always arises whether the convictions of man's mind, which has been developed from the mind of the lower animals, are of any value or at all trustworthy. Would any one trust in the convictions of a monkey's mind, if there are any convictions in such a mind?"[53]

Modern science, leading to technology, owes its existence to the Christian worldview. Virtually every major subdiscipline was founded by a committed apprentice of Jesus. Gregor Mendel, the father of genetics, developed genotype and phenotype traits while playing with pea pods in his monastery. Carl Linnaeus was the father of taxonomy. Louis Pasteur gave the world bacteriology. Rene Descartes is the father of modern geometry. Gottfried Leibniz is the father of calculus. Robert Boyle is the father of chemistry. Johannes Kepler is noted for astronomy. Isaac Newton began with the assumption of a moral law and predicted laws of physics according to which he began to test. His faith both informed and inspired what eventually became Newtonian physics.

Not only does history reveal that Christianity and science were not at odds, but it also reveals that Christianity spawned modern science. More than a fact of history, this record is best explained by a worldview that begins with mind, not matter. And it includes beings created in God's image, capable of mapping the external world, abstracting information, drawing inferences, and developing technology. Christians believed that God was the ground of rationality and had given human beings minds to discover His glory in the created order.

Remember, *ratio* is the Latin term for "reason." It is derived from the Greek *logos*, from which we get our English word "logic." John's Gospel begins highlighting Jesus as the *Logos*. Jesus is not only the central figure in history who underwrites love, but He is the foundation of logic as well. The case for reason, science, and human value seems more at home in Christianity than in secular humanism.

Astonishingly, the atheist historian Tom Holland makes clear his thinking about the value-impact of Christianity:

> That every human being possessed an equal dignity was not remotely self-evident a truth. The Romans would have laughed at it…The origins of this principle—as Nietzsche had so contemptuously pointed out—lay not in the French Revolution, nor in the Declaration of Independence, nor in the Enlightenment, but in the Bible.[54]

In a most amazing statement, Holland profoundly rebuffs Christianity's critics, saying,

> The founding conviction of the Enlightenment—that it owed nothing to the faith into which its greatest figures had been born increasingly came to seem to me unsustainable…Even as belief in God fades across the west, the countries that were once collectively known as Christendom continue to bear the stamp of the two-millennia-old revolution that Christianity represents…It is why we generally assume that every human life is of equal value. In my morals and ethics, I have learned to accept that I am not Greek or Roman at all, but thoroughly and proudly Christian.[55]

Today, two billion people profess allegiance to the revolutionary who has transformed individuals, societal structures, and the world more potently for good than any single person. The Christian gospel embraces the fact that Jesus paid the debt He did not owe because we owed a debt we could not pay. This is not to say that being a professing Christian is identical to being a Christian who possesses true saving faith in Jesus. But there is no doubt that the central message of the gospel concerning sin and grace is deeply intuitive to much of the world.

A clear case can be made to a reasonable person that even while critics can point to bad apples within Christianity or certain Christian-linked movements that were less than savory, Christianity is a significant net good for people individually and for the world more generally. But that by itself doesn't make the Christian worldview reasonable to believe, much less true. We're now able to answer those next two questions in turn.

11

IS CHRISTIAN BELIEF REASONABLE?

A decade ago, along with nearly a dozen atheist and Christian scholars, I coedited a book titled *Is Faith in God Reasonable? Debates in Philosophy, Science, and Rhetoric.* Many claim that Christians are guilty of wish fulfillment. But clearly that proverbial shoe can fit on the other foot as well. Aldous Huxley, author of *Brave New World* (1932), was an agnostic who coined the term prior to his death in 1963. He admitted his motives for not believing in God:

> I had motive for not wanting the world to have a meaning; consequently, assumed that it had none, and was able without any difficulty to find satisfying reasons for this assumption. The philosopher who finds no meaning in the world is not concerned exclusively with a problem in pure metaphysics, he is also concerned to prove that there is no valid reason why he personally should not do as he wants to do, or why his friends should not seize political power and govern in the way that they find most advantageous to themselves...For myself, the philosophy of meaninglessness was essentially an instrument of liberation, sexual and political.[1]

Thomas Nagel, a living and prominent atheist philosopher, admits the same:

> I want atheism to be true and am made uneasy by the fact that some of the most intelligent and well-informed people I know are religious believers. It isn't just that I don't believe in God and, naturally, hope that I'm right in my belief. It's that I hope there is no God! I don't want there to be a God; I don't want the universe to be like that. My guess is that this cosmic authority problem is not a rare condition and that it is responsible for much of the scientism and reductionism of our time. One of the tendencies it supports is the ludicrous overuse of evolutionary biology to explain everything about human life, including everything about the human mind…This is a somewhat ridiculous situation…[It] is just as irrational to be influenced in one's beliefs by the hope that God does not exist as by the hope that God does exist.[2]

Again, another atheist—perhaps the most prolific in writing, with more than 200 books—Isaac Asimov, proclaims,

> I am an atheist, out and out. It took me a long time to say it. I've been an atheist for years and years, but somehow, I felt it was intellectually unrespectable to say one was an atheist, because it assumed knowledge that one didn't have. Somehow it was better to say one was a humanist or an agnostic. I finally decided that I'm a creature of emotion as well as of reason. Emotionally I am an atheist. I don't have the evidence to prove that God doesn't exist, but I so strongly suspect he doesn't that I don't want to waste my time.[3]

The truth is that embracing Christianity for some might come down to wish fulfillment, but must it for everyone? That is, can it not be the case that Christianity is a rational position to hold?[4] One question is whether Christianity is true, but a separate question that is asked by many is whether it is even rational. Many sidestep the truth question entirely and simply claim that religion is a crutch for weak-minded people. Thus, both queries need a response.

One of the primary critics on the rationality of religious belief was Karl Marx, and in his spirit come many of the attacks today. Today, the rapid growth of Marx on college campuses requires addressing this. Indeed, one is hard pressed to advance cultural apologetics without understanding cultural Marxism. But fair warning. I'm going to a greater intellectual depth in this section than in the rest of the book.

Despite the facts that Karl Marx came from a Jewish religious background, that his father was a Lutheran convert in Germany, and that his mother was a practicing Jew, Marx had very little regard for religion. In fact, his use of criticism contrary to popular opinion to emancipate humanity does not begin with criticism of politics or economics. This is the case, although he had much to say in these fields. Rather, Marx begins his criticism with religion, for "the criticism of religion is the premise of all criticism."[5] His core views are still shared by his followers. The disciples of Marcuse have advanced Marx's thoughts to the next level in contemporary society in terms of how they seek to intellectually subvert Christian belief.

We'll deal with the ideas of Marx in several sections. In the first section, I will lay out what I perceive to be the chief characteristics of Marx's theory of knowledge about religion. Then, I will provide the larger context in which the epistemological issue is framed. Finally, I will provide a critique of Marx's criticism of religion and conclude that his and his followers' views are both false and irrational.

MARX'S EPISTEMOLOGY OF RELIGION

It is not as though Marx merely thinks traditional religion, which affirms that God made man in His image, to be false. Rather, he thinks that traditional religion is a man-made social construct. Today, that's the common view held to in the universities and the one that has propagated out into culture. That is, Marx claims that man had made God in man's image. Marx makes remarks such as this: "It is not religion which creates man but man who creates religion."[6] More generally, man's intellectual views are shaped by their natural and social environments; hence, one's epistemological viewpoints, generally, are to be contextualized via social structures.[7] I'm going to put Marx in his historical context, but the essence of the view holds true with his followers today, who are sweeping the university and pushing it into culture.

Marx's critical method begins with his criticism of religion before turning to a critique of the state and of the economic situation. His vision of human emancipation requires, as a necessary condition, that serious religion be given up. You might be wondering, *Why the harsh criticism of religion?* Marx addresses the issue within the context of the Jewish Question,[8] which considered the desire of many Jews for political emancipation within the German ("Christian") state. Ultimately, the question is about the place of religion in general within the state. Marx's vision entails a classless society that seems precluded by *serious religion* (a term that Marx sets in opposition to *nominal religion*).

Serious religion, with its self-consciously privileged position, is taken by Marx to proliferate rather than to exterminate class division. It commands one's ultimate allegiance, which is often in conflict with others or the state. Strong religious identity, as such, is divisive and contrary to human progress. Hence, humanity cannot be emancipated fully until serious religion is eradicated. This opposition of religion to human emancipation can only be had when the opposition itself is made impossible—namely, by "abolishing all religion."[9] This may seem like a huge feat to accomplish, given the hold that religion had on a great number of people in Germany at that time or in the world in general. There are at least two ways, however, in which such a feat is possible.

The first way, which is preferable, is for believers to view their religions as mere "stages in the development of the human mind."[10] Marx's humanist vision regards the human being as "scientific" and "non-religious man." It is a vision grounded in his materialist worldview.[11] The perfected state is the atheistic state.[12] Liberation from religion is a necessary first step toward political emancipation. Marx holds that only under one condition would religion be allowable—that it be relegated entirely to the private rather than the public sphere, thus constituting the utter renunciation of serious religion.[13] But even then, after gutting the core of serious religion, he sees the existence of even nominal religion as defective in some way. Theological questions need ultimately be turned into secular questions, and superstition into history.[14] Religion "is the expression of the limitations of reason, a product of arbitrariness and fantasy, a veritable life in the beyond."[15] Hence, the religious viewpoint, as mere superstition, is a fantastic limitation on human reason. It is defectively impractical in the world and contrary to human reason, so it should be discarded.

The second way to accomplish the abolition of religion, at least for Marx, is by radical political revolution. So important for Marx's goal of humanistic progress is the abolition of religion that he justifies the possibility of violent means to achieve that end.[16] This may not be ready at hand in America today, but it is certainly the case in Marxist-led countries around the world. Marx says,

> Certainly, in periods when the political state as such comes violently to birth in civil society, and when the men strive to liberate themselves through political emancipation, the state can, and must, proceed to abolish and destroy religion; but only in the same way as it proceeds to abolish private property, by declaring a maximum, by confiscation, or by progressive taxation or in the same way as it proceeds to abolish life, by the *guillotine* [emphasis Marx's].[17]

Clearly, the guillotine mentioned here is not merely figurative. Both Marx and Lenin looked approvingly on the French Revolution. We see similarities in Marxist governments today. For Marx, to halt the suffering of the oppressed by the oppressor, it is sometimes necessary to bring about the greater good by whatever means necessary.

Ironically, this does not mean that religious believers are oppressors according to Marx, for they are also oppressed. It may be that they are self-oppressed, having bought into what Marx takes to be a false sense of happiness based on the illusion of religion. In the context of his most famous passage on religion, Marx says, "Religious suffering is at the same time an expression of real suffering and protest against real suffering. Religion is the sigh of the oppressed creature, the sentiment of a heartless world, and the soul of soulless conditions."[18]

Both Karl Marx and Sigmund Freud were influenced by Ludwig Feuerbach's criticism of religion. Feuerbach's *The Essence of Christianity* construed religion as simply the projection of human need, a fulfillment of deep-seated wishes. Feuerbach saw the purpose of his book as the "destruction of an illusion." In sum, "We have shown that the substance and object of religion is altogether human; we have shown that divine wisdom is human wisdom; that the secret of theology is anthropology, that the absolute mind is the so-called finite subjective mind."[19] Like Freud's later book *The Future of an Illusion*,[20] Marx's writings also treat religion as an illusion of mankind. He takes it to be some epistemic defect, a cognitive dysfunction of the one holding theistic belief.

Famously, Marx claims that religion "is the opium of the people."[21] He calls people to seek real happiness and to abandon a condition that requires illusion (e.g., religion). Whereas in Marx's time, opium was a drug affordable only to the wealthy class, he felt that the poor used religion as their means of escape from miserable socioeconomic conditions. His epistemology of religion thus construes belief in God as a sort of vestigial remnant of the evolutionary process; it serves the purposes of a drug that people mistakenly think to be the way to get through this harsh world. One day, however, given the right conditions, they will no longer see the instrumental "need" for this illusion, and they will shed it like a snake does its skin.

Ultimately, religious belief is epistemologically defective, dysfunctional, and due to a malfunctioning society. People come to believe in God because of their impoverished or oppressive socioeconomic conditions; they are somehow unhealthily suffering from some cognitive and emotional consequence of these poor conditions. Man's cognitive equipment, we might say, is not working properly; it is not functioning as it ought to because of an inverted social order. If man's cognitive equipment were working properly, then the religious adherent would no longer be under the spell of this illusion. He would instead face the world and our place in it with the clear-eyed apprehension that in it we are alone, and that any comfort and help we get will have to come from our own devising. Marx claims that once man unmasks his illusions of the sacred, then he will be on his way to reason and act differently.[22] Today's cultural Marxism is the same conflict theory as before, but instead of focusing on economic class, as classical Marxism did, it focuses on the cultural capital of race, sex, gender, and so on.

THE CONTEXT OF THE THEORY OF KNOWLEDGE

The general criticism that Marx lodges against religious belief takes place in an overarching context. It does not concern itself with the truthfulness of religion. Rather, his concern was epistemic—that is, dealing only with the rationality or reasonableness of religious belief itself. His view emerges from a materialistic worldview and involves giving a *naturalistic* explanation of religious belief in terms of poor socioeconomic structure. For Marx, man's intellectual perceptions are shaped by their natural and social environments; hence, one's epistemological viewpoints are dependent on contextual social structures.[23] Of course, giving a naturalistic account of belief is not necessarily to make a criticism of that kind of belief. One could amass many examples of beliefs whose explanation is given via a naturalistic account. But by itself, this would not discredit the truth-claim made for that belief. An explanation in terms of natural processes might provide a sort of causal genesis or antecedents of the belief and can still be logically consistent with those beliefs having a perfectly respectable intellectual status.

So if we are truly to have a criticism of religion by way of a naturalistic explanation of religious belief, we need something that in some fashion discredits religious belief or casts doubt on it to show that it is not intellectually respectable because there is something wrong with it. Here, the relevant criticism is that religious belief is irrational. Religious belief is not produced by cognitive faculties of the mind that are functioning properly simply because of the poor socioeconomic conditions created by an "inverted world consciousness."[24] Take away those conditions and replace them with conditions that are suitable to human flourishing, and religious belief will cease to function as the opium (sedative) that people so badly feel that they need to proceed through this rough world.

Thus, it was thought that if the socioeconomic problem was fixed, then the people would reject religion, as it would no longer satisfy the felt need that drove people to it in the first place. Marx's criticism amounts to a de jure objection that concerns the rational status of religious belief (an epistemic issue concerning the rational status of religious belief), not a de facto objection concerning its truth or falsity (a metaphysical issue concerning the truth or falsity of religion). Nowhere does Marx offer decisive proof for the nonexistence of God. He probably assumes that the Enlightenment thinkers had somehow accomplished this task, and so he does not concern himself with the project of whether religious belief is true or false. Instead, he denounces acceptance of such belief as irrational. This is like what many students hear daily in university classrooms when they are told to "Check your religious belief at the door."

Marx's vision of a classless utopian society may be regarded as idealistic or as realizable, but there are questions about the philosophical foundations that he offers in support of the edifice that he is promoting. As a kind of humanist, Marx is very optimistic about man's potentiality and self-fulfillment. But this humanism is at odds with his recognition of the impoverishments brought about by socioeconomic conditions; these conditions tend to stifle human potential. While he holds that given the proper conditions, human beings are basically good, or at least that humanity has good potential, poor socioeconomic conditions often make the situation worse because of various forms of what he calls alienation.[25] But what if we were to say that man is basically sinful and that the causal relationship between man's negative moral disposition and his poor socioeconomic conditions should be the reverse of Marx's views on the matter? What if sinful inclinations are a causal factor in generating the poor socioeconomic conditions that further the alienation already existing between humanity and its Maker? Or what if man's deepest needs cannot be fulfilled by simply having better external conditions such as higher wages? What if human potential is realizable not through the means that Marx proposes for achieving it but, instead, only through the knowledge of God understood from an eternal perspective?

CRITICISM OF THE CRITIC

A different overarching context may help us develop the question of the epistemic status of religious belief. In the burgeoning literature on philosophy of religion, reformed epistemology has offered a distinctive contribution to this question. Alvin Plantinga, the reformed Christian philosopher noted for bringing about a revolution of Christian thought in academic philosophy, is perhaps its foremost proponent in terms of developing the view. But it also has roots in the thought of prominent thinkers of the Middle Ages and of the Reformation, such as Thomas Aquinas and John Calvin. In this view, something like the following theistic proposition is taken as true, given what Calvin calls man's sense of the Divine: God has implanted in us a natural tendency to see His hand in the world around us to the extent that everyone would believe in God if it weren't for sin.[26] Were it not for the existence of sin in the world, says Calvin, human beings would believe in God to the same degree and with the same natural spontaneity displayed in our belief in the existence of other persons, or an external world, or the past. This is the natural human condition. Given that belief in God is formed in us naturally, apart from sin, any epistemic ambiguity with respect to God's existence is not about the evidence per se but about the interpretation of the evidence. Human blindness caused by sin is the primary problem of what some call Divine hiddenness. It is a question as to why God is not more obvious to all persons.

In the reformed religious epistemology (often called the A/C model in reference to Thomas Aquinas and John Calvin) as propounded in his *Warranted Christian Belief*, Plantinga responds to both de jure and de facto objections to belief in God.[27] The de facto objection says that Christian belief is false; the truth-claims espoused are factually in error. It is a truth-dependent objection. The de jure objection is not that Christian belief is necessarily false but that it is unjustified, irrational, or unwarranted, regardless of its veracity. It is a truth-independent objection. It is irrational, unjustified, or unwarranted to believe in God, whether this belief is true. Of importance in dealing with Marx, Plantinga aims to refute de jure objections to Christian belief. He shows that there is no reason to think that Christian belief lacks justification, rationality, or warrant, apart from, and unless one presupposes, the falsity of Christianity. It shows that there is no successful de jure objection. For any objection to be successful it will have to be a de facto objection. In order to show that Christianity is unjustified, unwarranted, or irrational, one would have to show it to be false, but this is something that Marx has not done. Thus, if God exists, then properly basic belief in God is certainly rational. In fact, it would be, for some, warranted and even a case of knowledge!

In reformed epistemology, beliefs known as "basic beliefs" are not beliefs that are justified on the basis of other more basic beliefs. For example, my belief that George Washington was the first president of the United States is justified or inferred based on other beliefs I learned by reading a historian of the time. My belief that gravity is real is justified by my belief in the reliability and experience of my sense perceptions. These beliefs are thus based on the inference of other beliefs, and so are nonbasic beliefs. Properly basic beliefs, as opposed to those merely basic beliefs, are beliefs that are likewise noninferentially justified, but they also entail a normative notion respecting the proper functioning of the reason of the one holding them. And this is relevant to assigning rational culpability to belief or nonbelief in God's existence. Given the truth of theism, it seems quite reasonable that God could create us such that our rational mental structure is adequately aimed at truth rather than at mere survival, when we are properly functioning in the way that we were designed to function as bearers of God's image.

Plantinga outlines his case something like this. Suppose someone S knows some proposition p, where p represents some propositional truth-claim like "the grass is green." So S knows p if the following four conditions hold: (1) the belief that p is produced in someone by cognitive faculties that are functioning properly (working as they ought to work, suffering from no dysfunction such as color blindness); (2) the cognitive environment in which p is produced is appropriate for those faculties like being in normal daylight, as opposed to being in a room with colored lights shaping and modifying my perception of color; (3) the purpose of the epistemic faculties producing the belief in question is to produce true beliefs; and (4) the objective probability of a belief's being true, given that it is produced under those conditions, is high.[28]

The dispute as to who is rational and who is irrational, and who is epistemologically culpable and who is inculpable, cannot be settled only by attending to epistemological considerations. It is fundamentally not an epistemological dispute concerning the rationality of religious belief but an ontological or theological dispute concerning the existence of God. The notion of proper function in belief formation does not necessarily depend on taking a theistic stance. In fact, Marx himself, in castigating religious belief as dysfunctional on the grounds that it is produced by poor environmental conditions, assumes, as part of being dysfunctional, some notion of proper function. Of course, his view of proper function is no doubt construed using naturalistic means. But what can this amount to? Marx did not quite have the mechanistic resources for the explanation of this phenomenon that were available to him with Darwin, and consequently he was not adequately able to explain proper function in a materialistic world. But given Darwinism, it is perhaps open to Marx's followers to explain proper function within materialism in terms of aptness for promoting survival, whether at the level of the individual or the species.

Can Marx give an account that belief in God is indeed less likely to contribute to our individual survival or the survival of our species than is atheism or agnosticism? I do not see how. Surely the prospects for a nonquestion begging argument of this sort are bleak. For if theism—Christian theism, for example—is true, then it seems wholly implausible and counterintuitive to think that widespread atheism, for example, would be more likely to contribute to the survival of our race than widespread theism.

Further, this says nothing about the merits of our cognitive equipment being aimed at true belief (see condition three above). The allied notions of proper function and cognitive equipment aimed at true belief seem more adequately accounted for on theistic grounds than on atheistic grounds. Arguably, our cognitive operations are better accounted for by the conjunction of theism, with or without evolution, than by the conjunction of naturalism and evolution. This is because the conjunction of naturalism and evolution makes it much less probable that complex, intelligent beings such as humans would emerge purely by chance processes than in any version of theism. If God exists, then it is much easier to explain the emergence of rational creatures, whether via divine fiat or a guided evolutionary process. Hence, theism has greater explanatory power on this note than atheism.

The theist has a ready answer to the relevant set of questions: What is proper functioning? What is it for my cognitive faculties to be working properly (i.e., working as they ought)? What is cognitive dysfunction? What is it to function naturally? My cognitive faculties are functioning naturally when they are functioning in the way that God designed them to function. The theist does not see themselves as suffering from cognitive deficiency and is unlikely to accept the idea that they are under a sort of widespread illusion endemic to the human condition. As a matter of fact, they are quite naturally inclined to think it is the nonbeliever, and Marx in particular, who is suffering in this way, from some illusion, from some mental dysfunction, from an unhappy, unfortunate, and unnatural condition with intellectually defective consequences. The situation of epistemic health and sickness, as it were, is reversed. They will see the objector as somehow the victim of sin in the world, their own or the sin of others (even if they are only culpable for their own).

Therefore, since Marx's objection to theistic belief is a de jure objection, it is unsuccessful without presupposing an answer to the de facto question—namely, whether Christianity is, in fact, false. The epistemic consideration cannot be made outside of the overarching context of the ontological question of whether God exists. For if God does, in fact, exist, then doubtless, religious belief would be rational; it would be warranted and constitute knowledge. In such a case, then, Marx's view turns out to be not just false but irrational, suffering from some cognitive defect and self-deception explained by wish fulfillment and/or by sin on a Christian theistic account.

CIRCULAR REASONING

Perhaps the most obvious objection is that such an argument (that everyone would believe in God if it were not for sin) seems to be guilty of question begging or circular reasoning. Circular reasoning is a logical fallacy in which the reasoner begins with what they are trying to end with. But how is this relevant?[29] The theist may not think the skeptic will be convinced, given certain self-deceptive consequences of nonbelief. After all, "A man convinced against his will, is of the same opinion still," or so the saying goes. Do self-deceived people know that they are self-deceived? If they came to know this, then they would no longer be self-deceived, a phenomenon widely reported by those converting to Christianity.[30] Admittedly, the sword cuts both ways, and it may be the theist who is self-deceived. But this is not obvious. Moreover, the theistic account may well have more adequate resources, such that it offers better grounds for the allied notions of proper function and rationality than does the conjunction of naturalism and evolution.

Further, it is not the case that all circular reasoning is malignant. In fact, many times it is benign.[31] Belief in God is arguably one such case for those who hold that it is properly basic to believe in God when our cognitive faculties are functioning properly (working as they ought to work, suffering from no dysfunction), in an environment appropriate for those faculties, and when the purpose of our epistemic faculties are to produce true beliefs. This is a plausible Christian position. Thus, the objective probability of a belief's being true, given that it is produced under those conditions, is going to be relatively high if God made us to know in this way. How can the theist simply give up on a whim such a properly basic belief concerning their experience of God, especially given that most belief is involuntary?[32]

Thus, apart from presupposing the falsity of Christianity, Marx's (and his followers') objection to religious belief is ungrounded, and perhaps, in the end, his own view turns out to be not merely false but irrational as well. So it seems that Christianity is first good for the world, and second, it is rational or reasonable to believe (regardless of whether it is known to be true). Now we will address the third question: Is Christianity true? What if it is true?

12

IS CHRISTIAN BELIEF TRUE?

It is no exaggeration to say that there are quite literally hundreds of arguments for God's existence.[1] Not all will persuade everyone, but some will. And for others, no argument will do. They simply *will not* believe.

THE INTELLECTUAL SCENE AND THE EXISTENCE OF THE CHRISTIAN GOD

By several measures, Christianity seems to be fading in the West, whereas it is exploding in the East and in Africa in particular. The rise of the "nones" (those with no religious affiliation) in America has concerned many. The decline seems to parallel and perhaps reveal a causal relationship with the rise of the New Atheism that began at the turn of the century. The 9/11 terror attack renewed some sense in which religions can be a great cause for evil and destruction. Christians sought to evade this by pointing out that Jesus and Mohammed, the founders of the two largest world religions, are very different when it comes to violence. But the New Atheists were sufficiently clever to tie Jesus to the God of the Old Testament and began charging that the alleged slavery, misogyny, and genocide approved by the God of the Old Testament was every bit as bad as that of the Jihadists. Yet, Jesus embraced the God of the Old Testament. Therefore, the goodness of Jesus is now at stake according to these critics. Most of the New Atheists were also engaged in the hard sciences, and they sought to show that all religion was mistaken, or evil, or both. The dialectic went back and forth for a decade with numerous books written by key atheist authors making a big splash. While the New Atheism was somewhat short lived, its spate of bestsellers has no doubt made a substantial impact on American Christianity and the Western Christian world. One thinks of those referred to as the "Four Horsemen" of the New Atheism—Richard Dawkins (*The God Delusion*), Sam Harris (*The End of Faith*), Christopher Hitchens (*God Is Not Great*), and Daniel Dennett (*Breaking the Spell*). The distinguishing mark of these players, in contrast to ordinary atheists, was their candor and ridicule. For example, who can forget this memorable tirade by Dawkins:

> The God of the Old Testament is arguably the most unpleasant character in all fiction: jealous and proud of it; a petty, unjust, unforgiving control-freak; a vindictive, bloodthirsty ethnic cleanser; a misogynistic, homophobic, racist, infanticidal, genocidal, filicidal, pestilential, megalomaniacal, sadomasochistic, capriciously malevolent bully.[2]

At the time, given the sad situation in American Christianity and its anti-intellectualism, most Christians were unprepared and had no defense. The New Atheist movement made its impact. Of course, upon reading their literature in full, it started to become clear to the trained person that not only were their arguments poor, but even academic atheists took notice. Even years later when their more "mature" books were written, they were still deemed poor. Michael Ruse said about one of them, "If God wanted to destroy New Atheism, getting this book written was a good start."[3]

That movement whose reign of terror lasted nearly two decades saw its demise. During the second decade, they began cannibalizing themselves as sexual and financial improprieties emerged among some members, while factions of the emerging identity politics split the movement in yet other ways. Indeed, the guillotine set up by them for religionists eventually took their own heads, just like Robespierre during the French Revolution. Some of its players have sought alliance with the Christians whose views they sought to destroy. Peter Boghossian admitted in a recent podcast that it was their own New Atheism that was partially responsible for the rise of the new woke culture.[4] Eventually, others revealed they had converted to Christianity, such as Ayaan Hirsi Ali.[5] She watched and condemned the 9/11 terror attacks, which led her to being an atheist for two decades, until seeing that the godless and false gods bear equally bad fruit in society. She quipped, "Christianity has it all."[6] Even the infamous Richard Dawkins now claims to be a "cultural Christian," revealing his newfound affection: "I like to live in a culturally Christian country although I do not believe a single word of the Christian faith."[7] Note that he's not claiming to be a Christian believer but rather someone who has inherited a Christian culture and who has come, if only by comparison to radical Islam or cultural Marxism, to appreciate and prefer Christian culture. This is not insignificant. Christianity is being reconsidered in light of our cultural revolution that has given pause to the direction of America and the West after having turned from Christianity.

For example, the extremely successful podcaster Joe Rogan evinces this when he claimed in February 2024, "We need Jesus. I think for real."[8] In that show, Rogan bemoaned,

> The problem with living in a secular society and living in a society that has a lot of people that are atheists, that have no belief system at all, is you find a belief system. A lot of these people that call themselves atheists—they've subscribed to the religion of woke. Their God is equity and inclusiveness.

Note the worldview of cultural Marxism Rogan is referring to when he says "religion of woke." When Rogan had philosopher Steve Meyer as a guest on his show, Rogan was an advocate of New Atheism. Meyer was perhaps the first Christian intellectual to be interviewed in some 2,000 episodes. Since that time, Rogan has featured other Christians who have spoken apologetically about their faith in conversations with the popular host.

Justin Brierley pointed out a silver lining of that movement when he wrote, "The church was forced to put down its tambourines and guitars and pick up its history and philosophy books again."[9] Indeed, like his debate show called *Unbelievable*, apologetics movements began in earnest, such as my organization, Ratio Christi, or William Lane Craig's Reasonable Faith, or Frank Turek's CrossExamined.org. Dissertation work has been done substantiating the value of apologetics in the conversions of many educated atheists.[10] Brierley thinks the tide may be turning. But tides go out and tides come in. The culture has already changed, and some movements have made adjustments to adapt, while others will find themselves in reactionary mode—just as the church was when the New Atheism arose.

Further, even while New Atheists were emerging, they were blissfully arrogant and largely unaware of the revolution that had already begun in the halls of Anglo-academic philosophy. Those folks in the New Atheism were riding on the crest of the scientism of a past era, and that wave crashed.

One thinks back to 1966's *Time* magazine article with the black cover page and red letters that stated, "Is God Dead?" That was an allusion to Nietzsche's death of God movement from centuries before. The 1960s student protests and sexual revolution, products of the academic atheism in the universities, may have been too premature in their declaration about the death of God. In the 1940s and 1950s, many academics thought that even talk about God was dead because God wasn't something verifiable by the five senses, and it was an age of verificationism. God-talk was literally nonsense. This reigning philosophy called *verificationism* collapsed under its own weight after people realized it was self-defeating in that it couldn't be verified by the five senses either. With its collapse came an almost secret renaissance in Christian philosophy.

One year before major student protests in 1968, a seminal book was published by Alvin Plantinga, *God and Other Minds: A Study of the Rational Justification of Belief in God*. Not only had he written several other books, one of which was largely credited with destroying the age-old "logical problem of evil," but in his wake, a whole movement followed. Christian academic societies and journals were launched, and Christian philosophers were being published in the finest journals. That has not gone unnoticed. Atheist philosopher Quentin Smith announced his lament in what he denoted "the desecularization of academia that evolved in philosophy departments since the late 1960s."[11] It was a cry for atheists everywhere to wake up. Naturalist's passivity had been blind to a wave of some of the brightest thinkers in philosophy who entered the field of academic philosophy and established a beachhead. He laments, "God is not 'dead' in academia; he returned to life in the late 1960s and is now alive and well in his last academic stronghold, philosophy departments."[12] This has come along with a resurgence in natural theology, a subdiscipline that seeks to show God's existence from the natural world wholly apart from divine revelation (but that is complementary to it).[13] Let's pursue the contours of some cursory examples.

COSMOLOGICAL ARGUMENT(S)

While there is a variation of arguments like this that reason from the existence of the world to the existence of God, here we will draw in broad strokes.

1. If the universe has an explanation, then God is that explanation.

2. Whatever exists has an explanation either in or outside itself.

3. The universe exists.

4. Therefore, God is the best explanation.

Most coherent people will grant the third premise. Suppose you were walking along a trail and saw a watch. The most rational thing to assume is not that it's simply always been there without explanation. Rather, it is to assume that the watch has a maker. Enlarging the watch to the size of the universe does nothing to alleviate the need for explanation. So the second premise is plausible. The atheist already assumes that if God does not exist, then the universe is without explanation. But if there is an external explanation, that explanation would be outside of space and time, otherwise it would be part of the universe and would no longer be external. Hence, any external explanation must be spaceless and timeless. There are only two sorts of things outside this: Mind or abstract objects such as numbers. But the latter are causally impotent. The number nine has no causal power to bring about anything. Hence, the best explanation is Mind. The Mind of God.

The Kalam cosmological argument, though part of the family, deserves special merit because it has received much attention in recent years given new scientific discoveries. While the argument goes back to a medieval Islamic source, it actually goes back even further to Arabic Christians like John Philoponus.

1. Whatever begins to exist has a cause.

2. The universe began to exist.

3. Therefore, the universe has a cause.

It is valid in that the conclusion follows inescapably from the premises. Are the premises true? They are certainly more plausible than their opposites, even if we don't know the premises with certainty. Otherwise, one would have to believe both that effects can exist without causes (including something coming from nothing) and that contrary to the mass of scientific evidence, the universe is eternal.

Atheists like to claim Christians believe in magic. But at least in magic, there is a magician and a hat out of which a bunny emerges. The atheist must believe something worse than magic—namely, there is neither a magician nor a hat but that a rabbit (i.e., the universe) magically appeared without explanation and is somehow rationally plausible to believe. While many atheists opt for an eternal universe, there are various philosophical and relatively new scientific reasons for thinking it is temporal.

First, a universe with an infinite past is philosophically absurd. If eternal, then it has an infinite number of time slices. But how could the present moment have arrived if an infinite number of time slices have passed? Second, scientific evidence conducted over the last century overwhelmingly supports a universe that had a beginning. The Big Bang—a theory first developed by a Catholic priest and physicist, Georges Lemaître, even while the expression was first used derisively by Fred Hoyle (who favored the Steady State Model)—has been considered the standard model of the origin of the universe for a century for good reason: evidence.

If the premises are more plausible than their opposites, and the conclusion follows validly from the premises, then it follows that what caused the space-time-matter-energy universe cannot be space, time, matter, or energy but must be something or someone that transcends those and be spaceless, timeless, immaterial, and powerful. And because the only two sorts of causes are physical causes and personal causes, it must also be personal because physics is the effect and not the cause. We can know much about the nature of the first cause even without invoking revelation. The notion, multiverse, has in principle no evidence but was concocted out of blind faith simply to avoid this conclusion. The multiverse is the hypothetical set of all universes we don't observe but postulate that they do exist.

TELEOLOGICAL ARGUMENT(S)

Today, the argument from purpose to God or from design to a Designer is very strong. Like the watch found on the trail moving one to infer a watchmaker, consider also looking at the busts of past American presidents' heads that are found on the rocks of Mount Rushmore. Then, imagine being told that the explanation of that specific complexity is due to millions of years of wind and water erosion. And imagine remaining rational with a straight face. The strength of the fine-tuning of the initial conditions of the universe is not for simply a universe but a life-permitting universe. When the physical laws of nature are articulated in mathematical equations, they contain certain constants whose constants are not themselves determined by the laws which they articulate (e.g., the gravitational constant). Also, there are certain quantities that simply exist within those initial conditions (e.g., the amount of entropy). These constants and qualities fall into a range of life-permitting values that, if altered by a razor's edge, would not permit life. Yet we are here, and we are alive. We can formulate the argument thusly:

1. The fine-tuning of the universe is due either to physical necessity, chance, or design.
2. It is not due to physical necessity or chance.
3. Therefore, the fine-tuning is due to design.

The first premise exhausts plausible possibilities. The second premise is a conclusion based on mounds of evidence why it cannot be accounted for by chance or necessity. The conclusion follows. The reason why necessity won't work is because the laws of nature are consistent with a wide range of values for the constants and quantities, meaning that the present ones aren't necessary. And the reason why chance won't work is because of the odds that this hypothesis points to the miraculous, unless one is prepared to embrace the highly speculative idea that our universe is but one member of a potentially infinite number of randomly ordered worlds known as the multiverse. This is where we've arrived in order to explain away the fine-tuning well known to cosmologists. Why would anyone ever propose such a bizarre idea? Because the fine-tuning of the real universe is that hard to explain!

One of the earliest developers of the multiverse concept is Leonard Susskind, a world-renowned theoretical physicist at Stanford University. He readily acknowledges that the universe appears to be specifically designed to permit human life, but he insists that appearance is simply an illusion. Susskind repeatedly asserts that the fine-tuning of the universe is so severe that there are only two reasonable explanations: multiverse or a supernatural Creator. Here are some examples of his perspective:

> As I have repeatedly emphasized, there is no known explanation of the special properties of our [universe] other than [multiverse]—no explanation that does not require supernatural forces.[14]

> What are the alternatives to [multiverse]? My own opinion is that once we eliminate supernatural agents, there is none that can explain the surprising and amazing fine-tuning of nature.[15]

Susskind is very clear that he chooses the multiverse because he will not even consider the possibility of a supernatural Creator.

> Let me be up front and state my own prejudices right here. I thoroughly believe that real science requires explanations that do not involve supernatural agents.[16]

> Scientists resist the temptation to explain natural phenomena, including creation itself, by divine intervention. Why? Because as scientists we understand that there is a compelling human

need to believe—the need to be comforted—that easily clouds people's judgment. It's all too easy to fall into the seductive trap of a comforting fairy tale. So, we resist, to the death, all explanations of the world based on anything but the Laws of Physics, mathematics and probability.[17]

The critical issue here is whether multiverse is science or philosophy. Is multiverse a valuable insight into the physical universe or a deceptive attempt to exclude God from it? Burton Richter, a Nobel Prize–winning physicist, reflects on this, saying, "Some of what passes for the most advanced theory in particle physics these days is not really science…I see major problems in the philosophy behind theory, which seems to have gone off into a kind of metaphysical wonderland. Simply put, much of what passes as the most advanced theory looks to be more theological speculation." Regarding multiverse, he states clearly, "That is metaphysics, not physics."[18] So affirmation of multiverse shows the length of faith one must go to in order to deny God's existence.

MORAL ARGUMENT(S)

Again, this is one version of a family of such arguments known as the moral argument. It can be formulated thus:

1. If God does not exist, objective moral values and duties do not exist.
2. Objective moral values and duties do exist.
3. Therefore, God exists.

By objective, this means that the values and duties in question are binding independent of human opinion. For premise one, many things like torture, murder, and rape among humans are simply commonplace among animals. Thus, if we're simply animals, then they are simply morally neutral in the ethics of the jungle. It's just nature. Further, if no one exists transcendentally to command or prohibit such things, how can we make sense of obligations? To whom are we accountable for violating any such prohibitions? Premise two is widely accepted. If it weren't, then the atheist would have nothing for their argument on the "problem of evil." But they clearly think some things are objectively wrong. Indeed, the Christian can capitalize on the perceived prominence of the problem of evil in the atheist's quiver to persuade them of premise two.

Often, nontheists will counter with a dilemma. They ask, "Is something good because God wills it, or does God will something because it is good?" The first horn on the dilemma makes good and evil arbitrary (called voluntarism because it is a matter of God's will). The second makes it independent of God such that God becomes merely redundant to morality. This view is called Platonism, as it was held by Plato. But this is a false dilemma. Christians have taken the third option—namely, essentialism. God wills something because He is good, essentially. So it is part of who God is, and His commandments are simply expressions of His nature and character.

These are just a few theistic arguments. There are others. And there are many great arguments for topics such as the reliability of the Bible and the historical resurrection of Jesus. HarperCollins Publishers says on their website, "Philosopher and former atheist Antony Flew set the agenda for modern atheism with his 1950 essay 'Theology and Falsification,' which became the most widely reprinted philosophical publication of the last half century."[19] Flew converted to theism. Prior to his death, he claimed that the new evidence from intelligent design, consciousness, and other lines of thought finally led him to believe there is a God.[20] He also wrote, "The evidence for the resurrection is better than claimed miracles in any other religion. It's outstandingly different in quality and quantity, I think, from the evidence offered for the occurrence of most other supposedly miraculous events."[21]

EVIDENCE AND EXPLANATION FOR THE HISTORICITY OF JESUS' RESURRECTION

There are many ways one can marshal evidence for the resurrection without assuming the Bible is the Word of God. For the sake of argument, simply treat it like other historical sources that can be tested for relative accuracy. For memorization purposes, I'll use the acronym FEAST to organize several facts that are agreed upon by most scholars:

F = Fate: Jesus was killed by crucifixion. Most historians specializing in the life of Christ concur. The declaration by Islam that Jesus was not crucified has origins that are too late to be considered authoritative compared to early testimonial evidence of Scripture. Further, the tomb location was attested to by both Jew and Christian alike. It's part of Mark's source material (Mark 15:42–6:8) for the book of Mark, likely being the earliest written Gospel account. Further, many scholars believe that Paul's first letter to the Corinthians was written even earlier, which includes an early church tradition embedded in 1 Corinthians 15:3-4 that is a summary of the early Christian preaching that occurred prior to the New Testament writings. The passage mentions the burial. Paul likely received it no later than his visit to Jerusalem (cf. Galatians 1:18). It therefore goes back to within five years of the crucifixion. Matthew, Luke, John, and Acts are also independent sources. This, along with other reasons, are why liberal New Testament scholar John A.T. Robinson of Cambridge University said that the burial of Jesus is "one of the earliest and best-attested facts about Jesus."[22]

E = Empty Tomb: On the third day, as was reported very early on, the women who went to the tomb to anoint Jesus' body were the first to see that the tomb was empty. First, in that era, if one wanted witness credibility, they could not claim women as the first witnesses. Women weren't respected as witnesses in that culture. This fact favors the testimony being historical. Second, the Jewish explanation inside the New Testament, as well as in the Talmud, both seek to explain away the empty tomb by naturalistic explanation. This attempt presupposes the tomb being empty. The Romans and Jews had only to publicly parade the dead body of Jesus through the busy streets of Jerusalem to put Christianity out of business because Jesus would have been not merely a dead prophet but a false one too, since He predicted His resurrection. That would have sealed the coffin, and Christianity would have ceased to exist. Instead, they sought to give a naturalistic explanation of the obvious empty tomb. It comes from not the followers of Jesus but his opponents. According to Jacob Kremer, a New Testament critical scholar who specializes in resurrection studies, "By far most scholars hold firmly to the reliability of the biblical statements about the empty tomb."[23] Indeed, in a survey of more than 2,200 research publications on the resurrection in German, French, and English since 1975, resurrection researcher Gary Habermas found that 75 percent of relevant scholars accepted the historicity of the discovery of the empty tomb.[24] Habermas has just launched his first of four volumes culminating 50 years of research on the topic. In the first volume, itself more than 1,000 pages, he says that number is now closer to 80 percent.[25]

A = Appearances: Jesus' followers believed they saw Him alive only days after His death. He was seen numerous times by individuals (e.g., Peter, James, the Twelve, the women, and up to 500 at one time) over a period of 40 days. Paul reports this in 1 Corinthians 15:3-8 and claims that if the physical resurrection did not happen, then Christianity is false. He reminds his readers that most of the people living at that time were still alive for cross examination, a time when Christians were in the minority. In Luke 1:1-4, we're told that Luke investigated everything carefully, not that the disciples simply believed. The appearances were reported by at least five early independent sources: Paul, Luke, John, Matthew, and Mark. All these sources generously report names, dates, and people that were cross-checked by outside corroborating sources in the ancient world. The reporting is accurate. Now, one can explain away these appearances as hallucinations, but one is hard pressed to say that the experiences did not happen. These experiences included empirical means such as seeing, touching, hearing, and talking to Him. This lines up with a pre–New Testament report circulating well before the New Testament was written, and it was then embedded in the early New Testament writing. Scholars believe the followers experienced something of belief forming, even if many of them don't embrace the supernatural explanation forming their beliefs. For example, liberal scholar Gerd Lüdemann says, "It may be taken as historically certain that Peter and the disciples had experiences after Jesus' death in which Jesus appeared to them as the risen Christ."[26]

S = Skeptics: Paul, a Jewish leader and skeptic who oversaw the killings of Christians, and Jesus' brother James, another skeptic, both became followers who died for Christ after they reported resurrected appearances of Jesus. No other explanation on offer competes for why these skeptics converted other than that they believed that they encountered the physically resurrected Jesus. Foes, not just friends, came to faith based on what they believed to be powerful empirical evidence. Most scholars today affirm that the earliest followers—friends and foes, women and men, individuals and groups—experienced some apparent bodily resurrected Christ. The scholars simply disagree on what explains this: Was it natural or supernatural?

T = Transformation: The early church was born because of the phenomenal transformation of the many disciples who were willing to die for what they came to experience in a risen Christ. The contagious news spread primarily based on evidential accounts from those who claimed to experience the risen Lord. For the first time, thousands of Jews began celebrating not on Saturday (the traditional day of Sabbath) but on Sunday, becoming known as the Lord's Day because Jesus rose on that day. The origins of the early Christian movement were contingent upon their belief in a risen Christ.

Most critical scholars believe each of those five facts regardless of whether they believe the supernatural explanation for them. Evidence is one thing, explanation another. Given the evidence and barring any antisupernaturalist *a priori bias* (rebutted above in earlier arguments), the supernatural explanation is the inference to the best explanation. Although a leading handful of naturalistic explanations have been given to explain the facts,[27] they're all abundantly dealt with in the literature. Why accept these facts? Simply because standard criteria for supporting actual historical events support them. The following lists the contours of some of the historical criteria.

First, multiple attestations. Claims that have been recorded by multiple sources have greater reliability than claims with only one source. Given the degeneration of records over time, multiple-source attestation isn't always easy to find. An event recorded in Matthew, Mark, Luke, John, and Paul's writings constitute five unique sources, as these were all written independently. The collection of books known as the Bible came together later. Further, all five facts are recorded not only by those sources but by later Christian and non-Christian writers.

Second, early attestation. Information found in earlier sources is considered more reliable than later information (this is why the Islamic report six centuries later is highly dubitable and with no evidence). Paul's epistles were written earlier than the Gospels. Of the Gospels, Mark (or some argue Matthew) was the earliest one written, and John was the latest. As alluded to earlier, Paul's first letter to the Corinthian church was written in the early 50s; we have embedded an early Christian creed recording Christ's death, resurrection, and appearances (1 Corinthians 15:3-8). Some ascribe the date of that creed to around AD 30–33. This places the first written record of the account within six months to three years of the resurrection event itself. Perhaps surprisingly, skeptical New Testament scholar Gerd Lüdemann assigns an early date, claiming that "the elements in the tradition are to be dated to the first two years after the crucifixion of Jesus…not later than three years… the formation of the appearance traditions mentioned in 1 Cor. 15:3-8 falls into the time between 30 and 33 C.E."[28]

Third, enemy attestation. If your enemies agree with you about something that happened, then its reliability is strengthened. When Christ's followers proclaimed a risen Lord based on an empty tomb, neither the Jews nor the Romans claimed the opposite—that the tomb wasn't empty. They certainly could have paraded Jesus' body publicly and Christianity would have ceased to exist. Instead, they confirmed the empty tomb report as factual by claiming that the body must have been stolen by the disciples. Most scholars, skeptics and believers alike, affirm the empty tomb due to the evidence.

Fourth, the criterion of embarrassment. If one is fabricating an account, one wants to avoid embarrassing details that might cast suspicion on the account. Embarrassing information that might render claims less credible often strengthens reliability because sharing these details isn't what a listener might expect to hear if one is simply fabricating an account. As mentioned above, women were the first witnesses, which isn't something someone would do to strengthen their case given the low view of women's testimonies at the time.

Naturalistic alternative explanations have been offered on how to explain the consensus agreement on these broad facts, but most of the explanations were invented between the seventeenth and twentieth centuries, and they carry with them antisupernaturalist bias.

Given the historical factuality of the five facts mentioned above, it is plausible that the inference to the best explanation of such facts is the supernatural resurrection. This implies the existence of a supernatural Being, but as we've seen, that is already intellectually plausible.

ON THE RELEVANCE OF ARGUMENTS

While there is no consensus to the above arguments (there rarely is consensus on anything), the amount of literature expelled to counter these arguments shows that they are having an impact. But someone might still suggest that all this great development in natural theology is pointless in a postmodern era reflecting a radical relativism. However, a thoroughgoing postmodern culture is an oxymoron. It is unlivable. No one is really a relativist in math or engineering when it comes to building bridges or buildings. Usually, it is only in matters of religion and ethics that people claim relativism for convenience. But even the people who claim relativism have a threshold. For most, there is a concept of going too far. Who, for example, thinks it ethically neutral to physically assault homosexuals, or for parents to force their children into illegal acts, or to own people as property? Remember that the leading thinkers of postmodernism don't seem to really believe relativism either but use it instead as a sophisticated cover for their leftist ideology along the lines of postmodern cultural Marxism or something similar. The gospel is always presented not in a vacuum but in the cultural and ideological context in which it exists.

Because the three dominant thought currents in the university all spin off from naturalism, a sort of thoughtful Christianity that is presented as an intellectually viable option will find investigators displaying an openness to the gospel. In the sociological study of religion, plausibility structures are the sociocultural contexts for systems of meaning within which these meanings make sense or are made plausible (believable). To believe in God apart from the intellectual plausibility structure is tantamount to asking them to believe in Zeus. Thus, Christians who depreciate and deprecate natural theology on grounds that "you can't reason someone into the kingdom" undermine Christianity.

Natural theology is the attempt to establish religious truths by rational argument and without reliance on alleged revelations. The value of such theology extends beyond one's immediate evangelistic contacts. It creates a plausibility structure that is otherwise faced with the tension that the heart cannot embrace what the mind cannot believe. It must be believable, credible, and trustworthy. The bottom line is that the intellectual resources supporting Christianity are available. We should all be equipped to know where to find resources to get prepared to answer people's questions. If someone needs a hug, we can give them a hug. But if they need an argument, we should love them enough to help them with answers. Everyone should engage in evangelism (using apologetics when relevant) at the personal level. But at the cultural level, we need to understand and consider recapture at the institutional level—influencing and shaping downstream.

13

ALL HANDS ON DECK: EVERYONE PAY ATTENTION TO THE UNIVERSITY!

If you want to change the world, change the university. As go the universities, so goes the culture. As go the universities in the US, so goes the world. The university is so enormously influential that everybody needs to pay attention and consider how they might prepare to impact the university, which will, in turn, impact the culture and the world. The college years are the time when students are at their prime of intellectual curiosity and discovery. That also helps us understand why so many are leaving the faith after they enter the university. Everyone needs to be influential in their own sphere while, at the same time, realizing the power of the university and how we all might play a role in evangelizing the university. There are several ways that we can impact the university.

PARACHURCH OR CAMPUS MINISTRIES

A parachurch ministry or organization is one that comes alongside the church. Some churches directly seek to minister at universities, while not all parachurches are directly related to the campus. For university impact, I'm not thinking of organizations such as Compassion International that help the hungry, or adoption agencies that help children find homes. Rather, I'm thinking in terms of those most connected to a university campus like Cru, InterVarsity, Veritas Forums, or the Navigators, to name just a few, all of which are on the campus. Other organizations include worldview- or apologetic-type ministries—ministries that seek to give a rational defense of the Christian faith. Some examples of this include Ratio Christi, Reasonable Faith, Reasons to Believe, Discovery Institute, Stand to Reason, Colson Fellows, Summit Ministries, and CrossExamined.org, among others. These organizations have a primary focus on reasons for the Christian faith, evangelism, and discipleship.

To continue to be salt and light in the culture, these ministries should think about how they might make the greatest impact in focusing some of their attention upstream to the campus. And for those already on the campus, focusing some of their attention to worldview and apologetics resources and training to meet the needs of a changing campus. Sadly, some campus ministries have been infected by the woke-mind virus, by a new form of liberation theology. Yet given the task before us at the secular university, where possible, these ministries should collaborate. We can do bigger and better things together in cooperation.

Because I am the president and CEO of one such campus ministry and know it most intimately (even while having served on staff at other ones), I'll share ways in which making an impact upstream in the right way is most strategic in terms of cultural impact. Ratio Christi means the "reason of Christ." While we believe in loving God with our hands and heart, in the university setting, we emphasize the head of Christ. We have a staff that is highly trained, many possessing doctorates, so we can engage students' minds. Ratio Christi's vision is as follows: Thoughtful Christianity—Transforming Lives on Campus Today, Changing Culture Tomorrow. "Thoughtful" represents both a compassionate heart and a contemplative mind. Politics is downstream from culture, culture is downstream from education, and the university is the apex of education. So if there is pollution downstream, rather than pouring chlorine at the end, we seek to make our impact upstream where the source of the corruption often begins. What separates us from the standard apologetics and worldview ministry is that we're on the campus, seeking to impact the campus and thereby the culture downstream. We often cooperate with respect to resources and speakers with other noncampus parachurch ministries. What separates Ratio Christi as a parachurch ministry from all the other campus ministries is that we do apologetics-evangelism with students and also focus on helping professors and administrators integrate their faith, reason, and vocation. Our mission statement reflects our intent to equip students and faculty with historical, philosophical, and scientific reasons for following Jesus Christ.[1]

Since the time that many of the big campus ministries began 80 years ago, the campuses have changed. Many haven't innovated like Ratio Christi has in order to meet that challenge. The apostle Paul engaged with Jews in the synagogues by using the Scriptures, which they affirmed as proof that Jesus was the Messiah. To the Greeks, Paul brought his biblically informed mind, but he also mediated that with reason, making appeal to the Greek way of thinking. To the Jews he became as a Jew, and to the Greek as a Greek.

At one time, the university was a Christian theistic institute that believed in God, the Bible, and a Judeo-Christian ethics. No more. But the students entering the universities' campuses still characteristically possess those fundamental beliefs, such that a campus minister could deploy the proverbial "Four Spiritual Laws," or otherwise, and witness conversions. Before World War II, only 15 percent of high-school graduates went on to college. So the American populace and its children weren't influenced by universities to the degree they are today. Things have changed, even in the beliefs held by the entering students. We lost the millennial generation (or even the prior generation), in part, because we thought we were still in the synagogue, so to speak, rather than on Mars Hill. The university has been rapidly and radically departing from its origins over the last century, and to effectively reach it, we need to have a simple and working knowledge of Christian apologetics.

Ratio Christi reaches college students with the gospel through apologetics-evangelism. We see many come to Christ and many others come to appreciate the intellectual foundations of Christian belief, of which they were previously unaware and which moves them to a different place of consideration. I am convinced that the heart cannot embrace what the mind cannot believe. Belief comes in degrees, such that mild belief doesn't lead to robust action, whereas confident belief often does. We change beliefs and or reinforce beliefs through our approach. The local chapters on campuses meet weekly, with some groups having more nonbelievers attending than believers given the nature of the topics. They hold annual big events on their campuses. I once moderated a debate where some 14,000 were in attendance. Topics range from debates on God's existence with the top scholars in the field to conferences on human sex trafficking where we'll bring in ex–porn stars and ex–sex slaves to tell their stories of leaving slavery and moving to freedom in Christ. Then we'll follow the latter with a debate on God and morality, even that same weekend, to show why our moral intuitions and solutions for ending human sex trafficking make the most sense if God exists and Christianity is true. In short, we want to show why Christianity is good, reasonable, and true.

Ratio Christi College Prep is a division working with Christian churches and schools to prepare students to not merely survive the 23:1 ratio of professors unfavorable to Christian belief on college campuses but thrive in that environment. In polling, when students go off to college, the rate of apostasy from the faith ranges broadly between 50 and 80 percent of students. Given the problems that pastors and parents are facing, as we will discuss below, we aim to come alongside them and turn that statistic around.

Ratio Christi Prof is a division that focuses not so much on apologetics-evangelism as with our student ministry as it does integration and infiltration. That is, we help those professors who are Christians see the dire need and become missional Christian professors by helping them better integrate faith with their reason, vocation, and life. Most of them will never receive such training from their churches and certainly won't encounter it in their graduate programs. Consequently, they often function as methodological naturalists in their disciplines from Monday through Friday. Or now, given the changes in the universities that we analyzed in parts 1 and 2, they might share a hybrid of their Christian view combined with some woke philosophy. Many who possess a PhD have never taken a philosophy class and so can easily imbibe the progressive ideology without recognizing it. Our vision for these professors is for them to have a fully integrated world- and life view. Apologetics-evangelism becomes secondary. We provide them with the philosophical and theological foundations of a Christian worldview and show how it helps them integrate their faith and reason, faith and vocation, and faith and life. We give them tools. We are one of the few professors' ministries (of very few in existence) that has a formal track on how to train these teachers in missional professor theory and practice. We call it Missional Prof 1.0 and 2.0.

Ratio Christi also runs what we call the Malik Academic Fellows program, whereby we fund young, committed, Christian PhD students who get accepted into elite research universities (called R1) with doctoral programs. Why focus on R1 schools? Because if they graduate from one of these reputable programs, it is their ticket into the job market, effectively the Trojan horse, to infiltrate the institution. We train them over multiple years and connect them with various full-professor mentors in key universities. Their funding includes also launching Christian PhD student–only ministries to train fellows (with our oversight) as we've taught them. Every fellow is to launch a ministry that will outlast them when they graduate and move on to become a professor elsewhere. The design is such that each one trains (or sets in motion a movement to train) ten other Christian PhD students per year, making the ministry 100 students in only ten years. Because each professor will have approximately 15,000 students over the course of their careers, this means that 1.5 million college students will be exposed to at least one trained missional professor during their college experience. This is scalable such that if we fund 10 or 100 Malik Fellows, the impact is exponential.

This is one way of infiltrating the universities to reclaim the intellectual voice of Christ at the highest levels. These professors eventually become administrators as well. So we're developing a long-term approach and a movement of young missional professors that will eventuate in our own revolution. I use that term here not in a violent way but in the sense in which we've already discussed the first two ideological revolutions or changing of the guard in university faculty—first, scientific naturalism, and second, postmodern cultural Marxism. If it has happened before, it can happen again, and we're aiming for that to happen in the long term, only this time back toward a Christ-centered worldview. As the neo-Marxists have denoted in their own plans, this constitutes for us "the long march through the institutions." To change the world, change the universities. This is no exaggeration. The rise of the number of international students, including future political leaders, attending American universities is encouraging in terms of the global opportunity for impact.

Ratio Christi International extends the work that we do in the US around the world. But we also reach students in the US who then go to other countries. At Purdue University, for example (a school adjacent to our administrative headquarters), in 2024, among the 58,000 undergraduate and graduate students enrolled on the main campus, more than 20 percent were graduate students, and nearly 20 percent of all students were international students, coming from 135 countries.[2] The world and its future professors have come to universities in the US (the largest populations being from China and India). Of nearly 200 countries in the world, as of 2024, 70 of their leaders (monarchs, presidents, or prime ministers) studied in the US.[3] In 2023, three-fourths of international students in the US came from the 10/40 window,[4] a region that shows the largest section on earth of unreached people groups that need to be reached with the gospel. Most international students return home. We can and should capitalize on the fact that the world has come to the universities in the US.[5] Difficulty abounds for those who want to reach the world. Many nations have closed doors to missionaries and ministry can be very costly. But many of those same nations send students to the campuses of America—they are the future leaders of their respective nations. The university is among the most strategic mission fields in the world. Christians can reach the world while simultaneously reaching the campus for Christ.

Ratio Christi Press has unique resources available for all. Many people struggle to read books today, which is unfortunate. But short booklets are another story. We have approximately 50 digital and printable resources that are concise (25 pages), credible (most authors possess a PhD), accessible (eleventh-grade reading level), and relevant (classical and cultural apologetics). They deal with many, many topics. They range from classical topics like the problem of evil, the reliability of the Bible, and questions about science and faith, to novel cultural apologetic topics like race, class, sex, and gender. They answer questions such as the following: Why does God allow evil? Is social justice compatible with Christianity? How do I think biblically about LGBTQ+ matters? What is a woman? It is important that Christian communities have the resources addressing topics that campus ministries are facing today because the broader culture will face them tomorrow as ideas move from the campus to the culture.[6]

Campus ministries want to see souls saved at the university, but we also want to see the soul of the university saved, in that we want to see the university resume its purpose of pursuing truth. Christians should be, minimally, part of that conversation. We want others to think the same way, to be thinkers and followers of Jesus. Not by dominating others heavy-handedly and becoming like the cancel-culture world that often cancels Christians. We want to at least have a robust presence at the most influential institution in civilization, an institution that Christians played a significant part in starting in the first place. Again, we want to help the university achieve its original telos, its purpose, which is the pursuit of truth. Because we think that Christianity is true, then that telos is helpful in more ways than one. The cost of our failure, as Christians, to reach the people and institutions at the universities may be at the expense of sacrificing our culture and, more profoundly, our children and grandchildren.

Campus ministries need to focus on reaching not only students with apologetics-evangelism but also professors and administrators. If we can win the professor, we can win the classroom too. Professors can influence students for several decades. Failure for Christians to do so is, strategically, the greatest omission of the Great Commission in the Western world.

Perhaps you're not in a place where you can partner directly with a parachurch ministry. But you can pray for them, their work on campus, and even support the many efforts and ministries that exist on college campuses. And there are still other opportunities available.

PASTORS, CHURCH LEADERS, AND CHURCHES

Being a pastor is harder than many think. I've done it. But no one said it would be easy. One must nonetheless be faithful in one's stewardship through joy and struggle. So I offer a few sobering, yet helpful, words to strengthen the resolve of our churches in being salt and light to the world and an encouragement to consider a partial focus on our universities. The church is an institution ordained by God. But pastors must recognize that other institutions have emerged that are sometimes leveraging greater influence on the culture because of the social stratification of culture.

Are Christians (including Christian pastors) relevant? Half of Americans believe that the same levels of charitable giving would go on even if Christianity were absent. According to recent research, approximately 66 percent of Americans say that the presence of clergy is a benefit to a community but that their insights are not considered relevant to living real life. Or as one author put it, "Christian leaders are viewed like a smiling greeter at Walmart."[7] And only 20 percent strongly believe that clergy are a credible source of wisdom and insight when it comes to the most important issues of our day.[8] This is a huge problem. Who will replace pastors as guides for biblical living? We can only pray it is not social media.

Are Christians extreme? There is a growing disdain for religion in America and for Christianity in particular. To be an extremist today, you don't need to decapitate someone or blow up a building. You only need to be a Christian. For example, in 2016, data revealed that 40 percent of adults believe it is extremist to try to convert others to their faith, to proselytize. But that number rises to 60 percent for Christians who try to proselytize.[9] Most adults think that Christians providing food pantries is a good thing but that a Christian seeking to follow Jesus in the Great Commission is extremist. Give me your money and resources, otherwise, keep your extremist mouth shut.

The fact is, as demonstrated earlier, that Christianity is good *for* the world, even if it is not perceived as good *to* the world. Like vegetables are objectively good *for* our children, even if they are not subjectively desired as good *to* our children. Genuine Christians will demonstrate this, and it is also incumbent on Christians to show this to others. As for evangelism, we cannot fail to share the good news. If we claim to love people, do we limit that to our behaving well toward them? Do we not also tell them why we do what we do and what motivates our behavior? Do we not want them to know God's love rather than only our love? Further, in today's skeptical and cynical culture to Christian thought and life, we need to realize the value of apologetics in evangelism. The most recent data from the Barna research demonstrates this need significantly.

Practicing Christians' ideas about what is most important to people when considering Christianity do not always match up with reality. In a recent Barna report, non-Christians self-report that what intrigues them most about

Christianity is if "Christianity had better evidence to support it." In fact, when asked, "What factors could increase interest in Christianity?" there were 14 options to select from, and 44 percent (almost half) of nonbelievers picked "evidence." By contrast, the response from practicing Christians to the same prompt had that answer at almost dead last. Only 14 percent of practicing Christians thought that nonbelievers would be interested in evidence for Christianity. Most practicing Christians are woefully out of touch with what nonbelievers self-report that they want. Instead, we give them skinny jeans and fog machines or other gimmicks to attract them to our churches. The evidence is clear that apologetics is not only a command for today (1 Peter 3:15-16), but it is also a demand for today. But interestingly, even the Barna researchers themselves appear to be coming to grips with the data and evidence. They admit that almost half of non-Christians wish for credible and reasonable explanations of the Christian faith. But they add a caveat:

> This does not necessarily mean Christians should invest heavily in traditional apologetics, however. As demonstrated by non-Christians' distaste for street preaching and tracts, depersonalized outreach that feels intrusive or manipulative is likely to lower openness to the gospel rather than to encourage its further consideration.[10]

This is an overgeneralization. Yes, apologetic endeavors should be carried out without intrusiveness and manipulation. But traditional apologetics is not strictly street preaching, tracts, and depersonalized outreach. With respect to compelling "evidence," one pastor interviewed for the research said, "'Evidence' does not automatically mean 'proof' or something visible to draw a person to the sensibleness of a belief. In my experience…an understanding of how creation cares for us as we care for it shows the value of humanity to a 'Supreme Being.' This is evidence."[11] If such evidence is representative, then it is clear that there are pastors who need training in this area.

Pastors are to be virtuous in character, role models for others to follow. As Paul says, "Follow my example, as I follow the example of Christ" (1 Corinthians 11:1). Failure in this area has wrecked many a ship. The world is watching, and those in leadership will be held accountable. This involves moral character, but it also involves intellectual virtues and loving God with your mind. Pastors in America were once looked at as intellectual authorities. They thought Jesus was smart. They wanted to be smart like Jesus. If you want to be like Jesus, you need to think like Jesus. They realized that Jesus said that the purpose of life is knowing God, such that knowledge isn't something peripheral to Christian life but central. Every university president for nearly two centuries (1636–1840) was also a member of the clergy and taught the capstone senior class on moral philosophy. Times have changed, and pastors, like many Americans, have often become anti-intellectual, serving as the hands and heart of Christ, yet without the head of Christ.

Now, I realize that not all pastors fit this bill, but enough do to make this statement a necessity. Ready? Pastors need to jettison their churches from attractional ministry that pervades our culture. They must return to the business of their call "to equip the saints for work of ministry" (Ephesians 4:12 ESV). Our culture is dying, and our churches are capitulating. This call includes every pastor in your church. This entails a robust discipleship program. Anti-intellectualism had already become part of evangelical subculture such that the scandal of the evangelical mind was that there wasn't much left of the evangelical mind—at least for a great number of adherents.[12] The attractional ministry model has a short shelf life, for clear reasons, but something else has come along in its place that is a danger to the pastor of the empty mind.

In recent years, many became attracted to social justice, thinking that might well avoid conflict while pursuing some good deeds. Who wants to touch conflicting topics like divorce, abortion, or homosexuality—or so the reasoning goes—when you can focus on broadly accepted good deeds? Some might reason it may provide a good platform because people will like the church and see it as beneficial for society and, perhaps, even listen to us. Some very noble and laudable thinking. Never mind that the term *social justice* itself is not biblical. But it is what is smuggled via false ideology inside a Trojan horse that is the concern. We addressed this earlier in the book. It's become so embedded that the term *social* can now be dropped while retaining the same meaning, simply referring to it as *justice*. There is a growing trend in evangelical circles to now rebrand "mercy" or "compassion" ministries as "justice" ministries. Under this ministry is everything from feeding the poor to adoption, and from building water systems in the developing world to rescuing trafficked women. Such ministries were once identified as mercy ministries. Why are churches rebranding these as justice ministries? This shift reveals something else following on the heels of the shift away from education and thoughtful Christianity.

With the rise of social justice, mercy has taken a backseat. It is hip now to advocate for justice, a shortened form of social justice but with a different meaning than *justice* has been historically understood. As Christians, we should advocate justice when defined properly. That's the problem. Much of what passes for truth is political truth, for science is political science, and for justice is social justice. These pairs don't always correspond and much of what is denoted social justice is often injustice. Within Christianity, the problem is more subtle as we have blended mercy and justice together. Such confusion leads to a loss of both.

Justice is getting one's due, getting what you deserve. It is merit based. You earn it. It is owed. When Paul says, in Romans 6:23, that "the wages of sin is death," it is clear that justice based on what is due to us is wrath. Fortunately, he goes on to say, "But the gift of God is eternal life through Christ Jesus our Lord." Grace is getting what you don't deserve. Mercy is not getting what you deserve. Mercy forgoes merit and grace gives favor to those who are undeserving. The focus is on getting one's due. To make it plain, justice is something we can demand, while mercy and grace are not things for which we have a right to demand. It is this ability to demand justice that makes it more appealing.

If Christians make feeding the poor an issue of justice instead of mercy, then we are saying the poor have the right to demand satisfaction from others or the right to their money or property. Moreover, they have the right to demand that they receive what belongs to others. Such an action violates the eighth commandment and is therefore unjust.

Biblically, things like feeding the poor and adoption are acts of mercy and grace, not of justice. Poverty, or any inequality, are not necessarily caused by injustice. While some people become poor because of oppression, it is also true that some are poor because of justice. The acts of some people earn them poverty (Proverbs 6:9-11; 24:30-34). In such cases, helping the poor is an act not of justice but of mercy and grace. For Christians, justice, mercy, and grace are all virtues, but they are distinct virtues. Social justice confuses them because it has been infused by Marxist thought that inequality entails injustice. Christians often gullibly give in because we know God hates oppression and hates sin, but sin is not identical to oppression. Furthermore, it gets applied to everything like reproductive justice, environmental justice, gender justice, research justice, and so on.

It is unsurprising that false philosophies have infiltrated churches because most pastors simply do not hold a biblical worldview. It is incumbent on pastors to love God not just with their hands and hearts but also with their minds. Yet Scripture assigns pastors the role in equipping, shepherding, and teaching Scripture and Christian thought. Titus 1:9 says that a pastor "must hold firmly to the trustworthy message as it has been taught, so that he can encourage others by sound doctrine and refute those who oppose it." First Timothy 3:2 says that the pastor must be "able to teach."

The Barna Group publishes an *Annual Worldview Inventory*. For the purposes of the research, a "biblical worldview" was characterized by seven chief cornerstones: (1) a belief in God's existence and biblical understanding of God's nature, (2) all humans are sinners in need of a savior, (3) Jesus being the only way of salvation, (4) the Bible is God's Word and is historically reliable and true in all it teaches, (5) absolute truth (including moral truth) exists and is grounded in God, (6) the purpose of life is to know, love, and serve God, and (7) success is understood through faithful obedience to God.[13]

The following statistics are derived from the Barna research and cited above. In 2022, it was discovered that only 6 percent of Americans hold a biblical worldview (this dropped to 4 percent in 2023) and that slightly more than one-third (37 percent) of America's Christian pastors possess a biblical worldview. For nondenominational or evangelical pastors, that number is between 51–57 percent. That slight majority is not a great cause for celebrating. Most embrace some sort of syncretism with the world's views on crucial matters. That number is far lower for children's and youth pastors at 12 percent. In some cases, discovering how little difference exists between the life or belief of Christian pastors and the average American indicates how strongly the culture is influencing the American church and not vice versa. The salt has lost its saltiness.

What this reveals is that our transition away from thoughtful Christianity has led to poorly behaving Christianity. Belief precedes behavior. Our real (not merely declared) beliefs are the rails upon which our behaviors ride. The menace of mindless Christianity has got to go. Distinguished professor of philosophy at Biola University J.P. Moreland articulates the role of reason in the life of the soul in his book *Loving God with All Your Mind*. I recommend it as a resource. It should not need to be pointed out that Jesus commanded us to love God with our minds (Matthew 22:37), that knowledge is central to the Christian experience (John 17:3), that using our minds is part of the discipline God uses for His disciples to be transformed (Romans 12:1-2), and finally, that the world needs us to start placing a premium not only on the heart and hands of Christ but on the head of Christ. Peter commands us to be ready to give an apologetic or reasonable response for the logic of what we believe, but to do so out of hope from our heart and with gentleness and respect with our hands (1 Peter 3:15-16). The integrated Christian loves God with head, heart, and hands. Not only is it still a command, but it is back in demand in our culture—especially at the universities.

When it comes to apologetics, there are many ministries prepared to help churches (e.g., Reasonable Faith, Reasons to Believe, Colson Fellows, Stand to Reason, CrossExamined.org, and Discovery Institute). Ratio Christi is prepared and has booklets to help with small groups, Sunday-school classes, and resources that can even enable you to launch a Ratio Christi College Prep group in your church to prepare students for the onslaught of the universities. Remember that universities are training K–12 teachers and social media is adding to the complexity of the problem. We need to be addressing the hot, pressing topics with our youth.

Pastors need to equip their people, especially parents and young people, in order to thrive in universities, not simply survive. Our culture, especially university culture, has shifted to an Acts 17 Mars Hill model.[14] It's been there for a long time. That is, we live in a post-Christian culture, not only an era of a post-Christian university. When Paul went to the synagogues, he brought the Scriptures and reasoned from them to the Jewish people that Christ was the Messiah. When he went to Mars Hill in Athens, the people didn't embrace the Scriptures and so Paul commenced with a different starting point. We are living in an Acts 17 American culture. Given our culture, knowing doctrine and apologetics is vital. Indeed, given our Scripture, it isn't a suggestion, but a command. The apostle Peter's admonition has never been more relevant:

> In your hearts revere Christ as Lord. Always be prepared to give an answer to everyone who asks you to give the reason for the hope that you have. But do this with gentleness and respect, keeping a clear conscience, so that those who speak maliciously against your good behavior in Christ may be ashamed of their slander (1 Peter 3:15-16).

Pastors, part of your outreach strategy should include, if even a modicum of focus, the university. Consider the words of the great Princeton theologian J. Gresham Machen:

> False ideas are the greatest obstacles to the reception of the gospel. We may preach with all the fervor of a reformer and yet succeed only in winning a straggler here and there, if we permit the whole collective thought of the nation or of the world to be controlled by ideas which, by the resistless force of logic, prevent Christianity from being regarded as anything more than a harmless delusion. Under such circumstances, what God desires us to do is to destroy the obstacle at its root.[15]

The gospel is given in soil that either is or is not conducive to it taking root. Recall the parable of the soils and cultivate good soil.

PARENTS AND GRANDPARENTS

One of the greatest joys and challenges in life is raising children. Increasingly, American culture is making it difficult given educational, economic, and ideological challenges. It's become cultural (and some say required) to have two-parent incomes. Our economic standards often add pressure to conform to this phenomenon to make ends meet. Sometimes feeling exhausted, many

Christian parents have punted their responsibility of child rearing to the youth pastor or the state-funded educators. We've already shown where K–12 teachers are being educated and how few pastors, much less youth pastors, hold a biblical worldview. Admittedly, full-time work and nighttime visitation with children and teens can be exhausting. While two-thirds of parents of preteens claim to be Christian, only 2 percent of all parents of preteens possess a biblical worldview. Not only do many people fail to nurture their children's minds, but they also fail to nurture their own. Forty percent of parents of preteens believe the Bible is trustworthy and accurate, less than half of whom read the Bible at least once per week, according to research.[16] Oddly, far fewer of those believing the Bible to be trustworthy and accurate hold a biblical worldview, in part because they never read the Bible, which they claim such confidence in such that they hold the worldview that it teaches. Nonetheless, Scripture is clear that it is primarily the parental role to raise up godly offspring with a biblical worldview. One of the most central verses of the Old Testament says,

> Hear, O Israel: The LORD our God, the LORD is one. Love the LORD your God with all your heart and with all your soul and with all your strength. These commandments that I give you today are to be on your hearts. Impress them on your children. Talk about them when you sit at home and when you walk along the road, when you lie down and when you get up. Tie them as symbols on your hands and bind them on your foreheads. Write them on the doorframes of your houses and on your gates (Deuteronomy 6:4-9).

Further, Proverbs 22:6 says parents are to "train up a child in the way he should go: and when he is old, he will not depart from it" (KJV). And in the New Testament, Ephesians 6:4 tells parents to bring up children "in the nurture and admonition of the Lord" (KJV). The Bible assigns the worldview development process to parents and the faith community, yet in many cases neither seem up to the task. Only 2 percent of parents of children under the age of 13 have a biblical worldview (6 percent if attending an evangelical Protestant church), such that few parents have worldview development for their children on their radar. Many pastors struggle to help. The American Christian church and family are struggling with shockingly alarming levels of biblical illiteracy.

Many have sought to deny that critical race theory is taught in public schools. But no less than its cofounder Kimberlé Crenshaw has been clear about its influence in K–12 education. In 2021, the African American Policy Forum, where she is the executive director, affirmed,

> Critical race theory originated in law schools, but over time, professional educators and activists in a host of settings—K–12 teachers, DEI advocates, racial justice and democracy activists, among others—applied CRT to help recognize and eliminate systemic racism.[17]

For the students who go off to university, it's like they are fish in a barrel. This is especially so given that the vast majority of professors disregard, if not denigrate, the Bible. This has profound consequences. I've stated this before: Parents and grandparents are quite literally paying for the apostasy of their own children and grandchildren when sending them off to secular universities unprepared. Unprepared for what? Many professors and administrators hold worldviews subversive to Christian thought, and many politicize these views in academia where they hold a monopoly.

In 2023, the president of the University of Pennsylvania (an Ivy League school) resigned after appearing before Congress and failing to answer an otherwise obvious question—namely, Is calling for Jewish genocide morally wrong and violating the university's code of conduct? Instead of a simple "yes," she said that it is a "context-dependent" decision. Expectedly, that answer caused outrage.[18]

Today, Jewish people are often characterized as oppressive colonizers. Seemingly, the days of their being Holocaust victims are over, and their successes have placed them squarely in the "haves" rather than the "have nots" camp. Postcolonialism grows out of a Marxist view of conflict theory denoting certain nations (not just persons or groups of persons) as pervading oppression over other nations and peoples. This is why so many leftists in America hate America and educate others to that same end. It's also why we saw such a great lack of sympathy and compassion for Israel in the many student protests of a radical nature taking place on elite college campuses in 2024 following the October 7, 2024, Hamas massacre of Jewish people in Israel. At one time, when the Jewish people were the underdog after World War II, they were considered oppressed. Now that they've risen above most others in the Middle East, they're considered an oppressor nation, as occupiers and colonizers.

Briefly, postcolonial theory looks to deconstruct the West. Its purpose in postmodern thought is to "decolonize." That is, the systematic undoing of all European colonialism in all its manifestations and impacts in Western civilization from the fifteenth century onward. It rejects truth and perceives the world as constructed from systems of power and privilege that determine what can be known. Decolonizing everything, including family, is part of this thinking. It often involves an iteration of social justice called "research justice," whereby all Western and white books are replaced by minoritized authors and different "knowledges." One book called *Decolonizing the University* adopts a standpoint theory of knowledge from the lived experience of minoritized groups or cultures over and against "Eurocentric" ways of knowing. You can see where the family and the Bible as a metanarrative might come into view as a target facing scrutiny in these efforts.

Also at UPenn, Dr. Sophie Lewis is a writer and an independent visiting scholar at the Center for Research in Feminist, Queer, and Transgender Studies. She is a member of the teaching faculty of the Philadelphia branch of the Brooklyn Institute for Social Research (a Marxist think tank). She's a young and upcoming academic and author, known for her radical ideas of family abolition and the use of surrogacy on a societal scale. Lewis has published two relevant books recently when it comes to family titled *Full Surrogacy Now: Feminism Against the Family* (2019), and *Abolish the Family: A Manifesto for Care and Liberation* (2022).[19]

This is how she opens her book *Abolish the Family* (the blanks within the statements below represent where profanity and vulgar language were used):

> Abolish the family? You might as well abolish gravity or abolish God. So! The left is trying to take grandma away, now, and confiscate kids, and this is supposed to be progressive? What the ____!?...

> I don't want to deny that there is something "scary" (psychologically challenging) about this politics. This same scariness is present in all real revolutionary politics, in my view...

Continuing in all her erudition, saying,

> All of us—even those of us who own no property, receive no guaranteed care, and who subsist at the blunt end of empire, whiteness, cis-hetero-patriarchy, and class—will have to let go of something as the process of our collective liberation unfolds. If the world is to be remade utterly, then a person must be willing to be remade also.

Lewis goes on to speak to her young audience (i.e., your children) that reads her little red book for which she teaches a college course on the same content: "Listen, I get it. It's not just that you're worried about your dad getting all upset if he sees you with this book. It's that it's existentially petrifying to imagine relinquishing the organized poverty we have in favor of an abundance we have never known and have yet to organize." She's intent on changing young minds whose parents have no idea how universities are radicalizing our children with our money and tax dollars. I'll say it again: They are after your children!

Mollifying normal views of family, she says of family that it is merely "the name we use for the fact that care is privatized in our society."[20] But she denigrates the traditional nuclear family by claiming that it is often "where most of the rape happens on this earth, and most of the murder."[21] We can rename family and restructure caregiving such that society can reframe "family"; society can raise "children."

Now, it is well known that the late British Prime Minister Margaret Thatcher was no fan of socialism and communism. Marx once said that communism can be summarized as "abolition of private property." Lewis says, "When Margaret Thatcher, the 'milk snatcher,' of the eighties, said, 'There is no such thing as society, there are individual men and women and there are families,' she wasn't so much (alas) winning an argument against anti-family foes as triumphally making a capitalist reality explicit."[22] Lewis and many other university professor radicals believe that children are items of private property and need liberation and care. In the words of another radical, "Only once property love is abolished can we begin to invent a new love, a revolutionary love, a red love."[23] These aren't the views of only one or two radicals. These are representatives of a movement serious in their intent to push a kind of utopian community of comradeship that requires the abolition of the family. She goes on to discuss "queering motherhood," citing another book on *Revolutionary Mothering*. The book simply uses language and discourse prompting "abolition of the family as a decolonial imperative."[24]

But this is nothing new. Marx was all about family abolition and couldn't care less about his own family, parents (whom he'd scorned), wife (whom he'd cheated on), kids (who were neglected). In the very first footnote of Marx's *German Ideology*, it states, "That the abolition of individual economy is inseparable from the abolition of the family, is self-evident."[25] Remember these individuals see themselves as social justice liberators freeing society from Western institutions of oppression. That is because, as another writer quips, "The nuclear family turns children into property."[26] While she claims that there has been a 30-year lull from 1985 to 2015 in family abolitionism, today abolition has been taken back up in a big way: "We have entered a moment of abolition fervor and generalized abolitionism on a scale that was last seen in the nineteenth century."[27] This is much more common than most people realize in the halls of academia.

The postmodern neo-Marxist paradigm and its growing movement are to be taken seriously. The state (or a subcommunity), not the parents, can raise the children. Parents need to do their job or lose their children. This might require sacrificing a two-parent income for the proper training of our children. These are hard times, and we need to think creatively and carefully about this. How many of us have heard discussion in recent years over the fight for "parental rights"? What is behind it is what we've been discussing. *Abolish the Family* is literally a manifesto for replacing the traditional nuclear family with another kind of "care"; indeed, it is a liberation from traditional family, which is allegedly oppressive. Nobody is more likely to harm you than your family, the author argues. Are we too far removed to remember some of that which was scrubbed from the BLM website because it was a little bit too controversial? Remember, the founders who claimed to be "trained Marxists." Marxism holds that the family is a hierarchy that underwrites capitalism. Tearing down capitalism, therefore, requires dismantling its foundation, the family. The BLM website was open about this, initially saying, "We disrupt the Western-prescribed nuclear family structure requirement by supporting each other as extended families and 'villages' that collectively care for one another, especially our children, to the degree that mothers, parents, and children are comfortable."[28]

If this family abolition sounds outlandish, how much in only the last five years has America changed from what was apparently stable and normal to now wrestling with the outlandish? If you've not been to the university in the last five years, you don't realize the depth of ideology that is being indoctrinated. Like no other time in our nation's history have we witnessed an ever-widening gulf opening between parents and grandparents and their kids or grandkids. Millennials and Gen Z have been educated differently. Often, it is LGBTQ+ considerations that drive the wedge, with the younger educated generation thinking their elders are ignorant, traditional, nonscientific, and somewhat hateful and oppressive. But all of that is part of a bigger ideology, a postmodern cultural Marxist ideology that dominates our universities. Consequently, many Christian parents and grandparents are simply seeking to hold on to their family relationships by a shoestring and end up moving in a progressive direction themselves.

Parents and grandparents are investing heavy sums of money, energy, and love only to surrender their own children when they send them off to the secular baptismal font unprepared. Recall that the ratio of left to right professors is somewhere between 12:1 for those moving into retirement and 23:1 for those tenured with another 25 years ahead of them.[29] How can parents or the youth pastor, without proper equipping, compete with that?

Let's face it. Parenting is not easy—not if it is to be done well. But it is a sacrifice and an investment that is worthwhile and God honoring. It takes time, and many of us either don't have time because of lifestyle choices or don't make the time. If you don't educate your kids, their own social media will. If you don't educate your kids, the public or private school system will.

Don't depend on your church's youth pastor to educate your kids. Historically, youth ministry developed in a vacuum where there were increasingly large numbers of kids that were without Christian parents. Then, Christian parents sent their kids to the youth pastor too. In many cases, abdicating their role and responsibilities over to the youth pastor. This has been a colossal mistake.

Parents need help, but it is still the primary job of the parent to educate and prepare the children. Sadly, instead of not departing from the way in which they were trained up (Proverbs 22:6), what is happening is children are being raised for 18 years (sometimes with blood, sweat, and tears), and when they go off to university, they get conscripted to participate with the other side. Ratio Christi continuously receives testimonies like this from parents. What is the problem? We're not properly training them. Again, I realize parents need help, but the primary responsibility still lies with them, however it gets done in a biblically faithful way. This is something that my family has found works for us. Every Sunday, I meet with my youngest child for a meal, and we relate and read a book of the Bible or an age-appropriate book in Christian apologetics.

I've been a parent and a youth pastor. There are lots of resources to help.[30] If you can manage it, I recommend you get your high school or college students in touch with a Ratio Christi chapter or another ministry that embraces a biblical worldview and trains in Christian thought and apologetics. If you can do so, support Ratio Christi's efforts to plant chapters on university campuses. Insist that your pastor start a Ratio Christi College Prep group at your church. Grandparents can help fund ministries and organizations that help. Part of my role as president of Ratio Christi requires raising funds for the ministry. I meet with a lot of people, and I'm amazed at how many donate to their college alma maters. Far too many are funding those institutions whose worldviews don't simply fail to align with their own but, in fact, function to subvert it.

PHILANTHROPISTS AND OTHER DONORS

Stop funding those who hate you and your worldview. Fund those whose views align with your own, and especially that of Jesus.

In mid-2023, the US Supreme Court struck a blow—somewhat substantial and somewhat symbolic—to Harvard University when it declared to the chagrin of the university that it could no longer be racist in admissions policies.[31] University officials at Harvard and elsewhere have been scrambling since then to find loopholes around the ruling so that they can, in fact, continue operating with their harmful admissions policies. "One thing is certain, however," quips Heather Mac Donald, a *New York Times* bestselling author, "the university will pay no price in reputation or in philanthropic support for the Court's rebuke."[32] But following the major Hamas attack on Israel in October 2023, inspiring a lot of antisemitism on Ivy League campuses, haven't we seen a plethora of billionaires threaten to pull their millions from radical universities?[33] Pennies, comparatively.

In April 2023, hedge fund manager Kenneth Griffin gifted $300 million to Harvard, nearly the single largest financial gift in history, bringing his lifetime total to half a billion dollars. Even the antisemitism of students on that campus and others, chalking on the sidewalks "holocaust 2.0" and chanting "From the river to the sea, Palestine will be free" in reference to the death of Israel, isn't enough to get Harvard to stop being racist. The former president of Harvard merely stepped into a faculty position. And after the SCOTUS rendering from earlier in 2023, there is no evidence that the dozens of DEI full-time workers left their jobs. What will they do 40 hours per week? And where do people think these student radicals developed their ideas? Indeed, as Mac Donald says of Harvard, "Its animating credo is that every American institution is systemically racist." Despite other billionaires threatening to pull their funding over the obvious antisemitism present on that campus, it doesn't matter. Harvard's annual operating expenses of $6.4 billion dollars are larger than the Gross Domestic Product (GDP) of 33 countries, and an endowment of more than $53 billion dollars is larger than the GDP of more than 90 of the world's countries.[34] Harvard has more bureaucratic administrators and staff than undergrad students, and certainly more admin than professors (nearly 100 whose full-time work is in DEI).[35] It is a veritable Marxist headquarters. It is as though racism is their modus operandi. Even their medical library has a plethora of books by the high priest of antiracism Ibram X. Kendi, who is now failing to even make socialists happy due to his squandering of tens of millions of donor funds given to his center at Boston University, elicited through white guilt manipulation on the heels of the death of George Floyd.[36]

But to return to the megadonor, Griffin. He is not your typical Harvard leftist donor like George Soros, Bill Gates, or David Geffen. By every bit of evidence from the positions he stands for and supports, according to Mac Donald's glut of evidence, he is a conservative. Yet he gave an unrestricted gift that can be used anywhere at any time at the university. It's not that the university needs it. Prior to the gift, its 2022 endowment was around $51 billion dollars, and has only grown.[37] But to get his name on a brick, he could have at least investigated or else given to an institution that aligns with his views. He now laments it, but it is too late. After Harvard gave Griffin more than a brick, but the name on their business school (Harvard Kenneth C. Griffin Graduate School of Arts and Sciences), Griffin now says he won't give anymore because Harvard is "caught up in a rhetoric of oppressor and oppressee."[38]

Sadly, rather than nudging them toward their motto as founded by Christians, "Truth," he instead paid for their proliferation of political truth. He could have used his money to leverage Harvard even a bit to require a course in Western civilization as did the large donor at Yale that we discussed at the beginning of this book. Instead, Griffin gave Harvard $300 million to sabotage everything he stands for. Ironically, while Griffin left Chicago for Florida because of the politics and rise in crime in the former, Harvard hired the former Mayor of Chicago Lori Lightfoot to teach leadership, even after she was the first Chicago mayor in 40 years to lose reelection.[39] Griffin's gift tells other businessmen, including other conservatives, that the path to prestige still leads through the Ivy League. The university will pay no price for seeking to undermine America. It can make you wonder, What if more Christian or conservative philanthropists gave to organizations that align with their worldview?

It's not just institutions like Harvard; we should be concerned about Catholic and Christian schools too. This scenario is not unique to a rogue institution here and there. For example, take one all-women's Catholic school in Indiana that decided to start admitting males pretending to be females, inciting the bishop's rebuke that the school is no longer properly Catholic.[40] It is so widespread to one degree or another among far too many Christian colleges that I won't take the time to mention names here. Parents, attendees, and donors need to do their homework.[41]

Donors need to stand up, speak up, and be aware of who they are funding. You might be funding an organization that has drifted from its former position or the position they continue to declare while embracing a new view that subverts your view. Fund those whose views align with your own.

Yale Law School graduates created such an unsafe environment that when the president of Alliance Defending Freedom was speaking on campus (alongside an atheist attorney, as a joint venture), she had to be escorted away by armed security. Consequently, some federal judges have announced that they won't be hiring these protesting graduates.[42] Good for those judges! Some of you reading this may still be funding universities whose activities and ideologies no longer align with your own—indeed it is common to fund our alma maters. But have you considered what ideology your former university is promoting? There is a reason we are losing our youth, generation after generation, to these secular baptismal fonts.

Unfortunately, it's only getting worse. The ideologies being promoted on university and college campuses are responsible for the cultural degradation downstream. There are godly and smart Christian professors and administrators working within these universities, but they are effectively silenced and vastly outnumbered. That must change if we're to see significant change downstream in culture.

If you fund these institutions, evaluate why. Why continue to fund those who oppose and even hate you and your worldview but are perfectly happy to accept your money and your children or grandchildren?

When we give our support without seriously investigating the ideologies promoted in these institutions, we often unwittingly end up paying for the apostasy of our own children and the larger culture. Instead, I encourage you to support and fund organizations that better align with your worldview and who can facilitate positive change in the university upstream impacting culture and the world downstream.

God wants us to be good stewards. Stop funding those who hate and actively work against your worldview, and encourage your friends to do the same. Instead, give generously to those who align with your worldview and share your values. Add fuel to the right fire.

PROFESSORS AND EDUCATORS

Last but not least, professors. They are the frontlines upstream shaping culture downstream. They are the top of the ticket, the gatekeepers of ideas. Sociologist James Davison Hunter observes,

> The deepest and most enduring forms of *cultural* change occur from the "top down." In other words, the work of world-making and world-changing are, by and large, the work of elites: gatekeepers… Even where the impetus for change draws from popular agitation, it does not gain traction until it is embraced and propagated by elites…groups who have a lopsided access to the means of cultural production. These elites operate in well-developed networks and powerful institutions.[43]

It begins with the theorists and researchers whose work is most conceptual and invisible. It is passed on to more generalized teachers and educators. Then, to practitioners and popularizers whose work is most concrete and visible. Hunter realizes that a common view of social change among Christians that "changed lives in beliefs and hearts change cultures"[44] has its place but does not account historically for most macro-level cultural changes whose model involves institutional elites and networks.

The Founder of Cru, Bill Bright, recognized the professors' impact near the end of his life, saying, "If I could start [Cru] over again I would begin by working with professors."[45] Professors teach future business owners, political leaders, doctors, journalists, lawyers, K–12 educators, and many others. They are the gatekeepers of thought to cultural change. The teachers whom they teach will reach an even larger audience. Teachers are often underpaid and overworked. But many practicing Christians go into the teaching field because they care for others and see it as a way for them to bring added value to the world. But they need good, foundational training in Christian thought in addition to their formal studies required for teaching credentials. Colson Fellows is a ministry that is becoming increasingly focused on seeking to help teachers band together and develop a Christian worldview. Many teachers inadvertently adopted viewpoints from the university that are not in harmony with their Christian perspective. Teachers should reach out to such organizations that can help build up their Christian thought in worldview and apologetics.

Much of the methods, theory, and practice of teaching (i.e., pedagogy) in North America today is derived from the work of Brazilian Marxist radical, Paulo Freire. Whereas most in America may not have heard of him, he is legendary in colleges of education and in social science graduate schools. He's been called the father of critical pedagogy. Critical pedagogy is critical theory (i.e., neo-Marxism) applied to pedagogy. Freire is recognized as the third most-cited scholarly author in all the social sciences for his book *Pedagogy of the Oppressed*, being central in the colleges of education training those pouring into K–12 schools.[46] It is no wonder *Wall Street Journal*, *USA Today*, and *Publishers Weekly* bestseller James Lindsay wrote in his most recent book *The Marxification of Education* that "our kids go to Paulo Freire's schools."[47] As a good Marxist, he adopts conflict theory whereby people are either oppressed or oppressors. Indeed, with a simple cursory look at citations, one sees influential names from Marx, Mao, Lenin, Che Guevara, and all the stars from the Frankfurt School of critical theory. As Marcuse noted, the '60s radicals needed to redeploy into the universities for the "long march through the institutions." The last half century is a footnote to the progress made. Marcuse couldn't have been clearer in his 1972 book that the repurposing of the universities spreading to "all levels of education" was for the explicit plan of "political education."[48]

Stanley Aronowitz, distinguished professor of sociology from the City University of New York, comments on the back of *Pedagogy of the Oppressed*, "For any teacher who links education to social change, this is required reading. Freire remains the most important writer on popular education."[49] The strategy was not that the ideology remains in the ivory towers but that it spread like a virus by first capturing and transforming the colleges of education, forming a generation or more of teachers, and then programming K–12 students thereafter. According to Lindsay, while the teaching has been circulating throughout academia for some time, "colleges of education were captured almost entirely to the Freirean approach by no later than 1995, and the intervening quarter century has seen enough turnover of the teachers to have fundamentally remade our schools and thus education itself."[50] My daughter is an elementary education major, and the syllabi in many of her classes at her university confirm this. My other daughter, in secondary school, comes home and discusses what's being taught in her classes, providing further evidence that the teachers were trained in the Freirean school of thought. If this is the midwestern United States, imagine the Northeast and West Coast.

For Freire, who has written numerous books on the topic, his work is not merely a philosophy of education; it is also a liberatory social movement intent on emancipating the masses of oppressed from the hand of the oppressor. While near record numbers of kids in our schools are subpar or failing in the basics of reading, writing, arithmetic, history, and science, this is the sort of content that is replacing it. Many broadly dominant developments in education today can be traced back to Freire, even after word choices have changed. These include Culturally Relevant (and Responsive) Teaching, Social-Emotional Learning (SEL), especially "Transformative" SEL, Comprehensive Sex Education (CSE)—including practices like drag queen story hour.

Among several of Freire's concerns or contributions was the promotion of nonhegemonic knowledge and ways of knowing. Critical pedagogy is concerned with elevating marginalized "knowledges" and alternative ways of knowing. This includes concepts like "research justice" and the "decolonization of the curriculum" (i.e., the inclusion of certain texts and voices at the exclusion of others, modern inclusivity). As some authors writing in an academic teaching journal reveal, it calls for the revolutionary "pursuit of educational practices beyond white, Anglo-Saxon, middle-class and heterosexual educational norms" and is intentional in elevating "subjugated knowledges of women, minority groups, and indigenous groups."[51]

Remarkably, Neil Shenvi and Pat Sawyer, Christian scholars critical of critical social theories, point out in their recent book *Critical Dilemma*, Freire wrote the foreword to the 1986 edition of James Cone's *A Black Theology of Liberation*. As I mentioned earlier, liberation theology is a hybrid of Marxism and Christianity, whereby the former is the core and the latter but a shell. Recall also that two of James Cone's protégé students are Reverend Jeremiah Wright (Obama's pastor of 20 years) and Georgia Senator, Raphael Warnock. Whether Freire practiced much Catholicism, he certainly was involved with the Latin American liberation theology movement. According to Shenvi and Sawyer, the relationship was forged in Switzerland at the World Council of Churches in 1973, which hosted a dialogue between black liberation theology and Latin American liberation theology. It was there that Freire received Cone's book and later wrote,

> I was spellbound page after page, not putting it down until the early morning and finishing it some hours later…I read it for a second time and then wrote to Cone, giving him my impressions and stressing the importance of its immediate publication in Latin America, because black theology, of which Cone was the foremost proponent in the United States, is unquestionably linked with the theology of liberation flourishing today in Latin America.[52]

There is a religious characteristic about Freire as is the case for many in the movement. He was engaged in Latin American liberation theology (Marxism pretending to be Catholic). In his other famous book *The Politics of Education*, he discusses Easter. He claims that to be an effective teacher one must live through a kind of existential "Easter" that awakens (woke) them to a full political consciousness. Indeed, he says it is the only true meaning of Easter and that without which Christians and educators merely go through dead rhetoric. They need to die to the existing social order and resurrect themselves as people with (Marxist) consciousness—on the side of the oppressed.

> They really experience their own Easter, that they die as elitists so as to be resurrected on the side of the oppressed, that they be born again with the beings who were not allowed to be…I can only experience rebirth at the side of the oppressed by being born again, with them, in the process of liberation.[53]

This is a blatant replacement of the Christian central beliefs in the death, burial, and resurrection of Christ in which the Marxist counterfeit individual dies to the existing world. This becomes a new mission for the churches that run in parallel course with educational institutions, which is why it's in a book on educational theory and practice.

I'm reminded of Reverend Dr. Raphael Warnock's tweet that was deleted around Eastertime: "The meaning of Easter is more transcendent than the resurrection of Jesus Christ. Whether you are Christian or not, through a commitment to helping others we are able to save ourselves."[54] People can save themselves through good deeds isn't what the death, burial, and resurrection of Jesus was about. Warnock faced massive backlash from political pundits and Christian public intellectuals from his since-removed tweet only months after assuming a seat in the US Senate.

Christian professors, this is why your work is so gravely needed! You stand at the vanguard. More than simply K–12 educators are being targeted. "The contemporary Western intellectual world," writes noted philosopher Alvin Plantinga, "is a battleground or arena in which rages a battle for men's souls."[55] Defender of the faith William Lane Craig quips, "If the Christian worldview can be restored to a place of prominence and respect at the university, it will have a leavening effect throughout society…Because the gospel is never heard in isolation. It is always heard against the background of the cultural milieu in which one lives."[56] The former Harvard-trained philosopher and UN secretary general, warning American Christians of the danger of neglecting the mind, asked, "Who among the evangelicals can stand up to the great secular scholars on their own terms of scholarship and research? Who among evangelical scholars is quoted as a normative source by the greatest secular authorities on history or philosophy or psychology or sociology or politics?"[57]

What we need are not more professors who happen to be Christians in the universities. We need more Christian professors with a missional mindset, both excellent in their field and thinking of their job as a calling, their occupation as a vocation in Christian perspective. Missional professors. Craig encourages Christian scholars by advising in three areas. First, Christians serving vocationally in the universities must be mindful of attending to their own personal and spiritual formation. Second, they must engage intellectually not only with their disciplines but with their Christian faith. A Christian scholar must have at least a rudimentary knowledge of Christian theology and apologetics, knowing why he or she believes what is believed. Third, strive to integrate their faith with their discipline. Instructive is a famous statement made by C.S. Lewis for Christian thinkers:

> I believe that any Christian who is qualified to write a good popular book on any science may do much more by that than by any direct apologetic work...We can make people often attend to the Christian point of view for half an hour or so; but the moment they have gone away from our lecture or laid down our article, they are plunged back into a world where the opposite position is taken for granted...What we want is not more little books about Christianity, but more little books by Christians on other subjects—with their Christianity latent. You can see this most easily if you look at it the other way around. Our faith is not very likely to be shaken by any book on Hinduism. But if whenever we read an elementary book on Geology, Botany, Politics, or Astronomy, we found that its implications were Hindu, that would shake us. It is not the books written in direct defense of Materialism that make the modern man a materialist; it is the materialistic assumptions in all the other books. In the same way, it is not books on Christianity that will really trouble him. But he would be troubled if, whenever he wanted a cheap popular introduction to some science, the best work on the market was always by a Christian.[58]

Further resources to aid Christian professors in this regard are readily available and mentioned on websites by those engaged in faculty ministry, including Ratio Christi.[59] There are videos, books, and regular cohorts that meet in the process of developing a movement of missional professors—theoretically and practically—that are smart, winsome, and Christ-centered scholar activists.

Christians who are full professors and senior administrators need to focus on hiring to replace themselves before retiring. With baby boomers retiring, we're experiencing the biggest changing of the guard in the history of the American professorate. Assistant professors and PhD students need to consider integrating faith and reason, faith and vocation, and carrying that vision into action for decades to come. They need to move from being professors who happen to be Christian to missional Christian professors.[60] More young aspiring Christian thinkers need to consider careers in academia as a mission field. It might be a task like storming the beaches of Normandy. It will not be easy. But by God's grace, it can be done.[61] For those who object and think the university system simply needs to be tossed aside and started over, starting over will require scholars to publish in magazines like *Nature* and not only in *Christianity Today* for cultural cash value.

CONCLUSION

MAGA AND THE MORNING AFTER

Make America Great Again (MAGA) is the catchy slogan of the Trump administration's political campaign—with spinoffs like "Make America Healthy Again," "Make America Responsible Again," "Make America Safe Again," and a dozen others. This multiplication of the slogan doesn't merely confirm a successful marketing campaign, but it points to sentiment that America has been headed in the wrong direction. A fundamental question in closing is whether America can be made great again without it being made good again? Before this is answered, let's consider where we are.

With Trump's successful reelection in 2024, many wondered, *What's next?* The morning after resulted in the usual cries from celebrities threatening to leave the country, feminists shaving their heads and going on a sex strike until 2028, and elite universities canceling classes due to students perhaps feeling unstable. The Secular Student Alliance, who my organization recently won against in our court victory involving the Department of Education, even sent to its constituency a post-election newsletter with this fearful title: "White Christian Nationalists and the Trump Administration Openly Pursue an Agenda to Transform Our Democracy into a Christian Theocracy."[1] Even one of the largest campus ministries, Cru, sent a sympathetic letter only to its BIPOC staff, to comfort them in their felt affliction under a Trump victory. Some with large YouTube audiences criticized Cru, as if black and brown

Christians all felt or should feel a unified fear, and as if "diversity" is simply about skin color. Critics question, Why not send a letter to all staff declaring "Jesus as King" regardless of who won the election?[2]

These desperate cries seem somewhat unhinged from reality. Just where are all these scary "White Christian Nationalists" that are "openly" pursuing a theocracy? Or is this simply another political boogie man? "White" plays on the white-supremacy fear card, "nationalism" plays on the fears of Nazi Germany's abusive form of nationalism, and "Christian," being the majority is, at least according to critical theory, oppressive as it is the religion with power in America. This was simply one flavor of all the post-election hysteria in media, academia, and broader America.

The message of fear was infused. Perhaps this was received by some due to the policies advanced during the first term of Trump's presidency (2016–2020)—which, contrary to rhetoric, was hardly theocratic—or maybe it was due to the constant Democratic media, academic, and political opposition seeking to persuade the public that Trump was a Nazi, a fascist, and a convicted felon.[3] Whatever truth there is relative to the tidal wave of legal attacks against him, noted by some to be "lawfare" (similar to "warfare") because of the sheer amount and electoral timing of the mostly fruitless attacks, it was clear that at least much of it was believed to be more about political theater and real effort to harm Trump than about a genuine concern for justice. It gave the country a costly and massive cloud to sift through—often just a cloudy headache chalked up to another political season of rivals going after political opposition.

Now, if it is true that Trump is akin to Hitler, then is it inconceivable that some might seek to assassinate him for the sake of America? After all, it is easy to argue that Hitler was quite deserving of assassination. Even the once pacifist pastor Dietrich Bonhoeffer finally thought it through and was arrested in his heart by the prudential choice of the matter. He attempted assassination of Hitler and, like others, lost his own life trying, just as occurred in at least one of the failed Trump assassinations. Given that the election wasn't merely an Electoral College win but a majority population win, the Harris opposition went away quietly in the immediate aftermath without the prior usage of despairing rhetoric, an odd move if Trump really is as dangerous as Hitler.

Maybe they didn't really believe Trump was Hitler after all? Indeed, apparently most Americans didn't either because they elected Trump by wide margins. We can infer that such rhetoric is part of the miseducation of America by a party and partisans in media and academia who used extreme rhetoric to impact the election. No one wants the other side to win, but we've reached a new level of danger in American politics, the consequences of which were that Trump (and even billionaire Elon Musk, who supported him) had to increase personal security. Many of the cabinet picks subsequently received death threats.[4]

It wasn't just Democratic voters, but even some conservatives abstained from voting for Trump or anyone else for that matter out of protest to there being no morally viable candidate, while other such "never Trumpers" went to the polls for Kamala Harris.[5] Conservatives voting for Trump were challenged with being hypocritical because they voiced loudly the notion that character mattered during Bill Clinton's run up to his second term in office. Most conservatives, however, despite whatever questions about President Trump's character, wagered what was in the end a favorable argument that character matters, but it is not all that matters. They argued for policies-over-person on the assumption that perhaps both Trump and Harris had lackluster character, making all the more important the affirmation of policies-over-person. This drove them in mass to vote because they were more confident this time around not just based on wishful thinking but on evidence of governance compared to four years of what they deemed to be catastrophic governance under Democrats.

Trump was arguably not the first choice of conservatives in 2016. He was the only one left standing of over two dozen primary candidates to face off against Hilary Clinton. But now things have changed. First, there is a four-year track record of Trump's actual governance, which was unavailable in 2016, and there were many reasons why most conservative Christians broke for Trump and the Republican policies, thinking it was the best way of supporting policies good for the nation, the most consistent with the US Constitution (especially the most prominent in the Bill of Rights, the First Amendment), and the most consistent with biblical values.[6] Second, compared to the opposition and its apparent drift via evident postmodern cultural Marxist influence (for a reminder, revisit the beginning of the book on DEI, or DIE), many were elated the day after the election to feel a sigh of relief—at least a reprieve for a few more years. Perhaps there is something here.

Many say that even if Trump is not actually a Christian, he is at least similar to Cyrus the Great, the Persian king who conquered the Babylonians in the sixth century BC, not only freeing the Israelites but also permitting them to return to the land and rebuild their wall and the Second Temple. Cyrus was not a believer but, adopting a policy-over-person mentality, was friendly in policy toward God's people in the Old Testament. It is reasoned that we acquired Cyrus (Trump) and avoided Nero (Harris).[7] While I won't defend all of Trump's actions, he was helpful to Christian mission in many ways, including my own organization by changing the judiciary, which helped us win a case in the Ninth Circuit Court and inserting the *Free Inquiry Rule* for which Ratio Christi was the intervening defendant against atheist groups, a rule designed to protect campus organizations like mine from religious discrimination on campuses. In the final month of Biden's presidency, I was alerted by our attorneys that we achieved victory—victory for all campus ministries.[8] The US Supreme Court is viewed by many conservatives as the way to preserve the nation through decades of potential tumult, especially considering the current cultural revolution. They're not entirely wrong, but they're also not entirely right.

According to the exit polls, which determine voters' thinking and motivation, while the older generation (45 plus) voted more conservative, the younger generation (18–44) voted, and is voting, more progressive—especially the closer in proximity one is to college or graduate school—an institution with extreme bias and effectively persuading the world and life views of young people. This has profound implications for the future electorate and public policy, which in turn could solidify ideological control over our education system, underscoring the need for Christians to permeate the university if they want to have influence on lives and culture.[9] The administrators and professors didn't go away simply because Republicans won an election. Indeed, as much as people hear in the news that DEI is in retreat, the reality is that it is simply being repackaged and rebranded.[10] The nearly 100 DEI officers at Harvard mentioned earlier may not go away from their university posts (the professors certainly aren't). It's like changing lipstick on a pig. Trump's push to eradicate DEI (i.e., systemic Marxism) from all federal agencies, including the Department of Education, can bring about good outcomes, but whether it will be successful is another thing entirely.[11] One thing is certain. Unless we concentrate efforts on reinfiltrating our highest educational institutes with non-Marxist thinkers, especially Christian thinkers, yesterday's operation will continue tomorrow under stealth cover.

POLITICAL REALIGNMENT

What has happened to the Republican and Democratic Parties as of the close of the first quarter of the twenty-first century? Some say the Republicans look like Democrats, and the Democrats look like something foreign to American politics altogether. Consider that two former Democratic presidential candidates for whom Trump sought for and successfully positioned in his cabinet (Tulsi Gabbard and Robert F. Kennedy) and the former Democratic senate majority leader of California (Gloria Romero) all campaigned for Trump. Notably, so did Elon Musk, the world's richest man, who voted for Biden and Obama in previous elections. In fact, he considered a potential loss in some of his wealth to be worthwhile for the country for him to go all in for Trump in 2024, believing that civilization was on the line. The world's largest podcaster, Joe Rogan, who once advanced New Atheism and didn't feature a Christian intellectual on his program for more than 2,000 episodes before ever inviting a Christian intellectual on his show, also endorsed Trump. Even the skeptical philosopher Peter Boghossian, who was once very anti-right, anti-Trump, and anti-Christian (author of *A Manual for Creating Atheists*), began seeing the massive shift of many liberals moving into the Republican camp for Trump. Boghossian revealed on X, "So, so many centrists and liberals have whispered the 'unthinkable' to me—they'll be voting for Trump."[12] And many apparently did. Many felt that the Democratic Party left them as it moved radically left. And despite constantly being harassed by the media as a racist, Trump managed to win more black and Hispanic votes than any Republican in half a century.[13] Does that all really sound like a motley crew ready to advance a white Christian nationalist theocracy?

The RNC welcomed them just as it had reduced or eliminated the new Republican platform's statements on social issues like homosexuality and abortion while adding new components that oppose ideas like critical race theory and the practice of men claiming to be women dominating in women's sports. The Republicans broadened the tent to include many voices from the old left (liberal) but who are opposed to the New Left, the Marxist left (illiberal). These new voices comprehend the ideology that has swept the Democratic Party and feel it has moved away from them. It has given Christians who usually come out strongly Republican a slightly smaller slice of the pie of influence because of all the newcomers.

There has been a country-wide cultural shift to the left such that the Democratic Party has been highly infiltrated by an ideology that is foreign to America's history. It's not only the standard liberal and conservative divide, though there is that. But its sweeping DEI policies have revealed that identity politics (a.k.a. identity Marxism) has apparently become central to that party's DNA. This also explains why many Democrats have shifted to the Republican Party. Boghossian further commented shortly after Trump's landslide victory about education reform and the trajectory of our culture due to the universities, "For the first time in a long, long time, I am wildly optimistic."[14] He said Trump is 100 percent correct in eradicating the Marxism out of our education system. There is a real realignment taking place in this cultural revolution, and where it is headed is anyone's guess. But there is a great sense of relief or even optimism by many Republicans, conservatives, and Christians.

In 2023, we began seeing a trend away from DEI, a dismantling of it in the corporate world, including America's biggest corporation, Walmart.[15] *The Chronicle of Higher Education* has been tracking the dismantling of DEI on over 200 campuses in 33 states, possibly maneuvering away from it for fear of consequences relative to recent public sentiment or perhaps they've genuinely seen its failure in application.[16] Further, in response to the radical antisemitic protests at elite universities, leading many to see how students are being radicalized in these universities, many philanthropists have withheld funding and some state legislatures have taken action to sponsor and pass into law viewpoint diversity bills that relate to gaining and retaining tenure. DEI seems to be on the retreat, at least on the surface. Notably, even the leader of antiracism at the popular level, Ibram X. Kendi, was forced to move on from his formerly $30-million-dollar funded center at Boston University that closed in June 2025.[17]

This is significant in that, in some cases, diversity statements are now illegal.[18] They were used to select woke candidates and alienate others, while giving conservative and (classically) liberal faculty and students a route to complain if departments or professors are obviously inhibiting a lack of viewpoint diversity in favor of only diversity of skin color and body parts, which has become the focus for far too long. The political cover also provides safety and emboldens the vast minority of professors who aren't left leaning to pursue legal options that free them from having to sit under taxpayer-funded Marxist training.[19] This legal and political cover now not only provides conservative Christians in academia a chance to have a voice as students and faculty but opens the pipeline for Christians to enter and engage careers in academia more freely.[20] This recent cultural and political shift is important to note as a window of opportunity. Other state legislatures should follow suit. However, Christians must not be overly optimistic that a shift downstream in politics and culture is anything more than a brief window of opportunity, unless and until ideological change takes place upstream in the universities. That is, we must pursue a greater influence for at least partial yet substantial institutional change and, yes, institutional recapture. But among the opportunities most exciting are the spiritual opportunities among all those who, by comparative analysis brought on by this cultural revolution, are reconsidering the merits of both cultural and real Christianity.

MAKING AMERICA GOOD AGAIN

To resume our query now, can we really make America great without making it good? The groundswell of reaction to how radical this revolution in America has become creates a time not to rest on our laurels but to act. The philosophy of scientific naturalism (nature is all that is, was, or ever will be) gave us Karl Marx; Marx's later disciples gave us the postmodern cultural Marxism that we're experiencing today. The American church absorbed part of the first, which gave us theological liberalism, and absorbed part of the second, which gave us social justice or liberation theology. These two revolutionary ideologies that swept through our universities over the last 150 years cannot ground what America needs to become good, much less to become great again. James Lindsay, once a New Atheist (now agnostic), is one example of an allied thinker with Christians who has come to oppose the postmodern cultural Marxist revolution. He isn't alone but is joined with many public non-Christian figures favorable to Christianity, from Elon Musk (somewhat of an agnostic or transhumanist) to the influential public intellectual Jordan Peterson (mystic existentialist). Some of these people even refer to themselves, as has the atheist Richard Dawkins, as "cultural Christians" or "existential Christians," preferring its fruit after seeing the rotten fruit of what a cultural Marxism might look like if that revolution is successful. Taking America would be the greatest Marxist prize in its history.

But like Lindsay, some see the solution as returning to political liberalism (its major historical competitors being fascism and communism), but not simply a broad liberalism in the classical sense of *liber* or freedom in the thinking of intellectuals like John Locke, where the individual person's rights and universal humanity is valued, but one akin to Enlightenment humanism. That is, a form of secular humanism. Here we must remember that the alliance of coalition members pushing back on the postmodern cultural Marxist revolution still disagree on substantive matters. Lindsay quotes approvingly scientific naturalist and secular humanist Steven Pinker, "Faith, revelation, tradition, dogma, authority, the ecstatic glow of subjective certainty—all are recipes for error and should be dismissed as sources of knowledge."[21]

Recall my earlier discussion of Pinker, who ostensibly said that the most formidable enemies of Enlightenment thinking were religion and socialism (i.e., Marxism). But secular humanism cannot easily ground human value or dignity in an objective sense by grounding it in human beings, full stop. That is a mere preference for a species sometimes referred to as speciesism. It requires further grounding. As nontheist University of Toronto philosopher R.Z. Friedman has noted, "Without religion the coherence of an ethics of compassion cannot be established. The principle of respect for persons and the principle of the survival of the fittest are mutually exclusive."[22]

When Nietzsche proclaimed that God is dead at the end of the nineteenth century, he posited that one day, we would all come to realize that we cannot have the fruit without the root of Christianity. We cannot have a world of objective moral value and meaning to life, to the sanctity of human life, without a sanctifier of human life. If God is dead, everything is permissible, and life is objectively meaningless. Later French philosophers like Sartre would assert that we can freely create our own meaning by choosing a course of action. He chose Marxism. But even these existentialist philosophers cannot live consistently with their philosophy. This inconsistency is easy to see. Supposing I give one meaning and you another—then who is right? The universe has no objective meaning or value no matter how we subjectively regard it. Meaning isn't found in a vacuum. It is given by a mind. Unless that Mind stands outside this world, it is hard to see how it could be objective. Following World War II, Sartre wrote vigorously against antisemitism as if it were objectively evil in accordance with humanism.[23] Arguably, secular humanism only leads to a Nietzschean kind of nihilism, the only viable alternative being theism—a robust theism like Christian theism. That founding was indispensable to America even if America was not technically a "Christian nation." Its social contract, while not mentioning Jesus by name, was indubitably influenced by Jesus' movement of real Christianity. John Adams said, "Our constitution was made only for a moral and religious people. It is wholly inadequate to the government of any other."[24] It is therefore dubious to think that America will become great without it becoming good and equally dubious to think that goodness without God is enough.

What is America? America is a place. But most importantly, America is a philosophy of noble ideas. The Declaration of Independence is a philosophical defense of natural rights—rights held by nature, none of which have sound grounding outside of their being endowed by their Creator. Indeed, it is not surprising that one of the chief architects of the UN Declaration of Human Rights was none other than a Christian philosopher, Charles Malik. Civil rights come and go, but human rights have a deeper and more permanent nature. Rights must be grounded in what is good, which, in turn, is grounded in God. The government doesn't give them, nor can it take them away. As discussed earlier, human rights were derived from natural rights, which were derived from natural law, which were further derived from eternal law. We know the source. We know the rhetorical evolution of language.

But the foundation for human rights remains inescapably in God, as penned in the United States' Declaration of Independence:

> We hold these truths to be self-evident, that all men are created equal, that they are endowed by their Creator with certain unalienable rights, and that among these are life, liberty, and the pursuit of happiness. That to secure these rights, governments are instituted among men, deriving their just powers from the consent of the governed, and that whenever any form of Government becomes destructive of these ends, it is the right of the people to alter or abolish it, and to institute a new Government.[25]

Patriotism means more than a mere love for your country. It means a love for what makes your country your country. When Alexis de Tocqueville visited America and reflected on what it was that made America great, he realized America was great only because America was good.[26] But if America loses her goodness, she will lose her greatness. This is true regardless of whether de Tocqueville said it or not, just as it would be true that human dignity is grounded in God whether our founding documents said it or not. This is assumed in the First Amendment, even if it is a social contract.[27] Our freedoms that the world relishes begin with that indispensable theological grounding.

Take pride not in what is evil but in what is good. Robust freedom is not freedom from something but freedom to something. Like the Golden Rule trumping the Silver Rule, it is a positive and not a negative understanding of ethics and the sort of beings capable of living by it. It is freedom to do what we ought to do, not just what we want to do or freedom to be left alone. It is freedom in accordance with the sort of beings we are, beings made in God's image. Be all you can be! Be a Christian humanist because Christian humanism is the only sort of viable humanism.

POLITICAL ALLIES

The enemy of my enemy is my friend. This was the thinking of Franklin Delano Roosevelt and Winston Churchill relative to Joseph Stalin and Adolf

Hitler. The alliance with Stalin to "get the job done" was required, albeit temporarily and with a very watchful eye. To get legislation passed, it often ends with a simple majority of 51 percent. In our cultural revolution, we need to forge alliances of various sorts for practical purposes. Alliances don't always involve compromise, although they can, since, proverbially, "alliances make strange bedfellows." These alliances can be seen in more obvious forms, like the Alliance Defending Freedom with their robust theology of litigation at the right time and place to keep free speech, freedom of religion, and free thinking alive. At least on the political level, these alliances can even be conducted with atheists, pantheists, transhumanists, and agnostics, ones who are classical liberals when it comes to free thought, speech, and religion or irreligion, and see the value of rescuing institutions like universities and who are beginning to see the goodness of Christianity in shaping Western culture like they've never seen it before.

We're seeing many appreciate the fruit of what some call "cultural Christianity," but many others have come to appreciate the root, real Christianity, underlying the mere behavior or tradition that made America, and indeed the West, great. When it comes to institutional influence, we've already discussed permeation in existing universities, for example. But there is also ideation over starting new universities and colleges. One must question, however, how we can guarantee that those too won't be overtaken and succumb to mission drift, as well as question how advantageous institutional prestige will be with a new university as opposed to those centuries old (prestige matters for the job market and elements of persuasion; in other words, it matters). Other models include more hostile takeovers like what we've seen with Governor Ron DeSantis and free-thinking activists like Christopher Rufo of the Manhattan Institute, appointing new board members in red states over publicly funded colleges so that they can become even minimally open to Christian influence. Or again, other means include notifying key donors of failing universities, secular and Christian, to get them to put pressure on administrators at rogue universities. Christianity can compete in the marketplace of ideas if it has the opportunity. But this requires a solid open door to our entry and existence in those high-level places of influence.

America is undergoing a cultural revolution. Even when the political pendulum swings the other way, it is likely brief. America is big and has a durable history set up wisely by the founders. But it is not bulletproof. Some change is good; some change ends in death. In my view, the current Marxist revolution, if successful, will constitute the greatest Marxist revolution in history. Marx would've loved to see the day, as would Lenin, Mao, and a host of others. America is the prize because America is the single most influential nation in the world. Much is at stake and affords an opportunity for strength in numbers by some nonconventional alliances. But we must be cautious and keep a healthy distance while tackling common problems. While we needed Stalin temporarily, we knew from the start that it could not be a permanent tie to build a better world. Many such allies are in broad ways liberal and not necessarily Christian. But their liberalism—defined also in classical terms broader than the narrower view characteristic of what the Democratic Party used to predominantly resemble—is what helps combat the illiberalism of the new power brokers who've sought to take over our institutions in ways more perilous than the other, previous revolutionary ideas that have come to dominate our universities. We have much in common like classical liberalism, affirmation of the correspondence theory of truth, debate to discover the truth, respect for human dignity, freedom of speech and thought, and so on. But the Christian worldview has the best grounding for all of this. We must continue to encourage a move from mere cultural Christianity (while celebrating it over its rivals) to real Christianity, where one embraces the truth-claims of Scripture and of Christ Himself. Christ is the one who grants real freedom—the freedom for which we were all made.

PRAYERS

Above all we can pray. We can and should be praying. The book of Daniel describes everything from God's movement throughout history among kings and empires to interaction with individuals. Daniel prayed and had remarkable institutional influence, among other things like recognizing spiritual warfare. We're informed in Daniel 10 how his experience of delayed answers to his commitment to prayer and fasting was because there was a spiritual battle taking place in the heavenlies involving intelligent beings neither divine nor human. In our cultural engagement, we often fail to realize that beyond the earthly there are activities happening in the heavenly context. This echoes what we've been shown in the first two chapters of Job, who likely never knew—during this life anyway—what was behind the source of his troubles. Facing immense opposition to the brink of suicidality, Elijah prayed, and God showed up and showed off. Habakkuk, another biblical author who was challenged by cultural decay among his people, was given revelation by God as to why the troubles were happening and how God was using world powers to shape the world—sometimes to discipline His own people. We learn from the book of Habakkuk, ultimately, that the just (righteous) shall live by faith—a ventured trust in God's providence, a theme picked up by the apostle Paul in Romans 1 and again by Martin Luther in the Protestant Reformation.

What is before us may often seem to be an impossible task, especially when considering permeating universities with robust Christian presence and influence. But we must remember that what is actual entails what is possible. Ideological revolutions have occurred not only once but twice since our universities were originally founded on Christ. And a new revolution can and should happen again. In that moment, we pray, act, and trust God, who moves in human history. During what is called the silent period or the intertestamental period (when there were no prophets or prophecies for Israel, from the time of Ezra and Nehemiah until the announcement of the birth of John the Baptist), God's people seemed to be in perpetual exile for four centuries, but God was at work. Arguably, God works providentially in mysterious ways we don't always see except in retrospect—sometimes, not even then. I believe that during the split between the Greek religion of polytheism and the Greek philosophy that generated monotheistic thinkers, together with an objective and purpose driven world, God was at work. Socrates trained Plato, who trained Aristotle, who trained Alexander the Great, who conquered the world and forced everyone to speak and live like Greeks. The Romans took over, and with it, Roman law and order was established, including safe passageways throughout the empire. God was providentially acting in the world, then, something significant happened.

The apostle Paul tells us in Galatians 4:4 that at the right moment in time, God sent forth His Son into the world. We were given a New Testament, written in Greek, and the Christians largely invented, or at least popularized, the codex or spine of what we have today in books rather than scrolls. Indeed, instead of carrying 66 scrolls around the Mediterranean world, these mission-bound people put them together and formed the collection of books called the Bible. With safe passageway on the roads and having one spoken language for the first time since the Tower of Babel, Christian missions exploded. There was one language for which to communicate truth, and the gospel went out with willing hands and feet across the world to change the world—to invent hospitals and universities and to eventuate in Western civilization, along with representative government. God answers prayers and God moves in human history even when we don't recognize it. Our job is to be faithful and to think strategically about expanding the message of Christ, who transforms lives and cultures. Colleges and universities have often been connected to great revivals, and we should pray for this to happen again. We can overcome the progressive miseducation of America by proper education and by being strategically missional.

FINAL REMARKS

Culture and politics are downstream from education. The university is the apex at the top of education. If you want to change the culture, what might be the single most strategic place in culture (churches and families are already a given) to see that vision come to fruition is the university. For it is among the most influential, if not the single most influential institution shaping Western civilization. To forgo effort at even a small level of institutional recapture or influence there is to sacrifice not only our culture but the souls of our children and grandchildren, who will invariably be influenced by it even if they never attend university. That is where the fulcrum is placed at just the right point, like a seesaw or teeter-totter, to leverage weight heavier than yours and, in this case, move the world. It is the greatest location to impact potential leaders from other nations and influence world missions, as so many world leaders, not just citizens, of other countries attend American universities. It is a grandiose idea, a revolutionary idea, to seriously plan and pursue substantial Christian presence in the universities. A form of thoughtful Christianity must be reasserted on university campuses everywhere forming a third revolution in the universities.

Recall the book *Dominion* by agnostic historian Tom Holland, whose work demonstrates the subtitle *How the Christian Revolution Remade the World*. It didn't require hostile takeover of institutions. It certainly involved the gospel—no doubt. But in Western civilization today, given that the university is the single most influential institution and where students and future leaders are having their ideas challenged more than anywhere else, it requires the intellectual voice of Christ.

One can never know how long America will last. But the founders of America built something neither immortal, nor perfect, and yet it was built with significant durability. Pendulum swings often occur. There are signs of that happening now, which creates an open door for us if we choose to take it. Christians have a far more penetrating analysis of both the problem (the fall, not oppression) and the solution (redemption, not earthly liberation) of the human condition and the good life. This does not mean that we have nothing to learn about oppression and injustice from other quarters, but it does mean that we better understand both the underlying cause and its ultimate cure, and so have an infinitely better hope to proclaim in the here now as well as the hereafter.

We must not only be ready to answer those who inquire about our hope that Christianity is reasonable, good, and true, but realize that the gospel is still the power of God for the salvation of everyone who believes (Romans 1:16). The Bible declares that "there is no one righteousness" and that "all have sinned and fall short of the glory of God" (Romans 3:10, 23). God is holy, and we can't live up to His standards. That's bad news. But that's why the gospel is good news! It further declares that "God demonstrates his own love for us in this: While we were still sinners, Christ died for us" (Romans 5:8). We were unlovable, but God so loved us that He sent His Son, Jesus, to die for us (John 3:16). We cannot earn God's gift of grace, or it wouldn't be a gift. The Bible says, "The wages of sin is death, but the gift of God is eternal life in Christ Jesus our Lord" (Romans 6:23). In the face of a holy God, our sin merits only death and separation from God. But Christ gave His life so that we could live. For those who come into relationship with God, "there is now no condemnation for those who are in Christ Jesus" (Romans 8:1). We are assured, says Paul, that "if you confess with your mouth that Jesus is Lord and believe in your heart that God raised him from the dead, you will be saved" (Romans 10:9 ESV).

Jesus changes lives, cultures, and entire civilizations for good. But key institutions are vitally important for the Christian message to have a hearing. All Christians must prepare ourselves and our people (on defense) for what is coming out of the universities, but also strategically (on offense) stealthily permeate the universities and focus on "the long march through the institutions."

Jesus, the Savior, was born in the context of three great cultures: the Hebrews, Greeks, and Romans. For the Hebrews, the ideal was symbolized by light. God's first words in Genesis 1 were, "Let there be light" (verse 3). Throughout Scripture, light symbolizes God's presence, favor, and even salvation. Jesus is called the "light of the world" in John's Gospel (John 8:12; 9:5). For the Greeks, the ideal was knowledge. Indeed, elsewhere I've argued how Aristotle's famous *Nicomachean Ethics*, which was about happiness and the purpose of life, could not so much as get off the tarmac without appeal to God, the knowledge of God, as the ultimate human good.[28] For the Romans, the ideal was glory. The glory of Rome. These three great abstractions were light, knowledge, and glory. Paul was a Hebrew, a citizen of Rome, raised in a Greek city. Writing to the Corinthian church (and to us), he said, "God, who said, 'Let light shine out of darkness,' has shone in our hearts to give the *light* of the *knowledge* of the *glory* of God in the face of Jesus Christ" (2 Corinthians 4:6 ESV, emphasis added).

NOTES

DIVIDER PAGES

Quote on page 11: J.R.R. Tolkien, *The Return of the King*, 2nd ed. (Boston: Houghton Mifflin, 1993), 259.

Quote on page 27: George Orwell, *1984* (New York: Signet Classics), 80.

Quote on page 121: Charles Malik, *A Christian Critique of the University*, (Waterloo, Ontario: North Waterloo Academic Press, 1987), 100–101.

Quote on page 201: James Davison Hunter, *To Change the World: The Irony, Tragedy, and Possibility of Christianity in the Late Modern World* (New York: Oxford University Press, 2010), 41.

INTRODUCTION—THE DREAM TURNED NIGHTMARE

1. Mark Moore, "Traditional Values like Patriotism, Religion and Community Have Plunged Dramatically Among Americans: Poll," *New York Post*, March 27, 2023, https://nypost.com/2023/03/27/values-like-patriotism-religion-falling-out-of-favor-among-americans-poll/.

2. John F. Kennedy, "Address Before the Canadian Parliament in Ottawa," May 17, 1961. Although evidence suggests this quote is a misattribution, the idea can be deduced from Burke's thought. Scholars recognize that Burke said something like it in his pamphlet "'Thoughts on the Cause of the Present Discontents' (1770): 'When Bad Men Combine, the Good Must Associate; Else They Will Fall, One by One, an Unpitied Sacrifice in a Contemptible Struggle.'" Reuters Fact Check, "Fact Check: Edmund Burke Did Not Say Evil Triumphs When Good Men Do Nothing," *Reuters*, August 9, 2021, https://www.reuters.com/article/factcheck-edmund-burke-quote-idUSL1N2PG1EY.

3. Andrew Sullivan, "We All Live on Campus Now," *Intelligencer*, February 9, 2018, https://nymag.com/intelligencer/2018/02/we-all-live-on-campus-now.html.

4. James Davison Hunter, *To Change the World: The Irony, Tragedy, and Possibility of Christianity in the Late Modern World* (New York: Oxford University Press, 2010), 38.

5. Douglas A. Sweeney, *The American Evangelical Story: A History of the Movement* (Grand Rapids, MI: Baker Academic, 2005).

6. Sarah Vowell, *The Wordy Shipmates* (New York: Riverhead, 2008), 12.

7. Dan Hayes, *Fireseeds of Spiritual Awakening* (Orlando, FL: Cru Press, 2007), 7-8.

8. David Howard, "Student Power in World Missions," in *Perspectives on the World Christian Movement*, ed. Ralph D. Winter and Steven C. Hawthorne (Pasadena, CA: William Carey Library, 1992), B–87.

9. Jon H. Roberts and James Turner, *The Sacred and the Secular University* (Princeton, NJ: Princeton University Press, 2000), 16. See also Ronald Numbers, "Science Without God: Natural Laws and Christian Beliefs," in *When Science and Christianity Meet*, eds. David C. Lindberg and Ronald L. Numbers (Chicago: University of Chicago Press, 2003).

10. Helen Pluckrose and James Lindsay, *Social (In)justice: Why Many Popular Answers to Important Questions of Race, Gender, and Identity Are Wrong—and How to Know What's Right*, adapted by Rebecca Christiansen (Durham, NC: Pitchstone, 2022), 39.

11. Pluckrose and Lindsay, *Social (In)justice*, 39-40.
12. Pluckrose and Lindsay, *Social (In)justice*, 41.
13. Pluckrose and Lindsay, *Social (In)justice*, 42.
14. Helen Pluckrose and James Lindsay, *Cynical Theories: How Activist Scholarship Made Everything About Race, Gender, and Identity—and Why This Harms Everybody* (Durham, NC: Pitchstone, 2022), 40.
15. Winston Churchill, June 18, 1940. For the full text of Churchill's speech, see "Their Finest Hour," International Churchill Society, http://www.winstonchurchill.org/resources/speeches/233-1940-the-finest-hour/122-their-finest-hour.
16. Rod Dreher, *The Benedict Option: A Strategy for Christians in a Post-Christian Nation* (New York: Penguin, 2017), 2. See also Dreher, *Live Not by Lies: A Manual for Christian Dissidents* (New York: Penguin Random House, 2020), 213-214.
17. Albert Mohler, *We Cannot Be Silent: Speaking Truth to a Culture Redefining Sex, Marriage, and the Very Meaning of Right and Wrong* (Nashville: Nelson, 2015), 151.
18. Winston Churchill, "Tyranny Is Our Foe," *Harvard Magazine*, September 6, 2018, https://www.harvardmagazine.com/2018/09/churchill-harvard-september-6-1943.
19. Sarah Pulliam Bailey, "There Are More Atheists and Agnostics Entering Harvard Than Protestants and Catholics," *The Washington Post*, September 9, 2015, https://www.washingtonpost.com/news/acts-of-faith/wp/2015/09/09/there-are-more-atheists-and-agnostics-entering-harvard-than-protestants-and-catholics/.
20. "From John Adams to Massachusetts Militia, 11 October 1798," Founders Online, National Archives, https://founders.archives.gov/documents/Adams/99-02-02-3102.

CHAPTER 1—WOKE 101

1. Helen Pluckrose and James Lindsay, *Cynical Theories: How Activist Scholarship Made Everything About Race, Gender, and Identity—and Why This Harms Everybody* (Durham, NC: Pitchstone, 2022), 45.
2. Pluckrose and Lindsay, *Cynical Theories*.
3. Pluckrose and Lindsay, *Cynical Theories*.
4. Carl Trueman, "Words Matter: Definitions Matter," *World*, December 27, 2022, https://wng.org/opinions/words-matter-definitions-matter-1672146617.
5. Trueman, "Words Matter."
6. Özlem Sensoy and Robin DiAngelo, *Is Everyone Really Equal? An Introduction to Key Concepts in Social Justice Education*, 1st ed. (New York: Teacher's College Press, 2012), 48.
7. Susan D'Agostino, "Amid Backlash, Stanford Pulls 'Harmful Language' List," *Inside Higher Ed*, January 10, 2023, https://www.insidehighered.com/news/2023/01/11/amid-backlash-stanford-removes-harmful-language-list.
8. Kurt Vonnegut, "Shapes of Stories," lecture at Case Western University, 2004. Abridged video: Ernie Lausten, "Kurt Vonnegut on the Shapes of Stories," July 16, 2024, YouTube video, https://www.youtube.com/watch?v=4ec0lSd7qH4.
9. J.K. Rowling, "J.K. Rowling Writes About Her Reasons for Speaking Out on Sex and Gender Issues," *JKRowling.com*, June 10, 2020, https://www.jkrowling.com/opinions/j-k-rowling-writes-about-her-reasons-for-speaking-out-on-sex-and-gender-issues/.
10. See "Campus Cancel Culture Database," *The College Fix*, https://www.thecollegefix.com/ccdb. To be sure, not all cancellations are against conservatives or Christians even though the others are comparatively rare. Here is an example. This person was a colleague of mine, a noted anarchist who was a classmate in Marxism with me: Dr. Nathan Jun, a tenured professor of philosophy at Midwestern State University in Wichita Falls, Texas. In autumn 2020, Jun wrote on a friend's Facebook page, "I want the entire world to burn until the last cop is strangled with the intestines of the last capitalist, who is strangled in turn with the intestines of the last politician." This was intended as a riff on a quote from Diderot in relation to the French Revolution—"Men will never be free until the last king is strangled with the entrails of the last priest"—and was made in regard to the killing of George Floyd in May 2020 according to Jun, where he resigned due to the stress he felt from the university administration and community at large. Staff, "University Embattled MSU Professor Address Controversy over Social Media Comments," *Times*

Record News, October 1, 2020, https://www.timesrecordnews.com/story/news/local/2020/10/01/msu-addresses-controversy-over-professors-abhorrent-comments/5887105002/; and see correction to Diderot: Jean Meslier Quotes, *Quote.org*, https://quote.org/quote/the-last-king-should-be-strangled-with-624423.

11. The College Fix Staff, "The College Fix Campus Cancel Culture Database FAQs," *The College Fix*, August 15, 2021, https://www.thecollegefix.com/the-college-fix-campus-cancel-culture-database-faqs/.
12. Thomas Patrick Burke, *The Concept of Justice: Is Social Justice Just?* (London: Bloomsbury, 2011), 33.
13. Burke, *Concept of Justice*, 31-57.
14. Hanna Ziady, "Bud Light Boycott Likely Cost Anheuser-Busch InBev over $1 Billion in Lost Sales," *CNN.com*, February 29, 2024, https://www.cnn.com/2024/02/29/business/bud-light-boycott-ab-inbev-sales/index.html.
15. Siddharth Cavale, "Target Removing Some LGBTQ Merchandise Following Customer Backlash," *Reuters.com*, May 24, 2023, https://www.reuters.com/business/retail-consumer/target-remove-some-lbgtq-merchandise-after-facing-customer-backlash-2023-05-23/.
16. C. Douglas Golden, "DEI Disaster: Petition Circulating Within Secret Service Community Warns of 'Potential Insider Threats,'" *The Western Journal*, May 11, 2024, https://www.westernjournal.com/dei-disaster-petition-circulating-within-secret-service-community-warns-potential-insider-threats/.
17. Sarah Fortinsky, "Secret Service: DEI Criticism of Female Agents After Trump Assassination Attempt 'Disgusting,'" *The Hill*, July 18, 2024, https://thehill.com/homenews/administration/4780166-secret-service-defends-female-agents/.
18. Editors, "Chick-fil-A and Covenant House," *Ministry Watch*, November 25, 2019, https://ministrywatch.com/chick-fil-a-covenant-house/.
19. "Committed to Being Better at Together," Chick-fil-A, accessed November 30, 2024, https://www.chick-fil-a.com/dei. The previous time I accessed the site, July 10, 2023, it read, "Chick-fil-A, Inc.'s commitment to being Better at Together means embedding Diversity, Equity & Inclusion in everything we do." That is no longer present. The note about the hire of Erick McReynolds as vice president of DEI is also no longer obvious on the website. His LinkedIn page shows he was hired as executive director of DEI just over one month after George Floyd's death in May 2020 and then was promoted later in 2023 to VP of DEI. See https://www.linkedin.com/in/erick-mcreynolds-922a8140/. Last accessed November 30, 2024.
20. Larry Fink, "A Sense of Purpose," BlackRock, 2018, blackrock.com/corporate/investor-relations/2018-larry-fink-ceo-letter.
21. Joseph S. Nye, *Soft Power: The Means to Success in World Politics* (New York: PublicAffairs, 2004), ix, xi.
22. Christopher F. Rufo, "Obscene Federal 'Diversity Training' Scam Prospers—Even Under Trump," *New York Post*, July 16, 2020.
23. Rich Loury, "Biden's Shocking Push to Radicalize the Federal Bureaucracy," *New York Post*, February 20, 2023, https://nypost.com/2023/02/20/bidens-shocking-push-to-radicalize-the-federal-bureaucracy/amp/. And see Chris Rufo, "President Biden Issues Executive Order Creating National DEI Bureaucracy," February 23, 2023, YouTube video, https://www.youtube.com/watch?v=WH2RWBgg9jk.
24. Justin Dorazio, "How Federal Agencies Can Advance Equity Through Biden's Second Executive Order," The Center for American Progress, May 24, 2023, https://www.americanprogress.org/article/how-federal-agencies-can-advance-equity-through-bidens-second-executive-order/.
25. Becky Bowers, "President Barack Obama's Shifting Stance on Gay Marriage," *Politifact.com*, May 11, 2012, https://www.politifact.com/factchecks/2012/may/11/barack-obama/president-barack-obamas-shift-gay-marriage/.
26. Report, "Two-Thirds of Democrats Now Support Gay Marriage," *Pew Research Center*, July 31, 2012, https://www.pewresearch.org/religion/2012/07/31/2012-opinions-on-for-gay-marriage-unchanged-after-obamas-announcement/.
27. ABC News, "DNC 2012: DNC Platform Changes on God, Jerusalem Spur Contentious Floor Vote," September 5, 2012, YouTube video, https://youtu.be/t8BwqzzqcDs?si=CqKy7P9l5NDQJ_v3.
28. Buzz Bissinger, "Caitlyn Jenner: The Full Story," *Vanity Fair*, June 25, 2015, https://www.vanityfair.com/hollywood/2015/06/caitlyn-jenner-bruce-cover-annie-leibovitz.
29. Ryan Morik, "Caitlyn Jenner Launches 'Fairness First' PAC to 'Keep Boys Out of Women's Sports,'" *Fox News*, April 4, 2023, https://www.foxnews.com/sports/caitlyn-jenner-launches-fairness-first-pac-keep-boys-womens-sports.

CHAPTER 2—A CASE OF SEXUALIZED AND GENDERIZED INSANITY

1. David A. Levy and Paul R. Nail, "Contagion: A Theoretical and Empirical Review and Reconceptualization," *Genetic Social and General Psychology Monographs* 119, no. 2 (1993): 233-284.
2. See the course at https://arts.princeton.edu/courses/black-queer-in-leather-black-leather-bdsm-material-culture-sp-23/. See the department website at https://arts.princeton.edu.
3. This journalistic website is helpful for understanding generally what is happening on college campuses in addition to our immediate interest—see Abigail Anthony, "Ecological Restoration Is like 'Gender Confirmation Surgeries,' Trans River Scientist Tells Princeton Students," *The College Fix*, October 10, 2022, https://www.thecollegefix.com/gender-confirmation-surgeries-are-like-ecological-restoration-princeton-hosts-queer-trans-feminist-river-scientist/.
4. "William Crawley Meets Peter Singer (part 3)," April 21, 2007, YouTube video, https://youtu.be/gAhAlbsAbLM?si=0UvuUKj4lCUHNTwy. See also the review paper Singer wrote on bestiality: Peter Singer, "Heavy Petting," *Prospect*, April 19, 2001, https://www.prospectmagazine.co.uk/opinions/56258/heavy-petting.
5. Lewis Caroll, *Alice Through the Looking Glass* (London: Macmillan, 1871), 103, as cited in Anthony Flew, *There Is a God: How the World's Most Notorious Atheist Changed His Mind* (New York: HarperOne, 2007), 31.
6. Carl Trueman, *The Rise and Triumph of the Modern Self: Cultural Amnesia, Expressive Individualism, and the Road to Sexual Revolution* (Wheaton, IL: Crossway, 2020).
7. See Lisa Diamond's 2013 Cornell lecture, "Just How Different Are Female and Male Orientation?": Cornell University, "Lisa Diamond on Sexual Fluidity of Men and Women," December 6, 2013, YouTube video, https://youtu.be/m2rTHDOuUBw. See also her Ted Talk in September 2018 in Salt Lake City, Utah, at https://www.ted.com/talks/dr_lisa_diamond_why_the_born_this_way_argument_does_not_advance_lgbt_equality?
8. TEDx Talks, "Why the 'Born This Way' Argument Doesn't Advance LGBT Equality: Dr. Lisa Diamond; TEDx SaltLakeCity," December 18, 2018, YouTube video, https://youtu.be/RjX-KBPmgg4?si=KA8IWjKpVcA-FrRU.
9. Linn Tonstad, *Queer Theology: Beyond Apologetics* (Eugene, OR: Cascade, 2018), 48.
10. David M. Halperin, *Saint Foucault: Toward a Gay Hagiography* (New York: Oxford, 1995), 61, as cited in Tonstad, *Queer Theology*, 64.
11. John Adams, "Adams' Argument for the Defense: 3–4 December 1770," National Archives, https://founders.archives.gov/documents/Adams/05-03-02-0001-0004-0016.
12. Melinda C. Mills, "How Do Genes Affect Same Sex Behavior?," *Science* 365, no. 6456 (August 30, 2019): 869-870, https://www.science.org/doi/10.1126/science.aay2726.
13. Mills, "How Do Genes Affect."
14. Lincoln-Douglas debates of 1858. See the one in Ottawa: "Mr. Douglas's Opening Speech," Northern Illinois University Digital Library, accessed March 25, 2023, https://digital.lib.niu.edu/islandora/object/niu-lincoln:36541.
15. See summary of a recent 25-year study in Finland: "Suicide Mortality Among Gender-Dysphoric Adolescents and Young Adults in Finland," *Society for Evidence Based Gender Medicine*, February 23, 2024, https://segm.org/Suicide-Gender-Dysphoric-Adolescent-Young-Adult-Finland-2024. See study in which this is further based—S.M. Ruuska, K. Tuisku, T. Holttinen, and R. Kaltiala, "All-Cause and Suicide Mortalities Among Adolescents and Young Adults Who Contacted Specialized Gender Identity Services in Finland in 1996–2019: A Register Study," *BMJ Mental Health* 27, no. 1 (February 17, 2024): https://pubmed.ncbi.nlm.nih.gov/38367979/.
16. Christian Schneider, "Transgender Activists File Bias Report Against Lesbian Crafting Group," *The College Fix*, January 29, 2020, https://www.thecollegefix.com/transgender-activists-file-bias-report-against-lesbian-crafting-group/.
17. J.K. Rowling, "J.K. Rowling Writes About Her Reasons for Speaking Out on Sex and Gender Issues," *JKRowling.com*, June 10, 2020, https://www.jkrowling.com/opinions/j-k-rowling-writes-about-her-reasons-for-speaking-out-on-sex-and-gender-issues/.
18. Joanna Moorhead, "UK's Only Trans Philosophy Professor to JK Rowling: Harry Potter Helped Me Become a Woman," *The Guardian*, July 11, 2020, https://www.theguardian.com/education/2020/jul/11/uks-only-trans-philosophy-professor-to-jk-rowling-harry-potter-helped-me-become-a-woman.

19. Moorhead, "UK's Only Trans Philosophy Professor."
20. "San Francisco Launches New Guaranteed Income Program for Trans Community," *SF.gov*, November 16, 2022, https://www.sf.gov/news--san-francisco-launches-new-guaranteed-income-program-trans-community; Brooke Singman, "New California Law Allows Jail Time for Using Wrong Gender Pronoun, Sponsor Denies That Would Happen," *Fox News,* October 9, 2017, https://www.foxnews.com/politics/new-california-law-allows-jail-time-for-using-wrong-gender-pronoun-sponsor-denies-that-would-happen; Josh Blackman, "The Government Can't Make You Use 'Zhir' or 'Ze' in Place of 'She' and 'He,'" *The Washington Post,* June 16, 2016, https://www.washingtonpost.com/news/in-theory/wp/2016/06/16/the-government-cant-make-you-use-zhir-or-ze-in-place-of-she-and-he/.
21. The life expectancy of male homosexuals was deemed to be between 8 and 21 years less than for heterosexual men. See one significant study by Robert S. Hogg, Steffanie A. Strathdee, Kevin J.P. Craib, Michael V. O'shaughnessy, Julio Montaner, and Martin T. Schechter, "Gay Life Expectancy Revisited," *International Journal of Epidemiology* 30, no. 6 (December 2001): 1499, https://doi.org/10.1093/ije/30.6.1499. Although the mortality rate among males having sex with males (MSM) from, say, the '80s and '90s, during the AIDS crisis, until now has become significantly mitigated due to medical technology over the years, it is indisputably still linked with severe health concerns. Anal sex predominantly takes place among MSM. Those on receiving end of anal intercourse are particularly vulnerable to acquiring numerous STIs (sexually transmitted infections): hepatitis, herpes, HPV, Chlamydia, Gonorrhea, Syphilis, HIV, Herpes, lymphogranuloma venereum, and other infections. The most concerning is HIV, which can lead to AIDS. HIV and AIDS are related but distinct in that the former is the immune deficiency virus causing the latter, which is described in the advanced stage when the immune system is severely compromised. According to the CDC, active MSM accounted for 67 percent of estimated new HIV infections in 2022. See US Statistics, February 5, 2025, https://www.hiv.gov/hiv-basics/overview/data-and-trends/statistics. Some of the significant reasons why MSM are at the highest risk have to do with the anatomy and physiology mentioned in the body of this book, which is why anal intercourse isn't healthy for anyone, gay or not. Mary Anne Dunkin, "Anal Sex Safety: What to Know," medically reviewed by Zilpah Sheikh, MD, April 11, 2024, https://www.webmd.com/sex/anal-sex-health-concerns.
22. "Bronze Sculpture of Alfred C. Kinsey Marks 75th Anniversary of Kinsey Institute," September 9, 2022, https://news.iu.edu/live/news/28033-bronze-sculpture-of-alfred-c-kinsey-marks-75th.
23. Abigail Shrier, *Irreversible Damage: The Transgender Craze Seducing Our Daughters* (Washington, DC: Regnery Publishing, 2021), introduction, xxi. See also Lisa L. Littman, "Rapid Onset of Gender Dysphoria in Adolescents and Young Adults: A Descriptive Study," Vol. 60, Issue 2, in *Journal of Adolescent Health*, February 2017.
24. Alex Oliveira, "Nearly 40% of Brown University Students Identify as LGBTQ+," *New York Post* (July 15, 2023).
25. Shrier, *Irreversible Damage*, xxiii.
26. Henry Gleitman, Daniel Reisberg, and James Gross, *Psychology*, 7th ed. (New York: W.W. Norton, 1981), 425-428.
27. Ryan T. Anderson, "Sex Reassignment Doesn't Work: Here Is the Evidence," The Heritage Foundation, March 9, 2018, https://www.heritage.org/gender/commentary/sex-reassignment-doesnt-work-here-the-evidence; "Suicide Mortality Among Gender-Dysphoric Adolescents and Young Adults in Finland," Society for Evidence Based Gender Medicine, February 23, 2024, https://segm.org/Suicide-Gender-Dysphoric-Adolescent-Young-Adult-Finland-2024; see also reviews and commentary on the Finish study: Sami-Matti Ruuska et al., "All-Cause and Suicide Mortalities Among Adolescents and Young Adults Who Contacted Specialised Gender Identity Services in Finland in 1996–2019: A Register Study," *BMJ Mental Health* 27, no. 1, https://mentalhealth.bmj.com/content/27/1/e300940.
28. Henry Gleitman, Daniel Reisberg, and James Gross, *Psychology* (New York: Norton, 2007), 425-426.
29. Michael Rea, Facebook, https://www.facebook.com/runloganrun/posts/10209140940855184?pnref=story.
30. "Society of Christian Philosophers Invites Eminent Philosopher, Then Apologizes for His Views on Homosexuality," *The Stream*, September 28, 2016, https://stream.org/society-of-christian-philosophers-invites-eminent-philosopher-then-apologizes-for-his-views/.

31. Ed Feser, "Christina van Dyke Owes Richard Swinburne Her Resignation," October 1, 2016, http://edwardfeser.blogspot.com/2016/10/christina-van-dyke-owes-richard.html.
32. Rod Dreher, "'____ You, _____,' Argued the Yale Philosopher," *The American Conservative*, September 28, 2016, https://www.theamericanconservative.com/swinburne-jason-stanley-homosexuality/.
33. Victor Nava, "John Fetterman's Wife Slams *NBC* Reporter as 'Ableist,' Wants Network Apology After Husband's Interview," *New York Post*, October 17, 2022, https://nypost.com/2022/10/17/john-fettermans-wife-slams-nbc-reporter-as-ableist-wants-network-apology-after-husbands-disastrous-interview/.
34. Richard Dawkins, posted on X, April 10, 2021, https://x.com/RichardDawkins/status/1380812852055973888?lang=en.
35. Richard Dawkins, posted on X, April 12, 2021, https://x.com/RichardDawkins/status/1381665011127451652.
36. "American Humanist Association Board Statement Withdrawing Honor from Richard Dawkins," American Humanist Association, April 19, 2021, https://americanhumanist.org/news/american-humanist-association-board-statement-withdrawing-honor-from-richard-dawkins/.
37. Chris McGreal, "Rachel Dolezal: 'I Wasn't Identifying as Black to Upset People; I Was Being Me,'" *The Guardian*, December 13, 2015, https://www.theguardian.com/us-news/2015/dec/13/rachel-dolezal-i-wasnt-identifying-as-black-to-upset-people-i-was-being-me.
38. Rebecca Tuvel, "In Defense of Transracialism," *Hypatia: A Journal of Feminist Philosophy*, 2017.
39. Jillian Kay Melchior, "Fake News Comes to Academia: How three scholars gulled academic journals to publish hoax papers on 'grievance studies,'" *Wall Street Journal*, October 5, 2018, https://www.wsj.com/articles/fake-news-comes-to-academia-1538520950.
40. Andrew Theen, "PSU professor resigns, accuses school of becoming 'social justice factory,'" *The Oregonian*, September 13, 2021, https://www.oregonlive.com/education/2021/09/psu-professor-resigns-accuses-school-of-becoming-social-justice-factory.html.
41. Peter Boghossian writes about the cultures wars as he sees them and the ironic new alliances forming because of them. Peter Boghossian, "Welcome to Culture War 2.0: The Great Realignment," *The American Mind*, November 8, 2019, https://americanmind.org/salvo/welcome-to-culture-war-2-0/.
42. "Peter Boghossian: How the Academy Got Woke and Why the 'New Atheists' Are to Blame," *Spectator*, April 2023, https://www.spectator.co.uk/podcast/peter-boghossian-how-the-academy-got-woke-and-why-the-new-atheists-are-to-blame/.
43. Ashtyn Asay, "Student Protest, Controversial Event Both Unfold Quietly at USU," *HJ News*, February 7, 2020, https://www.hjnews.com/news/education/student-protest-controversial-event-both-unfold-quietly-at-usu/article_59233e04-e903-5c85-ba88-2ff1499cecc3.html.
44. In 2020, a group of several hundred Cru staff appointed a team to document how pervasive critical race theory had become throughout the organization and then sent the document to the Cru board of directors. That document in its fullness can be read here: https://languagendreligion.wordpress.com/wp-content/uploads/2021/05/seeking-clarity-and-unity.pdf; see also Curtis Yee, "Cru Divided over Emphasis on Race," *Christianity Today*, June 3, 2021, https://www.christianitytoday.com/2021/06/cru-divided-over-emphasis-on-race/.
45. Allie Beth Stuckey, "Campus Crusade for Christ's 'Diversity Team' Sent a Ridiculous Post-Election Note—to BIPOC Only," *Blaze Media*, November 27, 2024, https://www.theblaze.com/shows/relatable-christian-2669998934.
46. See at https://www.rileygaines.com/.

CHAPTER 3—THE EXPLOITATION OF RACE FOR REVOLUTION

1. "Stanford Stories from the Archives," *Stanford University Libraries*, https://exhibits.stanford.edu/stanford-stories/feature/1980s.
2. Jacques Steinberg, "Yale Returns $20 Million to an Unhappy Patron," *The New York Times*, March 15, 1995, https://www.nytimes.com/1995/03/15/us/yale-returns-20-million-to-an-unhappy-patron.html.
3. Douglas Murray, *The War on the West: How to Prevail in the Age of Unreason* (New York: HarperCollins, 2022), 13.

4. Joseph Ax, "New U.S. Census Data Shows White Population Shrank for First Time," *Reuters*, August 12, 2021, https://www.reuters.com/world/us/us-release-census-data-used-legislative-redistricting-2021-08-12/.
5. *The Tonight Show with Jimmy Fallon*, season 8, episode 180, NBC, August 12, 2021.
6. Thomas Sowell, *Discrimination and Disparities* (New York: Hachette Book Group, 2019), Preface vii. His most recent book is *Social Justice Fallacies* (New York: Basic Books, 2023).
7. Thomas Sowell, "Racism Isn't Dead—But It Is on Life Support," *National Review*, November 18, 2015, https://www.nationalreview.com/2015/11/racism-america-history/. Last accessed March 26, 2023.
8. Frank Newport, "Americans See Obama Election as Race Relations Milestone," *Gallup*, November 7, 2008, https://news.gallup.com/poll/111817/americans-see-obama-election-race-relations-milestone.aspx.
9. Hans A. von Spakovsky, "No Surprise in Holder's Black Panther Whitewash," The Heritage Foundation, March 31, 2011, https://www.heritage.org/crime-and-justice/commentary/no-surprise-holders-black-panther-whitewash.
10. Steven Seene, "Top Cop: Officers 'Pained' by Obama Remark," *NBC News*, July 22, 2009.
11. Barack Obama, *Dreams from My Father: A Story of Race and Inheritance* (New York: Crown Publishing, 2004), 100.
12. Kimberlé Crenshaw, "Demarginalizing the Intersection of Race and Sex: A Black Feminist Critique of Antidiscrimination Doctrine, Feminist Theory and Antiracist Politics," *University of Chicago Legal Forum* (January 1, 1989): 139. See also Janel Jorge, "A Lesson on Critical Race Theory," *American Bar Association*, January 11, 2021.
13. Kimberlé Crenshaw, ed., *Critical Race Theory: The Key Writings That Formed the Movement* (New York: New Press, 1995), xx, xxi.
14. Richard Delgado and Jean Stefancic, "Living History Interview with Richard Delgado and Jean Stefancic," *Seattle University Digital Law Commons*, January 1, 2011, 225, https://digitalcommons.law.seattleu.edu/cgi/viewcontent.cgi?article=1039&context=faculty.
15. Murray, *War on the West*, 17.
16. Richard Delgado and Jean Stefancic, *Critical Race Theory: An Introduction* (New York: New York University Press, 2001), 2-3.
17. Karl Marx, "Theses on Feuerbach," in *Karl Marx and Friedrich Engels: Selected Works* (Moscow: Foreign Languages Publishing House, 1962), 1:15.
18. Murray, *War on the West*, 19.
19. Mike Gonzalez, "Marxism Underpins Black Lives Matter Agenda," The Heritage Foundation, September 8, 2021, https://www.heritage.org/progressivism/commentary/marxism-underpins-black-lives-matter-agenda.
20. Zach Goldberg, "How the Media Led the Great Racial Awakening," *Tablet*, August 4, 2020, https://www.tabletmag.com/sections/news/articles/media-great-racial-awakening.
21. Lydia Saad, "Black Americans Want Police to Retain Local Presence," *Gallup*, August 5, 2020.
22. *Black Lives Matter 2020 Impact Report*, accessed February 12, 2025, 6, 20, https://blacklivesmatter.com/wp-content/uploads/2021/02/blm-2020-impact-report.pdf.
23. Samuel Kronen, "Reinventing Racism—A Review," *Quillette*, November 30, 2020.
24. *Black Lives Matter 2020 Impact Report*, 6.
25. Singh Arjun, "The Corruption of Black Lives Matter," *National Review*, May 26, 2022, https://www.nationalreview.com/2022/05/the-corruption-of-black-lives-matter/.
26. "It Is Time for Accountability," *BLM10+*, November 30, 2020, https://www.blmchapterstatement.com/no1/.
27. Robin DiAngelo, *White Fragility: Why It Is So Hard for White People to Talk About Racism* (Boston: Beacon Press, 2018), 11, 149-150.
28. Lia Eustachewich, "Coca-Cola Slammed for Diversity Training That Urged Workers to Be 'Less White,'" *New York Post*, February 23, 2021.
29. Jemima McEvoy, "Sales of 'White Fragility'—and Other Anti-Racism Books," *Forbes*, July 22, 2020, https://www.forbes.com/sites/jemimamcevoy/2020/07/22/sales-of-white-fragility-and-other-anti-racism-books-jumped-over-2000-after-protests-began/; see also NYS Writers Institute, "Conversation with Robin

DiAngelo: 'White Fragility,'" *New York State Writers Institute*, October 8, 2020, https://www.nyswriters institute.org/post/conversation-with-robin-diangelo-white-fragility.
30. DiAngelo, *White Fragility*, 81.
31. Robin DiAngelo, *What Does It Mean to Be White?* (New York: Peter Lang, 2012), 330.
32. Ijeoma Oluo, *So You Want to Talk About Race?* (New York: Seal, 2019), 216-217.
33. Justin, McCurry, "US and China Publicly Rebuke Each Other in First Major Talks of Biden Era," *The Guardian*, March 18, 2021, https://www.theguardian.com/world/2021/mar/19/us-china-talks-alaska-biden-blinken-sullivan-wang.
34. Kim Kyung Hoon, "Black Lives Matter Protesters March Through Tokyo," *Reuters*, June 14, 2020, https://www.reuters.com/article/world/black-lives-matter-protesters-march-through-tokyo-idUSKBN23L0FY/.
35. "Edinburgh University Renames David Hume Tower over 'Racist' Views," *BBC News*, September 13, 2020.
36. Too many to count; see Marx scholar Paul Kengor, "Why Not Cancel Marx?," *The American Spectator*, August 18, 2020, https://spectator.org/cancel-karl-marx/. See also Kengor's 500-page book, *The Devil and Karl Marx: Communism's Long March of Death, Deception, and Infiltration* (Charlotte, NC: Tan Books, 2018).
37. Sheryl Gay Stolberg and Marjorie Connelly, "Obama Is Nudging Views on Race, a Survey Finds," *The New York Times*, April 27, 2009, https://www.nytimes.com/2009/04/28/us/politics/28poll.html.
38. Jennifer Agiesta, "Most Say Race Relations Worsened Under Obama, Poll Finds," *CNN*, October 5, 2016, https://www.cnn.com/2016/10/05/politics/obama-race-relations-poll/index.html.
39. Bryan Caplan, "The Prevalence of Marxism in Academia," Econlib, March 31, 2015, https://www.econ-lib.org/archives/2015/03/the_prevalence_1.html.
40. Cristina Beltran, "To Understand Trump's Support, We Must Think in Terms of Multiracial Whiteness," *The Washington Post*, January 15, 2021, https://www.washingtonpost.com/opinions/2021/01/15/understand-trumps-support-we-must-think-terms-multiracial-whiteness/.
41. Murray, *War on the West*, 39-40.
42. Skeptic Research Center, "How Informed Are Americans About Race and Policing?" *Research Report CUPES-007*, February 20, 2021, https://www.skeptic.com/research-center/reports/Research-Report-CUPES-007.pdf. And see *The Washington Post*'s database of fatal shootings by police officers: https://www.washingtonpost.com/graphics/investigations/police-shootings-database/. See also "Officers Feloniously Killed," *Federal Bureau of Investigation*, accessed March 1, 2025, https://ucr.fbi.gov/leoka/2019/topic-pages/officers-feloniously-killed. See also Molly Stellino, "Fact Check: Police Killed More Unarmed Black Men in 2019 Than Conservative Activist Claimed," *USA Today*, June 24, 2020, https://www.usatoday.com/story/news/factcheck/2020/06/23/fact-check-how-many-unarmed-black-men-did-police-kill-2019/5322455002/.
43. Devon Link, "Fact Check: Yes, Kente Cloths Were Historically Worn by Empire Involved in West African Slave Trade," *USA Today*, June 18, 2020, https://www.usatoday.com/story/news/factcheck/2020/06/16/fact-check-kente-cloths-have-ties-west-african-slave-trade/5345941002/.
44. Vicky Osterweil, *In Defense of Looting: A Riotous History of Uncivil Action* (New York: Bold Type Books, 2020).
45. Also see the saga as it unfolded at his university where Jun had recently acquired tenure: Staff Reports, "University, Embattled MSU Professor Address Controversy over Social Media Comments," *Times Record News*, September 2, 2021, https://www.timesrecordnews.com/story/news/local/2020/10/01/msu-addresses-controversy-over-professors-abhorrent-comments/5887105002/.
46. "Being Black in America Should Not Be a Death Sentence: Officials Respond to George Floyd's Death," *CBS News*, May 26, 2020, https://www.cbsnews.com/minnesota/news/being-black-in-america-should-not-be-a-death-sentence-officials-respond-to-george-floyds-death/.
47. Kelsey Vlamis, "Minnesota's Attorney General Said There Was No Evidence to Charge Derek Chauvin with a Hate Crime in the Murder of George Floyd," *Business Insider*, April 26, 2021, https://www.businessinsider.com/no-evidence-to-charge-derek-chauvin-with-hate-crime-prosecutor-2021-4.
48. Cary Aspinwall and Dave Boucher, "'You're Gonna Kill Me!': Dallas Police Body Cam Footage Reveals the Final Minutes of Tony Timpa's Life," *Dallas Morning News*, July 30, 2019, https://

www.dallasnews.com/news/investigations/2019/07/31/you-re-gonna-kill-me-dallas-police-body-cam-footage-reveals-the-final-minutes-of-tony-timpa-s-life/.

49. Michael Sisak and Michael Balsamo, "Inmate who stabbed Derek Chauvin 22 times is charged with attempted murder, prosecutors say," *AP News*, December 1, 2023, https://apnews.com/article/derek-chauvin-stabbing-suspect-d458e9c8fba02a98d5dbabb1884dc1cc.

50. Billy Binion, "Tony Timpa Wrongful Death Trial Ends With 2 Out of 3 Cops Getting Qualified Immunity," *Reason*, September 27, 2023, https://reason.com/2023/09/27/tony-timpa-wrongful-death-trial-ends-with-2-out-of-3-cops-getting-qualified-immunity/.

51. Sean Campbell, "Tyre Nichols Was Brutally Killed by Five Black Police Officers. How Did We Get Here?," *The Guardian*, September 7, 2024, https://www.theguardian.com/us-news/article/2024/sep/07/tyre-nichols-black-police-officers-memphis-history.

52. "Officer Deaths by Year," National Law Enforcement Officers Memorial Fund, April 29, 2024, https://nleomf.org/memorial/facts-figures/officer-fatality-data/officer-deaths-by-year/.

53. Anders Hagstrom, "FBI Director Says Violence Directed at Police Officers Unlike Anything He's Seen Before," *Fox News*, April 25, 2022, https://www.foxnews.com/us/fbi-christopher-wray-police-officer-murders. For *The Washington Post*'s database: www.washingtonpost.com/graphics/investigations/police-shootings-database/. Filters used: year, race, gender, and victim armed/unarmed. Last retrieved October 12, 2024.

54. Kimberlé Crenshaw, "Fear of a Black Uprising," as cited in Heather Mac Donald's *When Race Trumps Merit: How the Pursuit of Equity Sacrifices Excellence, Destroys Beauty, and Threatens Lives* (Nashville: DW Books, 2023), 250.

55. Jennifer Newton, "'Students Be Careful, There's Someone Walking Around in KKK Gear with a Whip': Indiana University Student Triggers Scare After Mistaking Priest for KKK Man," *Daily Mail*, April 7, 2016, https://www.dailymail.co.uk/news/article-3528348/Students-careful-s-walking-kkk-gear-whip-Indiana-University-student-triggers-scare-mistaking-priest-KKK-man.html.

56. J.K. Trotter, "That KKK Robe Sighting at Oberlin Was Probably Just a Student Wearing a Blanket," *The Atlantic*, March 5, 2013, https://www.theatlantic.com/national/archive/2013/03/kkk-robe-oberlin-was-probably-just-student-wearing-blanket/317746/.

57. "University of Missouri Students Report Threats; Police Quell KKK Rumors," *CNN*, November 12, 2015.

58. Avery Anapol, "Kamala Harris: Violent Attack on Empire Start Is 'Attempted Modern Day Lynching,'" *The Hill*, January 29, 2019.

59. Tracy Swarz, "Osundairo Brothers Expose Jussie Smollett 'Attack' in 'Anatomy of a Hoax,'" *New York Post*, March 10, 2023, https://nypost.com/2023/03/10/osundairo-brothers-re-enact-jussie-smollett-attack/.

60. Karen J. Winkler, "Teachers in Germany Attracted to Nazi Party Before WWII," *The Chronicle of Higher Education*, September 20, 1989, https://www.chronicle.com/article/teachers-in-germany-attracted-to-nazi-party-before-wwii/.

61. Petra Mayer, "Welcome to Story Hour: 100 Books for Young Readers," *NPR*, August 31, 2020, https://www.npr.org/2020/08/31/905804301/welcome-to-story-hour-100-favorite-books-for-young-readers.

62. Amazon teachers' pick, *A is for Activist*: https://www.amazon.com/Activist-Innosanto-Nagara/dp/1609805399, Last accessed February 12, 2025.

63. Sara Rimer, "Ibram X. Kendi Named to Time100 List of Most Influential People," *Boston University Today*, September 22, 2020.

64. Ibram X. Kendi, *How to Be an Antiracist* (London: One World, 2023). For a good review, see Neil Shenvi, "The Gospel of Antiracism—A Short Review of Kendi's How to Be An Antiracist," https://shenviapologetics.com/the-gospel-of-antiracism-a-short-review-of-kendis-how-to-be-an-antiracist/.

65. Kendi, *How to Be an Antiracist*, 10.

66. Kendi, *How to Be an Antiracist*, 143.

67. Kendi, *How to Be an Antiracist*, 176.

68. Kendi, *How to Be an Antiracist*, 209.

69. Kendi, *How to Be an Antiracist*, 217-218.

70. Kendi, *How to Be an Antiracist*, 14-17.
71. Kendi, *Stamped from the Beginning: The Definitive Idea of Racist Ideas in America*, 2nd ed. (New York: Bold Type Books, 2023), 11. For a good review, see Neil Shenvi, "A Long Review of Kendi's Stamped from the Beginning—Part I," https://shenviapologetics.com/a-long-review-of-kendis-stamped-from-the-beginning-part-1/.
72. Kendi, *How to Be an Antiracist*, 21.
73. "'Pursuing Racial Justice Together' series Announced for Fall 2020 Semester," Purdue University, August 25, 2020, https://www.purdue.edu/newsroom/archive/releases/2020/Q3/pursuing-racial-justice-together-series-announced-for-fall-2020-semester.html.
74. Schedule 2020, "Pursuing Racial Justice Together," Purdue University, https://docs.lib.purdue.edu/prjt/prjt/.
75. Amanda Woods, "BU Professor Ripped After He Implies Amy Coney Barrett Is a 'White Colonizer,'" *New York Post*, September 28, 2020, https://nypost.com/2020/09/28/bu-professor-suggests-amy-coney-barrett-is-a-white-colonizer/.
76. Witness the Kendi empire collapse: Dominic Green, "Ibram X. Kendi's anti-racism center folds after millions in donations," *Washington Examiner*, September 29, 2023, https://www.washingtonexaminer.com/opinion/columnists/ibram-x-kendis-anti-racism-center-folds. Last accessed December 14, 2023.

CHAPTER 4—MATH AND MEDICINE SWOON UNDER THE SPELL

1. See Franklin Perkins, *Leibniz: A Guide for the Perplexed* (New York: Bloomsbury Academic, 2007), 22-23.
2. Douglas Murray, *The War on the West: How to Prevail in the Age of Unreason* (New York: HarperCollins, 2022), 195.
3. Chacour Koop, "Smithsonian Museum Apologizes for Saying Hard Work, Rational Thought Is 'White Culture,'" *Miami Herald*, July 17, 2020, https://www.miamiherald.com/news/nation-world/national/article244309587.html.
4. Kenneth Jones and Tema Okun, *Dismantling Racism*, https://resourcegeneration.org/wp-content/uploads/2018/01/2016-dRworks-workbook.pdf.
5. Sonia Michelle Cintron, Dani Wadlington, Andre ChenFeng, *A Pathway to Equitable Math Instruction*, May 2021, https://equitablemath.org/wp-content/uploads/sites/2/2020/11/1_STRIDE1.pdf.
6. See some screenshots of the Twitter battle: https://www.reddit.com/r/IntellectualDarkWeb/comments/i3w5tv/twitter_erupts_into_debate_about_225_so_that_math/. Last accessed July 11, 2023.
7. Brittany Marshall (@brittanylm3281), Twitter, July 5, 2020. And see the supportive professor: Amanda Jensen (@MandyMathEd), Twitter, July 9, 2020. It came to a head when 750 math professors and teachers set the record straight in an open letter. To see the letter: https://www.dailymail.co.uk/news/article-10288277/Hundreds-professors-sign-letter-blasting-woke-math-movement-eliminate-advanced-classes.html. To see a rational conversation about the radical philosophical background on why anyone would dare claim otherwise than 2+2=4, see mathematician James Lindsay's piece "2+2 never equals 5," *New Discourses*, https://newdiscourses.com/2020/08/2-plus-2-never-equals-5/.
8. American Mathematical Society (@amermathsoc), "2/2 We Recognize This Will Require Fundamental Change: The AMS Is Developing a Plan to Reckon with Our Own History of Racist Behavior and to Address Systemic Inequities That Exist in Our Mathematics Community," Twitter, June 11, 2020, https://twitter.com/amermathsoc/status/1271171913327484931.
9. Melissa Hellmann, "US Universities Are Reinstating SAT Scores: Experts Say It Will Exacerbate Racial Inequality," *The Guardian*, June 20, 2024, https://www.theguardian.com/us-news/article/2024/jun/20/university-require-sat-act-test-diversity.
10. Kehinde Andrews, "Racism Is the Public Health Crisis," *The Lancet*, April 10, 2021, https://www.thelancet.com/journals/lancet/article/PIIS0140-6736(21)00775-3/abstract.
11. See www.thelancet.com/racial-equality.
12. David Harsanyi, "Medical Ethicist: Elderly Shouldn't Get Vaccines First Because They're Too White," *National Review*, December 18, 2018, https://www.nationalreview.com/corner/medical-ethicist-older-people-shouldnt-get-vaccines-first-because-theyre-too-white/.

13. "Tackling Systemic Racism Requires the System of Science to Change," *Nature*, May 19, 2021, https://www.nature.com/articles/d41586-021-01312-4.
14. "Editor of JAMA Leaves After Outcry over Colleague's Remarks," *The New York Times*, June 2, 2021, https://www.nytimes.com/2021/06/01/health/jama-bauchner-racism.html.
15. Cary P. Gross and Ezekiel J. Emanuel, "The Missing Part of America's Pandemic Response," *The Atlantic*, June 5, 2022, https://www.theatlantic.com/ideas/archive/2022/06/nih-covid-vaccine-research-studies/661182/.
16. Mitch Kokai, "Musk Slams Boeing's DEI Obsession," John Locke Foundation, January 16, 2024, https://www.johnlocke.org/musk-slams-boeings-dei-obsession/.
17. "Quick Facts," United States Census Bureau, accessed February 13, 2025, https://www.census.gov/quickfacts/fact/table/US/RHI225223.
18. Office of Advocacy, "Frequently Asked Questions About Small Business, 2023," US Small Business Administration, March 7, 2023, https://advocacy.sba.gov/2023/03/07/frequently-asked-questions-about-small-business-2023/.
19. Gracie Martinez and Jeffrey S. Passel, "Facts About the U.S. Black Population," *Pew Research Center*, January 23, 2025, https://www.pewresearch.org/race-and-ethnicity/fact-sheet/facts-about-the-us-black-population/.
20. Heather Mac Donald, *When Race Trumps Merit: How the Pursuit of Equity Sacrifices Excellence, Destroys Beauty, and Threatens Lives* (Nashville: DWBooks, 2023), 13.
21. NAEP Report Card: Mathematics, "National Student Group Scores and Score Gaps," The Nation's Report Card, https://www.nationsreportcard.gov/mathematics/nation/groups/?grade=12.
22. "Black Students' Scores on the ACT Test Continue to Fall and the Racial Gap Widens," *The Journal of Blacks in Higher Education*, filed in *Research and Studies*, October 18, 2021.
23. "Survey of Earned Doctorates (SED)—2021," National Center for Science and Engineering Statistics, accessed March 1, 2025, https://ncses.nsf.gov/surveys/earned-doctorates/2021. See also "Academic Disciplines Where African Americans Received Few or No Doctorates in 2021," *The Journal of Blacks in Higher Education*, October 31, 2022, https://jbhe.com/2022/10/academic-disciplines-where-african-americans-received-few-or-no-doctorates-in-2021.
24. Richard Sander and Robert Steinbuch, "Mismatch and Bar Passage: A School-Specific Analysis," *Bar Passage Rate, Submission to the Journal of Legal Education*, August 2018, https://jle.aals.org/cgi/viewcontent.cgi?article=1778&context=home.
25. Mac Donald, *When Race Trumps Merit*, 28.
26. Ibram X. Kendi (@DrIbram), Twitter, September 19, 2019.
27. Kendi, *How to Be an Antiracist*, 113-114.
28. Kendi, *Stamped from the Beginning*, 11.
29. Thomas Sowell, *Discrimination and Disparities* (New York: Basic Books, 2019), 1.
30. Sowell, *Discrimination and Disparities*, 19-20.
31. Sowell, *Discrimination and Disparities*, 7.
32. Thomas Sowell, "The Legacy of Liberalism," November 18, 2014, https://www.creators.com/read/thomas-sowell/11/14/a-legacy-of-liberalism.
33. Brad Wilcox, "Less Poverty, Less Prison, More College: What Two Parents Mean for Black and White Children," Institute for Family Studies, June 17, 2021, https://ifstudies.org/blog/less-poverty-less-prison-more-college-what-two-parents-mean-for-black-and-white-children.
34. "The Consequences of Fatherlessness," Fathers.com., https://fathers.com/the-consequences-of-fatherlessness/.
35. "Poverty Rate of Black Married-Couple Families in the United States from 1990 to 2023," *Statista*, accessed July 11, 2023, https://www.statista.com/statistics/205097/percentage-of-poor-black-married-couple-families-in-the-us/.
36. Travis A. Hoppe et al., "Topic Choice Contributes to the Lower Rate of NIH Awards to African-American/Black Scientists," *Science Advances* 5, no. 10 (October 9, 2019): doi: 10.1126/sciadv.aaw7238.
37. Mac Donald, *When Race Trumps Merit*, 34.

38. Dowin Boatright, et al., "Racial Disparities in Medical Student Membership in the Alpha Omega Alpha Honor Society," *JAMA Intern Med* 177, no. 5 (2017): 659-665, https://doi.org/10.1001/jamainternmed.2016.9623.
39. Mac Donald, *When Race Trumps Merit*, 35.
40. Stanley Goldfarb, *Take Two Aspirin and Call Me by My Pronouns: Why Turning Doctors into Social Justice Warriors Is Destroying Medicine* (New York: Bombardier Books, 2022), 167.
41. "MCAT Psychology and Sociology: Everything You Need to Know," Shemmassian Academic Consulting, accessed July 16, 2023, https://www.shemmassianconsulting.com/mcat#mcat-content-guides.
42. Mark J. Perry, "New Chart Illustrates Graphically the Racial Preferences for Blacks, Hispanics Being Admitted to US Medical Schools," *American Enterprise Institution (AEI)*, June 25, 2017, https://www.aei.org/carpe-diem/new-chart-illustrates-graphically-racial-preferences-for-blacks-and-hispanics-being-admitted-to-us-medical-schools/.
43. Kathryn Watson, "Biden Says He'll Name a Black Woman as Supreme Court Pick by End of February," *CBS News*, January 28, 2022, https://www.cbsnews.com/live-updates/biden-supreme-court-black-woman-pick-february/.
44. Ted Frank, "Justice Jackson's Incredible Statistic," *Wall Street Journal*, July 5, 2023, https://www.wsj.com/articles/justice-jacksons-incredible-statistic-black-newborns-doctors-math-flaw-mortality-4115ff62.
45. Jay P. Greene, "Justice Jackson's Trifecta of Wrong on 'Research' on Racial Preferences," The Heritage Foundation, July 10, 2023, https://www.heritage.org/courts/commentary/justice-jacksons-trifecta-wrong-research-racial-preferences.
46. Ketanji Brown Jackson, "Students for Fair Admissions, Inc. v. President and Fellow of Harvard College—Dissent," *Politico*, 23, https://www.politico.com/f/?id=00000189-07c1-d330-a3bf-f7d73fd00000.
47. Greene, "Justice Jackson's Trifecta of Wrong."
48. "Birthweight," March of Dimes Peristats, updated January 2024, https://www.marchofdimes.org/peristats/data?reg=99&top=4&stop=54&lev=1&slev=4&obj=1&sreg=06. See also "Infant Health and Mortality and Black/African Americans," US Department of Health and Human Services Office of Minority Health, updated February 13, 2025, https://minorityhealth.hhs.gov/infant-health-and-mortality-and-blackafrican-americans.

CHAPTER 5—CHRISTIAN MINISTRIES AND MISSION DRIFT

1. Shaun Walker, "Gay People at Winter Olympics Must 'Leave Children Alone,'" *The Guardian*, January 17, 2014, https://www.theguardian.com/world/2014/jan/17/vladimir-putin-gay-winter-olympics-children.
2. Jenny Goldsberry, "WATCH: Child Touches Groin Area of Performer at Pride Event," *The Washington Examiner*, September 29, 2022, https://www.washingtonexaminer.com/news/2595501/watch-child-touches-groin-area-of-performer-at-pride-event/.
3. *The DCShorts* is affiliated with *The Daily Caller*, June 26, 2023, https://youtu.be/7NXNKnT28Kc.
4. Leonard Hamlin, "Pride Month 2023: The Antidote to Fear," Washington National Cathedral, June 7, 2023, https://cathedral.org/blog/pride-month-2023-the-antidote-to-fear.
5. Christie Smith, *NBCBayArea*, "San Francisco Church Hosts Its First Ever 'Drag Queen Bible Story Hour,'" *NBC*, June 18, 2023, https://www.nbcbayarea.com/news/local/san-francisco-drag-queen-bible-story-hour/3254933/.
6. Douglas Murray, "The Church of England's New Religion," *The Spectator*, April 22, 2021, https://www.spectator.co.uk/article/the-church-of-england-s-new-religion/. See the full report here: https://www.churchofengland.org/sites/default/files/2021-04/FromLamentToAction-report.pdf.
7. Note that the presiding bishop of the Episcopal Church at that time, Michael Curry, is black. The words *antiracism*, *intersectionality*, and a host of other familiar terms relative to CRT and critical theory in general are used more times than worth counting. See here for the report: https://www.episcopalchurch.org/wp-content/uploads/sites/2/2021/04/RR-Racial-Justice-Audit-Report_ENG.pdf. See here for Kendi recommended reading: https://saintthomaschurch.org/2020/08/22/saint-thomas-church-reading-group-how-to-be-an-anti-racist-by-ibram-x-kendi/?mo=2&yr=2025.
8. The movement is DIALOP, a traversal dialogue between Leftists and Marxists together with European Christians for common ethical goals of the left—see https://www.ncronline.org/vatican/vatican-news/pope-tells-marxist-group-good-policies-cannot-be-dictated-market. The slogan for the group founded by this pope is "In search of a common future in solidarity. Only together can we be saved." For a critique,

see https://europeanconservative.com/articles/commentary/popes-marxist-dreams/. As Catholic philosopher Ed Feser states: "Ten popes in a row over the course of more than a century and a half denied that Catholicism on the one hand and Marxism or related doctrines on the other can have any common mission."

9. James H. Cone, *A Black Theology of Liberation, Twentieth Anniversary Edition* (Maryknoll, NY: Orbis Books, 1990), 8. For a good summary of this book, see https://shenviapologetics.com/quotes-from-cones-black-theology-of-liberation/. For a good short read on the compatibility of contemporary critical theory and Christianity, see https://press.ratiochristi.org/product/engaging-critical-theory/..

10. Cone, *A Black Theology of Liberation*, 10.

11. Cone, *A Black Theology of Liberation*, 85-86.

12. Cone, *A Black Theology of Liberation*, 128.

13. Cone, *A Black Theology of Liberation*, 70.

14. Lucas Miles, *Woke Jesus: A False Messiah Destroying Christianity* (West Palm Beach, FL: Humanix Books, 2023), 40. On this note, see the downloadable eBook by Ratio Christi Press by black author H.C. Felder: *Is Christianity a White Man's Religion? The Facts and Fallacies of a Eurocentric Jesus*, https://press.ratiochristi.org/product/is-christianity-a-white-mans-religion/.

15. See here to download the nearly 200-page report put together by 350-plus Cru staff detailing, for the Cru board of directors, the levels of critical theory throughout Cru's conferences, trainings, leadership, and so on. Cru's global staff has gone from 23,000 when I was on staff to roughly 16,000. In fairness, that drop isn't entirely due to the tension within, but it is part of the explanation. There are some signs that things are improving and some signs that they are not. I hope and pray to God that Cru can overcome the obstacles and maintain the steadfast vision of its founder, Bill Bright. I believe that it can, but time will tell—see https://capstonereport.com/2021/05/11/cru-trainings-promote-anti-white-anti-american-rhetoric/36002.

16. Kirsten Powers, "My Complicated Feelings About Tim Keller," May 24, 2023, as cited in Megan Basham's *New York Times* bestseller *Shepherds for Sale: How Evangelical Leaders Traded the Truth for a Leftist Agenda* (New York: HarperCollins, 2024), 230-231.

17. Keller used the Bible, quoting "proof texts" in support of a sociological theory he took on. First, his use of the Bible on "race" is excessively allegorical, resulting in his belief that authors sort people by skin color rather than by nations and cultures. Influenced by antiracist sentiments, he takes it to imply that Christians should confess and repent the racism of past generations, which isn't biblical. Second, he implies his imbibing of identity politics by suggesting we can be grouped according to skin color. For biblical usage, see the fine article by theologian Gerald McDermott, "Misunderstanding Race and the Bible," *Public Discourse*, October 20, 2020, https://www.thepublicdiscourse.com/2020/10/72125/.

18. While rejecting CRT as a worldview, Keller nonetheless accepts some of its assumptions, without good argument, about systemic racism and the allegation that America is systemically racist. For the support raising, he simply appeals to an anecdotal story rather than extensive data. See, for example, "Tim Keller: Missionaries Raising Their Own Funds Is 'A Great Example of Systemic Racism,'" October 28, 2021, YouTube video, https://youtu.be/1YkyXQ5vlzs.

19. There really are too many to number, including but not limited to Wheaton, Calvin, and Azusa Pacific University, all of which have been more than friendly to LGBTQ+ and CRT movements within. Even some of the best ones nonetheless have token woke administrators or professors.

20. Earlier, I mentioned the Society of Christian Philosophers as just one example. Bethany Christian Services is the nation's largest Christian adoption agency. Its president, Chris Palusky, was in leadership at World Vision when it decided to open hiring of LGBTQ+ staff and quickly got pummeled by donors, moving World Vision to recant two days later. Then Palusky went to Bethany, turning it woke before returning to World Vision. In recent years, Bethany has been placing adoptive children up for grabs to the LGBTQ+ community and now, more recently, has followed Ibram X. Kendi's call out to limit white people from adopting children of color. As black author Ryan Bomberger says, "They're happy to place children into homosexual-led homes but find placing children of my complexion in white homes as something that can be 'dangerous' and violates Bethany's newfound dogma of 'equity.'" Ryan Bomberger, *Bethany Christian Services: All Whites Are Racists*, November 7, 2021, https://radiancefoundation.org/bethany-christian-services-all-whites-are-racist/.

21. "About: Our Work and Mission," *Council for Christian Colleges and Universities*, https://www.cccu.org/about/.
22. *Council for Christian Colleges and Universities*, accessed February 13, 2025, https://diversity.cccu.org/anti-racism-education/.
23. See the links, for instance, in Lucas Miles's *Woke Jesus*, 76-80.
24. See *Shepherds for Sale*'s chapter "Christian Media and the Money Men," 72-89. Basham's book has had its fans and detractors. Perhaps the best-balanced reflection on it can be found by Neil Shenvi: "Battle Lines: A Long Review of Basham's *Shepherds for Sale*," https://shenviapologetics.com/battle-lines-a-long-review-of-bashams-shepherds-for-sale/.
25. Viktor E. Frankl, *The Doctor and the Soul: Introduction to Logotherapy* (New York: Random House, 1982), xxi.
26. From Abraham Kuyper's famous quote, "There is not a square inch in the whole domain of our human existence over which Christ, who is Sovereign over *all*, does not cry: 'Mine!'" Abraham Kuyper, *Abraham Kuyper: A Centennial Reader*, ed. James D. Bratt (Grand Rapids, MI: Eerdmans, 1998), 461.

CHAPTER 6—THE UNIVERSITY AS THE MIND OF CULTURE

1. Charles Malik, cited in *The Two Tasks of the Christian Scholar*, eds. Paul G. Gould and William Lane Craig (Wheaton, IL: Crossway, 2007), 63.
2. Malik cited in *Two Tasks*, 60.
3. Paul Gould, *The Outrageous Idea of the Missional Professor* (Eugene, OR: Wipf and Stock, 2014), 47.
4. NCES.ed.gov.
5. Cited in John C. Lennox, *Gunning for God: Why the New Atheists Are Missing the Target* (Oxford: Lion Hudson, 2011), 18. See also Lennox, *Can Science Explain Everything?* (London: The Good Book Company, 2019).
6. Alex Rosenberg, *The Atheist's Guide to Reality: Enjoying Life Without Illusions* (New York: W.W. Norton, 2011), 2-3.
7. Baruch Aba Shaber, *100 Years of Nobel Prizes*, 3rd ed. (Los Angeles, CA: AmericasGroup, 2005), 57-61. When it comes to the Nobel Peace Prize, nearly 80 percent were Christian and only 6 percent nontheist.
8. See also John Lennox, *Can Science Explain Everything?* (London: The Good Book Company, 2019).
9. Indeed, one of the most prominent atheist philosophers of the past century, Antony Flew, claimed that it was a book by an Israeli scientist, Gerald Schroeder, *The Hidden Face of God: How Science Reveals the Ultimate Truth* (Mankato, MN: The Free Press, 2001), that was part of an instrumental process of his conversion. See Flew's personal interview concerning his conversion, "My Pilgrimage from Atheism to Theism," *Philosophia Christi* 6, no. 2 (2004): 197-212.
10. Alex Rosenberg, *The Atheist's Guide to Reality: Enjoying Life Without Illusions* (New York: Norton, 2011), 112.
11. *Naturalism Undefeated? Essays on Plantinga's Evolutionary Argument Against Naturalism*, ed. James Beilby (London: Cornell University Press, 2002). Critics and defenders provide essays, and Alvin Plantinga provides an extended response that metaphysical naturalism is self-defeating.
12. Alvin Plantinga, *Where the Conflict Really Lies: Science, Religion, and Naturalism* (Oxford: Oxford University Press, 2011).
13. C.S. Lewis, *Miracles* (New York: HarperCollins, 2001), 169.
14. This expression has a deep history going back to the Chinese revolution of Mao Zedong, who found himself on the losing side and, did a long tactical march—a retreat, which enabled a counterattack. With various iterations, it was known as something like "long march of the red army." Herbert Marcuse, a leading Marxist, felt like the New Left in America and Europe was in a similar position in America when, in the early 1970s, prospects for their postmodern cultural Marxist revolution were narrowing; he and a German student leader, Rudi Dutschke, dialogued about the new strategic retreat as a means of future victory. Dutschke applied Mao's tactical retreat toward victory to the new revolution. Marcuse wrote to Dutschke, "I regard your notion of the 'long march through the institutions' as the only effective way,

now more than ever." Herbert Marcuse, *Marxism, Revolution and Utopia: Collected Papers of Herbert Marcuse*, vol. 6, eds. Douglas Kellner and Clayton Pierce (New York: Routledge, 2017), 334-336, as cited in Chris F. Rufo, *America's Cultural Revolution: How the Radical Left Conquered Everything* (New York: Broadside Books, 2023), 36-37.

15. Brian Duignan, "Postmodernism," *Brittanica*, accessed December 14, 2023, https://www.britannica.com/topic/postmodernism-philosophy.

16. Roland H. Bainton, *Here I Stand: A Life of Martin Luther* (New York: Meridian Publishing, 1955). See also some of the historical controversy behind the statement: "Did Luther Really Say, 'Here I Stand'?," *Concordia Publishing House*, April 18, 2016, https://blog.cph.org/read/everyday-faith/lutheranism/did-luther-really-say-here-i-stand.

17. This is popularly attributed to the Russian philosopher Dostoevsky, but there is controversy surrounding whether he actually said it.

18. Richard Rorty, *Philosophy and the Mirror of Nature* (Princeton, NJ: Princeton University Press, 1979), 174.

CHAPTER 7—A BRIEF HISTORY OF THE UNIVERSITY AND EXTREME MISSION DRIFT

1. Charles Haskins, *The Rise of Universities* (New York: Henry Holt, 1923).
2. Mark W. Graham, "The Opening of the Western Mind: The Emergence of Higher Education in the 'Dark Ages,'" in *Faith, Freedom, and Higher Education: Historical Analysis and Contemporary Reflections*, ed. P.C. Kemeny (Eugene, OR: Pickwick Publications, 2013), 19.
3. Vishal Mangalwadi, *The Book That Changed Your World: How the Bible Created the Soul of Western Civilization* (Nashville: Thomas Nelson, 2011), 194.
4. George Marsden, *The Soul of the American University: From Protestant Establishment to Established Nonbelief* (Oxford: Oxford University Press, 1996), 43.
5. George Marsden, *The Outrageous Idea of Christian Scholarship* (New York: Oxford University Press, 1997), 3.
6. Graham, "Opening of the Western Mind," 19.
7. Roland H. Bainton, *Here I Stand: A Life of Martin Luther* (Nashville: Abingdon Press, 1950), 144. See also "Did Luther Really Say, 'Here I Stand'?"
8. "About W&M: History and Traditions," William and Mary, https://www.wm.edu/about/history/.
9. "Religious Studies," William and Mary, accessed February 14, 2025, https://www.wm.edu/as/religiousstudies/.
10. Nathan Harden, *Sex and God at Yale: Porn, Political Correctness, and a Good Education Gone Bad* (New York: St. Martin's Press, 2012), 208.
11. Linn Marie Tonstad, *Queer Theology: Beyond Apologetics* (Eugene, OR: Cascade Books, 2013).
12. See Peter Singer, *Unsanctifying Human Life* (Oxford: Blackwell, 2002); Peter Singer, "Heavy Petting," *Prospect Magazine*, April 19, 2001, https://www.prospectmagazine.co.uk/opinions/56258/heavy-petting. Singer writes an opinion piece on the latest taboo to reconsider as discussed in the book *Dearest Pet: On Bestiality*, authored by Dutch biologist Midas Dekker. He argues that so long as it is mutually consensual and no harm is inflicted on the animal, it is fair game (game animals or nongame animals).
13. Desheania Andrews, et al., "Columbia University refuses to condemn professor who called Hamas attack 'awesome,'" *New York Post*, October 16, 2023, https://nypost.com/2023/10/16/columbia-university-refuses-to-comment-on-growing-furor-over-professor-who-called-hamas-attack-awesome/.
14. David Freed and Idrees Kahloon, "Beliefs and Lifestyle," *The Harvard Crimson*, n.d., 2019 data accessed August 24, 2019, https://features.thecrimson.com/2015/freshman-survey/lifestyle.
15. Steven Pinker, *Enlightenment Now: The Case for Reason, Science, Humanism, and Progress* (New York: Penguin Random, 2018), front cover publisher's blurb.
16. Pinker, *Enlightenment Now*, 372.
17. Bradford Richardson, "Liberal Professors Outnumber Conservatives Nearly 12 to 1, Study Finds," *Washington Times*, October 6, 2016, https://www.washingtontimes.com/news/2016/oct/6/liberal-professors-outnumber-conservatives-12-1.

18. Cass R. Sunstein, "The Problem with All Those Liberal Professors," *Bloomberg*, September 17, 2018, https://www.bloomberg.com/opinion/articles/2018-09-17/colleges-have-way-too-many-liberal-professors.
19. Michael Bloomberg, *Commencement Address, Harvard University*, May 29, 2014, http://www.mikebloomberg.com/news/mike-bloomberg-delivers-remarks-at-harvard-universitys-363rdcommencement-ceremony/.
20. George Yancey, *Compromising Scholarship: Religious and Political Bias in American Higher Education* (Waco, TX: Baylor University Press, 2017).
21. Peter Boghossian, *A Manual for Creating Atheists* (Durham, NC: Pitchstone Publishing, 2014), 177.
22. Blake Mauro, "University Cancels Planned Talk on Christianity's Influence on Civilization," *The College Fix*, October 3, 2023, https://www.thecollegefix.com/university-cancels-planned-talk-on-christianitys-influence-on-civilization/.
23. The popular paraphrase is derived from a famous sermon by Moody, who said, "I came to understand that my Lord was coming back again. I look on this world as a wrecked vessel. God has given me a lifeboat, and said to me, 'Moody, save all you can.' God will come in judgment and burn up this world, but the children of God do not belong to this world; they are in it, but not of it, like a ship in the water. This world is getting darker and darker; its ruin is coming nearer and nearer; if you have any friends on this wreck unsaved, you had better lose no time in getting them off." D.L. Moody, "That Gospel Sermon on the Blessed Hope," sermon delivered at the Great Chicago Tabernacle, January 5, 1877, preserved by Mustard Seed Publications, https://www.mustardseedchristianpublications.com/post/that-gospel-sermon-on-the-blessed-hope-by-dwight-lyman-moody.
24. Marsden, *Soul of the American University*, 81.
25. Marsden, *Soul*, 104–105.
26. Marsden, *Soul*, 106.
27. Methodological naturalism is the view that only natural causes are admitted into scientific explanation. See Paul A. Nelson, "Life in the Big Tent," *Christian Research Journal* 24, no. 2 (2002): https://www.equip.org/article/life-in-the-big-tent/.
28. Julie A. Reuben, *The Making of the Modern University: Intellectual Transformation and the Marginalization of Morality* (Chicago: University of Chicago Press, 1996).
29. Ratio Christi's statement of beliefs: "Our Beliefs," Ratio Christi, accessed February 14, 2025, https://ratiochristi.org/about/beliefs/.
30. Thomas Aquinas, *Summa Theologica*, II-II, q. 58, a. 1, https://www.newadvent.org/summa/3058.htm.
31. Richard M. Weaver, *Ideas Have Consequences* (Chicago: University of Chicago Press, 1948).
32. George Santayana, *The Life of Reason* (New York: Scribner, 1905), 284.
33. For a great primer from The Gospel Coalition, see Robert S. Smith, "Cultural Marxism: Imaginary Conspiracy or Revolutionary Reality?," *Themelios* 44, no. 3 (December 2019): 436–466, https://www.thegospelcoalition.org/themelios/article/cultural-marxism-imaginary-conspiracy-or-revolutionary-reality/.
34. On Wikipedia, "Cultural Marxism" now redirects to "Cultural Marxism Conspiracy Theory." "Cultural Marxism Conspiracy Theory," accessed February 14, 2025, https://en.wikipedia.org/wiki/Cultural_Marxism_conspiracy_theory.
35. Dominic Green, "What's Wrong with 'Cultural Marxism'?," *Spectator*, March 28, 2019, https://thespectator.com/topic/whats-wrong-cultural-marxism.
36. Kenneth J. Barnes, *Redeeming Capitalism* (Grand Rapids, MI: Eerdmans, 2018), 50.
37. Karl Marx and Friedrich Engels, *The Communist Manifesto*, reprint ed. (1848; Oxford: Oxford University Press, 1992), 15.
38. Karl Marx, "Manifest of the Communist Party," in *The Marx-Engels Reader*, 2nd ed., ed. Robert C. Tucker (New York: W.W. Norton, 1978), 500.
39. Mao Zedong, "Report on an Investigation of the Peasant Movement in Hunan," *Selected Works*, vol. 1 (March 1927), 28.
40. Marx and Engels, *Communist Manifesto*, 39.
41. Elsewhere, Marx makes clear that this "dictatorship of the proletariat" is what he means by "socialism."

See "The Class Struggles in France, 1848–1850" (1895), in *Karl Marx and Friedrich Engels: Selected Works* (Moscow: Progress Publishers, 1969), 1:139-242.

42. Karl Marx, "Critique of the Gotha Program" (1875), in *Karl Marx and Friedrich Engels: Selected Works* (Moscow: Progress Publishers, 1970), 2:24.
43. Marx and Engels, *Communist Manifesto*, 18.
44. Marx and Engels, *Communist Manifesto*, 22.
45. Paul Kengor, *The Devil and Karl Marx: Communism's Long March of Death, Deception, and Infiltration* (Gastonia, NC: Tan Books, 2020).
46. Interview with Jared Ball, *The Real News Network*, July 23, 2015.
47. Anthony Leonardi, "Black Lives Matter 'What We Believe' Page That Includes Disrupting 'Nuclear Family Structure' Removed from Website," *Washington Examiner*, September 21, 2020, https://www.washington examiner.com/news/black-lives-matter-what-we-believe-page-that-includes-disrupting-nuclear-family-structure-removed-from-website.
48. Richard Dawkins, *River Out of Eden: A Darwinian View of Life* (New York: Basic Books, 1995), 133.
49. Marx and Engels, *Communist Manifesto*, 22.
50. François Furet, *Marx and the French Revolution*, ed. Lucien Calvie, trans. Deborah Furet (Chicago: University of Chicago Press, 1988). Furet was originally a member of the French Communist Party and later became critical of it. For more connecting Marx's fixation on some of the worst parts of the French Revolution and his own vision of revolution, see Karl Marx scholar Paul Kengor, *The Devil and Karl Marx: Communism's Long March of Death, Deception, and Infiltration* (Gastonia, NC: Tan Books, 2020). According to Kengor, Marx viewed the French Revolution's radicalism and use of violence as a necessary means for achieving societal change. It exemplified the conflict between the working class and the aristocracy, a core concept of his conflict theory shown in class struggle. He sought to understand it to replicate its revolutionary fervor toward a communist utopia.
51. Matt Ridley, "Marxism Belongs in History's Bin After 100 Years of Hellish Failure," *The Australian*, January 2, 2017, https://tinyurl.com/y4rbnyx3.
52. See Paul Johnson, *Intellectuals* (London: Phoenix, 1988), 69-75.
53. Al Mohler, personal interview, October 22, 2024. Used with permission.

CHAPTER 8—REASONS FOR FAILURE AND THE RISE OF THE NEO-MARXISM(S) OF THE EUROPEAN AXIS POWERS

1. Paul Johnson, *Intellectuals* (New York: Harper Perennial, 2007), 63.
2. "Millennial Socialism," *The Economist*, February 14, 2019, 9-10; "Life, Liberty and the Pursuit of Property," *The Economist*, February 14, 2019, 16-20. The latest survey by *Victims of Communism Memorial Foundation* (conducted by YouGov), released in 2020 showed that there was increased favorability of the term *socialism* (49 percent) among Gen Z compared to 2019 (40 percent). Opinions of capitalism declined slightly from 2019 to 2020 among all Americans (58 percent to 55 percent), with Gen Z slightly up (49 percent to 52 percent) and Millennials down (50 percent to 43 percent). Indeed, 35 percent of Millennials and 31 percent of Gen Zers support the gradual elimination of the capitalist system in favor of a more socialist system. Further, only 63 percent of Gen Zers and Millennials (compared to 95 percent of the Silent Generation—less than 20 million alive) believe that the Declaration of Independence better guarantees freedom and equality over the Communist Manifesto: https://victimsofcommunism.org/annual-poll/2020-annual-poll/. Last accessed September 6, 2023.
3. Samuel Gregg, "The Most Dangerous Socialist in History," *The Stream*, July 25, 2016, https://stream.org/dangerous-marxist/.
4. David McLellan, *Marxism After Marx* (Basingstoke, UK: Palgrave Macmillan, 2007), 2034.
5. Notebook 7, §16, cited in *Selections from the "Prison Notebooks" of Antonio Gramsci*, ed. Quintin Hoare and trans. Geoffrey Nowell Smith (New York: International Publishers, 1971), 238.
6. This phrase was first used by Rudi Dutschke, a prominent spokesperson of the German student movement of the 1960s and a great admirer of Gramsci.

7. Cited in Damien Tudehope, "What's Left of Western Culture? Just About Everything," *The Spectator*, October 9, 2017, https://tinyurl.com/y4jdlbhg.
8. Notebook 25, §5, cited in Pietro Maltese, "A Pedagogy of the Subalterns: Gramsci and the Groups 'on the Margins of History,'" in *Antonio Gramsci: A Pedagogy to Change the World*, ed. Nicola Pizzolato and John D. Holst (Berlin, Germany: Springer, 2017), 188.
9. Dante Germino, *Antonio Gramsci: Architect of a New Politics* (Baton Rouge, LA: Louisiana State University Press, 1990), 179.
10. Mao Zedong, "Report on an Investigation of the Peasant Movement in Hunan," *Selected Works*, vol. 1 (March 1927), 28.
11. Antonio Gramsci, "Audacia e Fede," *Avanti*, May 22, 1916; reprinted in *Sotto la Mole: 1916–1929* (Turin: Einaudi, 1960), 148, author's translation. Some have questioned this quote. But confirmation of the translation can be found at a prosocialist website discussing the various misuses of the quote and putting it in context. See "That 'Capturing the Culture' Quote from Gramsci Is Fake," accessed October 22, 2023, https://socdoneleft.substack.com/p/that-capturing-the-culture-quote.
12. Roger Scruton, *Fools, Frauds and Firebrands: Thinkers of the New Left* (London: Bloomsbury, 2015), 208.
13. Andrew Roberts, *A History of the English-Speaking Peoples Since 1900* (New York: Harper, 2007), 476.
14. Paul Kengor, *The Devil and Karl Marx: Communism's Long March of Death, Deception, and Infiltration* (Gastonia, NC: Tan Books, 2020), 387.
15. Stuart Jeffries, *Grand Hotel Abyss: The Lives of the Frankfurt School* (London: Verso, 2017), 71.
16. Martin Jay, *The Dialectical Imagination: A History of the Frankfurt School and the Institute of Social Research, 1923–1950* (Berkeley, CA: University of California Press, 1973), 21.
17. Max Horkheimer, "Traditional and Critical Theory" (1937), in *Critical Theory: Selected Essays*, trans. Matthew J. O'Connell (New York: Continuum, 2002), 227.
18. During the years of American exile, Horkheimer also "insisted that the M word and the R word (Marxism and Revolution) be excised from its papers so as not to scare the Institute's American sponsors" (Jeffries, *Hotel Grand Abyss*, 72).
19. Karl Marx, *A Contribution to the Critique of Political Economy*, trans. N.I. Stone (Chicago, IL: Kerr and Company, 1904), 11-12.
20. György Lukács, "Mon chemin vers Marx" (1969), *Nouvelles Etudes hongroises* (Budapest, 1973), 8:78-79, cited in Michael Löwy, *Georg Lukács—from Romanticism to Bolshevism*, trans. Patrick Camiller (London: NLB, 1979), 93.
21. William A. Borst, *The Scorpion and the Frog: A Natural Conspiracy* (Bloomington, IN: Xlibris, 2004), 105.
22. György Lukács, *Record of a Life* (New York: Verso Books, 1985) 63.
23. Lukács, *Tactics and Ethics: Political Writings, 1919–1929*, ed. Rodney Livingstone, trans. Michael McColgan (London: NLB, 1972), 27.
24. Scruton, *Fools, Frauds and Firebrands*, 119.
25. Scruton, *Fools, Frauds and Firebrands*, 120.
26. Cited in Frank Borkenau, *World Communism: A History of the Communist International* (Ann Arbor: University of Michigan Press, 1962), 172.
27. Jefrey D. Breshears, "The Origins of Cultural Marxism and Political Correctness: Part 2," The Areopagus, 2016, 31, https://www.academia.edu/64045216/The_Origins_of_Cultural_Marxism_and_Political Correctness Part_2_29.
28. Theodor W. Adorno, Else Frenkel-Brunswik, Daniel J. Levinson and R. Nevitt Sanford, *The Authoritarian Personality*, eds. Max Horkheimer and Samuel H. Flowerman (New York: Harper & Brothers, 1950).
29. Jay, *Dialectical Imagination*, 247.
30. Jay, *Dialectical Imagination*, 247-248.
31. Marcuse, *Eros and Civilization: A Philosophical Inquiry into Freud* (Boston: Beacon Press, 1974), 81.
32. Marcuse, *Eros and Civilization*, 226, 263 and passim. Marcuse also uses the terms *polymorphous sexuality* (xv, 201, 211) and *polymorphous eroticism* (215).

33. Sigmund Freud, *Three Essays on the Theory of Sexuality* (1905), cited in Albert Mohler, "The Age of Polymorphous Perversity, Part One," Albert Mohler, September 19, 2005, https://tinyurl.com/y5r7lxho.
34. These and many other documented allegations against Kinsey can be found in Dr. Judith A. Reisman and Edward W. Eichel. *Kinsey, Sex, and Fraud: The Indoctrination of People* (Alameda, CA: Huntington House, 1990). This was followed by her work *Kinsey: Crimes and Consequences* (Scottsdale, AZ: Institute for Media Education, 2003) and *Sexual Sabotage* (Chantilly, VA: WND Books, 2010).
35. See commentary by Robert Knight, "Fraud and Pervert Alfred C Kinsey Returns: Scientist Still Leading the Sexual Revolution of Today," *The Washington Times*, September 24, 2022, https://www.washingtontimes.com/news/2022/sep/24/fraud-and-pervert-alfred-c-kinsey-returns/. See also https://www.christian.org.uk/news/us-university-unveils-statue-of-paedophile-collaborator-alfred-kinsey/.
36. Christopher Turner, "Hugh Hefner in Six Volumes," *The Guardian*, July 16, 2010, http://www.theguardian.com/books/2010/jul/17/hugh-hefner-playboy-biography.
37. In 2023, the Indiana state legislature defunded the Kinsey Institute that Indiana University continues to fund because of the institute's controversial history, and in 2024, it required Indiana University to show that it was no longer using taxpayer funds for it: https://www.in.gov/comptroller/files/Attorney-General-Todd-Rokita-and-Comptroller-Elise-Nieshalla-tell-IUs-Kinsey-Institute-to-follow-State-law.pdf. Last accessed October 28, 2024.
38. Revealing that both bestiality and pedophilia are on Singer's ethics menu, in this BBC interview with William Crawley, Singer has a message to those objectors who say, "It's just wrong though, isn't it?" Singer replies, "No, I don't see that you can say that. That's not my view. My view is not that anything is 'just wrong' full stop." See at https://www.youtube.com/watch?v=gAhAlbsAbLM&t=452s. Last accessed August 31, 2023.
39. See William Crawley of the BBC interviewing Peter Singer at "William Crawley Meetings Peter Singer," April 1, 2007, https://www.youtube.com/watch?v=gAhAlbsAbLM&t=433s. For interviews with former colleagues, staff, and students on the depths of Kinsey's depravity, see "Secret History: Kinsey's Pedophiles," July 5, 2013, https://www.youtube.com/watch?v=W6J7qLv-2hA.
40. Marcuse, *Eros and Civilization*, xv.
41. Simon J. Williams and Gillian A. Bendelow, *The Lived Body: Sociological Themes, Embodied Issues* (London: Routledge, 1998), 104.
42. Marcuse, *Eros and Civilization*, 208.
43. Marcuse, *Eros and Civilization*, 201.
44. Marcuse, *Eros and Civilization*, 201.
45. Marcuse, *Eros and Civilization*, 202.
46. Marcuse, *Eros and Civilization*, 203.
47. Marcuse, *Eros and Civilization*, 211.
48. See Kevin Floyd, "Rethinking Reification: Marcuse, Psychoanalysis, and Gay Liberation," *Social Text*, 19, no, 1 (2001): 103-128.
49. Marcuse, *Eros and Civilization*, xxv.
50. Herbert Marcuse, "Repressive Tolerance," in *A Critique of Pure Tolerance*, eds. Robert Paul Wolff, Barrington Moore Jr., and Herbert Marcuse (Boston: Beacon, 1965), 81-117.
51. Marcuse, "Repressive Tolerance," 88.
52. Marcuse, "Repressive Tolerance," 100.
53. Marcuse, "Repressive Tolerance," 109.
54. Herbert Marcuse, "On the New Left," in *The New Left and the 1960s: Collected Papers of Herbert Marcuse*, vol. 3, ed. Douglas Kellner (London: Routledge, 2005), 124.
55. From Occidental College's areas of study departmental website, accessed February 14, 2025, https://www.oxy.edu/academics/areas-study/critical-theory-social-justice.
56. Logan Dubil, March 16, 2022, https://www.thecollegefix.com/cornell-to-hire-social-justice-equity-librarian-for-science-library/.

57. Karl Marx, "Theses on Feuerbach," in *Karl Marx and Friedrich Engels: Selected Works* (Moscow: Foreign Languages Publishing House, 1962), 1:15.
58. See Marx's letter to Arnold Ruge (Kreuznach, September 1843).
59. Stephen E. Bronner, *Critical Theory: A Very Short Introduction* (Oxford: Oxford University Press, 2011), 4.
60. Max Horkheimer, "On the Problem of Truth," in *Between Philosophy and Social Science: Selected Early Writings*, trans. G. Hunter, M. Kramer and J. Torpey (Cambridge, MA: MIT Press, 1993), 177-215.
61. Max Horkheimer, "Dämmerung," in *Dawn and Decline: Notes 1926–1931 & 1950–1969*, trans. M. Shaw (New York: Seabury, 1978), 18.
62. Jay, *Dialectical Imagination*, 63.
63. Jeffries, *Grand Hotel Abyss*, 18.
64. Georg Lukács, *The Theory of the Novel: A Historico-Philosophical Essay on the Forms of Great Epic Literature*, trans. Anna Bostok (Cambridge, MA: MIT Press, 1971), 22.
65. Whitfield, "Refusing Marcuse."
66. Jeffries, *Grand Hotel Abyss*, 4.
67. "Professors: One-Dimensional Philosopher," *TIME*, March 22, 1968, https://time.com/archive/6624660/professors-one-dimensional-philosopher/.
68. "100 Most Influential People 2020," *TIME*, accessed October 24, 2023, https://time.com/collection/100-most-influential-people-2020.
69. Erich Fromm, *Revolutionary Hope: Prophetic Messianism as a Critical Theory of the Future* (Rotterdam: Sense Publishers, 2014), 41.
70. Ben Agger, "Accidental Hero: Marcuse's 'One-Dimensional Man' at 50," *Truthout*, September 9, 2014, https://truthout.org/articles/accidental-hero-marcuses-one-dimensional-man-at-50/.
71. Agger, "Accidental Hero."

CHAPTER 9—CULTURAL MARXISM AND THE POSTMODERN TURN

1. "Political correctness" has long been associated with communism. Leninists used it to describe steadfastness to party affiliations, Stalinists used it to evoke a sense of historical certitude, and Mao Zedong used it in his *The Little Red Book*.
2. Damien Tudehope, "What's Left of Western Culture? Just About Everything," *The Spectator*, October 9, 2017, https://tinyurl.com/y4jdlbhg.
3. Alasdair MacIntyre, *Marxism: An Interpretation* (London: SCM, 1953), 18.
4. See Vodie Baucham, *Fault Lines: The Social Justice Movement and Evangelicalism's Looming Catastrophe* (Washington, DC: Salem Books, 2021), chapters 4–6 on the new religion, priesthood, and canon. See also Melvin Tinker, *That Hideous Strength: How the West Was Lost: The Cancer of Cultural Marxism in the Church, the World and the Gospel of Change* (Welwyn Garden City, UK: EP Books, 2018).
5. Stephen Hicks, *Explaining Postmodernism: Skepticism and Socialism from Rousseau to Foucault*, expanded ed. (Brisbane, Australia: Connor Court Publishing, 2019).
6. Michel Foucault, as cited in Hicks, *Explaining Postmodernism*, 2.
7. Richard Rorty, as cited in Hicks, *Explaining Postmodernism*, 2.
8. Jacques Derrida, *Moscou aller-retour* (Saints Etienne: De l'Aube, 1995), as cited in Hicks, *Explaining Postmodernism*, 5. See also Mark Lilla, "Review of Derrida's *Moscou Aller-Retour*" in *The New York Review of Books*, June 1998, from whence this statement was made.
9. Richard Rorty, *Philosophy and the Mirror of Nature* (Princeton, NJ: Princeton University Press, 1979), 175-176.
10. Hicks, *Explaining Postmodernism*, 3.
11. Frank Lentricchia, as cited in Hicks, *Explaining Postmodernism*, 3.
12. Hicks, *Explaining Postmodernism*, 24.

13. Hicks, *Explaining Postmodernism*, 84.
14. Mark Lilla, "The Politics of Jacques Derrida," *New York Review*, January 25, 1998, https://www.nybooks.com/articles/1998/06/25/the-politics-of-jacques-derrida/.
15. Hicks, *Explaining Postmodernism*, 85.
16. Friedrich Engels, "Utopian and Scientific," *The Marx-Engels Reader*, 2nd ed., ed. Robert C. Tucker (New York: W.W. Norton, 1978), 700.
17. Hicks, *Explaining Postmodernism*, 90.
18. Jacques Derrida, *Specters of Marx: the State of the Debt, the Work of Mourning and the New International* (New York: Routledge Classics, 1996), 15.
19. Marian L. Tupy, "100 Years of Communism: Death and Deprivation," Cato Institute, October 17, 2017, https://www.cato.org/commentary/100-years-communism-death-deprivation.
20. Herbert Marcuse, as cited in Hicks, *Explaining Postmodernism*, 171.
21. Pol Pot, communist leader of Cambodia who murdered millions of his own, was also a member of the French Communist party. He studied in France during the same time as Foucault was a member.
22. In 1977, both Foucault and Derrida called for decriminalization of "consensual" sexual relations between adults and minors. Foucault was gay and died of AIDS. He was also more recently discovered to have been a pedophile rapist who had sex with Arab children while living in Tunisia in the late 1960s. One French academic told interviewers that he witnessed Foucault throwing money at boys as young as eight and inviting them to meet him for nocturnal sex at the local cemetery, where he abused them on the gravestones. The question of consent wasn't even raised. Foucault enjoyed sadomasochistic bathhouses in San Francisco and died of AIDS. He published four volumes on the *History of Sex*, being every bit a Freudian sex fan himself. His fourth volume, in which he wrote much about sexual freedom, was delayed, locked in a vault, until published posthumously in 2018. Stuart Jeffries, "How Foucault Was Shielded from Scandal by French Reverence for Intellectuals," *The Spectator*, July 31, 2021.
23. Richard Rorty, *Contingency, Irony, and Solidarity* (Cambridge, UK: Cambridge University Press, 1989), 9.
24. Richard Rorty, "A Conversation with Richard Rorty," interview by Scott Stossel, April 23, 1998, https://www.theatlantic.com/magazine/archive/1998/04/the-next-left/306010/.
25. Hicks, *Explaining Postmodernism*, 182-183.
26. "The Republic," *Plato: Complete Works*, ed. John M. Cooper (Indianapolis, IN: Hacket, 1997), 983.
27. Frank Lentricchia, *Criticism and Social Change* (Chicago: University of Chicago Press, 1983), 12.
28. Richard Rorty, "Universality and Truth," in Robert B. Brandom, *Rorty and His Critics*, ed. Robert B. Brandom (Oxford: Blackwell, 2000), 21–22.

CHAPTER 10—IS CHRISTIANITY GOOD FOR THE WORLD?

1. Jaroslav Pelikan, *Jesus Through the Centuries: His Place in the History of Culture* (New Haven, CT: Yale University Press, 1999), 1.
2. Steven Pinker, *Enlightenment Now: The Case for Reason, Science, Humanism, and Progress* (New York: Random House, 2019).
3. Benjamin M. Friedman, *Religion and the Rise of Capitalism* (New York: Random House, 2021). Here, Friedman also discusses the seminal work by sociologist Max Weber, *The Protestant Ethic and the Spirit of Capitalism* (1905).
4. Karl Marx, "Critique of the Gotha Program," *Karl Marx/Frederick Engels: Collected Works*, vol. 24 (New York: International, 1989), 96.
5. Benjamin M. Friedman, *Religion and the Rise of Capitalism* (New York: Alfred A. Knopf, 2021); Max Weber, *The Protestant Ethic and the Spirit of Capitalism* (New York: Routledge, 2005).
6. Peter Singer, *The Unsanctifying of Human Life* (Malden, MA: Blackwell, 2002), 228-229.
7. Helen Alvare and Ryan T. Anderson, "The Lazy Slander of the Prolife Cause," January 7, 2011, https://www.thepublicdiscourse.com/2011/01/2380/.

8. "Who We Are," *Planned Parenthood*, accessed February 15, 2025, https://www.plannedparenthood.org/about-us/who-we-are.
9. Moira Gaul, "Fact Sheet: Pregnancy Centers—Serving Women and Saving Lives (2020 Study)," *Charlotte Lozier Institute*, July 19, 2021, accessed February 15, 2025, https://lozierinstitute.org/fact-sheet-pregnancy-centers-serving-women-and-saving-lives-2020/.
10. "Five Things You Need to Know about Adoption," *Barna*, November 4, 2013, https://www.barna.com/research/5-things-you-need-to-know-about-adoption.
11. Andrew Crislip, *From Monastery to Hospital: Christian Monasticism and the Transformation of Health Care in Late Antiquity* (Ann Arbor: University of Michigan Press, 2005).
12. Sara Zylstra, "How Southern Baptists Trained More Disaster Relief Volunteers Than the Red Cross," *The Gospel Coalition*, November 7, 2017, https://www.thegospelcoalition.org/article/how-southern-baptists-trained-more-disaster-relief-volunteers-than-the-red-cross.
13. Organizations like Compassion International and World Vision help people adopt children and serve, via child sponsorship, millions of babies, children, and youth in more than 100 countries.
14. For example, International Justice Mission, whose goal is to end human sex trafficking.
15. Arthur Brooks, *Who Really Cares? The Surprising Truth About Compassionate Conservatism* (New York: Basic Books, 2006), 34.
16. Brooks, *Who Really Cares?*, 34.
17. Brooks, *Who Really Cares?*, 36.
18. Brooks, *Who Really Cares?*, 39.
19. Brooks, *Who Really Cares?*, 40.
20. Brooks, *Who Really Cares?*, 97.
21. United Nations, *Universal Declaration of Human Rights* (Paris, 1948), https://www.un.org/en/about-us/universal-declaration-of-human-rights. Like other institutions of magnanimous origins, the UN is no stranger to questions about its faithfulness to its origins. The point is that it was undergirded by Christian thought and maps onto our intuitions.
22. See James Griffin, *On Human Rights* (Oxford: Oxford University Press, 2008), 1-2. Griffin writes, "The French marked the secularization of the concept by changing the name from 'natural rights' to 'human rights'…. The secularized notion that we were left with at the end of the Enlightenment is still our notion today. Its intension has not changed since then: a right that we have simply in virtue of being human."
23. Charles Darwin, *Descent of Man* (Amherst, NY: Prometheus Books, 1998), 101.
24. James Rachels, *Created from Animals: The Moral Implications of Darwinism* (Oxford: Oxford University Press, 1990), 70.
25. Pinker, *How the Mind Works* (New York: W.W. Norton, 1997), 21.
26. Richard Dawkins, *Outgrowing God: A Beginner's Guide* (New York: Random House, 2019), 99.
27. Jurgen Habermas, *Time of Transitions* (Cambridge, UK: Polity, 2006), 150-151.
28. For contemporary and historical treatments, see Jeffrey Wattles, *The Golden Rule* (Oxford: Oxford University Press, 1996); *The Golden Rule: The Ethics of Reciprocity in World Religions*, eds. Jacob Neusner and Bruce Chilton (London and New York City, Continuum, 2008).
29. Donald Pfaff, *The Neuroscience of Fair Play: Why We (Usually) Follow the Golden Rule* (New York: Dana Press, 2007), 3.
30. *Babylonian Talmud* (Shabbat 31a), The William Davidson Talmud, www.sefaria.org/Shabbat.31a. For Judaism, while Hillel's statement represents SR, one can argue that the ancient Jewish position suggests GR roots if grounded in Leviticus 19:18, "Love your neighbor as yourself" (NIV).
31. Jami Al-Tirmidhi, vol. 4, book 35, *Hadith* 2515.
32. Confucius, *The Analects* (London: Penguin Books, 1979), 12:2.
33. John Ireland, *The Udana: Inspired Utterances of the Buddha* (Kandy, Sri Lanka: Buddhist Publication Society, 1990), 68.

34. *The Mahabharata* (Book 13: Anusasana Parvan 113.8), trans. Kisari Mohan Ganguli, Sacred Texts, https://www.sacred-texts.com/hin/m13/index.htm.
35. Michael Ruse, *Darwinism as Religion* (Oxford: Oxford University Press, 2017), ix.
36. Charles Darwin, *The Descent of Man* (Princeton, NJ: Princeton University Press, 1981), 106.
37. Alex Rosenberg, *The Atheist's Guide to Reality* (New York: Norton, 2011), 95.
38. Michael Ruse, *The Darwinian Paradigm* (London: Routledge, 1989), 262, 268–269.
39. Explanatory scope pertains to the range of facts or evidence explained. Explanatory power relates to the likelihood of the evidence explained.
40. Sahih al-Bukhari, vol. 9, book 88, *Hadith* 6922.
41. Rosenberg, *Atheist's Guide to Reality*, 103.
42. Rosenberg, *Atheist's Guide to Reality*, 109.
43. Donald Hoffman, *The Case Against Reality: Why Evolution Hid the Truth from Our Eyes* (New York: Norton, 2019).
44. Aristotle, "Metaphysics," *The Complete Works of Aristotle: The Revised Oxford Translation*, ed. Jonathan Barnes (Princeton, NJ: Princeton University Press, 1984), I.1, 980a21-7.
45. Charles Haskins, *The Rise of Universities* (New York: Henry Holt, 1923).
46. Corey Miller, *In Search of the Good Life: Through the Eyes of Aristotle, Maimonides, and Aquinas* (Eugene, OR: Wipf and Stock, 2019).
47. Vishal Mangalwadi and David Marshall, eds, *The Third Education Revolution: From Home School to Church College* (Clovis, CA: Soughtaftermedia, 2021). Mangalwadi, mentioned in chapter 2, has noted how the Bible changed the world. In truth, I agree with its influence, but it is God in Christ through the Spirit who did that. The Bible was only the literary medium, which I'm sure Mangalwadi would agree with. We've seen how the rise and expansion of the universities was due primarily to Christianity. Mangalwadi et al. offer an approach of reclaiming the Christian mind through a more recent work that I was invited to participate in. Yet that book focuses on educational revolutions within and by the church institution proper to impact the world. The focus of Mangalwadi and Marshall is on the two educational revolutions in the eighth and sixteenth centuries, during which the church educated the minister to serve both church and state, and then subsequently in Luther's Reformation, through which every believer was educated by the church to serve God as priest and king. Now, Mangalwadi argues, it should be done by the church via new digital media methods as the universities are sending students online. There is much with which I concur. My present volume, however, focuses on the two anti-Christian ideological revolutions that swept the American universities in the epochs of modernity and postmodernity. These ideological revolutions, deriving ideology from post-Reformation European universities (i.e., scientific naturalism and postmodern cultural Marxism), are anti-Christian and have not only subverted but even now have infiltrated the church institution proper. The two ideological revolutions in American universities ironically sprang from European influence. It is the American universities' ideological revolutions, however, that are changing the world on account of leverage. As go the US universities (onsite and online), so goes the world. Given that nearly one-third of world leaders and prime "ministers" earn a degree from US universities and that America is the most influential country, these universities are vital and must be infiltrated by Christian believers. They are not the only aim for a third revolution as I advocate, but they are the primary focus for the purposes of this present book. We must have education within the church, as Mangalwadi argues, but we must reclaim the intellectual voice of Christ in these universities because of their massive leverage point. Arguably, these universities are influencing the church in the West more than vice versa.
48. Robert Woodberry, "The Missionary Roots of Liberal Democracy," *American Political Science Review* 106 (2012): 244-274.
49. Harvard's original motto, "Veritas," although it has retained only that term, cannot escape its theistic roots in that it emerged from the idea that all truth is God's truth and that at best we can and ought to seek to think God's thoughts after Him.
50. George Marsden, *The Soul of the American University: From Protestant Establishment to Established Nonbelief* (Oxford: Oxford University Press), 43.

51. Corey Miller, "How We Lost the Universities and How to Reclaim the Voice of Christ," *Christian Research Journal* online exclusive feature article, August 22, 2019, https://www.equip.org/article/how-we-lost-the-universities-how-to-reclaim-the-voice-of-christ.
52. Pinker is an atheist whose book seeks to make the case, an apologetic if you will, that humanism made the West best. Steven Pinker, *Enlightenment Now: The Case for Reason, Science, Humanism, and Progress* (New York: Viking, 2018), 385.
53. Letter to William Graham, July 3, 1881, in *The Life and Letters of Charles Darwin*, vol. 1, ed. Francis Darwin (New York, NY: D. Appleton and Company, 1887), 255.
54. Tom Holland, *Dominion: How the Christian Revolution Remade the World* (New York: Basic Books, 2019), 494.
55. Tom Holland, "Why I Was Wrong About Christianity," *The New Statesman*, September 14, 2016, https://www.newstatesman.com/politics/religion/2016/09/tom-holland-why-i-was-wrong-about-christianity.

CHAPTER 11—IS CHRISTIAN BELIEF REASONABLE?

1. Aldous Huxley, *Ends and Means* (New York: Harper & Brothers Publishers, 1937), 270.
2. Thomas Nagel, *The Last Word* (Oxford: Oxford University Press, 1997), 130–131.
3. Isaac Asimov, "An Interview with Isaac Asimov on Science and the Bible," *Free Inquiry* 2, no. 2 (Spring 1982): 9.
4. For more details, see Corey Miller, "A Critique of Marx's Epistemology of Religion from Reformed Epistemology," *International Philosophical Quarterly* 49, no. 3 (September 2009): 351-359.
5. Karl Marx, "Contribution to the Critique of Hegel's Philosophy of Right: Introduction," *Marx-Engels Reader*, 2nd ed., ed. R. Tucker (New York: W.W. Norton, 1978), 53.
6. Marx, "Contribution to the Critique of Hegel's Philosophy," 20.
7. Marx, "On the History of His Opinions," *Marx-Engels Reader*, 4.
8. Marx's "Jewish Question" is not to be confused with the Nazi perspective on Jewish people of 1930–1940s Germany. Marx wrote this nearly a century before. While both Marx's "On the Jewish Question" and Hitler's ideology touched on the concept of "the Jew," Marx's analysis was a critique of the societal structures that created the stereotype of the Jewish "huckster," focusing on economic factors and arguing for a societal transformation to dismantle these prejudices, whereas Hitler's views were explicitly racist and aimed at the systematic extermination of Jews, promoting a notion of a racially pure "Aryan" society that excluded Jews entirely.
9. Marx, "On the Jewish Question," *Marx-Engels Reader*, 28. While Marx seems to have a positive place for religion according to some passages, where he mentions its unproblematic existence, the context reveals that it is nominal, properly domesticated, or secularized, humanistic religion (see also pages 35-36, 39).
10. Marx, "On the Jewish Question," 28.
11. This is not to say that Marx lacked, at least conceptually, a place for spirituality. The most immediate example in contemporary times appropriating the Marxist ethos from Marx's thought is liberation theology as found in Latin America. For more on classic and contemporary Marxist spirituality, see *Marxism and Spirituality: An International Anthology*, ed. Benjamin Page (Westport, CT: Bergin and Garvey, 1987).
12. Marx, "On the Jewish Question," 36.
13. Marx, "On the Jewish Question," 29.
14. Marx, "On the Jewish Question," 31.
15. Marx, "On the Jewish Question," 39.
16. While many Marxists may, with good reason, want to deny this aspect, and while it certainly is not Marx's own ideal means to solving the serious religion problem, support for this position can be found in his text. Further, history shows that perhaps it is not as rare as we think when we consider the persecution in Eastern Europe during the Cold War and the purges under Stalin during the 1950s and 1960s; many were killed for their religious stance.

17. Marx, "On the Jewish Question," *Marx-Engels Reader*, 36.
18. Marx, "Contribution to the Critique of Hegel's Philosophy," 54.
19. Ludwig Feuerbach, *The Essence of Christianity*, trans. George Eliot (Amherst, NY: Prometheus, 1989), 270.
20. Sigmund Freud, *The Future of an Illusion* (New York: W.W. Norton, 1989).
21. Marx, "Contribution to the Critique of Hegel's Philosophy," 54.
22. The next step is, of course, the criticism or unmasking of the secular political realm toward the ultimate human emancipation.
23. Marx, "On the History of His Opinions," *Marx-Engels Reader*, 4.
24. Marx, "On the History of His Opinions," 53.
25. It may be inaccurate to say that Marx believes that man is basically good, but neither does he hold that man is basically evil. In fact, good and evil are social constructions, and Marx's own view is an optimistic humanism whereby he believes if the poor socioeconomic conditions were eliminated, then man would lose that one great impediment to greatness.
26. It might be suggested that this assumption can be easily made owing to the sociological factor of the times. Most people in Europe were Christians and that was their world. What else would they expect of the "minority" of nonbelievers but that they were somehow culpable? But this is not the case, because Aquinas, Calvin, and the Reformers took their cue from the New Testament, from a time when Christians were most certainly the minority, and the view was held then as well. Hence, this view is held on the basis of theological conviction rather than on any contemporary cultural analyses. John Calvin, *Institutes of the Christian Religion*, trans. Ford Lewis Battles (Philadelphia, PA: Westminster Press, 1960), 1.3, 43-44.
27. Alvin Plantinga, *Warranted Christian Belief* (Oxford: Oxford University Press, 2000), preface, 7-12. With respect to notions of rationality, see Alasdair MacIntyre, *Whose Justice? Which Rationality?* (South Bend, IN: University of Notre Dame Press, 1988).
28. Alvin Plantinga, *Warrant and Proper Function* (Oxford: Oxford University Press, 1994); *Warranted Christian Belief* (Oxford: Oxford University Press, 1994).
29. Epistemic circularity, which is at issue here, is different from logical circularity. The latter arises when the conclusion of an argument is also one of its premises. Not so with epistemic circularity. Epistemic circularity arises when a subject comes to believe that a particular source of knowledge is reliable through the use of that very source.
30. "I once was blind, but now I see." That is what John Newton wrote after his conversion, in the famous hymn "Amazing Grace." Newton, a former British slave trader, became a seminal figure in the abolition of slavery in Great Britain about one decade before Marx was born. He worked together on this with William Wilberforce. I am fairly certain that many slaves were quite happy for his religious conversion and newfound beliefs (much to the chagrin of Marx), which were directly responsible for delivering such slaves from alienation and oppression. See Armand M. Nicholi, *The Question of God: C.S. Lewis and Sigmund Freud Debate God, Love, Sex, and the Meaning of Life* (New York: Free Press, 2002), 78.
31. Our justification of the reliability of our sense perceptions rests on an epistemically circular argument. One cannot justify one's sense perceptions without appealing to them as the source of justification by some kind of track-record argument. Of course, the perception skeptic will not be convinced, but how does this make the one contending that his perceptions are reliable any less rational? How else can we justify the reliability of our sense perceptions apart from benign circular reasoning? The sort of belief that can get infected with epistemic circularity is a belief that one's belief source, x, is trustworthy. A context in which this is a bad thing is one in which the subject begins by doubting or being unsure of x's trustworthiness. But the theist need not doubt the source of his belief in God, because belief in God is properly basic. See Michael Bergmann, "Epistemic Circularity: Malignant and Benign," *Philosophy and Phenomenological Research* 69 (2002): 709-727.
32. This experience of God seems to be an overwhelming intrinsic defeater—a defeater such that when other defeaters come, unless they are exceptional, they are easily deflected. For example, if a murder took place and all the external evidence is against person S, S may still be in an especially unique position to know

whether he committed the crime or not despite the external evidence to the contrary. In such a case, how could someone simply give up her belief that she knew to be true even if she were not in a position to show it to be true? Ultimately, while there are good arguments, even if not demonstrable, for God's existence, it is not necessary to show God in order to know God.

CHAPTER 12—IS CHRISTIAN BELIEF TRUE?

1. See Chad Mcintosh's summary array of arguments at www.camcintosh.com/theistic/index.html.
2. Richard Dawkins, *The God Delusion* (Boston: Houghton Mifflin, 2006), 31.
3. Ruse was referencing the then-new book *The Moral Landscape*, written by popular New Atheist Sam Harris. Michael Ruse, "Little 'Value' in New Harris Book," *Religion Dispatches*, October 26, 2010, https://religiondispatches.org/little-value-in-new-harris-book/.
4. Peter Boghossian, "Peter Boghossian: How the Academy Got Woke and Why the 'New Atheists' Are to Blame," *The Spectator*, April 25, 2023.
5. Aayan Hirsi Ali, "Why I Am Now a Christian: Atheism Can't Equip Us for Civilisational War," *Unherd*, November 11, 2023, https://unherd.com/2023/11/why-i-am-now-a-christian/.
6. Aayan Hirsi Ali, "Why I Am Now a Christian."
7. Rachel Johnson, "Richard Dawkins: I'm a Cultural Christian," *Leading Britain's Conversation*, April 1, 2024, https://www.youtube.com/watch?v=COHgEFUFWyg.
8. Kurt Mahlburg, "'We Need Jesus': Joe Rogan Admits Value of Christ in 'Chaotic' World," *The Daily Declaration*, February 27, 2024, https://dailydeclaration.org.au/2024/02/29/we-need-jesus-joe-rogan-admits-value-of-christ-in-chaotic-world/.
9. Justin Brierley, *The Surprising Rebirth of Belief in God: Why New Atheism Grew Old and Secular Thinkers Are Considering Christianity Again* (Carol Stream, IL: Tyndale Elevate, 2023).
10. Jana Harmon, "Religious Conversion of Educated Atheists to Christianity in Six Contemporary Western Countries" (PhD diss., University of Birmingham, 2019), http://etheses.bham.ac.uk/id/eprint/9490.
11. Quentin Smith, "The Metaphilosophy of Naturalism," *Philo* 4, no. 2 (2001): 3–4.
12. Smith, "Metaphilosophy of Naturalism."
13. For example, see William Lane Craig and JP Moreland, *The Blackwell Companion to Natural Theology* (Hoboken, NJ: Wiley-Blackwell, 2012); see also William Lane Craig, *Reasonable Faith: Christian Truth and Apologetics,* 3rd ed. (Wheaton, IL: Crossway, 2008).
14. Leonard Susskind, *The Cosmic Landscape: String Theory and the Illusion of Intelligent Design* (New York: Back Bay Books, 2006), 363.
15. Susskind, *Cosmic Landscape*, 356.
16. Susskind, *Cosmic Landscape*, xi.
17. Susskind, *Cosmic Landscape*, 355.
18. Burton Richter, "Theory in particle physics: Theological speculation versus practical knowledge," Physics Today, October 1, 2006, https://doi.org/10.1063/1.2387062.
19. "Antony Flew," HarperCollins Publishers, accessed February 15, 2025, https://www.harpercollins.com/blogs/authors/antony-flew-880000001845.
20. Antony Flew and Roy Varghese, *There Is a God: How the World's Most Notorious Atheist Changed His Mind* (New York: HarperOne, 2007).
21. Antony Flew, "My Pilgrimage from Atheism to Theism," *Philosophia Christi* 6, no. 2 (2004): 197-211. Flew stopped short of becoming a Christian because he still had a problem with the existence of evil. He believed in something closer to deism.
22. John A.T. Robinson, *The Human Face of God* (Philadelphia, PA: Westminster, 1973), 131.
23. Jacob Kremer, *Die Osterevangelien—Geschichten um Geschichte* (Stuttgart, Germany: Katholisches Bielwerk, 1977), 49-50, as cited in William Lane Craig, *Did Jesus Rise from the Dead? Examining the Evidence for Life Everlasting* (West Lafayette, IN: Ratio Christi Press, 2023), 7. One of Craig's two doctoral dissertations, this one in German, was on the evidence for the resurrection.

24. Gary Habermas, "Experience of the Risen Jesus: The Foundational Historical Issue in the Early Proclamation of the Resurrection," *Dialog* 45 (2006): 292.
25. Habermas, *On the Resurrection, Volume 1: Evidences* (Brentwood, TN: B&H Academic, 2024).
26. Gerd Lüdemann, *What Really Happened to Jesus?*, trans. by John Bowden (Louisville, KY: Westminster John Knox Press, 1995), 80.
27. See William Lane Craig's *Did Jesus Rise from the Dead* for examination of naturalistic alternatives such as the apparent death, displaced body, and hallucination hypotheses. A PDF version can be downloaded for free at RatioChristiPress.com.
28. Gerd Lüdemann, *The Resurrection of Jesus: History, Experience, Theology*, trans. John Bowden (Minneapolis, MN: Fortress, 1994), 38.

CHAPTER 13—ALL HANDS ON DECK

1. "Our Mission," Ratio Christi, https://ratiochristi.org/about/.
2. To view Purdue's 2024 enrollment statistics, see "Student Enrollment, Fall 2024," *Purdue University*, https://www.admissions.purdue.edu/academics/enrollment.php; "International Enrollment and Statistical Report: Fall 2024," Purdue University, https://www.purdue.edu/gpp/iss/_documents/EnrollmentReport/iss_statisticalreportfall24.pdf.
3. Nick Hillman, "HEPI Soft-Power Index 2024: The US Pulls Further Away, While the UK Stands Still and France Slips Back," Higher Education Policy Institute, October 10, 2024, https://www.hepi.ac.uk/2024/10/10/the-us-pulls-further-away-in-the-latest-soft-power-index-while-the-uk-stands-still-and-france-slips-back/.
4. "International Students," The Traveling Team, accessed February 15, 2025, https://www.thetravelingteam.org/internationals-in-the-usa.
5. Ed Stetzer, "Reaching International Students in Our Own Backyards," *The Exchange* (blog), *Christianity Today*, January 30, 2019.
6. To see a full listing of helpful resources, go to https://press.ratiochristi.org/.
7. David Kinnaman and Gabe Lyons, *Good Faith: Being a Christian When Society Thinks You're Irrelevant and Extreme* (Grand Rapids, MI: Baker, 2016), 29.
8. Kinnaman and Lyons, *Good Faith*, 14.
9. Kinnaman and Lyons, *Good Faith*, 41.
10. All of the data and the quote can be found on the same page of *Reviving Evangelism: Current Realities That Demand a New Vision for Sharing Faith* (Dallas–Fort Worth, TX: Barna Group, 2019), 55.
11. *Reviving Evangelism*, 26.
12. Mark Noll, *The Scandal of the Evangelical Mind* (Grand Rapids, MI: Eerdmans, 1995).
13. *American Worldview Inventory 2022–2023*. This work is done by Arizona Christian University. See the online versions for continuous studies at https://www.arizonachristian.edu/culturalresearchcenter/.
14. See Acts 17:16-34. For discussion, see Douglas Groothuis, "Learning from an Apostle: Christianity in the Marketplace of Ideas (Acts 17:16-34)," *Christian Research Journal*, 35, 4 (2012; updated April 3, 2024), https://www.equip.org/article/learning-from-an-apostle-christianity-in-the-marketplace-of-ideas-acts-1716-34/; cf. Brian Godawa, "Storytelling as Subversive Apologetics: A New View from the Hill in Acts 17," *Christian Research Journal* 30, no. 2 (2007), https://www.equip.org/article/storytelling-as-subversive-apologetics-a-new-view-from-the-hill-in-acts-17/.
15. J. Gresham Machen, "Christianity and Culture," *Princeton Theological Review* 11 (1913): 7.
16. George Barna, *American Worldview Inventory 2022–23* (Glendale, AZ: Arizona Christian University Press, 2023), 7.
17. Kimberlé Crenshaw, "#TruthBeTold Messaging Guide," *African American Policy Forum*, 2021, 2–3, https://www.aapf.org/_files/ugd/0813a9_6b0ea3c8b15a48cab92db4f0fd7991b7.pdf. The forum even has a CRT summer school each year dedicated to CRT education from K–12 to higher education and even legislation. See http://www.aapf.org/crtsummerschool.
18. The president of the University of Pennsylvania, Liz Magill, resigned, as did the president of Harvard,

Claudine Gay, for similar pressures over antisemitism on campus and the leaders' lack of moral clarity. Note, however, they remained as faculty. See Daniel Arkin, "University of Pennsylvania President Steps Down amid Criticism of Antisemitism Testimony," *NBC News*, December 9, 2023, https://www.nbcnews.com/news/us-news/university-pennsylvania-president-steps-criticism-antisemitism-testimo-rcna128712; Emma H. Haidar and Cam E. Kettles, "Harvard President Claudine Gay Resigns, Shortest Tenure in University History," *The Harvard Crimson*, January 3, 2024, https://www.thecrimson.com/article/2024/1/3/claudine-gay-resign-harvard/.

19. Sophie Lewis, *Abolish the Family: A Manifesto for Care and Liberation* (London: Verso, 2022).
20. Lewis, *Abolish the Family*, 4. All block and in-paragraph quotes after the citing of the book itself until now derive from page 4.
21. Lewis, *Abolish the Family*, 9.
22. Lewis, *Abolish the Family*, 7-8. Philosopher Roger Scruton argues that Thatcher didn't literally mean that there are no societies. Rather, she meant that there is such a thing as a society, but that society is not identical with the state. Society is composed of people of free association forming communities of interest that socialists have no right to control or outlaw. See Scruton, *How to Be a Conservative* (London: Bloomsbury, 2014), 8.
23. Michael Hardt, "Red Love," *South Atlantic Quarterly*, 116, no. 4 (2017): 781, as cited in Lewis, *Abolish the Family*, 20.
24. Lewis, *Abolish the Family*, 43.
25. Karl Marx and Friedrich Engels, *The German Ideology*, ed. C.J. Arthur (New York: International Publishers, 1970), 50.
26. Lola Olufemi, *Experiments in Imagining Otherwise* (London: Hajar Press, 2021), 137, as cited in Sophie Lewis, *Abolish the Family*, 87. Hajar Press appears to be motivated by the same radical revolutionary spirit we've been seeing throughout this book. On their website, it says, "An independent political publishing house run by and for people of colour…We don't believe in upholding an either/or distinction between beautiful and revolutionary." "Homepage," Hajar Press, accessed February 15, 2025, https://www.hajarpress.com/.
27. Lewis, *Abolish the Family*, 79.
28. Anthony Leonardo, "Black Lives Matter 'What We Believe' Page That Includes Disrupting 'Nuclear Family Structure' Removed from Website," September 21, 2020, *Washington Examiner*, September 21, 2020, https://www.washingtonexaminer.com/news/black-lives-matter-what-we-believe-page-that-includes-disrupting-nuclear-family-structure-removed-from-website.
29. Bradford Richardson, "Liberal Professors Outnumber Conservatives Nearly 12 to 1, Study Finds," *The Washington Times*, October 6, 2016, https://www.washingtontimes.com/news/2016/oct/6/liberal-professors-outnumber-conservatives-12-1.
30. Parents can be helped by booklets and eBooks published by Ratio Christi Press (https://press.ratiochristi.org; other helps include books for parents by Natasha Crain such as *Keeping Your Kids on God's Side* (Eugene, OR: Harvest House, 2016); *Talking with Your Kids About Jesus* (Grand Rapids, MI: Baker, 2020); Lee Strobel's books *The Case for Faith* and *The Case for Christ*, all available in adult or student editions. For elementary-age children, see Foundation Worldview by Elizabeth Urbanowicz at: https://foundationworldview.com/about/meet-the-founder. Finally, see the partnership curriculum for children and teens by Sean McDowell and Awana at: https://seanmcdowell.org/blog/announcement-new-apologetics-curriculum-for-students#google_vignette.
31. Amy Howe, "Supreme Court Strikes down Affirmative Action Programs in College Admissions," *SCOTUS blog*, June 29, 2023. SCOTUS determined that colleges like Harvard and the University of North Carolina were violating the equal protection clause of the Fourteenth Amendment by creating race-based admissions policies.
32. Heather Mac Donald, "Conservative Donors: Wake Up!," *City Journal*, Summer 2023, https://www.city-journal.org/article/conservative-donors-wake-up.
33. Numerous big donors pulled funding in the wake of the Hamas attack on Israel, the radical student responses on Ivy League campuses, and the paltry responses from the leadership of those schools. But those universities still have plenty of money. Nathaniel Meyersohn, "Harvard and UPenn Donors Are Furious:

It May Have a Financial Domino Effect," *CNN*, October 12, 2023, https://www.cnn.com/2023/10/19/business/harvard-upenn-donors-israel/index.html.

34. These GDP figures are based on sources from the World Bank and the United Nations data in 2022 and 2023 at https://www.worldometers.info/gdp/gdp-by-country. Harvard's figures are based on their recent October 2024 financial report: https://finance.harvard.edu/files/fad/files/fy24_harvard_financial_report.pdf.

35. Terrance Kible, "At Harvard, There Are 2,600 More Administrators Than Undergrads," *The College Fix*, October 24, 2023, https://www.thecollegefix.com/at-harvard-there-are-2600-more-administrators-than-undergrads/.

36. It didn't take long to spot the scam of the "antiracist" Ibram X. Kendi. Where did the money go? Much like BLM founders, Kendi received millions and millions of dollars from white virtue-signaling donors made to feel guilty after George Floyd's death in 2020. These donors gave countless millions to race Marxists making out like capitalists. The so-called antiracists (i.e., new racists), far from wanting to eradicate racism, make bank on perpetuating it. Tom Mackaman, "Ibram X. Kendi's 'Antiracism Research Center' Squanders $43 Million, Lays off Staff," September 22, 2023, *World Socialist Website*, https://www.wsws.org/en/articles/2023/09/23/rvlf-s23.html.

37. See Harvard's 2022 Financial Report: https://finance.harvard.edu/files/fad/files/fy22_financial_overview.pdf.

38. Molly Bohannon, "Billionaire Ken Griffin Becomes Latest to Stop Harvard Donations—Worries Elite Students Becoming 'Whiny Snowflakes,'" *Forbes*, January 31, 2024, https://www.forbes.com/sites/mollybohannon/2024/01/30/billionaire-ken-griffin-becomes-latest-to-stop-donations-to-harvard-calls-students-whiny-snowflakes/.

39. Natasha Korecki, "Lori Lightfoot Becomes the First Chicago Mayor in 40 Years to Lose Re-Election," *NBC News*, February 28, 2023, https://www.nbcnews.com/politics/elections/lori-lightfoot-becomes-first-chicago-mayor-40-years-lose-re-election-rcna71997.

40. Joe Bukuras, "Indiana Catholic Women's College Now Accepting Men Who Identify as Women," *Catholic News Agency*, November 17, 2023, https://www.catholicnewsagency.com/news/256112/catholic-women-s-college-now-accepting-men-who-identify-as-women.

41. We all should practice good stewardship with resources and recommendations after investigating the organizations we consider giving donations to. For example, when you hear charges that an organization is going woke, do your homework. Talk with people. Talk with faculty. Don't simply take someone's word for it. In our age of social media, it is easy for people to put together isolated bits and pieces of information to tell a narrative that might not be representative of the whole. If necessary, hold the organization to account. Sometimes even adjacent friendly organizations to an accused organization can be considered guilty by association. For instance, one charitable foundation told us they weren't going to give Ratio Christi a large grant simply because at the time we had ties with Biola University, and the foundation deemed Biola University and Talbot School of Theology as going woke, so we were also deemed susceptible to the accusation. To determine whether allegations against any group are true or not, a prospective donor should do their homework before they give money. If the organization or ministry checks out, great. If not, address the matter with the organization, or don't donate. In the case involving Ratio Christi, I think the charitable foundation was concerned in part because donors, alumni, and supporters of Biola launched a petition in July 2020—with more than 2,000 signatures—seeking to get President Barry Cory and donors' attention regarding claims that Biola was, in part, embracing CRT. See https://www.change.org/p/biola-board-of-trustees-a-call-for-biola-to-affirm-essential-human-equality-and-denounce-critical-race-theory. This petition served as a counterpetition to one that seemed to favor CRT, which garnered more than 4,000 signatures written in June of 2020, shortly after the death of George Floyd—see https://www.change.org/p/biola-board-of-trustees-a-call-for-biola-to-affirm-essential-human-equality-and-denounce-critical-race-theory. To see a similar petition launched in April of 2025 with 1,500 signatures calling on major change at Wheaton College, see https://forwheaton.org/.

42. The guests were speaking about the preceding case that Ratio Christi supported with an amicus brief and that SCOTUS ruled in favor of free speech. The case involved an ADF Supreme Court win, *Uzuegbunam v. Preczewski*. William Porayouw & Ines Chomnalez, "Federal Judges Boycott Yale Law Grads, Citing Free Speech Concerns," *Yale News*, October 10, 2022, https://yaledailynews.com/blog/2022/10/10/federal-judges-boycott-yale-law-grads-citing-free-speech-concerns. More than a dozen judges won't hire

law students from Columbia University, saying that they "lost confidence" in the institution over its handling of student protests tied to antisemitism and the Israel-Hamas war. See Jacqueline Thompson, "Conservative Judges Won't Hire Columbia Law Clerks Over Protests," *Bloomberg Law*, May 6, 2024, https://news.bloomberglaw.com/us-law-week/conservative-judges-wont-hire-columbia-law-clerks-over-protests.
43. James Davison Hunter, *To Change the World: The Irony, Tragedy, and Possibility of Christianity in the Late Modern World* (New York: Oxford University Press, 2010), 41.
44. Hunter, *To Change the World*, 16, 41.
45. "Groups to Reach: Faculty," Cru, https://www.cru.org/us/en/opportunities/explore-your-interests/groups-to-reach/faculty.html.
46. That was in 2016, when it was cited more than 72,000 times, now up to more than 130,000 times, with each year surpassing the previous. His works have been cited more than half a million times—see https://blogs.lse.ac.uk/impactofsocialsciences/2016/05/12/what-are-the-most-cited-publications-in-the-social-sciences-according-to-google-scholar. See also Paulo Freire's page on his most famous and influential book: https://scholar.google.com/citations?view_op=view_citation&hl=en&user=IdMflV7YL6MC&citation_for_view=IdMflV7YL6MC:u5HHmVD_uO8C
47. James Lindsay, *The Marxification of Education: Paulo Freire's Critical Marxism and the Theft of Education* (Orlando, FL: New Discourses, 2022), 1.
48. Herbert Marcuse, *Counter-Revolution and Revolt* (Boston: Beacon Press, 1972), 55-56.
49. Paulo Freire, *Critical Pedagogy*, 1968, 50th anniversary ed. (London: Bloomsbury Academic, 2018).
50. Lindsay, *The Marxification of Education*, 2.
51. Peter McLaren, Gregory Martin, Ramin Farahmandpur, and Nathalia Jaramillo, "Teaching in and Against the Empire: Critical Pedagogy as Revolutionary Praxis," *Teacher Education Quarterly*, 31, no. 1 (2004): 138, as cited in Neil Shenvi and Pat Sawyer, *Critical Dilemma* (Eugene, OR, Harvest House, 2023), 51.
52. Paulo Freire in James H. Cone, *A Black Theology of Liberation*, 20th anniversary ed. (Maryknoll, NY: Orbis, 2010), xi, as cited in Shenvi and Sawyer, *Critical Dilemma*, 52.
53. Paulo Freire, *The Politics of Education: Culture, Power, and Liberation* (Greenwood, NY: Bergin & Garvey Publishers, 1985), 122-123.
54. Michelle Boorstein, "Sen. Raphael Warnock's Deleted Easter Tweet Reflects Religious and Political Chasms About Christianity," *The Washington Post*, April 5, 2021, https://www.washingtonpost.com/religion/2021/04/05/raphael-warnock-deletes-tweet-easter-resurrection-jeremiah-wright/. Prior to joining the US Senate, Warnock preached a sermon referring to Jesus as "a poor Palestinian prophet." See https://www.jewishpress.com/news/us-news/hey-georgia-candidate-warnock-has-another-shocker-for-you/2020/11/16.
55. Alvin Plantinga, "The Twin Pillars of Christian Scholarship," in *Seeking Understanding: The Stob Lectures 1986–1998* (Grand Rapids, MI: Eerdmans, 2001), 124.
56. William Lane Craig, "Concluding Thoughts on the Two Tasks," in *The Two Tasks of the Christian Scholar: Redeeming the Soul, Redeeming the Mind*, 178.
57. Charles Malik, "The Two Tasks," in Craig, *Two Tasks of the Christian Scholar*, 64.
58. C.S. Lewis, *God in the Dock* (Grand Rapids, MI: Eerdmans, 1970), 93.
59. See https://prof.ratiochristi.org/resources/.
60. Paul Gould, *The Outrageous Idea of the Missional Professor* (Eugene, OR: Wipf and Stock, 2014). Ratio Christi has a training program to help with this.
61. Indeed, it is happening in small pockets. Since the late 1960s, Christian philosophers like Alvin Plantinga and others have established a significant beachhead in philosophy departments. In one atheistic journal, an atheist philosopher lamented the "desecularization of academia that evolved in philosophy departments since the late 1960s." Quentin Smith, "The Metaphilosophy of Naturalism," *Philo* 4, no. 2 (2001): 3-4.

CONCLUSION—MAGA AND THE MORNING AFTER

1. "Our Students Face the Next Wave of Christian Nationalism's Agenda," November 6, 2024. This ill-defined nebulous expression was used by Politico's Heidi Przybyla this way: "The thing that unites them as Christian

nationalists... is that they believe that our rights as Americans, as all human beings, don't come from any earthly authority. They don't come from Congress; they don't come from the Supreme Court. They come from God." See https://www.foxnews.com/media/reporter-lashes-claiming-christian-nationalists-believe-rights-come-god.

2. Allie Beth Stuckey, "Cru's 'Diversity Team' Sent a Ridiculous Post-Election Email | Ep 1105," *Relatable*, November 22, 2024, YouTube video, https://youtu.be/Go6RPMdEpJ4?si=McgD8DrIxbCEefkL.

3. According to the Media Research Center, Trump was given mostly negative coverage, while Harris was given mostly positive coverage. Rich Noyes, "TV Hits Trump With 85% Negative News vs. 78% Positive Press for Harris," *MRCNewsbusters*, October 28, 2024.

4. Alice Herman, Joanna Walters, and Rachel Leingang, "Trump's Picks for New Administration Are Focus of Bomb Threats and 'Swatting,'" *The Guardian*, November 27, 2024. Ironically, the very media reporting on this took the effort to add an insert article at the end of this one by its editor-in-chief, Katharine Viner, to raise money at the end of the year for *The Guardian* by seeking to instill more fear about the incoming Trump administration. The insert article was titled "How the Guardian Will Stand Up to Four More Years of Donald Trump" and said, "Trump is a direct threat to the freedom of the press." See https://www.theguardian.com/us-news/2024/nov/27/trump-cabinet-bomb-threats. Last accessed November 28, 2024.

5. David French and Russell Moore, the editor of *Christianity Today*, promoted a miniseries on voting Democrat. *The Bulletin*, podcast episode 117, October 22, 2024, https://www.christianitytoday.com/podcasts/the-bulletin/117-stop-look-listen-voting-democrat/.

6. Wayne Grudem, "20 Reasons to Vote for Republicans—and Especially for Donald Trump," *TownHall*, October 27, 2024, https://townhall.com/columnists/waynegrudem/2024/10/27/20-reasons-to-vote-for-republicans-and-especially-for-donald-trump-n2646824.

7. Cyrus is mentioned in Isaiah, Ezra, 2 Chronicles, and Daniel. Nero was emperor of Rome when the apostle Paul wrote about human government in Romans 13. Nero was believed by many historians to have illuminated the roads to Rome by impaling Christians by the thousands and lighting their bodies on fire.

8. "Secular Student Alliance v. U.S. Department of Education," Alliance Defending Freedom, February 19, 2025, https://adfmedia.org/case/secular-student-alliance-v-us-department-education.

9. "Exit Polls," *NBC News*, November 22, 2024, https://www.nbcnews.com/politics/2024-elections/exit-polls.

10. Owen Anderson, "DEI is dead—long live DEI: How universities are rebranding their diversity, equity, and inclusion policies," *World*, April 4, 2025. https://wng.org/opinions/dei-is-dead-long-live-dei-1743730693.

11. See press release issued from the US Department of Education: "U.S. Department of Education Takes Action to Eliminate DEI," US Department of Education, January 23, 2025, https://www.ed.gov/about/news/press-release/us-department-of-education-takes-action-eliminate-dei.

12. Peter Boghossian (@peterboghossian), August 9, 2024, "So so many of my friends..." *X*, https://x.com/peterboghossian/status/1821773140613013966.

13. Dan Gooding, "Donald Trump Won More Black Voters Than Any Republican in 48 Years—Analyst," *Newsweek*, November 8, 2024.

14. Peter Boghossian, "Breaking Down Trump's Education Plans," November 19, 2024, YouTube video, https://youtu.be/55FCS9sAkrc?si=N5oxkwvCUAmlbW10.

15. See several examples, including, significantly, Walmart. Ryan Foley, "5 Companies That Are Scaling Back DEI, LGBT Advocacy," *The Christian Post,* September 6, 2024; Danielle Genovese, "Walmart Rolls Back DEI Policies, Says It's 'Willing to Change' After Activist's Anti-Woke Campaign," *The Christian Post*, November 25, 2024. See also a report on over 100 companies in 2023 and 2024, https://www.christianpost.com/news/company-support-for-dei-programs-on-the-decline-report.html.

16. Regardless of motives, positive change is in the air. Erin Gretzinger, Maggie Hicks, Christa Dutton, and Jasper Smith, "Tracking Higher Ed's Dismantling of DEI," *The Chronicle of Higher Education*, November 22, 2024, https://www.chronicle.com/article/tracking-higher-eds-dismantling-of-dei?utm_source=Iterable&utm_medium=email&utm_campaign=campaign_11802215_nl_DEI_date_20241122&sra=true.

17. Matt Lamb, "Ibram Kendi Will Shut Down Functionally Inactive 'Antiracist' Center, Move to Howard," *The College Fix*, January 21, 2025, https://www.thecollegefix.com/ibram-kendi-will-shut-down-functionally-inactive-antiracist-center-move-to-howard/.

18. Goldwater Institute, "Five More States Prohibit 'Diversity Statements' in Admissions and Hiring Decisions," Goldwater Institute, April 26, 2024, https://www.goldwaterinstitute.org/victory-goldwater-defeats-diversity-statements-in-5-states/.

19. One Christian philosophy professor took Arizona State University to court claiming that it is in violation of the law by requiring faculty to take DEI training. See Janae Joachim, "Conservative Professor's Lawsuit Against ASU's DEI Training May Proceed, Judge Rules," *The College Fix*, January 16, 2025, https://www.thecollegefix.com/conservative-professors-lawsuit-against-asus-dei-training-may-proceed-judge-rules/.

20. Tyler Coward, "Indiana's SB 202 Holds Promise, but Needs Changes to Protect Academic Freedom," Foundation for Individual Rights and Expression (FIRE), February 7, 2024, https://www.thefire.org/news/indianas-sb-202-holds-promise-needs-changes-protect-academic-freedom. Provided here is an example at Purdue University of how one can complain if one is feeling censored or if one feels an environment isn't "viewpoint friendly." See https://www.purdue.edu/ethics/resources/procedures-for-intellectual-diversity.php.

21. Steven Pinker, *The Better Angels of Our Nature: The Decline of Violence in History and Its Causes* (London: Allen Lane, 2011), as cited in Lindsay's chapter, "An Alternative to the Ideology of Social Justice," in *Cynical Theories: How Activist Scholarship Made Everything About Race, Gender, and Identity—and Why This Harms Everybody* (Durham, NC: Pitchstone, 2020), 246.

22. R.Z. Friedman, "Does the 'Death of God' Really Matter?" *International Philosophical Quarterly* 23 (1983): 322. See also the debate between philosophers William Lane Craig, a Christian, and Paul Kurtz, a humanist, as recorded in Nathan King and Robert Garcia, *Is Goodness Without God Good Enough?* (Lanham, MD: Rowman and Littlefield, 2009).

23. Jean Paul Sartre gave a lecture, "Existentialism as a Humanism," in 1946. He cannot at once say life is absurd and then say life is meaningful, or that there are no objective moral values and turn around to defend objective moral values—see https://www.marxists.org/reference/archive/sartre/works/exist/sartre.htm.

24. John Adams, "Letter from John Adams to Massachusetts Militia," October 11, 1798, https://founders.archives.gov/documents/Adams/99-02-02-3102.

25. "Declaration of Independence: A Transcription," National Archives, https://www.archives.gov/founding-docs/declaration-transcript.

26. In truth, the evidence is scanty that he ever made this exact statement himself. The idea may be present, perhaps, but the popularization of the statement has become so mainstream. For a brief critical history of this, see "America Is Great Because America Is Good," *Faith and History: Thinking Christianly About the American Past*, July 27, 2016, https://faithandamericanhistory.wordpress.com/2016/07/27/america-is-great-because-america-is-good-part-one.

27. See Thomas G. West, *The Political Theory of the American Founding: Natural Rights, Public Policy, and the Moral Conditions of Freedom* (Cambridge: Cambridge University Press, 2017); see also Michael D. Breidenbach and Owen Anderson, eds., *The Cambridge Companion to The First Amendment and Religious Liberty* (Cambridge: Cambridge University Press, 2020).

28. Corey Miller, *In Search of the Good Life: Through the Eyes of Aristotle, Maimonides, and Aquinas* (Eugene, OR: Wipf and Stock, 2019).